THE
EMPERORS AND
EMPRESSES
OF RUSSIA

The New Russian History

Series Editor: Donald J. Raleigh,
University of North Carolina, Chapel Hill

This series makes examples of the finest work of the most eminent historians in Russia today available to English-language readers. Each volume has been specially prepared with an international audience in mind, and each is introduced by an outstanding Western scholar in the same field.

THE EMPERORS AND EMPRESSES OF RUSSIA

REDISCOVERING THE ROMANOVS

Edited by **Donald J. Raleigh**

Compiled by **A. A. Iskenderov**

M.E. Sharpe
Armonk, New York
London, England

Original publication information:

Peter I: "Petr I" was published in *Voprosy istorii*, 1993, no. 6, pp. 59–77, and has not previously appeared in English. Anna: "Anna Ivanovna" was published in *Voprosy istorii*, 1993, no. 4, pp. 19–33, and translated in *Russian Studies in History*, vol. 32, no. 4, pp. 8–36. Elizabeth: "Elizaveta Petrovna" was published in *Voprosy istorii*, 1993, no. 5, pp. 51–72, and translated in *Russian Studies in History*, vol. 32, no. 4, pp. 37–72. Peter III: "Petr III" was published in *Voprosy istorii*, 1991, no. 4/5, pp. 43–58, and translated in *Russian Studies in History*, vol. 32, no. 3, pp. 30–56. Catherine II: "Ekaterina II" was published in *Voprosy istorii*, 1989, no. 3, pp. 62–88, and translated in *Soviet Studies in History*, vol. 30, no. 3, pp. 30–65. Paul: "Pavel I" was published in *Voprosy istorii*, 1989, no. 11, pp. 46–69, and translated in *Soviet Studies in History*, vol. 30, no. 3, pp. 3–48. Alexander I: An earlier version of "Aleksandr I" was published in *Voprosy istorii*, 1990, no. 1, pp. 50–72, and translated in *Soviet Studies in History*, vol. 30, no. 3, pp. 49–91. Nicholas I: "Nikolai I" was published in *Voprosy istorii*, 1993, no. 11/12, pp. 27–49, and translated in *Russian Studies in History*, vol. 34, no. 3, pp. 7–38. Alexander II: "Aleksandr II" was published in *Voprosy istorii*, 1992, no. 6/7, pp. 58–79, and translated in *Russian Studies in History*, vol. 32, no. 3, pp. 57–88. Alexander III: "Aleksandr III" was published in *Voprosy istorii*, 1992, no. 11/12, pp. 46–64, and translated in *Russian Studies in History*, vol. 34, no. 3, pp. 39–67. Nicholas II: "Nikolai II" was published in *Voprosy istorii*, 1993, no. 2, pp. 58–76, and translated in *Russian Studies in History*, vol. 34, no. 3, pp. 68–95.

Library of Congress Cataloging-in-Publication Data

The emperors and empresses of Russia : rediscovering the Romanovs / compiled by A.A. Iskenderov and edited by Donald J. Raleigh.
    p.   cm.—(The New Russian history)
"Comprises portraits of the Romanov tsars that appeared in the journal Voprosy istorii beginning with the reign of Peter the Great"—CIP pref.
Includes bibliographical references and index.
ISBN 1-56324-759-3 (cloth : alk. paper).—ISBN 1-56324-760-7 (pbk. : alk. paper)
1. Romanov, House of. 2. Russia—Kings and rulers—Biography. 3. Russia—History—1613–1917. I. Iskenderov, Akhmed Akhmedovich. II. Raleigh, Donald J. III. Series.
    DK37.8.R6E46   1996
    947'.046'0922—dc20
    [B]   95-41894
                  CIP

Printed in the United States of America

Contents

About the Editors and Contributors

Donald J. Raleigh is professor of history at the University of North Carolina, Chapel Hill, and former editor of *Soviet (Russian) Studies in History*.

Akhmed Akhmedovich Iskenderov is a corresponding member of the Russian Academy of Sciences and editor-in-chief of *Voprosy istorii*.

Boris Vasilievich Ananich is a corresponding member of the Russian Academy of Sciences.

Evgenii Viktorovich Anisimov, Doctor of Historical Sciences, is a senior research associate at the St. Petersburg Branch of the Institute of Russian History, Russian Academy of Sciences, and a member of the Russian Writers' Union.

Valentina Grigorievna Chernukha is a doctor of historical sciences and leading research associate at the St. Petersburg Branch of the Institute of Russian History, Russian Academy of Sciences.

Vladimir Aleksandrovich Fedorov is a doctor of historical sciences and professor at Moscow State University.

Rafail Sholomovich Ganelin is a corresponding member of the Russian Academy of Sciences.

Aleksandr Borisovich Kamenskii, Candidate of Historical Sciences, teaches at the Moscow Historical–Archival Institute.

Tatiana Aleksandrovna Kapustina is an historian and archivist.

Aleksandr Sergeevich Mylnikov is a professor and doctor of historical sciences at the St. Petersburg branch of the Institute of Ethnology and Anthropology, Russian Academy of Sciences.

Viktor Petrovich Naumov is a candidate of historical sciences and chief archivist at the State Archives of the Russian Federation.

Iurii Alekseevich Sorokin is a candidate of historical sciences and associate professor at Omsk University.

Iaroslav Evgenievich Vodarskii, Doctor of Historical Sciences, is a leading research associate at the Institute of Russian History, Russian Academy of Sciences.

Larisa Georgievna Zakharova is a doctor of historical sciences and professor at Moscow State University.

Preface

From the 1930s until the dawn of glasnost, a complex and mostly unfortunate fate befell biography as a genre of historical writing in the USSR. Unable to break out of the intellectual confines of Stalinist scholarship, historians in the Soviet Union neglected serious analysis of the country's prerevolutionary rulers. The exceptions to this rule were Tsars Ivan the Terrible and Peter the Great, the study of whom was often motivated by contemporary political considerations. But perestroika radically altered this situation, as the reading public's rapidly shifting tastes and interests posed new challenges to practitioners of both popular and scholarly historical writing in Russia. Insatiably hungry for fresh accounts of the country's past, readers demanded answers to topics once taboo or at least discouraged. As their expectations rose, ferment within the historical profession itself brought about important changes in the country's major historical publications. For example, in striving to recapture a readership that had lost interest in what professional historians had to say, the journal *Voprosy istorii* (Problems of History)—an important barometer of change for the Russian historical profession—enlisted prominent specialists to author historical portraits of both Russian tsars and Soviet commissars whose careers had been distorted and even patently falsified by Soviet historiography.

This collection of essays on the Russian tsars merits consideration because most of the historical sketches represent the first serious efforts of the post-1985 period to reassess Imperial Russia's rulers. Focusing on the Romanov emperors' and empresses' human qualities and legacies, the accounts draw heavily from the country's prerevolutionary historical tradition, and thus help to rehabilitate historical scholarship of the pre-1917 period. Some of the authors also seek to place their work within the context of foreign historical writing. Although the originality of the articles varies considerably, their commonality lies in their authors' attempts to present nonideological, scholarly reassessments of Russia's leaders that would appeal to the reading public and serve as starting points for future research. Eschewing the naive romanticization of the past often found in popular writing in the wake of the collapse of the Soviet Union, the authors of the portraits of the tsars composing this anthology depict their protagonists as complex human beings, not as flat, wooden representatives of "feudal" or "capitalist" Russia's ruling class.

These dispassionate rediscoveries of the Romanovs contribute to the revitalization of the historical profession in Russia, place serious study of the tsars on the research agenda, and initiate beneficial dialogue with foreign scholars. Collectively, they underscore several prominent themes in Russian history. First, in emphasizing the rulers' upbringing, education, and personalities they clearly show that many of the Romanovs who occupied the Imperial throne were ill-prepared to rule. The consequences of this often proved tragic for the individuals, and for Russia as well. To be sure, some of the Romanovs were victims of historical circumstance; however, it was at such times that their shortcomings as individuals especially made themselves felt. Second, military affairs and preparedness for war permeated all aspects of life in the empire, affecting its social structure and shaping the various rulers' attitudes toward reform. War had been the midwife of change for Peter the Great, and in similar ways it affected Tsar-Liberator Alexander II's decision to emancipate the Russian peasantry in 1861. Third, there were structural and even institutional limitations to autocratic power; the Romanov emperors and empresses had to take into account the attitudes of the ruling strata and even the broader population at times. Failure to do so cost more than one ruler his crown—and life. Fourth, the problem of reform in Russia looms large already by the reign of Catherine the Great. We are reminded of several historical turning points during which the introduction of systemic political reform might have resulted in the evolution of a constitutional order in the country, thereby deflecting Russia from the path of revolution. Yet the institutional as well as the personal impediments to reform become adumbrated as we view Russian history through this bright spotlight focused on the country's rulers. Fifth, the question of Russia's relationship to the West—or how western Russia was—moves to center stage with the wrenching changes introduced by Peter the Great. The unanticipated consequences of his relentless improvisations made Russia more western at a superficial level, but less so in regard to the role played by autonomous social groups in public life. In time, many among the educated strata used the West as a yardstick with which to measure Russian developments, seeking to redefine and renegotiate society's relationship to the autocratic system. Sixth, growing disaffection with the Imperial system constructed by Peter I serves as a subtext and counterplot to the lives and reigns of the tsars, first within government circles, and then among a growing educated stratum of the population. This dissension evolved against a backdrop of mass discontent, which periodically exploded into paroxysms of violence.

Despite the common threads woven through all the essays presented here, no attempt was made to put together a team of authors who agreed about the past, let alone Russia's path to revolution. The reader will therefore encounter authors who decry the uncritical stereotypes in circulation about a particular ruler only to discover that other authors in this same volume repeat them. This would suggest that the essays will contribute to what promises to be a lively debate among Russian authors.

This volume comprises portraits of the Romanov tsars that appeared in the journal *Voprosy istorii* beginning with the reign of Peter the Great (1689–1725), which marks the start of the Imperial period of Russian history. Three Romanovs who reigned during brief transition periods—Catherine I (1725–27), Peter II (1727–30), and Ivan VI (1740–41)[1]—are not treated separately; however, they are mentioned in the other essays and in the introductory remarks to the individual articles included in the anthology.

Unless otherwise indicated, all dates in this book are given in the so-called Old Style, according to the Julian calendar, which was eleven days behind the Gregorian calendar of the West in the eighteenth century, twelve days behind it in the nineteenth century, and thirteen days behind it in the twentieth century. A list of suggested readings identifying the most important scholarly accounts of the emperors and empresses of Russia can be found at the end of the book.

I would like to take this opportunity to extend my sincerest thanks to Patricia A. Kolb, Executive Editor at M. E. Sharpe Inc., who backed this project from the start and who facilitated its publication in many ways. Thanks, too, to Ana Erlić who saw the volume through production. Kim Braithwaite translated the essays, except for the one on Peter I, which Carolyn J. Pouncy translated. She and Atherton Noyes assisted in copyediting them when they were first published in English. Carolyn Pouncy later carefully copyedited the entire volume. I also received much appreciated research and editorial assistance from Elizabeth Jones Hemenway, Amy Lewis, Anthony Young, and Susan Beam Eggers who, as editorial assistants, helped me put out *Russian Studies in History* during the past several years, where these articles, again with the exception of the one on Peter I, first appeared in translation.[2] Elizabeth Hemenway also prepared the name index to this book. A special thanks as well goes to Professors Joseph Bradley and Christine Ruane, who succeeded me as editors of *Russian Studies in History*, for inviting me to serve as guest editor of the Winter 1995–96 issue of the journal (vol 34, no. 3). This issue first published the essays on Nicholas I, Alexander III, and Nicholas II.

Donald J. Raleigh
Chapel Hill, NC

Notes

1. Recently published, these portraits have not yet appeared in English translation. They are V.I. Buganov, "Ekaterina 1," *Voprosy istorii*, no. 11 (1994), pp. 39–49; A.B. Kamenskii, "Ivan VI Antonovich," same issue, pp. 50–62, and E.V. Anisimov, "Petr II," *Voprosy istorii*, no. 8 (1994), pp. 61–74.

2. It should be noted that virtually all of the essays as published here incorporate authors' corrections and changes, and that, in particular, V.A. Fedorov's essay on Alexander I has been extensively revised by the author since its initial publication.

Introduction

Akhmed Akhmedovich Iskenderov

For a long time, the history of the Romanov dynasty was a topic all but forbidden to official Soviet historiography, which in principle reacted negatively to dynastic history in general, and to the history of the Romanovs and the reigns of its individual representatives in particular. They were subjected to severe criticism, fundamentally denunciatory in nature. What epithets were not bestowed upon the Russian tsars! They were accused of every vice—stupidity, spinelessness, petty tyranny, incompetence in and disinclination to occupy themselves with affairs of state, even dislike of Russia. Only a few Romanovs, for example Peter I, attracted the attention of historians and writers, but in most cases the portraits that were created reflected the biased political and ideological directives that prevailed in society at that time.

Particularly harsh criticism was applied to the last Romanovs, whose activity was perceived as entirely negative. This served the goal of demonstrating that Russia, as it strove to reach the level of the industrially developed countries of Europe and the world, had no alternative other than a violent, revolutionary break with its existing way of life and prior system of social relationships.

Only recently, in the wake of the changing situation in the new Russia and society's growing interest in the fatherland's true history, have publications (including reprints) of memoirs and monographs previously unknown to Russian readers begun to appear. These publications have made it possible to examine our country's past anew and to characterize without bias the state and public figures who performed on the political stage, including the members of the Romanov dynasty and this dynasty's role and place in Russian history.

Unfortunately, we have not always reached this point without going to extremes: often a minus sign has simply been exchanged for a plus sign, and one or another representative of the Romanov dynasty has been transformed, by the stroke of an author's pen, from a reactionary to a progressive. Such a metamorphosis, of course, does not add to objective knowledge or promote the restoration of truth, but merely complicates the process of discerning historical reality.

The essays included in this book were originally published in the journal *Voprosy istorii* (Problems of History). During preparation of the present volume, some corrections and additions were made to several of the articles, primarily because it was necessary to consider new archival documents that have been made available only recently. When the editors of *Voprosy istorii* set out several years ago to present Russian and world history first and foremost through the fate of individuals, and thus overcome the "facelessness" of historical writing at that time, they created a new feature called "Historical Portraits." The editors sought to avoid artificial schemata and to overcome the false constructions that distorted and impoverished Russian history, minimized the roles of many historical figures, and sapped the dramatic content from real historical processes. The study of the behavior, psychology, and affiliations of historical figures and their milieux makes it possible to perceive more clearly and to comprehend more deeply the essence of historical processes, phenomena, and facts often hidden from a cursory glance.

The non-Russian reader of this book should keep in mind the set of circumstances that influenced the content of the essays included here.

In preparing this volume, the authors made an effort to ensure that their assessments and conclusions would be based on an impartial analysis of all the relevant facts and documents, including those previously not only unknown to the general reader but unavailable even to scholars, and on the objective comparison of various viewpoints and ideas. This, of course, entailed considerable difficulties. The greatest of these, perhaps, was that already during the lifetimes of the Russian tsars and tsaritsas, all sorts of rumors, gossip, and even legends appeared and achieved wide circulation. In time some of these versions became so familiar that they were no longer perceived as inventions; moreover, they often appeared to be confirmed by documentation. Even now, one cannot always be sufficiently certain that one has succeeded in separating fact from fiction.

Russian readers find it very difficult, even painful, to free themselves from the grip of the view of history formulated over decades under the influence of false ideological stereotypes and various myths that found their way into the literature, especially into popular literature. Because of this, the Russian public's historical consciousness often proves incapable of perceiving views, assessments, and approaches that are unfamiliar and that contradict the impressions deliberately instilled over the years. Fortunately, a new understanding of many events, facts, and the very role played by historical figures, including the members of the Romanov dynasty that ruled Russia for more than three hundred years, is gradually being established. The essays presented here to the non-Russian reader offer tangible evidence that, despite the problems, a new conception of Russian history is beginning to take hold.

The book includes eleven essays on the lives and reigns of the Romanovs, from Peter I to Nicholas II, ending with the February Revolution of 1917. By this means, readers may trace almost the entire history of the Romanov dynasty, comparing and contrasting its individual rulers' activities, world views, and personal qualities, and thereby make their own judgments.

The authors rejected the preconceived, predetermined, and one-sided evaluation of historical personages that is fatal to history. The issue is not at all about idealizing the Russian autocrats, about closing one's eyes to their mistakes and keeping silent about errors they made in both foreign and domestic policy or even about crimes they committed. As is well known, even the august figures themselves evaluated their ancestors in a far from monolithic way. Nicholas II, for example, reacted to Peter I quite dispassionately, reproaching him for his excessive enthusiasm for Western modes of life and accusing him of contempt for Russian traditions and customs and of an unwillingness to study fully Russian conditions and peculiarities before implementing reform.

It would be inaccurate, however, to forget the enormous contribution that the members of this dynasty made to Russia's history. And in fairness, this applies not only to the epoch immediately following the Time of Troubles, when the early Romanovs essentially saved the Russian state from complete disintegration. Not only did they restore the collapsed structure of the Russian state system, but they infused it with new life, boldly discarding the old foundations and structures. Under the Romanovs' scepter, Russia was transformed into one of the great powers—not only in Europe but in the entire world. Each of the Romanovs—within the limits of his or her understanding of the state, of the essence and meaning of the mission laid upon the ruler, of Russia's role in Europe and the world, and, indeed, of his or her personal qualities—made a contribution to the development and strengthening of the state. It is still incumbent upon historians to portray these contributions with sufficient thoroughness and scholarly objectivity. Here it is important that the authors of the published essays tried not simply to describe the Romanov emperors and empresses who ruled Russia, but to contextualize them by viewing them first as representatives of their own times.

For all the diversity of the Romanovs, both as individuals and as political figures, a distinct historical continuity may be discerned in the political course they set, making it possible to view this dynasty's annals as the single and unified story of this crucial institution of state power, reflecting the general tendencies of Russian society's development and expressing its interests and demands. Thus, Peter I's reforms cannot be understood in all their depth if we examine them in isolation from that which occurred during the reign of Aleksei Mikhailovich and evolved under Fedor Alekseevich, nor should the activities of Catherine II properly be assessed without considering the actions of her predecessors. During the later stages of Russia's historical and cultural development, when the necessity of reforming society and the state became ever more vital, this continuity may be even more keenly perceived.

One of the fundamental distinctions of Russian history was the exclusive role played by monarchs in all aspects of public life. The autocracy's nature changed, and this or that monarch's influence on political, economic, social, and spiritual life waxed or waned, but royal figures and their immediate entourages invariably remained central. The reasons that the ruling dynasty had so important and influential a role demand thorough and fundamental historical analysis. It is perfectly clear, however, that the history of the Romanov dynasty is not only inseparable from the main line of the Russian historical process, but also that, taken as a whole, the evolution of the institution of monarchical power expresses the main content of this process.

One may, for example, evaluate variously Nicholas I's activities and historical role, but one will hardly find a historian who will deny that it was precisely in the second quarter of the nineteenth century that the reform of Russia's state system, begun under Peter the Great and continued by Catherine II and Alexander I, was completed. Nicholas I's reign may be considered the apogee of autocratic rule in

Russia. It is not at all accidental that precisely as this historical stage drew to a close, a turning point in Russian history occurred, encouraging the development of tendencies that bore fruit in the reforms realized by his successors. Perhaps, because of this organic link between the evolution of the Romanov dynasty and the main line of the country's historical path, the sharp break in this crucial institution of state power determined, to no small degree, the catastrophic character of Russia's later history.

It may be that not all the authors' positions, conclusions, and assessments will satisfy the non-Russian reader. We hope, however, that, in making this volume's acquaintance, the reader will examine Russia's history anew, seeing it as it really was, and acquire a deeper understanding of the country's present and a greater ability to imagine its historical destiny.

THE
EMPERORS AND
EMPRESSES
OF RUSSIA

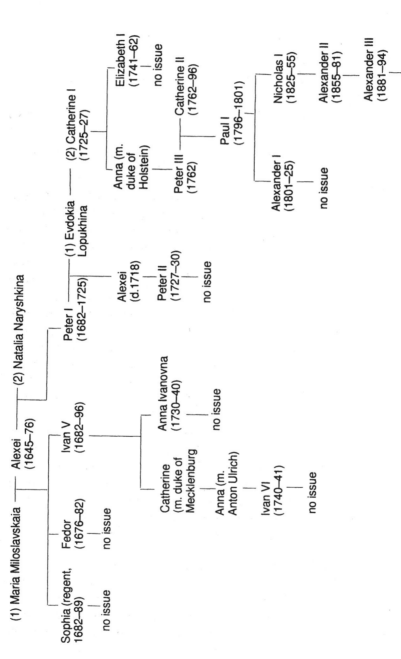

Emperors and Empresses of Russia

Emperor Peter I, 1682–1725

It is fitting that this volume opens with a portrait of that giant of Russian history, Peter the Great, whose reign marks the beginning of the history of Imperial (rather than Muscovite) Russia, a period characterized by expansion westward and the moving of the nation's capital from Moscow to St. Petersburg near the Baltic Sea. Peter's daunting image has played a central role in the evolution of Russian historical writing and in how Russians have understood their country's place in the world. As historian Marc Raeff observed years ago, "the historiography of Peter the Great provides an almost perfect mirror for the Russian intelligentsia's views on the past and future of Russia, their relationship to the West, and the nature of the social and political problems confronting their country."[1] Raeff's remark remains valid today as historians search for ways to explain how Russia's political culture and historical traditions contributed to the rise of Bolshevism and shaped Marxism's peculiar development in Russia after the Revolution of 1917.

Emphasizing that Peter the Great "cannot be evaluated unidimensionally," Iaroslav Evgenievich Vodarskii accents Peter's formative years and experiences, and closes with a probing assessment of the long-term consequences of Peter's reforms on the course of Russian history. Vodarskii draws on the evaluations of Peter made by prerevolutionary Russia's premier historian, V.O. Kliuchevskii, as well as on a serious study from the Soviet period by N.I. Pavlenko, and a powerfully argued post-Soviet account by E.V. Anisimov. In his striving to present a multifaceted portrait of Peter, Vodarskii weighs the emperor's accomplishments and failures. The author believes that neither Peter's upbringing nor his education "sufficed to separate him from the class of serfowners to which he had been born." Viewed through this lens, Peter's policies fall into focus. But Vodarskii's explanation of Peter's shortcomings is not a justification of his statecraft. Indeed, while casting Peter as a "great statesman," the author

3

*nonetheless concludes that Peter's actions "obstructed Russia's progressive evo-
lution to the greatest extent possible, creating conditions that continued to
hinder it for 150 years!" Vodarskii's negative assessment complements other
contemporary Russian studies of Peter I as well, and this, as Raeff suggests,
undoubtedly reflects current concerns over the cost of Peter's extending a military model of organization to society at large.*

D.J.R.

Note

1. Marc Raeff, ed., *Peter the Great Changes Russia*, 2d ed. (Lexington, Mass., 1972), p. 195.

Peter I

Iaroslav Evgenievich Vodarskii

One cannot evaluate Peter I, either as a political figure or as a person, unidimensionally. Indeed, how would it be possible to do so?
Among both contemporaries and heirs his reforms evoked altogether contradictory opinions. These were formulated most dis-
tinctly during the Westernizer–Slavophile debates in the middle of
the nineteenth century. The Westernizers connected Peter to the
best in Russian history; in the Slavophiles' opinion, he betrayed the
national principle of Russian history, distorted Russian culture by
borrowing from the West, and damaged the country's natural path of
development. As one modern scholar correctly noted, many legends
and stereotypes surround his name: "the tsar carpenter, the worker
on the throne," "a stern man, but fair and democratic," "the voice of
the ruling class's interests," "the one who fleeced" the peasants, and
so on.1 By themselves, these assessments are, on the whole, accurate,
but each presents only part of his character.

Overall, Russian historians have evaluated Peter's activities positively: his reforms "placed Russia on a path of accelerated economic,
political, and cultural development"; "Peter sharply intensified the
processes already under way in the country and forced it to take a
giant leap, carrying Russia through several stages at once"; "even so
odious an instrument of the absolutist state as despotic, autocratic

power was transformed into a force for progress thanks to Peter the Great's activities, which were historically justified and served Russia's developmental interests to the highest degree."[2] In considering their analyses against the facts cited, however, one is struck by how poorly the conclusions fit the assessments, which also are stereotypes.

Peter was born on 30 May 1672, the product of Aleksei Mikhailovich's (Alexei's) second marriage, to Natalia Kirillovna Naryshkina. In health and vitality he diverged sharply from his elder brothers, Fedor and Ivan, born during Alexei's first marriage to [Maria] Miloslavskaia (Fedor, who assumed the throne in 1676 upon his father's death, expired one month before his twenty-second birthday; Ivan was sickly from birth and incapable of ruling), and rumors circulated that Tsar Alexei was not Peter's father. Nothing definite may be said about this, but the argument made about Peter's great energy is unconvincing, since Tsarevna Sophia, also born of Miloslavskaia, was a very energetic woman.

Fedor Alekseevich died on 27 April 1682, and Peter was proclaimed tsar, but on 15 May a long-expected uprising among the musketeers broke out in Moscow. The musketeers, an infantry unit in the Russian army, occupied a unique position. The major part of them (twenty regiments) lived in Moscow in their own households, and in peacetime, when the entire army (except for two regiments) was released to their homes, they occupied themselves with trade and crafts. The uprising resulted from the bad treatment they received from their commanding officers, who oppressed the musketeers, exacted money from them, forced them to work for the officers themselves, and so on.

On 23 April, four days before Fedor's death, the musketeers sent him a petition. On 29 April they sent a second petition, and on 15 May, armed, they burst into the Kremlin. Opponents of the Naryshkins, who were now in power, had circulated rumors that Tsarevich Ivan had been murdered, and Tsaritsa Natalia was forced to bring Tsar Peter and Tsarevich Ivan out on the balcony. But this did not quiet the musketeers, who burst into the palace, killing two of the tsaritsa's brothers and many dignitaries whom they hated. This happened in front of Peter, and probably the shock it caused was why he was subject to fits during moments of stress: his mouth twisted; his cheeks, neck, and legs twitched; he suffered convulsions and lost self-control.

The Naryshkins' supporters were ousted from power, which was taken over by Tsarevna Sophia. Ivan and Peter were declared co-tsars, and Sophia became their regent. Peter and Tsaritsa Natalia were sent to the Moscow suburb of Preobrazhenskoe. Sophia formed an alliance with Prince V.V. Golitsyn, who became head of the government. The musketeers were pacified by a series of concessions and by mustering the gentry as a warning; Sophia did not win their favor with these measures. Her position was still further eroded by Golitsyn's two unsuccessful campaigns against the Crimean Tatars. Russia had to undertake these after entering into a coalition with Poland, Austria (more accurately, the Holy Roman Empire, the emperor of which was Leopold of Austria), and Venice against Turkey. But Poland refused to help Russia because of its claims to Kiev.

Peter's mother requested a gentle and pious tutor; Nikita Zotov, an under-secretary, was chosen. Peter's studies began on 12 March 1677, when he was less than five years old. As was customary, he learned by heart the alphabet, the Book of Hours, the Psalter, the Gospels, and the Acts of the Apostles. In later years, he "freely joined the choir, and read and sang, in his thin baritone, no worse than any deacon."[3] When it came to book-learning, however, Peter made horrific spelling mistakes throughout his life. Zotov's indisputable service was his teaching Peter Russian history. This undertaking was evidently not limited to his teacher's narrations; Peter said that he himself even read the Russian chronicles. One might argue that precisely then, the foundation was laid for the love of his native land that characterized Peter I.

Once ensconced in Preobrazhenskoe, Peter was left to his own devices. Like all boys, he loved to play war games, and his opportunities were great: he had not tin, but live soldiers assigned to him, usually of his own age. As the years passed, the games became more complicated. The Russian army at that time included gentry cavalry, musketeers, regiments of "foreign composition" (ashamedly dubbed by Soviet historians regiments of "new composition"), as well as artillery units in which many foreigners served. Gradually Peter formed two battalions of "boy soldiers," which later became the Preobrazhenskii and Semenovskii Regiments, and a corps of bombardiers. Under the command of foreign officers (who lived in the German Quarter near Preobrazhenskoe), he started serious military study, beginning his "service" as a drummer boy.

The foreign officers taught him arithmetic, geometry, the art of fortification, and the handling of artillery shells. He learned to set off "fires for amusement"—fireworks—which became one of his favorite pastimes. His studies were defined broadly: in 1686 large boats were even constructed in the ponds surrounding Preobrazhenskoe. In 1688, in the village of Izmailovo, Peter found an old boat and recognized with astonishment that ships existed that could go against the wind. This little boat and the tales of great seagoing vessels so captured his imagination that he decided that he himself should learn how to build large ships. A master shipbuilder was immediately found in the German Quarter. When Peter later visited Arkhangelsk and saw the sea with his own eyes, his love at first sight was transformed into a genuine passion; so it remained until the end of his life.

Peter's third great source of enthusiasm (after the sea and military affairs) was the study of crafts; he loved to work with his hands and to do everything himself. By his own count, as a youth he knew fourteen crafts; most of all, he loved to work with a lathe, as a carpenter, building ships. How can one explain Peter's tendency to experience such things for himself, not shrinking even from manual labor? As one scholar aptly remarked, "One cannot imagine his pious father, the 'Quietest One' Aleksei Mikhailovich, doffing his magnificent royal robes and picking up a mason's trowel or a blacksmith's hammer."[4] Here Peter's having been surrounded not by haughty boyars but by master craftsmen played an important, if not crucial, role. The playmates of his childhood games were those who worked in the tsar's enormous household and their children: stablehands, falconers and gyrfalconers, herders, artisans, and so on.

Usually between a tsar's son and such people there was a screen of tutors and personal servitors—gentlemen of the bedchamber, gentlemen of the table, and other courtiers of equally lofty rank and from the most exalted families—who observed court etiquette and prevented the tsarevich from contact with mere servants. Between them and Peter no such screen existed, and the curious boy found himself face to face with people who knew and handled horses and could repair objects of all sorts. Naturally, he wished to learn all that his playmates knew how to do. This meant, first of all, the art of war: once he began to play soldiers, he needed to know all that a soldier should know. Shooting off cannon was more interesting than marching, so Peter became a bombardier. Is it not really fascinating to build a boat oneself? In 1691 Peter sailed on the Iauza [River, near Moscow] in a yacht he himself had built.

In 1689–90 a company of Peter's closest friends was formed. Soon, the most important among them were the son of the court stablemaster, Alexander Menshikov, the foreign captain Franz Lefort, and the gentleman of the table Prince F.Iu. Romodanovskii. With a quick understanding and much initiative, Menshikov, a year younger than Peter, was boundlessly devoted and industrious. When Peter gave him an order, he could be sure that it would be fulfilled, and if unforeseen circumstances arose, then Menshikov would handle them as Peter himself would have done. When such circumstances did arise, Peter's confidence was validated. The Swiss-born Lefort was a mercenary, twice Peter's age. This intelligent man loved gaiety more than anything; one of his contemporaries, Prince B.I. Kurakin, dubbed him "the French debauchee." Lefort understood Peter's character and quickly won his trust, becoming completely essential to him. The third person whom Peter trusted absolutely, entrusting political investigations to him and leaving him in power when he himself went abroad in 1697, was Romodanovskii, whom the same Prince Kurakin described as "a monster in appearance, an evil tyrant in his habits, a person who wished no good toward anyone and was drunk every day."

Members of the old noble families (F.M. Apraksin and others) also entered the tsarevich's company, as did half- or completely Russified foreigners (such as General Patrick Gordon, who had lived in Russia for three decades, or Jacob Bruce, who was born there) and the Russians who had belonged to Peter's make-believe army. The company operated according to comradely principles, which even included the tsar, "bombardier Peter Mikhailov." The tsar insisted on this and sternly rebuked any failure to observe it. The comical head of the company was Prince Romodanovskii, who held the title "prince-caesar"; Peter received his "orders" like any ordinary soldier in the ranks.

While serving in his pretend army, working in the shipyards, and enjoying himself with his company, Peter continued to study the construction of fortifications and shipbuilding. The same year that he built his yacht on the Iauza, he began constructing a warship on Lake Pleshcheevo. When he visited Arkhangelsk in 1693, he ordered that a large ship be built in Holland and began a vessel in the Arkhangelsk shipyard. In 1694 he returned to Arkhangelsk, where the ship he had begun was finished and where the ship from Holland had been taken. That fall Peter participated in large-scale war games in Kozhukhovo, near Moscow. For three weeks the storming of the fortress continued, involving thirty thousand soldiers and musketeers, of whom twenty-four were killed and fifty wounded. Some scholars have argued that these were the first such war maneuvers in Europe, but while this may be literally true, Peter himself later noted that he considered the maneuvers a game.

Besides military affairs and shipbuilding, another game began to develop greatly at this time: the "Most Drunken Council of Fools and Jesters." In October 1691 Peter produced its "rules of order." On 1 January 1692 he placed at its head his former tutor, Nikita Zotov, awarding him the titles "Most holy lord Ianikita, archbishop of Pressburg and patriarch of all the Iauza region and Kukui" and "prince-pope" (Pressburg was the fortress on the Iauza River that Peter's army had stormed, and Kukui a stream that ran through the German Quarter, which was thus also called "Kukui"); the "Council" likewise had a conclave of twelve cardinals. Peter himself performed a deacon's duties. The first commandment for members of the "Council" was daily drunkenness. Upon initiation, new members were asked, not "do you believe?" but "do you drink?" Some of its rituals cannot be described, because of their indecency. The "Council" went from party to party, not limiting itself to holidays, but throwing "feasts of Bacchus" and "struggles against Ivashka [Johnny] Khmelnitskii."*

In structuring the "Council" Peter used not only concepts from Orthodoxy (the patriarch and the like) but those from Catholicism (pope, conclave, cardinals). N.N. Molchanov justly considered the "Council" a vicious parody of the entire Church hierarchy and an "extraordinary sacrilege."[5] But why did Peter, who of course believed in God and who participated in church services (he sang in the choir), make up such a game? Historians get lost in speculation. Of course, their statements as to the almost perpetual drunkenness of not only the highest clergy but monks and many priests are justified. It is well known that in Western Europe there were organizations that parodied church institutions.[6] Peter may have known about these. Some historians have argued that the establishment of the "Council" was intended to dethrone the patriarch then in power. It is true that, according to the customs of the time, on Palm Sunday a ceremonial procession took place, during which the tsar led the donkey on which the patriarch rode. Peter held a procession of his "councillors," during which the "prince-pope," the "jesters' patriarch," rode high on an ox, accompanied by a cart to which pigs, bears, and goats were hitched.

The "Council" had, of course, as one of its goals vilification of the Church hierarchs, particularly the patriarch, and the denigration of

---

*A play on the word *khmelet'*, to get drunk or tipsy. (Bogdan) Khmelnitskii was also the name of a Ukrainian Cossack who led a revolt against the Poles. His son Iurii later ruled over the "right bank" Ukraine west of the Dnieper River, which remained Polish.—D.J.R.

the Church as an institution that claimed to share power with the tsar. It was also, however, a way to humiliate the boyars, or aristocracy, whose members either joined the "Council" or were subject to the "councillors'" sorties and to humiliation within their own homes. Needing recreation after hard physical labor, war exercises, and intellectual efforts, Peter sometimes chose this form of entertainment. The crudity of the forms that these games assumed can be explained, as N.I. Pavlenko noted, by the deficiencies in Peter's upbringing, by his crude tastes, and by his unbridled energy.[7] One should not forget that Peter was raised in a far from regulated environment and that he had opportunities to engage in all kinds of pursuits.

Thus Peter's childhood and youth passed in games, military service, physical labor at the shipyards, and wild and indecent parties. What did he learn during these years? He became a soldier, a drummer boy, and a gunner; he was even wounded during one of his war games (an exploding shell hit him in the face). He became a carpenter who built ships and mastered other crafts as well that he needed in order to construct small vessels. He became a patriot, a committed supporter of Western culture and science, and an opponent of his ancestors' customs, which stood in the way of adopting that culture and those sciences. He did not receive the upbringing that had previously been obligatory for Russian tsareviches, but he was raised in an environment composed of household servants, stablehands, and other simple folk, along with foreign adventurers, rude mercenaries, and artisans, with whom he—himself soldier, officer, sailor, and artisan—felt himself at home. He smoked tobacco and drank vodka, just like them; he served as a soldier and worked, physically, just as hard as they; in a word, he was one of them, and he earned their respect, not only because he was tsar, but because, like them, he was a laborer. And he amused himself as they did, rudely, drunkenly, with youthful enthusiasm violating the limits of prudence and decency as he mocked those whom he saw as ill-wishers: the Church, the boyars, and the customs that confined him.

In 1689 Peter turned seventeen, and he could then lay claim to real power. Sophia's followers tried to retain the musketeers' support, so as to prevent any power shift toward Peter, and perhaps even to kill him. During the night of 7/8 August 1689, news that the musketeers were gathering in the Kremlin suddenly reached Peter, and he fled the palace in his undergarments, heading for a grove near Preobrazhenskoe. There he was brought clothes and, accompanied by several others, he took off for the Trinity–St. Sergius Monas-

Peter I

tery, placing himself behind the protection of its walls. In response to his call, soldiers and several regiments of musketeers came to his aid and met him at the monastery. No one continued to support Sophia, and she was incarcerated in the Novodevichii Convent. Power returned to the Naryshkins, but Peter did not immediately take the reins into his own hands; he had priorities of his own.

He was unhappy in his family life. In 1689 his mother, hoping he would settle down, married him to Evdokia Lopukhina, a young girl from an impoverished gentry clan. Peter did not meet with understanding from her nor find in her a life companion, and because of his youth and preoccupation with his own affairs, he paid no attention to reeducating her (whether such an attempt would have been successful is unknown). Instead, he washed his hands of his wife and his son Alexei, born in 1690, spending his free time in the German Quarter with his mistress Anna Mons. (There is some evidence that she was Lefort's mistress first, and that Lefort gave way to his young friend[8]; Peter's friends are known to have shared their lovers with him subsequently.) Peter's affair with Anna Mons, which began in 1692, continued until early 1703. In examining the papers of the Saxon envoy, Königsach, who had drowned near Schlüsselberg, Peter discovered his connection with Anna and immediately broke with her.

In 1694 Tsaritsa Natalia died, and Peter took power into his own hands. (His co-ruler, Tsar Ivan, who died in 1696, did not take part in state affairs.) Peter wanted to visit Western Europe, but Russia was embroiled in responsibilities to the coalition fighting against Turkey. It would, of course, be best to appear before the European monarchs as a victor. But where should he strike a blow? The experience of Golitsyn's campaigns illustrated the danger of a strike in the direction of the Crimea, yet the Tatars, while vassals of Turkey, were not Turks. This meant Russia had to take Azov, where there were Turks, as well as an exit to the sea and an opportunity to build a base from which to attack the Crimeans.

In 1695 the Russian army moved toward Azov. General Gordon had jokingly called the maneuvers around Kozhukhovo a "military ballet," cautioning the tsar of its serious consequences. It seems that Peter treated even the campaign against Azov as a continuation of the game. No one considered that the Turks might easily obtain reinforcements and provisions by sea; no one sized up the fortress they intended to storm. The first campaign ended with a retreat from Azov. We may consider this event the end of Peter's war games, the end of his adolescence and youth. He began to think and act like a statesman.

Even in Tsar Alexei's time shipyards had appeared in Voronezh for the construction of river vessels. Now bigger ships as well were built there. Peter himself participated in building them. In the spring of the next year, 1696, an entire squadron was made ready: two large ships, twenty-three galleys, and four fire ships. With their help Azov was taken. Thus the glorious three-hundred-year history of the Russian navy began.

During the Azov campaigns, Peter proved himself a statesman and a good organizer; he did not allow his spirit to flag in the face of failure or lose his self-confidence. Peter considered the Azov campaigns in particular the beginning of his military service.

Azov's fall made it possible to construct a base for the navy on the shore of the Sea of Azov (at Taganrog) and to begin the mission to Western Europe. First of all, however, came the celebration of the victory. For Moscow's residents, who feared the drunken revelry of Peter and his companions, the celebration came as yet one more shock. They saw a triumphal ark decorated with biblical sayings and with pictures of unknown naked people (Greek and Roman gods subduing their enemies), "Patriarch of the Jesters' Council" Nikita Zotov's luxurious carriage, the no less luxurious coach of Admiral Lefort—and the tsar, who, amid the opulently equipped, magnificently armed, and beautifully dressed boyars, walked in a simple shirt, carrying a lance in his hand!

Although he could ignore the feelings of the people and the boyars, Peter nonetheless had to reckon with the Boyar Council, or Duma. He convened it on 20 October, and it ratified his decisions, agreeing to place a garrison in Azov, to send twenty thousand men to construct a naval base at Taganrog, and—a historic decision—"that there should be naval vessels!" Where, however, was the money to build them to be found? Where were the naval officers and shipbuilders? On 4 November the Boyar Council affirmed another of Peter's decisions: owners of one hundred or more serf households would be combined into "companies," each of which (that is, every ten thousand households owned by lay proprietors and every eight thousand of the Church's households) would give the money to build one ship. All the urban homesteaders (traders and artisans) would together pay for fourteen vessels. By this means fifty-two warships were built during the next two years. By 22 November Peter had already commanded that sixty-one young members of noble clans (including twenty-three princes) be sent abroad to study naval service and the command of ships.

Although most of the army consisted of regiments "of foreign composition," the musketeers, who had supported Sophia in 1682, represented a sizable force. After the taking of Azov, Peter did not dismiss the musketeer regiments, sending part of them to govern the western border. Tsikler, a colonel in the musketeers, along with two gentlemen of the table, Sokovnin and Fedor Pushkin, planned to raise a revolt against Peter taking advantage of the musketeers' discontent. On 23 February 1697 the plan was discovered, and at the beginning of March the conspirators were subjected to a most cruel execution.

A few days later, the "Grand Embassy" set out for Western Europe. It included three senior ambassadors—Franz Lefort, F.A. Golovin, and P.B. Voznitsyn—and a large retinue of about 250 people, among whom was "sergeant Peter Mikhailov" (the tsar). Thirty-five young volunteers traveled with them. The Grand Embassy's official purpose was to strengthen the coalition against Turkey and the Crimea, but it was all really a cover for Peter's visit. Still fond of games, he made a seal for himself with the elegant words, "For I am a student and ask to be taught."

Peter studied the use of artillery in Brandenburg, receiving a certificate recognizing him as a "master of firepower." Then he visited Saardam, about which he had heard much from the master-craftsmen who worked in Russia. In Saardam, however, they built only merchant ships, so after a week Peter moved to Amsterdam, where he worked in the shipyards for more than four months. While he was there, and with his participation, a warship was built. Amsterdam, however, did not content him either, because the master-craftsmen there could not teach him the theory of shipbuilding. He left for England (leaving the Embassy behind and taking only the volunteers), where he spent another three months working.

Both in Holland and in England, Peter did not limit his interests solely to shipbuilding, but absorbed literally everything he encountered. He visited factories, workshops, whaling fleets, hospitals, foundling homes, the botanical garden, Leeuwenhoek's instruments (Leeuwenhoek invented the microscope), and autopsy rooms (in one of them he delightedly kissed a "very well-prepared," to quote S.M. Soloviev, child's corpse; in another, seeing revulsion on his companions' faces, he forced them to touch the corpse). He also studied engraving and the like. Along the way, he induced more than nine hundred specialists, from vice admirals to ships' cooks, to accept service in Russia. From England he returned to Amsterdam, and from there he traveled with the Embassy to Vienna, where he met with the emperor. There Peter received news of a musketeers' uprising, and instead of visiting Venice, he returned to Russia.

What impressions did Peter form during his first trip to Western Europe? To answer this question, we must imagine the difference between Russia's economic and cultural level and that of the advanced Western countries that Peter visited. This difference was considerable, and although Peter had become partially familiar with West European culture in Moscow's German Quarter, it was only partially, because the foreigners who lived in the German Quarter were all from the lower and middle strata (the "outcasts" of Western Europe, as V.O. Kliuchevskii put it), and Western Europe's economic development came as a surprise to him. In Holland hundreds of ships were built at once (Amsterdam alone had several dozen shipyards); many towns had manufactories making sailcloth, rope, paper, glass, textiles, dyes, bricks, and lumber; they produced navigational instruments; the country had thousands of workshops. As early as the beginning of the century, England had begun to smelt coal and iron in large quantities, with more than a thousand furnaces pouring iron and many textile, wool, and other manufactories, including large ones employing thousands of workers.

As Kliuchevskii described it, "on his return to Russia, Peter must have imagined Europe as a noisy and smoky workshop full of machines, ships, shipyards, and factories."[9] But in both countries book publishing, too, was highly developed (England produced about forty agronomic tracts in the first half of the century); the classic philosophical and political economic works of Hobbes, Spinoza, and Petty were published, as were authors like Milton. Newspapers were printed, and theaters operated.[10] Undoubtedly Peter also knew about France's economic development, particularly the results of Colbert's activities. His encouragement of trade and creation of large factories to supply the military resulted in the creation of a great navy.

What was Russia like back then? It had several ironmaking factories near Tula, Kashira, Moscow, and Voronezh, as well as several factories for salt, leather, glass, papermaking, and copper smelting. These were not thousands, not even hundreds, but individual factories. Russia had no proper standing army, only a few regiments of soldiers, the musketeers, and the gentry cavalry units, all poorly armed. Between wars, these units returned to their homes. There was no navy. Russia had few schools, and those, controlled by the Church, taught only reading and writing; there were no universities, no scholars, and no doctors. The country had one pharmacy, which belonged to the tsar. It had no newspapers, and only one publishing house, which primarily issued ecclesiastical books. Merchants and artisans lived at the mercy of the military governors, who ruined them through frequent requisitions. Western European culture could be found only among the upper levels of the nobility, and then rarely, as it encountered fierce opposition. As to Peter's own cultural level and that of his companions, after their departure from England, the owner of the house in which they had stayed drew up a list detailing the damage they had caused. According to Kliuchevskii, "Even allowing for exaggeration, reading this list makes one shudder. The floors and the walls were spattered and smeared from their parties; the furniture was smashed and the curtains torn; the pictures on the walls had holes in them because they had been used for target practice; and the lawn was torn up, as though an entire army wearing iron boots had drilled on it."[11]

During his trip abroad, Peter saw with his own eyes how far Russia's economic and cultural development lagged behind that of the advanced West European countries. He understood how the development of trade was linked to that of industry and culture, and how all three affected a state's international position (its security); he understood the significance of having an army and a navy, education and scholarship or, as he himself put it, "I would never have become more than a carpenter, had I not studied with the English."[12] Evidently, however, the most important result was that he recognized that Russia lay in grave danger of falling into economic dependence on the advanced countries, that it could be turned into a colony or even vanquished by its neighbors, and that he had a personal responsibility for his country's fate. Not only did he recognize this, but he made a firm decision to act, without delay and decisively, brooking no obstacle.

Peter returned early because of a revolt of the musketeers on the western border, where four Moscow regiments had been sent after the fall of Azov. Messengers sent by the musketeers had arrived in the capital beforehand. Sophia's supporters took advantage of this and invited the musketeers to march on Moscow. They began to move toward the capital, but Shein's and Gordon's troops defeated them at the Istra River. By then Peter was already rushing home. Shein and Romodanovskii began a perfunctory investigation, and with Peter's arrival the inquest was reopened, uncovering evidence that linked the musketeers to Sophia. Peter himself interrogated the prisoners and participated in the unbelievably cruel tortures inflicted on the musketeers. When the main part of the investigation was finished, he joined the executioners and cut off the heads of the condemned, forcing his nearest comrades-in-arms to do likewise. Altogether, more than a thousand musketeers were executed; several were strung up on the walls of the Novodevichii Convent, where Sophia lived as a nun, in front of the tsarevna's windows. The regiments of the Moscow musketeers were disbanded, and they and their families were dispersed to various towns, where they were inscribed in the town registers as artisans and traders. (The musketeers stationed in other towns, however, remained in existence until 1713, when they were incorporated into regiments of regular soldiers.)

After returning from abroad, Peter immediately turned his attention to reform, launching an attack on local customs with his decrees on the shaving of beards and the wearing of European-style dress (peasants and those inscribed on the urban tax rolls who wished to keep their beards could do so if they paid a special tax). He introduced a new calendar and moved the beginning of the year to 1 January. Urban workers were removed from the control of their grasping military governors; institutions of self-government were established in the towns—local houses, subordinate to the Moscow Ratusha,* were assigned to collect taxes.

While implementing reform, Peter concluded the negotiations he had begun abroad for an alliance against Sweden. After the death in 1697 of Polish king Jan Sobieski, Russia and Austria succeeded in securing the election to the Polish throne of Augustus II, elector of Saxony. In 1699, anticipating the imminent death of the Spanish king and a Franco-Austrian war (the Austrian emperor's son and the French king's son were nephews of the Spanish king, and both had laid claim to his throne), Austria, Poland, and Venice, Russia's allies against Turkey, signed a peace treaty with the Ottomans. Peter found himself with a choice: whether to continue fighting Turkey one-on-one or to take advantage of the opportunity created in Europe as Austria and France, then England and Holland, became embroiled in the War of the Spanish Succession to find allies and begin a war with Sweden in order to regain access to the Baltic Sea. The latter was more important for Russia. The Black Sea littoral, much farther from

---

*Often translated as Board of Accounts, which handled state finances.—D.J.R.

Russia's central regions, was also threatened by the Crimean Tatars. The exit from the Black Sea via the Bosporus was closed by Turkey; for these reasons, the Black Sea offered a longer and more dangerous route to the advanced countries.

Weighing all these factors, Peter decided on war with Sweden. Therefore, in 1699 he concluded negotiations with Saxony and Denmark, sent a diplomatic mission to Istanbul on the forty-six-gun warship *Fortress*, built in Voronezh (which had the desired effect), and on 8 August 1700 concluded a peace treaty with Turkey in which the latter acknowledged the loss of Azov.

After disbanding the musketeers' regiments, Peter found himself, in effect, without troops. He had two regiments of former "make-believe soldiers," several regiments of "foreign composition" (long since dispersed), the gentry muster, and that was all. In November 1699 Peter instituted a levy of "volunteer" soldiers as well as a gathering of "conscripts" from selected peasant households. Nine regiments (consisting of thirty-two thousand men) were formed in the spring of 1700. The foreign officers whom Peter had brought quickly trained them. The gentry muster was called up, as well as 3,500 Cossacks. The army set off for Narva on 9 August and reached it on 23 September. A siege began.

On 16 November Peter received news of Charles XII's advance; at dawn on 19 November he left for Novgorod, and by the middle of the next day the Swedes had attacked the Russian positions. Toward evening the gentry cavalry retreated to the opposite shore of the Narva. The mercenary commander-in-chief of the army, the Duke de Croy, was captured, along with almost all of the foreign officers and some of the Russians; only the Preobrazhenskii and Semenovskii Regiments and Golovin's division were still in a condition to defend themselves. Their commanders began negotiations with Charles XII. As a result, these units left Narva with their personal arms and their banners; almost one-third of the army, about 80 officers, including 10 generals, and 135 cannon were lost.[13] This defeat probably did not take Peter by surprise. Later, he acknowledged that "this whole matter was like a little boy's game."[14] As had happened after the first Azov campaign, however, this incident revealed a characteristic feature of his: he did not lose heart in the face of failure.

Why did Peter leave the army on the eve of battle? Later, in *The History of the Swedish War*, which he edited, he explained that it was necessary to hurry the remaining regiments of the Russian army along the road to Narva and "especially, to greet the Polish king."

This explanation, however, sounds unconvincing. One cannot accuse Peter of personal cowardice: he proved that in later battles, for example, by his participation in the fight at Poltava, where he led the troops himself and was almost killed (a bullet pierced his hat). One may suggest that the main reason for Peter's departure was his awareness of his own uselessness in battle because of his lack of experience in commanding warriors. He may at that time have thought that his presence would hinder the Duke de Croy, whom he had invited to lead the army and on whose experience, it seemed, he could depend (Peter never again pinned all his hopes on foreign commanders). But as he studied the evidence of the orders he had given and reviewed the events of his life, he could not, either then or later, acknowledge this.

After Narva, Charles XII faced a dilemma. Should he march into the depths of Russia, knowing a Saxon army, much more war-ready than the Russian one, was at his back, or should he turn against Augustus II? Choosing the second option, the Swedish king became "bogged down" in Poland. He managed to compel Augustus II to make peace and abandon his alliance with Russia only in 1706. Meanwhile, Peter acted with astonishing energy. He took full advantage of the breathing space that the Swedes had given him. As Kliuchevskii wrote, "Leaving his generals and admirals to act at the front, Peter . . . gathered recruits, drew up plans for troop movements, built ships and factories to supply the army, and procured ammunition, provisions, and military supplies. He stored everything and equipped everyone; he urged, quarreled, fought, promised, and coaxed from one end of the state to the other; he was general-fieldmaster, general-quartermaster, and master shipbuilder all at once."[15] Despite this, he still found time to enact reforms.

The results of this activity became evident very quickly—by the end of 1701 the Russian army began in places to beat the Swedes. In 1702 Peter took Oreshok (and renamed it Schlüsselberg); he began constructing St. Petersburg at the mouth of the Neva in 1703. Iam, Kopore, and Marienburg were also taken, and in 1704 he stormed and seized Narva. An uprising in Astrakhan was savagely put down in 1705, and 1707–8 saw the suppression of K.I. Bulavin's revolt.* In 1708 Peter defeated the Swedes at the village of Dobroe, then Löwenhaupt's corps at the hamlet of Lesnaia, and on 27 June 1709 Charles XII's army at Poltava.

---

*Kondraty Bulavin was a Don Cossack leader who sought to join the Cossacks of the Don and Dnieper into a united front to halt the expansion of the Muscovite state.—D.J.R.

The victory at Poltava became a turning point in Russian history. As V.G. Belinskii aptly noted, "It was a victory for the existence of an entire people and for the future of a whole state."[16] After Poltava, Russia's international standing rose dramatically. Saxony and Denmark renewed their alliance. Prussia then joined it, binding itself not to allow the Swedish troops to pass through its territory, and in 1714 itself entered the war with Sweden (although it engaged in hardly any military action). In 1710 Russia concluded an alliance with Hanover, the elector of which soon became king of England. Peter's son Alexei married the princess of Wolfenbüttel, Emperor Leopold's sister-in-law.

In 1710 the Russian forces took Vyborg, Kexholm (the old Russian town of Korela), Riga, and Reval. Peter allowed the Baltic German nobility to keep their privileges, and they acknowledged Russia's annexation of Estonia and Livland. This was also made possible because the local gentry and bourgeoisie received great profits from the transit trade between Russia and Western Europe, and because the landowners benefited from duties that had formerly gone to the Swedes.

Fearing that Russia would grow even stronger, the Turkish government declared war in the fall of 1710. Peter's reliance on help from the hospodars of Moldavia and Wallachia, themselves pressured by the Turks, proved mistaken, and the Russian army was surrounded on the banks of the Pruth. Although the Turkish attacks were beaten back, Peter decided not to risk his army and began negotiations. According to the peace treaty, Russia had to return Azov to the Turks and tear down the fortress at Taganrog, that is, to lose its access to the Sea of Azov. Peter evaluated his situation soberly: "This event is not without pain, to be deprived of those places where so much effort and loss occurred; however, I hope that this hardship will have as its other side a great strengthening, which will be of incomparable benefit to us."[17] And indeed, peace untied his hands for the war with Sweden.

Ignoring his perilous situation, Charles XII refused negotiations for peace. In 1712–14 the Russian army fought in Finland and northern Germany. The Baltic fleet constructed by Peter also engaged in the action: on 27 July 1714 ten Swedish ships were seized at Hangö. As 1716 approached, the combined Russian, Saxon, and Danish forces had swept the Swedish army out of Germany, and the Russian army and navy had driven them out of Finland. Peace talks with Sweden began in 1718. At the end of 1718, however, Charles XII was killed while besieging a fortress in Norway (which belonged to Denmark), and negotiations broke off. In 1719 the Russian navy gained new victories against the Swedes near the islands of Oesel and Grengi. The Russian ships fought off the very shores of Sweden, putting ashore landing parties there.

Continuing the war required soldiers, arms, ammunition, and money. Along with his military actions, therefore, Peter imposed new taxes and implemented reforms. Altogether, between 1700 and 1720, more than 1,700 legal acts were promulgated, either by Peter himself or by the Senate, the governmental institution he established in 1711. Most of these acts dealt with the most important facets of the country's life. Factories were built, as well as shipyards and ships, canals, and towns. A capital, St. Petersburg, emerged at the mouth of the Neva, and the elite and traders were forced to move there. Tens of thousands of people were mobilized to carry out this construction, many of whom perished. Thousands more fled to escape taxes, the army, or conscription in Peter's building projects. Those caught were savagely punished.

The opposition that congregated around Peter's son Alexei were among those executed. Alexei himself fled abroad and was lured back by the tsar, who then broke his promise to forgive his son, ordered Alexei cruelly tortured in his own presence, and then confirmed the death warrant prepared by a court composed of high government servitors. The tsarevich expired under torture (according to another version, he was murdered) in a chamber in the Peter and Paul Fortress.

In 1703 Peter became involved with Marta, a woman from Livland who had been captured after the storming of Marienburg, the mistress of Field Marshal B.P. Sheremetev, who yielded her to Menshikov, who in turn gave her to Peter. Marta, known after her baptism [into Orthodoxy] as Ekaterina Alekseevna (Catherine), won Peter's heart and became essential to him. Although they had eleven children, only two daughters, Anna and Elizabeth, survived. (Anna was given in marriage to the duke of Holstein, and her son, Peter's grandson, became emperor as Peter III; Elizabeth usurped the throne in 1741 with assistance from the Guards.) In 1711, before the campaign on the Pruth, Peter publicly revealed that Catherine was his wife, and in 1712 they were married in church.

On 30 August 1721 the Treaty of Nystadt concluded the peace negotiations with Sweden. According to the treaty, Russia acquired the Baltic coast from Vyborg to Riga, part of Karelia, Ingria, Estonia, and Livland, with the islands of Oesel, Dago, and Men. Russia was to return Finland to Sweden, pay approximately 1,500,000 rubles, and permit the Swedes to buy and export up to 50,000 rubles worth of grain, duty-free, from the Baltic region. Peter compared the Northern War to a harsh school. "All other students," he noted, "usually end their studies in seven years, but our school lasted three times that (twenty-one years); however, praise be to God, it ended as well as it possibly could have."[18] The victory in the Northern War, the establishment of a regular Russian army and navy, and their military experience made Russia one of the strongest states in Europe. As A.S. Pushkin said, "Russia entered Europe like a ship set free with a stroke of the axe and with guns blaring."[19] The Senate bestowed on Peter the titles of Great, Father of the Fatherland, and Emperor of All Russia.

Muscovy, which to West European eyes had appeared a barbarous kingdom at the level of Crimean and Nogai "Tataria," was transformed into the Russian Empire, becoming the equivalent in international relations of the Holy Roman Empire (the head of which stood higher than kings), England, France, Holland, and Spain. The view expressed in 1670 by one of the most advanced scholars in Europe, Gottfried Wilhelm Leibniz, was typical: he suggested that Russia's destiny was to become a Swedish colony.[20] How this changed as a result of Peter's actions is beautifully illustrated by France's ambassador to Russia, Jean-Jacques Campredon, who wrote, after the end of the Northern War, "Faced with the smallest demonstration by its [Russia's] navy, the first movement of its troops, neither the Swedish, nor the Danish, nor the Prussian, nor the Polish crown dares to take hostile action against it or to move their troops from their places, as they had done before present conditions prevailed."[21]

After the victory at Poltava, Peter could pursue an imperial policy, with the goal of widening and strengthening Russia's influence in both neighboring and distant lands. One example of this policy was the Persian campaign of 1722–23, when the Russian army captured Derbent, Baku, and Rasht; Iran agreed to transfer these cities to Russia if Russia helped the shah against Afghan insurgents. In 1724 Peter agreed with Turkey on mutual recognition of the possessions he had won from Iran and ordered the carrying out of reconnaissance of passages through the Caucasus suitable "for military actions." He also sought a route through Central Asia, considered India, and prepared an expedition to Madagascar.[22]

With renewed strength Peter prepared to continue his reforms: between 1720 and 1725, he had 1,200 legislative acts published, almost as many as during the preceding decade. A new state apparatus was created; new groups of the population were enserfed; and a new tax was introduced—the poll tax. Peter ordered cartographers be trained and began mapping Russia's territory. He sent Vitus Bering's expedition to verify whether Asia was joined to America (S. Dezhnev's 1648 discovery of the strait between them had by then been forgotten). He founded the Academy of Sciences and invited distinguished foreign scholars to join it; he opened the Kunstkamera and its library to visitors.

After the death of the last son from his marriage with Catherine, Peter promulgated a special decree in 1722, in which the emperor could name his own heir. Evidently he did not want the throne to pass to his grandson Peter, Alexei's son. In 1723 he declared Catherine empress, and in the next year formally crowned her. This, the last year of his life, proved to be very difficult for him. Menshikov, the tsar's closest friend and aide, his "brother," the "child of [his] heart," as Peter often called him, was again caught embezzling, this time on a large scale; a group of the tsar's closest companions was also involved.

Catherine, whom Peter had obviously intended as his successor (why else would he have crowned her?), was discovered to be romantically involved with her chamberlain, William Mons, the younger brother of Anna Mons. Peter undoubtedly found this a severe blow; although he himself had not maintained fidelity during his marriage, he could not excuse his wife's infidelity, especially because she was newly crowned. Mons was executed for bribe-taking in 1724; in dealing with the problem in this way Catherine's name was not mentioned. By then Peter was already seriously ill, and on 28 January 1725 he died in agony from uremia, not having managed to name his heir (male or female).[23] His last "testament," published later, was a forgery.[24]

Peter was, of course, a remarkable person. As one of his recent biographers correctly noted, "he was simultaneously hot-tempered and cold-blooded, extravagant and careful to the point of stinginess, cruel and soft-hearted, demanding and humble, rude and polite, prudent and hasty," but "despite all the motley features of Peter's character, his was a surprisingly whole nature. The idea of serving the state, in which the tsar profoundly believed and to which he subordinated his activities, was the cornerstone of his life."[25] This ideal of state service when combined with Peter's temperament and upbringing explains much of his behavior.

Contemporaries left many portraits of Peter at various times during his life. Here is, perhaps, one of the most complete descriptions of his outward appearance: "Tsar Petr Alekseevich was of great height, more thin than fat. He had thick, short, dark chestnut hair and big, black eyes with long eyelashes. His mouth was well formed, except for his lower lip. His face was handsome, inspiring respect at first glance. Given his great height, his legs seemed to me to be very thin. His head often jerked convulsively to the right."[26] Peter was a head taller than all those around him (2m. 4cm., or 6 feet, 8 inches) and had great physical strength. His natural physique gave him excellent health, but in time heavy drinking and his irregular life style weakened it, and as the Northern War wound down, he began to ail frequently; he underwent water cures and took his pharmacy with him.[27]

The distinguishing features of his character included his love of work, his remarkable capacity for work, his curiosity, his strength of purpose, and the absolute modesty of his private life. Peter lived as a soldier and a laborer: he served in the army, gradually rising through the officers' ranks of both land and sea forces as he accumulated experience; he worked as a shipmaster, drawing a salary only sufficient to cover his personal expenses. He lived in simple houses and disliked lavish lodgings; when assigned residences in foreign capitals, he always chose the most modest rooms, those intended for his servitors. Receptions usually took place at the palaces of his closest companions (Menshikov and the others), so he required them to live in grand style. Peter's diet was adequate, but simple. He slept little and rose early, at five o'clock in the morning; by six he was about his business—off to his building, to the shipyards, to the Senate, or to the Admiralty. He loved physical labor and took pride in his calloused hands. At one in the afternoon (sometimes even earlier) he dined on cabbage soup, buckwheat groats, fried meat with sauces and spices, pickled cucumbers, salt meat, or ham. He disliked fish and sweets. Before dinner he drank vodka, and during the second half of the day he might drink beer and wine. He loved fruit and black bread.

After dinner he napped for about two hours, then worked in his office. He read reports and wrote or edited decrees and instructions. He spent his evenings either with guests or in his own workshop, turning out something of wood or bone. This was his favorite pastime, his form of relaxation. His remaining hours were spent in Senate sessions, or editing *The History of the Northern War*, compiled under his direction, or in diplomatic matters. Usually he returned home about nine o'clock at night. Peter demonstrated a surprising ability to occupy himself simultaneously with different tasks; he could continue thinking about his work even during a banquet or entertainment.[28]

Peter demanded ongoing service, beginning at the lowest ranks, disdain for personal comforts, and great responsibility for the business at hand from all his servitors, regardless of who they were or where they served, and his own view of service provided a personal example. He probably learned in childhood to obey those higher in rank during his games, and later continued this type of behavior so as to offer a personal example. He demanded that his own military promotions be earned, receiving them from "prince-caesar" Romodanovskii. This, of course, was also a game, but one played in all seriousness.

In his upbringing Peter was a soldier, a sailor, and a ship's carpenter, but not in any sense a refined aristocrat. "With all the qualities with which nature has endowed him," said the elector of Brandenburg's mother-in-law when she met the twenty-five-year-old Peter during his first trip to Europe, "one might wish that his tastes were less crude."[29] The crudity, of both the epoch and Peter personally, meant that wild drunkenness accompanied any celebration. Contemporaries, shuddering, described how a guard stood at the doors of Peter's banquet hall while soldiers from the Preobrazhenskii Regiment carried tubs of vodka around, and at the tsar's insistence his guests drank themselves into a stupor. Peter himself drank heavily, but he had a powerful constitution, and in the morning, when his guests could not stagger from their beds, he returned to work as if nothing had happened.

Peter was cruel by nature. Of course, at that time cruelty was enshrined in the law: an investigation was always accompanied by torture; even those who confessed immediately were tortured, lest they had concealed something. Peter was merciless toward those who resisted reform. He ordered his son Alexei's torture, was personally present during that torture, and the day after his son's death celebrated the anniversary of one of his victories! (Even after this, some historians have argued that Peter was a kind person.) Peter ordered the lover of his first wife, tonsured long before, subjected to severe tortures, then impaled on a stake—and, so that he would suffer longer, ordered that he be dressed in a fur coat for the execution (which took place in winter). When unfortunate residents tried to save themselves from the waters during one of the St. Petersburg floods by climbing trees, Peter found the sight funny. His decrees were filled to the brim with threats of harsh punishment, and even of death for their nonfulfillment. The punishments included prohibiting members of the gentry who did not learn arithmetic and geometry from marrying.[30]

Peter was not accustomed to taking anyone else into account. During his second trip to Holland and his visit to France in 1717, he attracted attention because of his unceremonious behavior. For example, when he was involved in business, he did not wait for his retinue, but stopped the first carriage he saw, unseated those in it, and sat down.

Peter chose his aides from his own circle or from among those who distinguished themselves by quick-wittedness, efficiency, and industry. The members of elite clans who were closest to him were, besides Romodanovskii, F.A. Golovin, F.M. and P.M. Apraksin, N.I. Repnin, and P.A. Tolstoy; among those of lesser ranks were P.P. Shafirov, P.I. Iaguzhinskii, and others. Among them Menshikov held first place; Peter trusted him more than he did anyone else, and Menshikov exceeded the others in initiative, energy, and in his tendency to take responsibility. But at times Menshikov's embezzlement of state funds set him apart even during a period when almost everyone was an embezzler and a bribe-taker, and toward the end of Peter's life the tsar's attitude cooled toward him.

Possessing a phenomenal memory and a remarkable capacity for work, Peter monitored every detail. His view of state matters was an outgrowth of his attitude toward military affairs, where an unforeseen and at first glance meaningless circumstance might have lethal consequences. He regulated his subjects' every step. Alongside the major edicts, decrees were issued on the plastering of ceilings, the proper placing of tombstones, and so on. This tendency of Peter's to resolve all issues personally often sapped his subordinates' initiative. Peter "taught" those who blundered or neglected their service with his own cudgel; he punished extraordinary embezzlement of state funds and bribe-taking, even among his closest aides, severely (sometimes with death). But even he could not prevent them from doing this. While signing a reform into law, Peter included an explanation as to why the change was necessary and what advantage it would bring. Sometimes he did not mince words. For example, he demanded that the "Council of Ministers" (the restructured Boyar Duma) affirm his decision, "lest their stupidity otherwise be revealed."[31]

One of Peter's contemporaries portrayed the tsar's attitude toward women very clearly, noting that "His Highness loved the female sex," yet relayed the tsar's statement, "To forget service for a woman's sake is unforgivable."[32] Even after his marriage to Catherine, Peter did not consider himself under any obligation to preserve marital fidelity, and he had many lovers. Not only did Catherine not protest, but she herself presented him with "little mistresses" (evidently, women whom she did not perceive as rivals). When, however, she herself betrayed her husband, she was saved only because, not knowing, Peter had recently had her crowned; for him to make her behavior public would have made him the laughingstock of Europe.

It is typical of Peter that, of all people, he chose to marry Catherine, a former "washerwoman" of low social origins. In his eyes her "sort" meant nothing. With her unusual insight into his complex, contradictory character and his ideal of state service, Catherine succeeded in pleasing him. He believed in her devotion to him and his concerns and was devastated by her infidelity.

For all his faults, Peter had (as one of his contemporaries justly expressed it) "many merits and an extraordinary natural intelligence."[33] Most important to him was service to one's country, "to the common weal," as he understood it, that is, to the preservation and improvement of the state structure. In pursuit of this end he did not spare himself. For it, too, he enacted his reforms. What kind of effect did these have on Russia?

The reform of the military and of national defense. Peter replaced the occasional levies of "conscripts" with yearly recruitment levies and established a trained standing army in which soldiers served for life. He created a navy and set up special schools for the training of officers and subalterns, as well as a printing press to publish technical manuals. The "army of make-believe soldiers" became the Guards regiments. Peter reworked the Army Code and the Navy Code, introducing orders and medals. The army and navy that Peter established defeated the Swedish army, one of the best in Europe.

During Peter's reign, Russia entered the ranks of the most powerful states in Europe. As a result of his efforts, Russian diplomacy rose to the Western European level, and Russian embassies began to appear in the European capitals. With Peter, Russia began to pursue an imperial policy. Peter was a talented general and fleet commander, one of the founding fathers of the Russian military arts.[34] Similarly, he was a gifted diplomat, accurately defining the main direction of Russian foreign policy and successfully realizing it. In his diplomatic activity, Peter revealed a capacity for limitless patience, flexibility, and the ability to make concessions and to compromise. In 1648 at the Peace of Westphalia, the "Grand Prince of Muscovy" had been assigned the next to last place on the list of European monarchs, followed only by the Prince of Transylvania; at the end of Peter's reign, Russia was one of the great powers of Europe.[35]

The reform of industry. During his visit to Europe, and perhaps even earlier, Peter grasped the necessity of developing industry, most importantly to arm and supply the army and navy. On his return from abroad, he immediately began to act. One of Russia's characteristics became the decisive role played by the state. Factories, both state-supported and private, had existed in Russia before Peter's reign, but his intervention sharply accelerated their creation. In the first five years, eleven metal-processing plants were built to satisfy the need for iron, and the construction and expansion of ammunitions factories in 1712 supplied the military with arms. The building and expansion of plants producing textiles, linen, rope, leather, paper, cloth, buttons, hats, glass, and other objects also occurred; sheep and horse ranches were established, and so on. At the end of Peter's reign, Russia had more than two hundred factories (half of them private), that is, about ten times as many as it had had before him. It was precisely during his reign that the Urals emerged as an industrial region.

Peter pushed the development of industry along the same path it had followed before him, that is, that of preserving and expanding factories owned by serfowners. Because Peter's social policy pursued the goal of enserfing previously free population groups (the "vaga-bonds," the "people of various ranks," and others), which dried up the pool of wage laborers, he had to permit the purchase of serfs for factory work, leading to the formation of a new group of serfs, who became known as "possessional peasants." In addition, the reliance of factory production on serfdom was in line with the state regulation of the whole process of industrial development, from investing in enterprises to defining the list of manufactured articles.[36]

The reform of trade. As with industry, Peter devoted considerable attention to developing the state's role in trade. State monopolies on salt and tobacco were introduced, as well as on foreign sales of leather, hemp, linen, grain, potash, caviar, and many other goods. Traders were obliged to sell a portion of their goods to the state. Internal customs duties were retained. Traders, it is true, were released from the military governors' control; organs of self-government were established for them, as well as magistrates, responsible to the Main Municipal Administration, but the tsar appointed their members, which made them one of the state's central governmental bodies.

The state required traders and artisans to render service during the collection of taxes and to form trading and manufacturing companies. It moved them by force from one town to another and told them what routes they could take, what goods they could transport for sale, and what prices they could charge the state. Crafts production in the towns was restricted by the introduction of guilds. In 1721 a regulation from the Main Municipal Administration noted that "the traders and artisans among the tax-paying population in all the towns . . . are all but destroyed." As modern scholars have argued, the result of the trade reform was "the impoverishment and fall of what had once been the wealthiest commercial firms, the destruction of the towns, and the flight of their inhabitants."[37]

The reform of the tax system. War required money, and during most of the time it was under way, Peter sought ways to increase the flow of revenue into the treasury. He began by substituting copper money for silver; he introduced new taxes; he ordered a new census (in 1710), which revealed a decrease in taxable households; he tried to expand the range of taxable persons at the expense of the "people of various ranks"; he began yet another census (in 1715), but it too showed a decrease in the number of households; finally, after considering various projects, Peter ordered a census of the entire male population and introduced a poll tax, which replaced most of the previous taxes.

During the compilation of the census and its first revision, large groups of peasants who had been personally free, and even small landowners who owned no serfs, were reclassified, either as serfs or as belonging to the new category of state peasants. This expansion of serfdom significantly increased the number of people who paid the poll tax. The size of the tax was determined by dividing the sums necessary to maintain the army and navy and for other expenses among the number of taxpayers.

During Peter's reign (more specifically, from 1680 to 1724), the sum of all taxes increased 2.7 times; of these, the sum of direct taxes increased 3.7 times. The poll tax levied in 1727 garnered 28.6 percent more than the household tax collected in 1724, and if one includes extraordinary taxes, this increases to 64.3 percent. With the introduction of the poll tax, levies on every male "soul" in the population rose, on average, threefold.[38] The uninterrupted growth in taxes and obligations, the cruelty with which uprisings were suppressed, the massive peasant flight—all these promoted the ruin of the rural population.

The reform of the state administration. In the beginning, this resulted from the need to structure and to perfect the apparatus of tax collection; later, a second reason appeared—the need to ensure that its servitors would fulfill their obligations as Peter understood them. Historians have suggested that Peter's understanding of the state reflected the influence of West European thinkers, as well as the tsar's traditional attitude that the country was his patrimony.[39] Peter departed from the latter tradition in that he saw himself as obligated to serve the state, just like all other servitors. At the same time, the servitors, in serving the state, served the autocrat; military and civil-service oaths of allegiance were made to the tsar, not to the nation.

Peter reformed—more accurately, created anew—the entire state apparatus, utilizing for this purpose Swedish institutions but adapting them to Russia's particular customs. At the base of the reform lay the idea that each of the four estates should fulfill its own duties: the peasants should till the soil; the traders and artisans should produce goods and engage in trade; the clergy should inculcate in the population fidelity to the monarch; and the nobility should bear the burden of military and civil service. Military service was separated from civil service, and since all nobles, without exception, were obliged to perform military service and therefore could not be sent into the civil service, the apparatus created by Peter was above all a military–bureaucratic one.

The highest governmental body was the Senate, which substituted for the tsar during his absences from the capital. Its branch institutions were the colleges, where business was conducted by voting. Military affairs fell under the jurisdiction of the Army and Admiralty Colleges, while international relations belonged to the College of Foreign Affairs; industry to the Mines and Manufactures Colleges; trade to the Commerce College; finances to the Camer-College, Staffing-Office College, and Revision Colleges; judicial servitors to the Justice College; and landowning to the Patrimony College. The Main Municipal Administration was established for the administration and judgment of traders and artisans, and the Holy Synod for the administration of ecclesiastical matters (the patriarchate had been abolished). Soon a Little Russian College was created to govern Ukraine. The bureaucrats' and military servitors' duties were spelled out in regulations.

The country was divided into provinces, subprovinces, and military districts (later, Peter abolished the last of these and restored the earlier division into districts), with corresponding local institutions. In 1724 the country was again divided into military districts, in each of which a regiment was quartered, which was to collect the taxes to support itself. (After Peter's death, this also was abandoned.) A procuracy and fiscals were introduced to supervise the work of these institutions; denunciation became an obligation, and failure to perform it was severely punished. Peasant movement was restricted by a passport system (which had existed before Peter, but was now expanded and strengthened). In the civil service, as in the military, a clearly defined hierarchy of ranks was established, opening a path by which officers and non-noble bureaucrats could acquire noble status. A police force was set up in the towns to serve, according to one of the Main Municipal Administration's regulations, as "the conscience of the citizenry and of all good organizations."[40]

Peter created, therefore, not only a bureaucratic but a police state. Its institutions lasted a long time: the division into provinces until 1924–29, the Holy Synod until 1918, the Senate and Table of Ranks until 1917, the poll tax until 1887, and the colleges until 1802.

The reform of the social structure. Peter did not leave the social structure untouched, but fundamentally strengthened it. Society's basic groups were consolidated by blending small estate groups into them; reassignment from one group to another occurred as a result of the census and strict regulations.

The peasantry was split into two groups: serfs and state peasants. Slaves were included among the enserfed peasantry; serfdom became harsher and serfs in effect became slaves.

The people inscribed in urban registers were divided into traders and artisans. Traders were assigned to merchants' guilds, and artisans joined into crafts guilds, although in Western Europe both had already disappeared. The self-government given to the traders and artisans in the form of the Main Municipal Administration and the town administrations served the purpose of subjecting them to the state apparatus; the magistracies, in essence, were state institutions.

The clergy, which in the person of the patriarch had claimed to share power with the tsar, was transformed into a branch of government. The procurator-general of the Clerical College—the Holy Synod, the work of which took place under the leadership of the tsar's representatives—became the head of the Church, and the priests were forced to denounce their flocks to the secular authorities, breaking the secrets of the confessional and strengthening the autocracy in every way.

The nobility perhaps suffered the most changes of all. All the small and large groups of people who served "as their fathers had" (the boyars and junior boyars, the nobility and state secretaries in the

Boyar Duma, the gentlemen of the table, the gentlemen-in-waiting, the palace guards, the Moscow gentry, the "elected" gentry, the gentry and "boyars' sons" of the towns) were joined into one nobility (originally named after the Polish *szlakchta*, but this name was later dropped in favor of the traditional Russian name for the gentry). Estates acquired through service were made the equal of estates acquired through inheritance. As before, the nobility had to enter military service at a young age, but Peter required them to serve for life, and not only in wartime. They had to shave their beards and dress in foreign clothes (the full-dress uniform); they had to study and serve eagerly, following the tsar's example and living under the threat of severe punishment. In return for this they received lands and peasants, new titles (as barons and counts), orders and medals, and authority as officers and as civil servants. The Table of Ranks regulated their movement within the service.

Much more devoted servants of the autocracy—traders, state peasants, and soldiers, who, having reached the appropriate rank, received first personal, then hereditary nobility—rounded out the nobility. Inasmuch as the basic means of production—land, serfs, the state apparatus, and the army—were concentrated specifically in the nobility's hands, they became the ruling class. The obligation to serve for life was abolished in 1762.[41]

These measures of Peter's made possible the tsar's final transformation into an absolute ruler and the strengthening of the absolutist state and of the power of the nobility.

The reforms in education, science, and culture. These include the introduction of the West European calendar; the shift of the new year to 1 January; the building of elementary and military schools; the establishment of secondary schools specializing in artillery training, engineering, navigation, and medicine; the creation of a printing-press to print translated technical manuals, maps, grammar books, and instructions; the institution of newspapers; the introduction of Arabic numerals and the new civilian alphabet; the shift to record-keeping in business and double-entry bookkeeping in accounting; the organization of research expeditions; the training of cartographers and the beginnings of mapping the country; the establishment of a museum (the Kunstkamera) and a library; the opening of pharmacies in the large towns and for the army; the establishment of the Academy of Sciences; the organization of a theater in Moscow; the introduction of assemblies (balls); the forced shaving of beards and adoption of Western-style dress; the permission for and encouragement of study abroad;

and many others. All did not change at once: the government forced pupils to attend the few schools, and they studied from fear of punishment; the members of the Academy of Sciences were foreigners; and the traders and peasants refused to shave their beards or to adopt Western dress. Education and culture affected only 0.5 percent of the population, but a foundation was laid.

Peter had no systematic plan for his reforms. Their progression was dictated by military needs and the necessity to find money for military expenses (as Peter himself wrote, "money is the artery of war"). The administrative reforms proceeded "haphazardly," correlated neither among themselves nor with the tax reform.[42]

Peter's reforms evoked no serious opposition from the ruling class—"three or four conspiracies," to quote Kliuchevskii.[43] Even Tsarevich Alexei and his few followers found no support, which indicates that the nobility accepted Peter's reforms. The peasantry and the townspeople, who bore the brunt of the burden of "service" for the "common weal" and the major cost of the reforms, were another matter. The massive Cossack and peasant rebellion led by Bulavin and the uprising in Astrakhan were drowned in blood, and by the end of Peter's reign the number of runaway peasants reached 200,000.

Let us summarize. Peter guaranteed Russia's independence and made it one of the strongest countries in Europe. He created large-scale industry, but built it on serfdom and "placed it on such a footing that it in effect could not develop in any other way than through serfdom, on a path . . . where the circumstances for the development of capitalism (and therefore for the formation of a bourgeoisie) did not exist." His policies concerning the towns and trade "slowed down" "the process of formation of capitalist relations."[44] The towns were ruined. The peasantry, too, was destroyed: "The destruction . . . seemed to be a consequence of the chronic strain placed on agriculture."[45] The tax reform "reinforced and strengthened serfdom, . . . and capitalism did not encounter conditions favorable to its development."[46] Peter created a state apparatus and a bureaucracy, which strengthened the autocracy and the structure based on serfdom while successfully preventing the development of capitalism and the "formation" of a bourgeoisie. In the cultural realm, the conditions were created for the development of culture, at least among the privileged estates, but "the foundations of a new infrastructure were laid, on which a new culture could develop."[47]

How much did Peter's activities shape Russia's development? One must admit that he did not set the country on a path of accelerated economic, political, and social development, nor cause it to "leap" over several stages, and in general did not even intensify the processes already under way (except, perhaps, in developing the army, navy, industry, and culture). His actions did not prove to be historically justified nor to have corresponded very well to Russian developmental interests (again, except for the areas mentioned above). On the contrary, his actions obstructed Russia's progressive evolution to the greatest extent possible, creating conditions that continued to hinder it for 150 years!

In Kliuchevskii's words, Peter "wanted the slave to remain a slave, but to work consciously and freely. How despotism and freedom, enlightenment and slavery, can operate simultaneously is a puzzle still unsolved."[48] Could Peter have acted otherwise? Could he have set Russia on the path of capitalist development? Modern historians have given a negative answer to this question: "Peter had no other alternative."[49]

One may nonetheless argue that such an alternative did exist: the elements of capitalist production were developing in Russia; capitalism already reigned (or almost reigned) in England and Holland— he had examples. Developing them to an exceptional degree, Peter could only continue the reforms that had begun timidly and haphazardly under his father, which had rested on the strengthening of serfdom. Neither his upbringing nor his education sufficed to separate him from the class of serfowners to which he had been born.

It is interesting that the people separated their assessment of Peter's personality from their view of his reforms. On the one hand, "now, there was a real tsar! A man worth his salt, who worked harder than a peasant." On the other, "the fantasy of the popular multitude, for whom knout and monk defined the bounds of permitted thoughts, arrayed Peter in its own hateful images, found in the debris of its ideas. . . . Peter's great works and ideas for benefiting the people were not even mentioned by the milling crowds."[50]

Nevertheless, the act of securing the country's political and economic sovereignty, the restoration of its window to the sea (absolutely essential for a realm with such great resources), the formation of industry (although based on serfdom, it provided a base for the development of capitalism), the vigorous acceleration of cultural development, and the creation of opportunities for its further growth— all these offer sufficient grounds to consider Peter I a great statesman.

Notes

1. E.V. Anisimov, *Vremia petrovskikh reform* (Leningrad, 1989), p. 9.

2. N.I. Pavlenko, *Petr Pervyi* (Moscow, 1976), p. 6; Anisimov, *Vremia*, p. 13; N.N. Molchanov, *Diplomatiia Petra Pervogo* (Moscow, 1986), p. 10.

3. V.O. Kliuchevskii, *Sochineniia* (Moscow, 1958), vol. 4, p. 8. According to other evidence, Peter's schooling began in 1683 and his first tutors were N. Zotov and A. Nesterov (Pavlenko, *Petr Pervyi*, p. 14).

4. Pavlenko, *Petr Pervyi*, p. 15.

5. Molchanov, *Diplomatiia*, p. 50.

6. Ibid., p. 52.

7. Pavlenko, *Petr Pervyi*, p. 78.

8. N.G. Ustrialov, *Istoriia tsarstvovaniia Petra Velikogo* (St. Petersburg, 1858), vol. 3, p. 621.

9. Kliuchevskii, *Sochineniia*, vol. 4, p. 27.

10. *Vsemirnaia istoriia* (Moscow, 1958), vol. 5, pp. 25, 81–86.

11. Kliuchevskii, *Sochineniia*, vol. 4, p. 26.

12. Molchanov, *Diplomatiia*, p. 100.

13. Kliuchevskii, *Sochineniia*, vol. 4, p. 54; Pavlenko, *Petr Pervyi*, p. 87.

14. *Istoriia SSSR s drevneishikh vremen do nashikh dnei* (Moscow, 1967), vol. 3, p. 308.

15. Kliuchevskii, *Sochineniia*, vol. 4, p. 28.

16. Quoted in *Istoriia SSSR*, vol. 3, p. 325.

17. Ibid., p. 331.

18. Ibid., p. 337.

19. A.S. Pushkin, *Polnoe sobranie sochinenii*, 16 vols. (Moscow, 1949), vol. 11, p. 269.

20. Molchanov, *Diplomatiia*, p. 428.

21. *Sbornik Russkogo istoricheskogo obshchestva*, vol. 52, p. 146.

22. Anisimov, *Vremia*, pp. 396–432.

23. The tales that Peter died from other diseases, specifically syphilis, are evidently unfounded (for more detail, see ibid., p. 435).

24. Pavlenko, *Petr Pervyi*, pp. 347–75.

25. Ibid., p. 246.

26. Ibid., p. 58.

27. Ibid., p. 111.

28. Ibid., pp. 230, 223–24, 281–82.

29. Ibid., p. 52.

30. Anisimov, *Vremia*, p. 304.

31. Pavlenko, *Petr Pervyi*, p. 133.

32. Ibid., p. 193.

33. Ibid., p. 52.

34. *Istoriia Severnoi voiny, 1700–1721 gg.* (Moscow, 1987), p. 187.

35. Molchanov, *Diplomatiia*, pp. 14, 15, 18, 19.

36. Anisimov, *Vremia*, pp. 121–23.

37. Ibid., pp. 127–33.

38. E.V. Anisimov, *Podatnaia reforma Petra I. Vvedenie podushnoi podati v Rossii, 1719–1728 gg.* (Leningrad, 1982), pp. 287–92.

39. See, for example, N.I. Pavlenko, "Petr I (k izucheniiu sotsial'no-politicheskikh vzgliadov)" in *Rossiia v period reform Petra I* (Moscow, 1973), pp. 40–102; idem, *Petr Velikii* (Moscow, 1990), p. 497; E.V. Anisimov, "Petr Velikii: Rozhdenie imperii," in *Istoriia otechestva: Liudi, idei, resheniia* (Moscow, 1991), pp. 186–220.

40. Quoted in Anisimov, *Vremia*, pp. 352–53.

41. For doubts as to whether the nobility was the ruling class, see ibid., p. 313.

42. Pavlenko, *Petr Pervyi*, p. 224; idem, *Petr Velikii*, p. 442; P.N. Miliukov, *Gosudarstvennoe khoziaistvo Rossii v pervoi chetverti XVIII stoletiia i reforma Petra Velikogo* (St. Petersburg, 1892), p. 729. One must admit that Miliukov was right to call this "a reform without a reformer," that is, without a preliminary plan.

43. Kliuchevskii, *Sochineniia*, vol. 4, p. 217.

44. Anisimov, *Vremia*, pp. 295, 298, 326.

45. Anisimov, *Podatnaia reforma*, p. 286; Miliukov, *Gosudarstvennoe khoziaistvo*, p. 735.

46. Molchanov, *Diplomatiia*, p. 403.

47. Anisimov, *Vremia*, p. 361.

48. Kliuchevskii, *Sochineniia*, vol. 4, p. 221.

49. Anisimov, "Petr Velikii," pp. 197–98.

50. Kliuchevskii, *Sochineniia*, vol. 4, p. 234.

Empress Anna Ivanovna, 1730–1740

Peter the Great's decision in 1722 to name his own successor doomed eighteenth-century Russia to recurrent succession crises. More immediately, his failure to name an heir before his death caused a rift in the Romanov dynasty and involved the elite Imperial Guards regiments in the resulting palace intrigues. With their backing, the Senate named Peter's wife Catherine—a former servant—empress of Russia. When she died in 1727, the throne passed to Peter's grandson, a boy named Peter, the only surviving male Romanov and the son of Peter the Great's estranged son, Alexis. Peter II's short reign (1727–1730) was dominated by the powerful Dolgorukii family. Political crisis ensued when Peter suddenly died in 1730, before an heir had been named, resulting in the designation of Anna of Courland, the second daughter of Ivan V (Peter's half-brother and co-ruler during the early part of his reign), empress of Russia.

Not surprisingly, the historical literature has devoted only limited attention to the reigns of Russia's rulers during the interval between the death of Peter I and the rise of Catherine II (the Great), an "era of palace revolutions" when "lovers ruled Russia." In seeking to reclaim this period from popularizers, E.V. Anisimov has written a nuanced reassessment of Anna Ivanovna and her reign that is highly revisionist. After identifying the most vital features of Anna's unhappy years in Courland, Anisimov brings her to Russia when "the Muscovite seventeenth century and the coarse manners of the new Russian capital city and the European eighteenth century" came together. A hapless agent of history devoid of ambition and drawn to rumor and gossip, Anisimov's Anna more than anything else feared loneliness, and therefore sought out "reliable protection and support." Anisimov challenges Russian historical writing that depicts the period as a reactionary one dominated by

foreigners, denunciation, persecution, and a plundering of the state's wealth.
He denies the existence of the so-called "German party"; he denies the nobility
were ruined through extravagance; he denies the Orthodox Church was perse-
cuted; he denies there was any departure from Petrine principles in foreign
affairs. In examining the dark notoriety of Anna's influential lover Ernst-
Johann Biron, Anisimov admits Biron was enormously influential, crafty,
and cautious, but dismisses the sinister designs some historians attribute to
him. With humor, irony, and the detachment of a modern observer who
understands the eighteenth century, Anisimov offers an alternative view of the
reign of Anna Ivanovna that cannot go unheeded.

D.J.R

Anna Ivanovna

Evgenii Viktorovich Anisimov

It surprised everyone when Anna Ivanovna became empress. On the night of 19 January 1730, the fourteen-year-old emperor Peter II died in Moscow after an illness that lasted several days. With his death, the male line of the Romanov dynasty came to an end. There were two legitimate heirs to the throne: Peter I's daughter, the nineteen-year-old Elizabeth; and her nephew Karl Peter Ulrich (the future Emperor Peter III), the two-year-old son of Karl Friedrich, the duke of Holstein, and Elizabeth's late sister Anna. However, the members of the Supreme Privy Council, the leading governmental body from 1726 to 1730, who gathered in Lefortovo Palace would not even consider the daughter and grandson of Peter I and the Swedish "washerwoman" Catherine.

Some of the Supreme Privy Council members from the Dolgorukii clan attempted to place Ekaterina Alekseevna Dolgorukaia—Peter II's betrothed—on the throne, and to that end they even forged the late emperor's will to favor his intended. But the plan fell through as soon as it was announced at a council meeting. The official who put down this internal "rebellion" by his colleagues was Prince D.M. Golitsyn, an advocate of limiting the emperor's power. Fate had suddenly offered him a chance to realize his own plan by attempting an oligarchical coup that would serve the interests of the narrow circle of aristocratic families then in power, and particularly the Dolgorukii and Golitsyn princes, who in effect occupied all the seats on the Supreme Council.

It was acknowledged that the most suitable candidate for a monarch with limited powers was Anna Ivanovna, Duchess of Courland, whom they planned to proclaim empress but without the power enjoyed by her predecessors. The Supreme Privy Council would oversee her. To reinforce these limitations on the empress's powers, the officials drew up what were known as conditions regulating Anna's prerogatives. All the members of the Supreme Privy Council then approved the Duchess of Courland's candidacy.[1] This was no accident: nobody in the capital city took Anna Ivanovna seriously; she cut an insignificant figure in Russian politics and went practically unnoticed at the Russian court, which she occasionally visited from Mitava (Mitau), the capital of Courland. Many, therefore, thought that it would be simple to control the empress, who would be completely dependent on the council members.

The officials' choice came as a complete surprise to Anna herself. The second daughter of Tsar Ivan Alekseevich, the half-brother and co-ruler of Peter the Great, and Praskovia Fedorovna Saltykova, she was born in 1692 and, along with her sisters (the elder was Catherine, Duchess of Mecklenburg, and the younger, Praskovia), she was an outsider to power. "The Ivanovnas" was what the grandees of the Petrine court called them, rather disdainfully. Although Peter I was kindly disposed toward the widow of his brother, who had died in 1696, and his brother's daughters, he arranged their fate to serve his own political goals. As soon as they matured, he decided to give them in marriage to foreign princes and sovereigns in order to link the Romanov dynasty by blood to the most important royal and princely families of Europe.

Anna was given in marriage to Friedrich (Frederick) Wilhelm, Duke of Courland, the ruler of Russia's neighboring state located on the territory of present-day Latvia. In this way Peter I strengthened Russia's influence in the Baltic region. Hardly anybody, naturally, was interested in the tsarevna's own opinion concerning her forthcoming marriage. An investigative file from 1739 preserved in the Privy Office reveals the history of Anna's unhappy marriage. The office was investigating the "indecent words" of a song a peasant woman named A. Maksimova remembered from 1710: "Please, dear Uncle, Sovereign Tsar Petr Alekseevich, do not send me to a foreign land, an un-Christian, un-Christian, infidel land. Please, Sovereign Tsar, give me to a general, a noble prince, of our own."[2]

The wedding took place in St. Petersburg in late 1710, but by early 1711 Anna was already a widow: after setting out from St. Petersburg with his young wife, Frederick Wilhelm died unexpectedly at the first station on the road to Mitava. Anna returned home but not for long, since Peter I believed that Russia's state interests required the duchess of Courland to live in her own residence—Mitava—under the supervision of the appointed Russian representative, P.M. Bestuzhev-Riumin, who became her lover soon afterward. Upon finding herself in a foreign country, in the unfamiliar circumstances of a backwater European principality, Anna immediately suffered from a sense of humiliation and dependency. On the one hand, she was greeted in an extremely unfriendly manner by the nobility of Courland, apprehensive about strengthened ducal authority and Russian influence, who therefore tried to drive Anna from Mitava by restricting her rights and income. On the other hand, Anna was completely dependent on Peter I, who viewed his niece solely as an instrument of his will and was completely disinterested in her feelings, her opinions, or her actual situation in Courland.

For many years, Anna was tormented by her dismal status and by a level of poverty intolerable for a duchess. The portion of the revenues of the ducal domain allotted to Anna in accordance with her marriage settlement could not provide a fitting standard of living. Anna repeatedly wrote humble letters to Peter I, Empress Catherine, Menshikov, Ostermann, and other high-placed persons, begging for their help and support. "I have arrears of fourteen hundred rubles coming to me," she wrote to the tsar's cabinet secretary, M. Makarov, in 1724, "but if our Sovereign Little Father and Uncle may be so kind, please grant me another six hundred out of your gracious benevolence."[3] Although economical and even tight-fisted with his relatives, this time Peter gave her the money she had requested, but he did not always do so. In a letter to the Empress Catherine, Anna wrote:

> Dear Little Mother, I beseech you as I would God himself, dear Auntie, grant me a mother's kindness—please, dear heart, ask our dear Sovereign, our Little Father and Uncle, a favor for me, that he might do me the kindness of bringing my matrimonial case to an end, so that I may no longer be in torment and suffering from those who do me ill, nor quarrel with Little Mother. . . . Please also, dear heart, deign to consider: do I not have needs here? You are aware, dear lady, that I have nothing except the things you have graciously ordered for me, but what if the occasion demands and I have no decent jewelry, or laces, or

linens, or decent clothing . . . and with my village revenues it is all I can
do to keep a proper house and table. . . . And I beg of you, dear heart,
Mama must know nothing of this.[4]

That was yet another sad aspect of Anna's life. Her mother,
Tsaritsa Praskovia Fedorovna, was affectionate and considerate of her
elder and favorite daughter, Catherine, but she did not love Anna;
she did everything she could to make life hard for her and, whenever
Anna did manage to get away from hated Courland and come home
for a time to Praskovia's palace, she was received coldly, with reproaches and nagging from her mother, whom Anna both feared and
disliked. The aforementioned letter to Empress Catherine, essentially
the only person who ever supported Anna, contained the duchess's
request that the empress do something to resolve her "matrimonial
case." That matter, too, was most painful and sad for Anna. It would
be wrong to say that Peter was not thinking about a husband for his
widowed niece, but choosing someone for her—and any other path
would have been out of the question—was not easy: the new marriage
must not harm Russia's influence in Courland.

This consideration was chiefly to blame for the breaking of a marriage contract with the Prussian prince in 1723. Another marriage
proposal failed in 1726, when Anna's hand was requested by Moritz
of Saxony, the illegitimate son of Poland's King Augustus II, who had
already been elected duke by the nobility. This marriage was blocked
by the Russian government, which feared that the Polish king's influence might be strengthened in Courland. For Anna the prospects of
years of dreariness in Mitava Castle still loomed. If D.M. Golitsyn had
not taken notice of her on that memorable night when Peter II died,
she would probably have spent the rest of her life as an impoverished
duchess, and her lover, the chamberlain Ernst-Johann Biron
(Bühren), whom she acquired after Bestuzhev was recalled in 1726,
would never have gained such dark notoriety among historical novelists and the readers of their works.

The year 1730 elevated Anna to the Russian throne. After signing
the "conditions," she arrived in Moscow in early February. The members of the Supreme Privy Council tried to keep her in isolation, so as
not to allow contacts between the "limited empress" and their political adversaries—the scheming noblemen who immediately undertook
to wage battle against the oligarchs. In the clash between those who
advocated and those who opposed limiting the Imperial powers,
Anna managed to find a comfortable position that enabled her to

Anna Ivanovna

draw support from the advocates of autocracy and then, with the help of the Guards, to carry out a palace coup celebrated by a public and triumphant destruction of the "conditions."

In the heat of the political battle, Anna was important not as a person but as a symbol of traditional rule, one that many were ready to defend. It is not likely, however, that observers were delighted. None of the palace sycophants would have called Anna a beauty. That would have been too much. Gazing down upon us from all her official portraits is a sullen and bulky woman with a short neck, stiffly arranged coal-black ringlets, a long nose, and a baleful gaze. Countess N.B. Sheremeteva, who later became Princess Dolgorukaia, was horrified when she looked out the window and caught sight of the empress passing by: "She was frightful to look at, with a disgusting face, and she was so big that when she walked among men she was a head taller than everybody else and extremely fat."[5] Count E. Münnich (the son of the field marshal) offers a more balanced opinion: "She was handsome and tall in stature. She made up for her lack of beauty with noble and magnificent features. She had large, brown, bright eyes, a nose that was somewhat too long, a pleasant mouth, and fine teeth. Her hair was dark, her face was somewhat pockmarked, and her voice was strong and piercing. In terms of her physical makeup she was tough and could withstand many blows."[6]

Only a rare woman could stand a gun's kick to the shoulder, but Anna shot every day for many years. Nastasia Shestakova, the intimidated wife of a palace manager who once visited the empress, recalled: "She allowed me to kiss her hand, and she got playful, grabbing me by the shoulder so hard that my whole body winced, it was so painful."[7] In general, there was something mannish about Anna. The Spanish envoy de Liria wrote that "her face is more masculine than feminine." Other contemporaries commented on her rather crude face and voice, her oversized figure, and the absence of the charm and refinement that were then so prized. This woman's entire life prior to her ascension to the throne had been subverted by the higher goals of serving the state pursued by Peter the Great. Living in an alien and unfriendly country in complete dependency and poverty did not foster the flowering of the future empress's personality. Plain, unfeminine, with a morose character and a suffocated self-esteem, Anna was capricious and suspicious of those around her.

During her early years she had received neither a proper education nor an appropriate upbringing, and she did not have the ability or the urge to improve herself through books or interaction with interesting people. In general, Anna's behavior, manners, and interests reflected the various cultural eras that those who lived through Peter's reforms encountered during their lifetimes. This affected Anna, too: the childhood of one of the last of the seventeenth-century Muscovite tsarevnas, who lived according to the ancient laws, in "silence and cold," was suddenly replaced by the commotion of a disorderly youth in the new city of St. Petersburg, where Peter I moved and settled Tsaritsa Praskovia's family. Without even having time to get accustomed to the new manners and rather crude customs of Peter's court, Anna quite unexpectedly found herself in another country, in an unfamiliar and alien cultural environment with different traditions, faith, and customs. Without a profound intellect or thirst for knowledge, she did not know how to act amid all this cultural and domestic confusion, which left its mark on her tastes, interests, character, and personality.

It was as if different eras came together in Empress Anna's court: the Muscovite seventeenth century met the coarse manners of the new Russian capital city and the European eighteenth century. Academicians' scholarly discourses occurred alongside the obscene jokes, fist-fighting, and amusements of numerous "jesters and fools." The customs of an opulent European court were mingled with the manners of the old-time "tsaritsa's room," where chamberlains and maids of honor found themselves brushing shoulders with hangers-on, "pilgrims," beggars, dwarfs, and monkeys. Ballet and opera alternated with buffoonish processions and the primitive shows of commedia del'arte, in which permanent characters such as Harlequin and Columbine existed to make the audience laugh in response to fisticuffs, indecent gestures, and crude jokes.

But the overall tone and lifestyle of Anna's court after she moved to St. Petersburg in 1732 was nonetheless more like the lifestyle of an eighteenth-century Russian landowner, with its unsophisticated concerns and amusements, scandals, and inquiries into servants' squabbles. In 1732 the Privy Council examined the case of a soldier who had witnessed a remarkable scene under the windows of the imperial palace: "A peasant was passing by, and Her Imperial Majesty happened to glance out of the window and asked the peasant who he was, and he answered, 'I am a tradesman.' 'Why is your hat so poor and your shirt no better?' [Anna inquired.—E.A.] And she gave the fellow about two rubles for a hat."[8]

This homely scene would have been more characteristic of a merchant's wife, a bourgeoise, or a landowner gawking at infrequent passers-by on a boring afternoon. Somehow it is hard to imagine it involving, for example, Catherine II or even Elizabeth. Anna's psychology and manners had in them much of the landowner, but a landowner whose estate embraced not the village of Ivanovskoe and its hamlets but a whole vast nation. That is just how Anna appears in her letters, notes, and resolutions—petty, lazy, superstitious, and not especially intelligent. Quite remarkable are her letters to S.A. Saltykov, who was her relative and "commander in chief of Moscow." One has the impression one is reading the correspondence between a nobleman's wife and her steward, who lives on another noble's estate in a neighboring province. Trivial interests, a wretchedly narrow horizon, and an absence of intellect—these catch one's eye: Anna requests jesters, monkeys, and lamp oil for the icon.

Anna especially liked playing matchmaker, bringing couples together as she saw fit. On 7 March 1738 she wrote to Saltykov, "Send someone to find the governor's wife Kologrivaia, summon her to you, and tell her she is to give her daughter to Dmitrii Simonov, who serves in Our court. Inasmuch as he is a good man We, by Our grace, will not abandon him."[9] In general, everything connected with her subjects' marriages and love affairs keenly interested the empress. In such matters she involved herself in literally everything, and her chief sources of information were gossip and rumors.

As a diligent and strict mistress of a vast estate, Anna became absorbed in every detail. For example, she noted that someone named Kondratovich, who had been sent to Siberia along with V.N. Tatishchev, was now "hanging around in Moscow," that "in Moscow, at the Petrovskii Tavern a starling is perched on a window; it can speak so well that everybody who passes by stops to listen to it," that there was "a fellow who can put out fires," that "Vasilii Abramovich Lopukhin has a psaltery in his home," and so on. The empress issued stern commands: the psaltery, the starling, and the fellow in question were to be immediately dispatched to St. Petersburg, and Kondratovich and many others were to be immediately sent to their service assignments.

The empress's wrath thundered down on any disobedient lackey or subject who tried to ignore her orders or deceive her. "Investigate the latter," Anna wrote to Saltykov regarding some priest who had offended her, "without respect to who is to blame. I want nothing other than the truth, and I shall grant mercy to whomever I please."[10] The chief principle of autocracy, expressed long before by Ivan the Terrible—"We are free to grant mercy to Our lackeys, and We are free to punish them"—became quite firmly imprinted on the former duchess of Courland.

When she came to power, Anna Ivanovna found herself in a rather difficult situation. She had been proclaimed autocratic empress by political forces that during discussion of the nobility's plans had favored limiting her powers but that had withdrawn their demands at the last minute under pressure from the Guards. The logic of political behavior unerringly suggested to Anna and her associates a need to compromise with the nobility and accommodate even former adversaries. For this reason, when the abolition of the Supreme Privy Council, the center of the oligarchic movement under Peter II, was carried out on 4 March 1730, it was presented as an ordinary reorganization directed at restoring all the powers of the Senate, which was also composed of Supreme Privy Council members. But it was clear that the empress could not entrust the administration to the Senate, which, on the one hand, was filled with her "persecutors"—the members of the Supreme Privy Council—and, on the other hand, was structured, and functioned, inefficiently. Efficiency, moreover, was required under conditions of autocratic rule by a woman who was almost entirely lacking in the abilities and skills necessary for state administration.

The formation of the Cabinet of Ministers in the autumn of 1731 alleviated the administrative problem. The people who composed the new institution—Chancellor G.I. Golovkin, Vice Chancellor A.I. Ostermann, Prince A.M. Cherkasskii, and later P.I. Iaguzhinskii (and A.P. Volynskii, who replaced him)—were experienced administrators who assumed all the work of governing the empire. At first, Anna participated in the cabinet's work, but it was not long before this "bored" her, and she gave the ministers the right to handle matters in her name. By an edict of 9 June 1735, the signatures of three ministers were equivalent to that of the empress. In practice, however, two ministerial signatures, and later even one on an edict were sufficient. This did not, however, limit the autocrat's powers. After all, autocrats were free to turn over particular rights to an institution or representative while reserving the prerogative not to limit themselves in any way. The concept of autocracy was based on the belief that neither the range of matters subject to the monarch's jurisdiction nor the actual separation of powers into legislative, executive, and judicial branches was ever precisely defined, for that act would itself constitute a limitation on the monarch's powers, after which he or she could no longer be called an autocrat.

During Anna Ivanovna's reign her favorite, Ernst-Johann Biron, occupied a special place in the system of administration. Before Biron appeared, her long-time favorite had been Petr Mikhailovich Bestuzhev-Riumin, who was the Russian government's representative in Courland, the chief steward of the duchess's court, and the de facto ruler. The respected father of the family that produced the well-known Russian diplomats Mikhail and Aleksei Bestuzhev-Riumin, Petr Mikhailovich was himself an experienced courtier. Nineteen years older than Anna, he subjected her entirely to his will, which was one of the reasons for Anna's conflict with her mother. Tsaritsa Praskovia, who had numerous occasions to be jealous of Bestuzhev, asked Peter I and Catherine to expel him from Mitava. But Peter had his own views of Bestuzhev, a clever diplomat who placed Russia's interests above morality, which suited the tsar admirably.

"Anna Ivanovna cannot be excused her promiscuity," wrote Prince M.M. Shcherbatov, well known for his denunciations of court morals, "for it is true that Bestuzhev, who was with her previously, enjoyed her favors."[11] Anna, a widow, cannot be excused her promiscuity, if her liaison with Bestuzhev, himself a widower, can be called that. Nevertheless, she was not a bacchante or a Messalina; pride of place in this went to Elizabeth I and Catherine II. Anna was a simple woman, unsophisticated, not especially intelligent, and definitely not flirtatious. She lacked Catherine II's ambition and Elizabeth's desire to pursue first prize for beauty. All her life she dreamed only of reliable protection and support, the kind that a man, a master of the house and lord of her fate, could give her.

Requests for defense, for "protection," and a readiness to "submit to your will" were a constant theme in her letters to Peter I, Catherine I, Peter II, members of the Supreme Privy Council, and in general all the powers that were. That was why she was so eager to get married. Yet all her attempts to wed were unsuccessful: her suitors were unacceptable to Peter I and his successors. And in time, Bestuzhev did become the protector and support she needed. Anna closed her eyes to the enormous difference between their ages, to the hopelessness of a liaison with one of her subjects, and to her chief steward's numerous faults.

The unsuccessful match with Count Moritz of Saxony was also a painful blow to Anna Ivanovna. It was bad enough that this enviable suitor was driven from Courland in disgrace by Russian troops, but Bestuzhev was likewise recalled from Mitava. Menshikov could not forgive Bestuzhev for allowing Moritz to come to Courland. After

Bestuzhev left in the summer of 1727, Anna wrote a series of twenty-six letters to anybody she could, pleading that Bestuzhev be returned to her. She sent them to Menshikov, to his wife and his daughter Maria, even to his sister-in-law Varvara Arsenieva, as well as to other influential persons among His Highness's associates, asking that Bestuzhev be sent back to Mitava, because without him the entire palace household was falling apart.

Though she was a tsar's daughter, in her letters to Vice Chancellor Ostermann she desperately resorted to turns of phrase more fitting for the petitions of a soldier's widow: "I most humbly beg Your Excellency to petition His Highness on my behalf, alone as I am. . . . Please have mercy, Andrei Ivanovich, show mercy to me in my most humble and lonely pleading. Make me glad, do not make me weep in my solitude." Her desperate loneliness is poured out in the frank admission, "Truly I am in great grief and emptiness and fear! Do not have me weep forever! I am so accustomed to him!"[12] That was the heart of the matter: she longed for Bestuzhev, but not because of his personality or the special, undying love Anna had for her aging favorite. Her vital urgency came from something else: she could not and did not want to be alone; she was terrified of loneliness. And therein lay her great tragedy.

By the end of 1727 the wailing from Mitava died down. Bestuzhev was permitted to return to Courland, but—alas—his place there was already occupied. He wrote to his daughter, "I am unbearably sad, I can hardly bear to live, for evil people have caused my dear friend to turn away from me, while your friend [a sarcastic reference to Biron—E.A.] is now more in her favor. . . . Do you not know how much I love that person [i.e., Anna—E.A.]?"[13] The experienced old courtier was in deep despair, for it was he who had taken that scoundrel Biron under his wing. "Neither a nobleman nor a Courlander," as Bestuzhev described him, "he came from Moscow with nothing to his name and, through my efforts, was accepted into the palace without rank, and from year to year, out of my love for him and at his pleading, I brought him up to this grade—and after I had done so, as you see, he has repaid my great favor with grave offenses . . . and has come into favor during my absence [from Courland—E.A.]."[14]

Although a small landowner, Biron actually was both a nobleman and a Courlander, but his past is nonetheless quite obscure. All that is known is that while he was a student at the University of Königsberg, he took part in a fight between the students and members of the night watch and killed a soldier. After significant effort he managed a release from prison, and around 1718 he arrived in Anna's court thanks to Bestuzhev's patronage. Later he married the duchess's lady-in-waiting Benigne-Gotlieb von Trotta-Treiden and performed diligent service, carrying out assignments for Anna and Bestuzhev. But in the latter's absence, Biron—almost the same age as Anna (he was born in 1690)—consoled the grief-stricken widow. His influence on her grew steadily.

Bestuzhev, who knew his rival well, feared Biron. And not without reason: in August 1728 Anna sent her servant to Peter II's court with a message denouncing her former favorite and requesting an investigation into "how Bestuzhev managed to rob me and leave me deeply in debt."[15] The chief steward's machinations with the duchy's treasury came to light. Naturally, this was about more than stolen raisins or sugar: the point was to "get rid of" Bestuzhev entirely, and Biron, who had taken his place, began a skillful intrigue against him.

"Never in this world, I expect, has there ever been such a harmonious pair, sharing completely in gaiety and grief, as the empress and the duke," E. Münnich wrote (Biron became duke of Courland in 1737—E.A.). He continued, "Neither was ever able to dissemble. If the duke appeared with a gloomy face, the empress would instantly take on a look of anxiety. If the duke was happy, the monarch's face clearly revealed her own pleasure. If the duke did not like someone, that person would immediately detect a change in the way the monarch greeted and looked upon him. . . . The duke had to be petitioned for all favors, and it was with him alone that the empress made her decisions regarding them."[16]

After Biron joined Anna in Moscow in the middle of March 1730, they were never apart for a single day. Moreover, many contemporaries noted that the empress could not even stand to spend an hour without Biron; they were often observed walking hand in hand. This became the object of malicious gossip in society, which in turn became an object of investigation within the Privy Council's torture chamber. Biron's influence on the tsaritsa was enormous. Its sources lay not so much in the character of the favorite, an intelligent and resourceful man, as in Anna's prior life. Once having submitted to her lord and master, she had made her choice irrevocably and never betrayed him. They were together winter and summer, come rain or shine. They even took ill at the same time—or, more accurately, Biron's illness made Anna ill, and she never left her chambers during that time. Münnich wrote that Anna "did not even have her own table; she had dinner and supper only with Biron's family, and even in the apartments of her favorite."[17] It is remarkable to note that when the Supreme Privy Council summoned her to Moscow, Anna took Biron's one-year-old son Karl Ernst with her as well as other necessary things. There is good reason to believe that Karl was Anna's son by Biron and that she was taking along the person most dear to her. It is also well known that Karl Ernst later enjoyed special favor at Anna's court; until the day she died, he slept in her room.

Biron was married to an ugly, sickly woman, by whom he had another son, Peter, and a daughter, Hedwig Elizabeth. With Anna, they gave the impression of being a single family. Together Anna, Biron, Bironsha (for that was what his wife was called in society), and the children attended celebrations, took sleigh rides on the Neva, attended concerts, received the dentist, who treated each of them in turn, and so on. This triangle may surprise uninformed observers, but history has witnessed numerous such triangles, in which everyone long knew all that was going on and each had his or her own role, place, and destiny. Biron complained to some of his acquaintances that he was forced to spend whole days with Anna while affairs of state awaited him. But this reflected either a momentary weakness or craftiness. Bearing in mind his predecessor's sad fate, he never left the empress unattended: whenever he himself had to travel, either his wife or a spy whom he trusted stayed nearby. He always remembered what he had written to Russia's ambassador to Warsaw, G. Kaiserling, who enjoyed his special favor: "It is vital to be most cautious about the great favors of great personages, lest an unfortunate change ensue."[18]

In the scholarly literature there is a certain tendency to belittle Biron's importance as a statesman, portraying him as a man who was either far removed from administration or not very knowledgeable about state affairs. Neither is true. Biron had enormous influence both in foreign and domestic politics. In the system that emerged under Anna, not a single important decision was made without Biron, an ambitious person and her confidant. In his letters, the favorite complained constantly about being overburdened with duties, but at the same time he revealed himself as a very cautious man who tried to remain in the shadows and not overemphasize his role in administration.

The problem of the Biron era has continually attracted the attention of historians. In the 1991 edition of the *Soviet Encyclopedic Dictionary*,[19] "the Biron era" is characterized as a reactionary regime with "domination by foreigners, plundering of the country's wealth, universal suspicion, espionage, denunciation, and savage persecution of malcontents." This entry reflects in miniature historiographic stereotypes and clichés that came into being long before the struggle with "the West's pernicious influence."

The effort to portray Anna's reign as a period in which national interests were ignored and the Russian people were oppressed can be detected most clearly in the first steps that Elizabeth took after she ascended the throne as a result of a coup d'état. Only by asserting the need to liberate Russians "from the night-owls and bats sitting in the Russian eagle's nest and scheming against the state" in order "to release the sons of Russia from bondage and lead them to their original prosperity" was it possible to argue in favor of the palace coup on 25 November 1741. During the nineteenth century, historical fiction played a special role in portraying "the Biron era" as a time of domination by foreigners. K.P. Masalskii, in his story "Biron's Regency," and I.I. Lazhechnikov, in *The Icehouse,* gave their readers the patriot Artemii Volynskii, who perished due to the intrigues of that foreign hanger-on, Biron. Thanks to Lazhechnikov's novel, generations of Russian readers were nurtured with a solid "anti-Biron spirit," which was likewise fostered by popular notions about the harm Western influence did to Russia. Further traces were left in historiography and in the public consciousness by the Soviet campaign against cosmopolitanism.*

The first stereotype, then, is that "the Biron era" can be equated with domination by foreigners, primarily Germans. Many people remember V.O. Kliuchevskii's compelling, but unfortunately facile, description: under Anna "the Germans littered Russia like dust from a sack with holes in it, infested the court, clustered around the throne, and grabbed all the lucrative jobs in administration."[20] Yet Germans had "littered" Russia long before Anna ascended the throne, and their number had never frightened the Russian people before. From time immemorial, foreign specialists had come to Russia to work, but Peter the Great opened the doors to them all the way. Their fate once in Russia took various turns. Some left the country forever, insulted and with hatred in their hearts; for others, Russia became a second motherland, where their talents flourished and where they gained recognition and glory both during their lifetimes and after. The visitors included scientists, military commanders, architects, performing artists, doctors, and engineers. Russian history is inconceivable with-

---

*This refers to an ugly anti-Western campaign with anti-Semitic overtones that took place in the late 1940s.—D.J.R.

out them; through marriage, their blood mingled with Russians' blood, and alongside "native" Russians they created a magnificent Russian culture. Some extraordinary people of foreign origin "littered" Russia in the eighteenth century—architects D. Trezzini and B.F. Rastrelli, scientists J.-N. Delisle, D. Bernoulli, G.S. Bayer, J. Gmelin, and G.F. Müller, and musicians and composers G.A. Ristori, F. Araja, and J.-B. Laudé. When it comes to military men (engineers, commanders, and seamen), it is impossible even to list them. And most of these were foreigners who had been accepted into Russian service, knew their jobs, and earned their money.

During Anna's reign, just as before, foreigners were eagerly accepted into the army and into the state apparatus, but they did not find themselves in special circumstances thanks to Biron. It was under Anna, and at the initiative of the German Münnich, that the difference in salaries, a sore point for Russian officers, was abolished: they began to receive the same pay as foreigners rather than half as much, as had been the case under Peter I. Numerous governmental decrees have been preserved concerning the impermissibility of special privileges for foreign specialists in Russian service. Registers have been preserved reflecting the composition of the officer class on the eve of "the Biron era" and during its "heyday." According to the registers of 1728, the field army had 71 generals; 41 of them, or 58 percent, were foreigners. By 1738 the percentage of foreign generals had actually gone down—31 of the 61 generals were foreigners—in other words, in absolute terms they were fewer than before the "Biron era." If we count foreign generals and staff officers (including majors), in 1729 the army had 371 generals and staff officers, of whom 192 were foreigners—37.3 percent. This is clearly not sufficient to claim that foreign influence in the Russian army strengthened during Biron's time, although the number of foreigners in the army, especially in the newly created Izmailovskii Regiment, was in fact rather large.

A similar situation also developed in the navy. In 1725, twelve ship-of-the-line commanders and two frigate commanders were assigned to the summer campaign. The only Russian captain was the frigate commander Lodyzhenskii; all the rest were foreigners—Englishmen, Danes, Dutchmen, and so on. In the summer of 1741, a squadron of fourteen ships and six frigates was sent out. Thirteen of the twenty captains were Russians![21] And so the "Biron era," far from damaging Russia's naval pride, actually served to enhance it. As a matter of fact, power does not depend directly on the number of any particular national group in the army, navy, or civil service.

But one sphere attracted both Russians and foreigners. This was the court, which was not confined to the Table of Ranks of the court administration but rather remained a special community with its own atmosphere, rules, and traditions. The principal goal of all members of the clique was to secure their own well-being through the monarch's "good favor"; without it, absolutism in general, and Russian autocracy in particular, was inconceivable. Naturally, that a number of foreigners immediately showed up at court and among Anna's entourage could hardly fail to attract attention, and it displeased influential Russians—not because it offended their national sensibilities but because these new "favorites" were crowding them from the throne. Their annoyance is understandable: through the nobility's efforts and against the intentions of the Supreme Privy Council members, Anna had become the autocratic sovereign. Yet she immediately summoned Biron from Courland and surrounded herself with foreigners who had not previously played eminent roles in Russian politics.

But the events of 1730 had another side as well. The nobility had not been protecting Anna personally but rather the principle of autocracy that the oligarchs had violated. For this reason, the empress did not especially trust most of her allies met by chance. She sought support among those whom she knew personally, people with whom she had had ties for a long time. It is only natural for a new person in power to put together a "team" of relatives, fellow countrymen, comrades-in-arms, old friends, and so on. Loyalty and personal devotion to her were the principal criteria used during the formation of the circle of persons closest to Anna. This circle came to include her relatives, the Saltykovs; P.I. Iaguzhinskii (an uncompromising foe of the Supreme Privy Council); A.M. Cherkasskii; her favorite, Biron; the Levenvolde brothers; and Münnich, who had demonstrated his sincere devotion. A.I. Ostermann, a man of experience and therefore essential to the administration of the state, was also brought in.

It can be said with certainty that under Anna there was no such thing as a "German party"—that is, a relatively united and homogeneous national–political group that could control the upper levels of government. In the eighteenth century the ethnic concept "Germans" only partly coincided with inhabitants of Germany, since at that time Germans did not yet have a sense of ethnic unity within a single country. They were the subjects of numerous German principalities divided by religious, economic, and historical circumstances.

The motley company around Anna's throne consisted of the Livonian Levenvolde brothers, the Courland German Biron and his brothers, Münnich from Oldenburg, and Ostermann from Westphalia, as well as the Russians Golovkin, A. Ushakov, and Volynskii and Cherkasskii, a descendant of Kabardian princes. Moreover, this company was not unified but a typical court clique rent by an eternal struggle for power, influence, and "favor." "Devourers of happiness" were somehow alike, without regard to nationality, whether this meant Biron or the man fighting his influence, Volynskii.

The Spanish envoy de Liria had this to say about one of Anna's most influential courtiers, Count K.R. Levenvolde: "He did not scorn any means and would stop at nothing in the pursuit of his personal benefit, for the sake of which he was willing to sacrifice his best friend and benefactor. His only mission in life was his personal well-being. Deceitful and duplicitous, he was extraordinarily ambitious and vain; he had no religion and hardly even believed in God."[22] The same could have been said of other participants in the clique—Biron and Volynskii, Ostermann and Ushakov, Münnich and Iaguzhinskii, and many others. What divided them was not the nationality to which they belonged; this is confirmed by the history of the court struggle—or more accurately, the savage scrabbling for power—that immediately began at the foot of Anna's throne.

In the beginning, Biron, Levenvolde, and Iaguzhinskii plotted against Ostermann, who teamed up with Münnich; later, Iaguzhinskii was forced onto the sidelines, as was Münnich, who was abandoned by Ostermann. Biron became close to Ostermann but did not trust him, plotting against him through Golovkin, Iaguzhinskii, and then Volynskii, who at first was the favorite's "devoted vassal." While tracing the minute details of this struggle, one somehow forgets the nationality of the strugglers—that was not what divided or united the people of the court.

Consider the following historiographical clichés: the "trading away of the country's interests" and the "plundering of its wealth" by German opportunists under Anna. We can say with certainty that the foreign policies of the "German opportunists" were the policies of the Russian Empire at that time. The consolidation of the Russo-Austrian alliance, the concerted actions of the allies in Poland in 1733–34 during the War of the Polish Succession, and the Russo-Turkish War of 1735–39 all point in one direction: the principles and methods of imperial resolution of the "Polish" and "Black Sea" questions constituted an elaboration and perfecting of Peter's foreign policy doctrines applied to the new historical realities and along the most promising geopolitical lines. The same route was later taken by other "patriotic" governments, in particular that of the German Catherine II.

The accession to power by Anna, duchess of Courland, strengthened Russia's influence within that duchy on the empire's borders. After he became duke of Courland, Biron used Russia's treasury to remodel and decorate his palaces, built by the architect B.F. Rastrelli. But the money invested in Courland was not wasted; later it paid dividends, because from then on Courland was recognized in Europe as a state within Russia's sphere of influence. When Catherine II returned control of Courland to Biron, she no longer had to worry about Russia's interests in that region, for Biron—and later his son Peter—well knew who their true suzerain was, and they faithfully served that monarch until the end of the duchy's existence, when it was merged with the Russian Empire as a result of the third partition of Poland.

The scholarly literature has also characterized the country's domestic situation during "the Biron era" as a time of dramatic crisis: "The national economy, and along with it the state," Kliuchevskii writes, "was falling apart. Trade declined." Information provided by historians, and in particular the latest studies by N.N. Repin, have shown convincingly that any notion about declining trade is totally unfounded. St. Petersburg's general volume of trade between 1725 and 1739 increased from 3.4 million to 4.1 million rubles, and the amount of customs duties grew from 228,000 rubles in 1729 to 300,000 rubles in 1740. Iron exports during the 1730s rose more than fivefold, and grain exports (via Arkhangelsk) rose more than twenty-two times. Exports of tallow, caviar, and other goods doubled. There was also an increase in imports of foreign goods through St. Petersburg, Arkhangelsk, Revel, Narva, and Riga.[23]

Many people are most convinced by indicators of economic growth, in particular statistics on industrial output, which forms the foundation of a country's might. The production of pig iron in the state's smelters in the Urals increased from 252,800 poods* in 1729 to 415,700 poods in 1740. During Peter I's reign, in 1720, Russia produced 10,000 tons of pig iron, while England produced 17,000 tons; in 1740, Russia reached the level of 25,000 tons, whereas the furnaces of Sheffield and Leeds produced only 17,300 tons.[24]

A.K. Shemberg, a repulsive individual who was a protégé of Biron

---

*A Russian weight equivalent to 36 lbs. avoirdupois.—D.J.R.

and his associates, played a prominent role in the mining industry in the second half of the 1730s. Shemberg's name is rightly linked to many abuses and thievery in this lucrative sector. But as often happens in real life, here, too, there are two sides that are difficult to separate from one another. Shemberg's department undertook to revise mining legislation for the purpose of making conditions easier for private enterprise; this was reflected in the Berg Regulation of 1739. N.I. Pavlenko, an eminent expert on the history of Russian industry, believes that:

> the new concessions in favor of the industrialists, as established by the Berg Regulation, give every reason to believe that the policy of protection carried out by Peter's government in regard to the industrialists and the metallurgy industry, remained basically unchanged during the second quarter of the eighteenth century. Anna Ivanovna's government took into consideration the fact that "many other countries are getting rich and prosperous" by developing industry, and therefore deemed it essential to take steps to develop industry in Russia.[25]

The role played by administrators such as Shemberg is quite evident in this regard.

Of particular interest is the work of the special commission on the privatization of state enterprises. One of the most painful issues concerned the principles by which plants were turned over to private owners. As the head of the General Berg Directorate, Shemberg insisted that he and his department should be in charge of transferring the plants. The commission objected on grounds that this would open the way for all kinds of abuses by functionaries in that department, and that anybody who wished to acquire a plant must apply to the authoritative commission, which would hand down its decision "by consensus." Shemberg proposed that fixed prices be set on the factories, while the commission, on the contrary, was in favor of selling the factories at an auction benefiting the state. Ultimately, a dispute arose between Shemberg and the commission over whether officials in the mining department could themselves form mining companies and become factory owners. The commission rightly asked the General Berg director about such persons: "Once they become interested parties, who will supervise them?"[26]

The Berg Regulation that Anna approved opened the way to privatization of state industry, and the first person who hastened to take that route was Shemberg himself. Biron guaranteed his honesty and ability to pay.[27] As a "beginning" entrepreneur, Shemberg received considerable benefits and subsidies from the state, and to claim that Biron's friendship with Shemberg was without avarice would be hypocritical. Shemberg's machinations did not last long; Elizabeth stripped him of both his power and his property. This was not because he was Biron's friend and a thief, but because his factories had caught the eye of people from another clique—this time, purely Russian—that surrounded the throne of Peter I's daughter.

The new factory owners—Counts Shuvalov, Vorontsov, and Chernyshov—replaced the "German freebooters who had plundered the country." Shemberg's and Biron's activities looked like child's play compared to the machinations to which the Russian "patriots" resorted once ensconsed on this bountiful industrial soil. Gigantic subsidies from the treasury, gross violations of the mining laws, reprisals against the merchants who were their defenseless competitors, and all kinds of abuses—this shameless bacchanale gave N.I. Pavlenko reason to conclude: "A.I. Shuvalov's government graphically illustrates the shamelessness of the executive branch. . . . It is hard to detect even one feature of Shuvalov's government that had a positive effect on the development of Russian metallurgy."[28]

When one reads in Kliuchevskii that during the "Biron era" the "sources of state revenue were extremely depleted," that "the whole pack in that dissolute court . . . gorged itself and indulged in endless revels on the arrears money squeezed out of the people," and that, finally, "Biron cast his eyes on the numerous arrears monies [sic!—E.A.],"[29] one cannot help asking whether the great Russian historian was not making too much of the national question. Was it only under Biron that the sources of state revenues were so depleted? Was it only German opportunists, so hated by the patriots, who mercilessly extracted arrears monies using the hands of Russian army officers and men?

The problem of arrears monies was a difficult one all through the eighteenth century and was not solved by any government. The peasant farms could not cope with the burden of duties and taxes. It would be a mistake to think that arrears were collected differently under Peter I or Catherine II than under Anna; the method was always the same—messengers, army teams, mass floggings, confiscation of the debtor's property to the treasury, shackling in "irons," and incarceration in prison. In 1727 a special Arrears Office was created, and in 1729 a Confiscation Office, and they zealously indulged in behaviors for which Anna and Biron were later reproached. In the early 1730s, meanwhile, the government found itself in an extremely difficult financial position: by 1732, despite revenues of six to seven million rubles per year, arrears for the five preceding years came to seven million rubles. The money was not needed for merrymaking or revelry at court; it was needed for the army, which fought almost continually from 1733 to 1740. Under these circumstances, it would be unfair to expect humanity from the collectors of arrears.

Only Anna's regime is accused of thievery and the embezzlement of public funds. But Russia's history is replete with these vices. The same is true of another charge levied against the "Biron era" in the literature. E. Belov, fearful of the horrors of domination by German opportunists, has this to say: "There followed the systematic ruination of the higher nobility through an extravagance that was theretofore unheard of."[30] In Belov's opinion, the crafty German opportunist, by leading an extravagant life and putting on stupendous balls, induced simple-hearted Russian nobles to indulge in similar spending, and so they ruined themselves by spending money on entertainment, excursions, costumes, and receptions. Yet Elizabeth actually did more to "ruin" the Russian nobility, with her banquets, masquerade balls, and changing clothes two or more times a day, which became legendary. Examples of "ruination" due to extravagance have been cited by Prince M.M. Shcherbatov, the denouncer of palace depravity. Compared with Elizabeth's Lucullian banquets, Anna's entertainments look like evenings of fasting and temperance.

There are no grounds for believing that the "Biron era" witnessed any persecution of the Orthodox Church. This is another historiographical myth. The Holy Synod and the Church hierarchy were rife with intrigues and scheming. Many clergymen who were unhappy with Peter I's reforms did everything they could, even by dishonest means, to remove Archbishop Feofan Prokopovich, the theoretician of Peter's church reforms, from power, but Feofan was himself an unprincipled man experienced in intrigue who skillfully protected himself by assigning his adversaries to distant monasteries and to the Privy Council. It is no exaggeration to claim that Peter I's conversion of the Church into an office of religious affairs completely under state control served to introduce into ecclesiastical affairs those customs most characteristic of the court—malice, immorality, and filth. Otherwise, church policies under Anna changed hardly at all in comparison with preceding rulers.

The defense of the Orthodox Church chiefly involved, as before, reprisals against heretics, who were burned at the stake or sent to monastery prisons to rot. In addition, the "Biron era" proved to be a tragic period in the history of the Old Believers. In 1735 raids began on small forest monasteries in the Urals and Siberia that were unprecedented in scale and ferocity. The arrest, torture, and persecution of thousands of people resulted in "burnings"—self-immolation—of schismatics. "One can perceive a kind of ironic logic of history," N.N. Pokrovskii wrote, "in the fact that it was Vasilii Nikitich Tatishchev, a most enlightened advocate of the state approach and the state's interests, who was the active implementer of the very conservative line of Anna Ivanovna's government in this matter, and to some extent the actual initiator of the police action, which was unprecedented in scope."[31]

The patriot Tatishchev was merciless against the defenseless schismatics, as he was also in the case of the Bashkirs, not only putting down their uprising but actually proposing a plan to wipe them out entirely.

Nor could the members of the Russian nobility be unhappy with the "Biron era." The dramatic events of 1730 brought to the fore the problem of the nobility, who were demanding new estate privileges. Yesterday's servitors, decked out in uniforms, were demanding that their term of military service be reduced to twenty years, and that burdensome service as privates in the Guards be replaced by training in special institutions. But the most substantial point was that the members of the nobility, as one, demanded the repeal of Peter's 1714 law of primogeniture, according to which a landowner could transfer his estate to only one of his sons, thus dooming the rest to making their living through service in the state offices and in the regiments. Anna's government undertook to satisfy the nobility's demands, thereby substantially expanding the social base of her rule.

In 1730–31, to the landowners' general delight, the edict on unogeniture was repealed as "not being useful." In December 1736 an edict was issued that, in S.M. Soloviev's words, "created a distinct era in the history of the Russian nobility in the first half of the eighteenth century."[32] The edict allowed people to keep one son on the estate "to maintain the operation." Young nobles were permitted to stay at home until the age of twenty, and their term of military service was set at twenty-five years, after which they were free to return to their estates or engage in another activity. As a result, Russia's nobility, having achieved a substantial lessening of their service obligations and gained full property rights, took yet another step toward their emancipation, toward Peter III's famous charter granting them freedom. The "Biron era" did not prevent that step.

Russia's foreign policy during Anna's reign underwent no substantial changes in comparison with Peter's time and did not represent a departure from the principles of the Reformer Tsar. In 1726 Russia concluded a treaty of alliance with Austria, thanks to Ostermann's efforts. The St. Petersburg–Vienna axis imparted particular stability to Russia's politics. The alliance was based on common imperial interests in the south, in the struggle with the weakening Ottoman Empire over the Black Sea region and the Balkans, as well as in the struggle for spheres of influence in Poland and in Germany. In this groping manner the principal direction of Russia's foreign policy was established, and the country's governments—whether ruled by the Russian Anna Ivanovna or the German Catherine II—successfully developed it throughout the eighteenth century.

During the 1730s Russia, having intervened in Poland after Augustus II's death in 1733, came closer than ever before to the question of partitioning Poland. In that war, called the War of the Polish Succession (1733–35), Austria acted in concert with Russia and also sent her troops into Poland. The expulsion of Stanislaw Leszczyski, the candidate for the Polish throne whom the allies found inconvenient, and the enthroning of King Augustus III were achieved through joint efforts, and vigorous punitive measures against all of Russia's opponents showed what lay in store for Poland in the near future. The first harvest from its fields of battle was gathered in 1737: Courland acquired a new duke—Biron. This represented not only a triumph for Anna's favorite but also a solid success for Russia: from then on, Courland became Russia's satellite, and it was not difficult for Anna's successors to incorporate it into the empire.

Almost immediately after the War of the Polish Succession, war broke out with Turkey (1735–39). Russia started the war, with Austria's support. Anna's government did not conceal the fact that it was a war of retribution for Peter I's defeat on the Pruth in 1711. Just before the campaign, Field Marshal Münnich drew up a war plan that was to end with the taking of Istanbul and the expulsion of the Turks from Europe. This desire to erect "a cross on Hagia Sophia" did not reflect the influence of "the Biron era"; rather, it reflected the deeper goals of Russia's imperial policy. By its defeat of the Crimean khanate in 1736–38, Russia showed clearly that it would not tolerate rivals on the northern coast of the Black Sea and that the Crimea's fate would be decided in Russia's favor. Although the victories under Ochakov and Khotin yielded no real results during the peace negotiations with Turkey at Belgrade in 1739, the overall strategy of fighting the Turks in alliance with Austria was definitively established, and Catherine II systematically pursued the policies that the government of Anna and her favorite had begun. All this shows once more that the empire's interests were paramount for those in power in St. Petersburg, no matter to which nationality they belonged.

Another issue concerning the "Biron era" is its frequent depiction as a repressive regime somewhat similar in its brutality to that of Ivan the Terrible. It is true that during Biron's dominance there was spying, denunciation, and "savage prosecution of malcontents." But when has this not been the case in Russia? The history of the Privy Office—the principal repressive agency of the eighteenth century—shows that the whole system of political investigation, from the laws to the methods of conducting interrogations, was not invented by Biron but rather by his predecessors in power.

The history of political investigation in the eighteenth century shows that Anna's accession to power did not result in more repressive work by the investigation department, nor did the Privy Office increase its staff (15–20 officers and about 150 soldiers guarded approximately 250–300 prisoners). The number of persons arrested for political reasons during the ten years of Anna's reign did not exceed ten thousand, and not more than one thousand of these were sent to Siberia. Figures from the Privy Office's casebook led T.V. Chernikova to conclude that the number of political cases during Anna's reign did not exceed 2,000, whereas 2,478 were instituted during the first ten years of Elizabeth's reign and 2,413 during her second ten years.[33] Thus, any assertion that there was massive repression of malcontents during "the Biron era" is groundless.

The principal "criminal" offense that brought people into General Ushakov's torture chamber was rumor-mongering and gossip concerning the lives of Anna and her associates. Only rarely did the scandal-mongers' attention focus on the empress's favorite's German origin. Later, too, there were many similar cases; the people spoke no less harshly of the "nighttime emperors" during Elizabeth I's or Catherine II's reigns. Naturally, there was considerable condemnation of the privileges that the "Germans" enjoyed at court, but this was never the main cause of repression during the 1730s.

Anna's reign was clouded by investigations of and reprisals against the Golitsyn and Dolgorukii princes and Volynskii, which were also generally attributed to the "Biron era." But in this regard as well, her reign was no more one of "terror" than were the reigns of her predecessors and her successors. An inclination toward political investigation as a means of intimidating and suppressing political opponents and putting a stop to undesirable rumors has been exhibited to some extent or other by all the tsars. The bloody executions of the musketeers, the affair of Tsarevich Aleksei under Peter I, the reprisal against Menshikov and his comrades-in-arms P. Tolstoy, A. Devier, and others under Catherine I, and, finally, the case of the Lopukhins and the sad fate of Ivan Antonovich's family under Elizabeth—all become a single chain with links that include the case of the Dolgorukiis, the Golitsyns, and Volynskii under Anna.

When she came to power, Anna acted just as her predecessors had, favoring those who suited her and ridding herself of those who did not. The overall political situation at the start of her reign, when the new empress personified, so to speak, the restored unity between society and monarch, prevented her from immediately settling accounts with those who would have persecuted her—the Dolgorukiis and the Golitsyns. Suspicious and bearing a grudge, Anna waited for the right moment, limiting herself to exiling to Siberia those members of the family of A. Dolgorukii—the father of Peter II's favorite, Prince Ivan—who had most compromised themselves under Peter II. The exiling of a whole family, including women and children, was not because of any villainy on Biron's part. Rather, it reflected the tradition of political repression, according to which not only was the disgraced grandee exiled or executed, but also his brothers, his family, and his clan became victims of the tsar's wrath.

The Dolgorukiis' careless behavior in Berezovo, their quarrels and drunken parties, resulted in their being denounced, and in 1738 they were arrested and taken to Schlüsselburg. The first to break under interrogation was Prince Ivan, who during the investigation revealed the circumstances of the attempt to elevate Peter II's betrothed, Ekaterina Dolgorukaia, to the throne. A "General Assembly"—a high court consisting of Russian dignitaries—sentenced the Dolgorukiis to death, and their execution took place on 8 November 1739 in Novgorod. Anna's reprisals against the Dolgorukiis, as in the earlier case with D.M. Golitsyn, who had been sent to the Solovetskii Monastery, produced a gloomy impression on society, although it was clear to everybody that the actual motives in these cases were political rather than national, the revenge taken by an empress who had been humiliated by the members of the Supreme Privy Council, although the exiled Dolgorukiis and the ailing Golitsyn did not threaten her power (or Biron's).

Also largely political—or, more accurately, court-motivated—was the case of Cabinet Minister A.P. Volynskii, which started in the spring of 1740. Volynskii was a contradictory man. An excellent administrator, a "fledgling of Peter's nest," he was at the same time a petty tyrant and an embezzler; he knew how to keep his nose to the wind and skillfully accommodate those who were strongest. All of this was combined with immoderate arrogance, ambition, and imperiousness. In 1733 S.A. Saltykov, a relative of Volynskii's wife, wrote a letter in which he obsequiously asked Biron to watch out for Volynskii, who was being investigated in connection with abuses of office in Kazan where he had been governor. Biron liked Volynskii: intelligent, vigorous, and able to get things done, he was, according to the language of the times, a "get-up-and-go" person, willing to accommodate his new master.

It marked the start of a brilliant career, culminating in the post of cabinet minister and the good favor of Anna and her own favorite, to whom Volynskii regularly reported on the state of affairs. During the "dominance of the German opportunists," his career annoyed patriotic historians brought up on Ryleev's *Thoughts* and Lazhechnikov's novel in which Volynskii is depicted as an unwavering fighter for truth and fatherland. That is why they started the rumor that Volynskii had decided from the beginning to acquire high state posts and then to "attempt to change the situation in the country,"[34] to begin to fight the German opportunists. The facts, however, indicate otherwise: Volynskii curried favor with, intrigued against, then as a member of the court dispatched the Dolgorukiis to the scaffold without any underlying "patriotic thought." He was just like all the others who sought royal favors and were willing (as Volynskii himself said) to grab as much good fortune as would fit in their hands and mouths.

But by late 1739 the situation began to change: more and more, Biron became displeased with Volynskii. Volynskii himself, moreover, showed displeasure with his patron. People such as the arrogant and proud Artemii Petrovich rather quickly, under the spell of their own success, delude themselves into thinking that they owe it not to someone else's whim but exclusively to their own abilities; they think themselves irreplaceable. Volynskii came into sharp conflict with his cabinet colleague Ostermann and had a falling-out with Biron. Biron had been annoyed by many of the formerly obedient Volynskii's actions, in particular his attempts to ingratiate himself with the potential heiress to the throne, Anna Leopoldovna, and her husband Anton Ulrich.

One reason for Volynskii's fall from grace was an impudent letter that he sent to Anna Ivanovna, in which he complained about certain enemies who were wronging him at court. Anna, who valued Volynskii's businesslike qualities, hesitated a little before agreeing with Biron that it was necessary to get rid of him. When the investigation began, a story came to light that was unknown to the court concerning midnight meetings in Volynskii's home during which Volynskii, surrounded by his "confidants"—P. Eropkin, P. Musin-Pushkin, A. Khrushchov, and others—drafted a "General Plan" to rectify affairs of state. The drafting of this plan was judged to be a criminal act, an attempt to plot Anna's overthrow, and during torture Volynskii was made to confess that he wished to occupy the throne himself.

The denunciations of V. Kubanets, Volynskii's butler, did much to fill out his dossier, and all his frank talk about the stupid old woman on the throne, her crude and impudent opportunistic German, and other "dangerous materials," sealed the fate of Volynskii and his friends. The "General Assembly" (this time without Volynskii as a member), meeting in its full complement together with the Senate—and, remarkably enough, all were Russian dignitaries as well as Artemii Petrovich's acquaintances and friends—sentenced him to impaling. Patriotism, friendship, and all other feelings were silenced in these people, and only fear spoke. Had not Volynskii recently sat among them and signed the Dolgorukii's death warrant? Each of them probably thought, "Who will be next?"

Volynskii, Khrushchov, and Eropkin were executed on 27 June 1740. Anna had mitigated their sentence, commanding that they be decapitated. The executions made the atmosphere in St. Petersburg oppressive. And when Anna Ivanovna died on 17 October 1740 after a brief illness, having bequeathed the throne to Anna Leopoldovna's recently born son Ivan VI Antonovich and having made Biron regent, everybody knew that the opportunist's power was bound to collapse sooner or later. Three weeks later, Münnich carried out a coup d'état by arresting the regent at night and placing him in the Peter and Paul Fortress. The "Biron era" had come to an end. A new round of palace intrigue began, the victor of which, when all was said and done, was Elizabeth.

Notes

1. D.A. Korsakov, *Votsarenie imperatritsy Anny Ioannovny* (Kazan, 1880).
2. RGADA, f. 7, d. 670, ll. 5–6 ob.

3. Arkhiv S.-Peterburgskogo filiala Instituta rossiiskoi istorii, RAN, f. 270, d. 107, l. 268.

4. M.I. Semevskii, *Tsaritsa Praskov'ia (1664–1723)*, 2d ed. (St. Petersburg, 1883), pp. 68–69.

5. *Bezvremen'e i vremenshchiki* (Leningrad, 1991) p. 262.

6. Ibid., p. 165.

7. A.F. Shestakova, "Cherty domashnei zhizni imp. Anny Ioannovny," *Russkii arkhiv*, 1904, bk. 1, no. 3, pp. 523–26.

8. RGADA, f. 7, d. 281, l. 7.

9. "Perepiska imperatritsy Anny Ioannovny s Moskovskim gubernatorom grafom S.A. Saltykovym," *Russkii arkhiv*, 1863, no. 2, pp. 1648 ff.

10. Ibid.

11. M.M. Shcherbatov, *O povrezhdenii nravov v Rossii*, facsimile ed. (Moscow, 1984), p. 47.

12. *Pis'ma russkikh gosudarei i drugikh osob tsarskogo semeistva* (Moscow, 1862), pt. IV, pp. 176–203 ff.

13. S.N. Solov'ev, *Istoriia Rossii s drevneishikh vremen* (Moscow, 1963), bk. X, vol. 19, pp. 133–34.

14. K. Arsen'ev, *Tsarstvovanie Ekateriny I* (St. Petersburg, 1856), p. 82.

15. *Pis'ma russkikh gosudarei*, pp. 252–53.

16. *Bezvremen'e i vremenshchiki*, p. 163.

17. Ibid., p. 62.

18. *Sbornik Russkogo istoricheskogo obshchestva* (Sb. RIO), vol. 33 (St. Petersburg, 1888), p. 475.

19. *Sovetskii entsiklopedicheskii slovar'* (Moscow, 1991), vol. 1, pp. 140–41.

20. V.O. Kliuchevskii, Sochineniia (Moscow, 1989), vol. 4, p. 272.

21. RGVIA, f. 489, op. 1, dd. 7387, 7395.

22. Quoted in Korsakov, *Votsarenie*, p. 83.

23. N.N. Repin, *Vneshniaia torgovlia Rossii cherez Arkhangel'sk i Peterburg, v 1700–nachale 60-kh godov XVIII veka* (doctoral diss., Leningrad, 1985), vol. 1, p. 523 and tables.

24. S.G. Strumilin, *Istoriia chernoi metallurgii v SSSR* (Moscow, 1954), vol. 1, pp. 185–204; N.I. Pavlenko, *Razvitie metallurgicheskoi promyshlennosti Rossii v pervoi polovine XVIII veka* (Moscow, 1953), p. 82.

25. Pavlenko, *Razvitie*, pp. 124–26.

26. Ibid.

27. *Sb. RIO*, vol. 126 (Iuriev, 1907), p. 569.

28. N.I. Pavlenko, *Istoriia metallurgii v Rossii XVIII veka* (Moscow, 1962), p. 329.

29. Kliuchevskii, *Sochineniia*, vol. 4, pp. 295–96.

30. E. Belov, "Otnoshenie Fridrikha II do vstupleniia ego na prestol k russkomu dvoru," *Drevniaia i novaia Rossiia* (1875), vol. 2, p. 373.

31. N.N. Pokrovskii, *Antifeodal'nyi protest uralo-sibirskikh krest'ian-staroobriadtsev v XVIII veke* (Novosibirsk, 1974), pp. 68–69.

32. Solov'ev, *Istoriia Rossii*, bk. X, vol. 20, pp. 467–68.

33. T.V. Chernikova, "Gosudarevo slovo i delo vo vremena Anny Ioannovny," *Istoriia SSSR*, 1989, no. 5, pp. 155–63.

34. E.N. Epshtein, *Artemii Petrovich Volynskii—gosudarstvennyi deiatel' i diplomat.* (Candidate's diss., Leningrad, 1949), p. 235.

Empress Elizabeth I, 1741–1762

Anna Ivanovna was succeeded by the grandson of her sister, a baby crowned Ivan VI (1740–41). At first, Biron served as regent, but only a few weeks into the reign he fell in yet another palace revolt and was exiled to Siberia. Ivan VI's mother, Anna, now became regent—but not for long: within months another coup brought the daughter of Peter the Great, Elizabeth, to the throne.

Dismissed as "superficial," Elizabeth's twenty-year rule is often remembered for the huge debts she ran up for the Russian treasury and for palace wardrobes crammed with 15,000 gowns and dresses. In an attempt to redress the shallow assessments of Elizabeth, historian Viktor Petrovich Naumov, after painting a sympathetic portrait of Elizaveta Petrovna based on contemporaries' observations, challenges the notion found in the historical literature that Elizabeth was unprepared for the role of empress. Naumov's Elizabeth was the belle of the ball, but one with powerful political ambitions, too. Cautious by nature, Elizabeth "never made a single hasty or unconsidered move." The author emphasizes the empress's independent policies and their departure from those of her father, in particular in the state's administration of Ukraine and other matters. He also addresses the empress's piety, which he suggests might have been behind her critical attitude toward the death penalty. To be sure, the self-promotion as Peter's heir that she encouraged while in power proved long-lasting, for it nurtured the political canonization of Peter the Great and cast the 1727–1741 period in the most negative light. Guardedly positive, Naumov's rediscovery of Elizabeth underscores the "unhurried and measured development" of Russia that took place while she reigned as empress.

D.J.R.

Elizabeth I

Viktor Petrovich Naumov

> *"Such a happy tsaritsa*
> *Was Elizabeth:*
> *She would sing and make merry,*
> *But order was there none."*

This quatrain by A.K. Tolstoy from *The History of the Russian State from Gostomysl to Timashev* reflects better than anything else a widespread notion about the daughter of Peter the Great. The tsaritsa's costumes and balls against the background of the high-handed actions of her favorites and the decline of state affairs—such is the textbook portrayal of the reign of Elizaveta Petrovna (Elizabeth I), which in most general works on Russian history is almost completely lost among the political storms of what is called the era of palace coups. Yet the reign of Elizabeth represented a twenty-year period in Russian life that on closer examination proves to be an important page in the country's past.

Elizabeth, the daughter of Peter I and the former Livonian peasant woman Marta Skavronskaia (christened Ekaterina Alekseevna [Catherine I] after she converted to Orthodoxy), was born on 18 December 1709 in the village of Kolomenskoe near Moscow. When Elizabeth was born, Peter I and Catherine's marriage was not yet official, which later affected Elizabeth's fate. Together with her older sister Anna, she was brought up by "nannies" and wet-nurses from among the common folk, and as a result she was familiar with and fond of Russian customs from early childhood. From approximately 1716 onward, governesses from France and Italy, a Livonian to teach German, and a French dance master were recruited to educate the tsarevna. V.O. Kliuchevskii correctly noted that "Elizabeth fell between two opposing cultural tendencies; she was brought up amid both the new European currents and the legends of Russia's pious antiquity."[1] However, the "foreign" upbringing predominated: the tsarevnas were chiefly taught foreign languages, dances, and court etiquette. These types of knowledge and skills were deemed necessary for

Peter I's daughters as preparation for marriage with scions of the European dynasties. Elizabeth's father intended to give her in marriage to the French king, Louis XV, or to one of the Bourbon princes, but lengthy negotiations on this matter were unsuccessful.

Contemporaries commented that Elizabeth was perfectly fluent in French and German and understood Italian, Swedish, and Finnish. Her instruction in dance was also not in vain, and the future empress could dance better than anybody in St. Petersburg. Overall, however, Peter's daughters received a superficial education. D.V. Volkov, who was very closely associated with the top levels of power from 1756 through 1762, noted that Elizabeth "did not know that Great Britain is an island."[2] She learned to read and write, however, by the time she was eight years old, and by late 1717 she delighted her father by writing him a letter, as we know from his letter in response.[3] We have preserved, from that same year, Anna's and Elizabeth's first letter, signed by the tsarevnas although not written in their own hands. It was addressed to A.D. Menshikov, whom the little girls begged to grant clemency to a woman who was being subjected to a slow and agonizing death—burial up to her neck in the ground. Anna and Elizabeth wrote that she had been buried "for a considerable time now and is on the verge of death," and they beseeched him to "free her from that death . . . and send her to a monastery."[4] Hence, the first document known to have been signed by Elizabeth testifies to her mercifulness.

The first time the beauty of the tsar's daughter was mentioned also dates to the year 1717. By age twelve, Elizabeth was charming B.-Kh. Münnich, who had come to Russia. Later, the eminent field marshal recalled that "while still of tender years . . ., despite being overweight, she was nevertheless nicely built, attractive, and full of health and liveliness. She walked so swiftly that everyone, especially the ladies, found it difficult to keep up with her; she was an excellent rider and was not afraid of the water." Later still, the wife of the English Resident in St. Petersburg, Claude Rondeau, had equally high praise for the good looks of Peter I's daughter: "Princess Elizabeth . . . is very handsome. She is very fair with light brown hair, large, sprightly blue eyes, fine teeth and a pretty mouth. She is inclinable to be fat but is very genteel and dances better than anyone I ever saw before."[5]

According to descriptions by contemporaries, Elizabeth's character matched her appearance. People who came to know her stated that she was of "an extraordinarily merry temperament," that her "speech is intelligent and pleasant," that the tsarevna "treats everybody courteously but hates the ceremonies of the court," that she was "gracious and very coquettish but fickle, ambitious, and has a heart that is too tender."[6] This last statement means that Elizabeth was amorous and knew how to dissemble. More important here is the comment on the tsarevna's ambition, because that trait of her character largely predetermined the path her life would take.

In August 1721 Peter I assumed the title of emperor, after which Anna and Elizabeth began to be called the "tsesarevnas." This title separated Peter I's offspring from the other members of the Romanov house. Peter, the son of Tsarevich Alexei, who was executed, was only given the title Grand Duke, while Peter I's niece Anna Ivanovna was the tsarevna.

Peter I's death on 28 January 1725 did nothing to disrupt Elizabeth's happy world, because her mother, Catherine I, ascended the throne. Not long afterward, her older sister Anna was married to Karl Friedrich, duke of Holstein. Catherine was passionately fond of her daughters, and after the elder's wedding her younger was always at her side. It is frequently recorded that Elizabeth read state papers to her semi-literate mother and even signed edicts in her name. It is also well known that under Catherine I, Elizabeth wielded a certain amount of influence. In June 1725 A.P. Volynskii, the governor-general of Astrakhan, pleaded with the princess to petition the empress to improve his station.[7]

Actually, affairs of state were hardly much of a burden to the seventeen-year-old beauty, who sparkled at social gatherings and was generally acknowledged to be the belle of the ball. Some dignitaries openly condemned her for her excessive fascination with dances and her frivolous character, but others treated Elizabeth quite seriously. Those most attentive to her had taken part in the reprisal against Tsarevich Alexei and feared retribution from his son, whom the "semi-sovereign lord" Menshikov intended to be heir to the throne. During Catherine I's fatal illness in April 1727, Supreme Privy Council member P.A. Tolstoy and his associates expressed a desire that the empress "deign to make her daughter Elizaveta Petrovna the heiress."[8]

Catherine I died on 6 May 1727. Rumors circulated that a few days before she died she really had intended to turn the throne over to Elizabeth, but the empress's last will stated otherwise. According to her will ("Testament"), the heir to the throne was Peter I's grandson, the eleven-year-old Peter II. Until the young emperor came of age, a regency was to be established for him, consisting of nine personages, including Anna Petrovna and her husband, Elizabeth, Menshikov, and other members of the Supreme Privy Council. The Testament also stipulated the future succession to the Russian throne. If Peter II died without issue, the throne was bequeathed to Anna Petrovna and her children; if they too died without continuing the line, the throne would be inherited by Elizabeth.[9] Given these stipulations, Elizabeth's chances of ascending the Russian throne were slim.

Anna's and Elizabeth's involvement as members of the regency did not last long. The two sisters signed only one protocol of the Supreme Privy Council, dated 15 May 1727, and that document concerned only the transfer of a state-owned building to private hands.[10] The actual ruler during the reign of the underage tsar was Menshikov, who did his best to keep Peter I's daughters removed from affairs of state. The intrigues of "His Eminence" against Anna Petrovna and her husband forced them to leave Russia on 5 August 1727.

After her sister's departure, Elizabeth, in M.I. Semevskii's felicitous words, "remained alone amidst the delusions of society."[11] But she had no grounds for grumbling about her fate. The "royal lad," who was physically and mentally developed beyond his years, fell in love with his charming aunt, who was only six years older than he. Elizabeth lorded over the young tsar in clever company and would make the young people roar with laughter by imitating and mimicking members of high society. She did not even spare people close to her such as her brother-in-law, the duke of Holstein. One contemporary wrote on 10 January 1728, "Russians are afraid of the great power that Princess Elizabeth has over the tsar: her intelligence, beauty, and ambition frighten them, and they would like to marry her off and get rid of her."[12] They were unsuccessful in finding an appropriate suitor for her, however, and Elizabeth herself evinced no inclination to marry. She was having fun in the company of the emperor, who was growing more and more attached to her.

In early August 1728, the English Resident, C. Rondeau, informed London: "Princess Elizabeth is in great favor now. She is very beautiful and likes everything the tsar likes—dancing and hunting, which are her principal passions. . . . The princess is not yet involved in affairs of state, inasmuch as she is given over entirely to pleasures; she accompanies the young tsar everywhere he wants to go."[13]

Rondeau's information was obsolete the moment it was dispatched, because at that very moment the people of the court noticed that Peter II had unexpectedly cooled toward Elizabeth. To a large extent this was fostered by the intrigues of the Princes Dolgorukii, who were trying to have the emperor marry a girl from their own house. In addition, the young tsar had solid reasons for jealousy, inasmuch as Elizabeth was seriously attracted to Major General A.B. Buturlin. From then on, Peter II began to show his young aunt definite signs of disfavor.

The following year, Peter II was betrothed to Ekaterina Dolgorukaia, Buturlin was sent off to serve in Ukraine, and Elizabeth removed herself from the court and settled on her estate in the village of Aleksandrova, near Moscow. There she spent her days hunting rabbits and grouse in the company of a new favorite, guardsman A.Ia. Shubin. She spent her evenings in the company of the young women of the village, with whom she sang folk songs, and on feast days she would perform Russian dances with them "in a lively and skillful manner."[14] She did not disdain the common folk, and she loved her people.

After Peter II's unexpected death on 19 January 1730, Elizabeth became the lawful heir to the throne in accordance with the Testament, because her sister Anna had relinquished the right to the Russian throne for herself and her posterity. However, the Supreme Privy Council settled the question of succession to the throne by declaring Elizabeth illegitimate and denying her right to it. D.M. Golitsyn, who chaired the meeting of the council members, declared that with Peter II's death "Tsar Peter I's family has died out," and his statement met with no objection. After lengthy debate, it was decided to "invite" Peter I's niece Anna Ivanovna, the widowed duchess of Courland, to rule.

The French Resident, Magnan, informed his court that "Princess Elizabeth did not express herself one way or another in this case. She was having a good time out in the country at the time, and even those who were making an effort on her behalf were unable, in view of the circumstances, to get her to come to Moscow."[15] K.-G. Manshtein stated that I.-G. Lestok, Elizabeth's personal physician and friend, tried to get her to "call up the Guards, address the people, go to the Senate, and there assert her claim to the crown. But she would not even agree to leave her bedchamber." The memoirist suggested that "at that time she preferred having a good time to the glory of reigning."[16] It is more likely, however, that she simply lacked the courage to take such a decisive step. In addition, the princess was then ill.

Elizabeth did not come to the capital until after Anna Ivanovna's coronation, and she congratulated her cousin on her ascension to the throne. At that point, the princess entered the gloomiest ten years of her life. The new empress did not like her cousin and always saw her as a potential threat. Elizabeth was granted a yearly allowance of 30,000 rubles, whereas under both Catherine I and Peter II she had received 100,000 annually. One of the worst blows she suffered was Shubin's exile in 1731; evidently she loved him very much. Elizabeth again withdrew to Aleksandrova, but no longer with the same gaiety as before. The princess sought consolation in religion, attending daily worship services in the Monastery of the Dormition of the Virgin and spending her time reading religious books. Actually, her turn to Orthodox worship may also have served as a means of self-defense, a manifestation of obedience to the empress, inasmuch as Anna Ivanovna wanted to have Elizabeth made a nun. She was saved only by the intercession of the all-powerful Ernst-Johann Biron. Subsequently Elizabeth acknowledged that she owed him a great deal.

Elizabeth's grief over the loss of Shubin proved short-lived. Her heart was soon won, and then held for a long time, by A.G. Razumovskii, a Ukrainian Cossack who found himself at the princess's court thanks to his voice. A church chorister in one of the Chernigov villages, he caught the attention of Colonel F.S. Vishnevskii and was brought to St. Petersburg to sing in the court chapel, where he caught Elizabeth's attention. (One rumor has it that after she ascended the throne she secretly married him.) Yet the improvement in her personal life could not make up for the constant suffering she endured. Elizabeth was threatened with the convent or a forced marriage "with a prince . . . who could never pose any kind of danger"[17]—that is, a member of an impoverished family. She had no right to approach the empress without making an advance request or by special invitation. She was forbidden to arrange parties at her home. She was under financial strain as well. Not without reason, N.N. Firsov noted that "this personal unhappiness was the principal motive for the ambitious princess to exercise her right to the throne at the earliest opportunity."[18]

When Anna Ivanovna died on 17 October 1740 she designated as her heir her grandnephew Ivan Antonovich, who was only two months old at the time. Biron was regent, but his tenure lasted only three weeks. Field Marshal Münnich, who overthrew Biron, turned power over to Anna Leopoldovna, Anna Ivanovna's niece and Ivan Antonovich's mother. The new ruler treated Elizabeth sympathetically, but the latter hardly reciprocated. Probably, the princess never stopped thinking about ascending the throne; according to the English ambassador, she was already "very popular both in her own right and because she was Peter I's daughter, for his memory was becoming ever more dear to the Russian people." Catherine II claimed that during Elizabeth's excursions around St. Petersburg "people called out to her to ascend the throne of her ancestors."[19]

During Anna Ivanovna's reign, which was a difficult time for the people, broad segments of Russian society became convinced that all their troubles stemmed from the usurpation of power by the "foreigners." While Empress Anna was Russian, the half-German Anna Leopoldovna and her husband Prince Anton Ulrich of Braunschweig were foreigners in the eyes of the people, and were wrongly ruling Russia in the name of the baby emperor. The sympathies of the masses were with Elizabeth, who was "Russian in heart and in habits."[20]

The barracks of the Preobrazhenskii Guards Regiment became the center of the movement in favor of Peter I's daughter. According to E.V. Anisimov, most of those involved in Elizabeth's ascension to the throne came from groups subject to the poll-tax, and so were able to express the patriotic sentiments of large segments of the capital's population.[21] Elizabeth herself did everything she could to win the Guards' sympathies. She often spent time in the barracks "without fuss or ceremony," gave the guardsmen gifts of money, and stood godmother to their children. The soldiers never called her anything but "Little Mother." The threads of the plot did not extend to the heart of high society, and the circle of Elizabeth's proponents was restricted chiefly to the "cavaliers" of her court. Lestok and Razumovskii took part in preparing the coup as did the brothers A.I. and P.I. Shuvalov and M.I. Vorontsov. Lestok and Elizabeth herself led it.

Other people as well, however, were interested in elevating Peter I's daughter to the throne. The French ambassador, the Marquis de la Chêtardie, who arrived in St. Petersburg in December 1739, had confidential instructions to seek out Elizabeth's secret allies. French diplomacy hoped, by means of a coup, to change Russia's foreign policy orientation, because at that time Russia was allied with England and Austria, which were hostile to France. One of French politics' traditional goals, moreover, was to weaken Russia and prevent it from intervening in European affairs. The best way to accomplish this was through a coup in favor of Elizabeth, who, it was thought, "on the basis of her way of life and customs, would not mind returning to a pre-Petrine Rus and did not like foreigners."[22]

Chêtardie established close contacts with Elizabeth and Lestok and provided the plotters with 2,000 gold coins. Although not a large amount of money, it somewhat alleviated the princess's financial difficulties, which had made her withhold the courtiers' salaries in order to give presents to the guardsmen. Chêtardie's ally in preparing the coup was the Swedish envoy E.-N. Nolken. Chêtardie encouraged the Swedes to start a war against Russia and to elevate Elizabeth to the throne with the help of Swedish arms. As grateful payment for her help, Sweden hoped to regain the Baltic territories ceded to Russia by the Treaty of Nystadt in 1721.

In secret negotiations with the foreign diplomats, Elizabeth showed herself to be a subtle politician. She gratefully agreed to accept Sweden's help, but she gave no firm promises. Attempts by Nolken and Chêtardie to obtain a signed document from her guaranteeing territorial concessions were unsuccessful. Later, P.I. Panin noted that "Elizabeth refused to give written promises, pleading that it was extremely dangerous to lay out such a vital secret on paper, and she insisted that they trust her word in everything. Subsequent events showed that Elizaveta Petrovna outfoxed the wily Frenchmen and duped the Swedes."[23]

Sweden declared war against Russia in July 1741; one of the causes Sweden cited was "the banishing of Princess Elizabeth and the duke of Holstein (the son of Anna Petrovna) from the Russian throne, and the power that foreigners wielded over the Russian nation."[24] The Swedes, who had suffered defeat in the Northern War, had been harboring the idea of military revenge since 1727. The plans of the top Swedish rulers included seizing St. Petersburg and conquering Russia's northern territories as far as Arkhangelsk. The Swedes' military actions proved to be unsuccessful, however, and they had to confine themselves to hopes of weakening Russia through internal turmoil that the coup might cause. Meanwhile, the Guards were already in a mood for resolute action. In June 1741 several guardsmen met Elizabeth in the Summer Garden and told her, "Little Mother, we are all ready and are only awaiting your orders." She answered them, "Disperse now and conduct yourselves peaceably: the time is not yet ripe for action. I will let you know beforehand."[25]

The hour of the coup struck unexpectedly. The plans of the plot were revealed by Austrian and English diplomats, who warned Anna Leopoldovna of the danger that threatened her. On the evening of 23 November, the kindly and simple-hearted regent candidly told Elizabeth about the foreign ambassadors' suspicions and demanded an explanation. With considerable restraint and composure, the princess replied that the charges against her were slander, that to believe them would be foolhardy, and even that she was "too religious to break the vow she had given."[26] The confrontation between the two women ended with tears and embraces. Returning home, Elizabeth gathered her allies for a conference, and in view of the clear danger because of the disclosure of the plotters' plans, it was decided to carry out the coup on the evening of the following day. The sagacity of this move was confirmed, because the next day the Guards regiments were ordered to leave St. Petersburg and fight the Swedes.

On the night of 24 November, Elizabeth came to the barracks of the Grenadiers Company of the Preobrazhenskii Regiment and addressed her followers: "Men, you know whose daughter I am—follow me!" The guardsmen answered: "Little Mother, we are ready; we will kill all of them." Elizabeth objected: "If you intend to do that, I will not go with you." Realizing that her allies' hatred was directed against foreigners, she immediately declared that she was "taking all these foreigners under her special protection."[27] The coup was accomplished without bloodshed, and without Chêtardie's participation.

On the morning of 25 November 1741, a manifesto was published announcing that Elizaveta Petrovna had ascended the throne "by legitimate right, by blood kinship with her autocratic . . . parents." On 28 November a second manifesto was published in which the right of Peter I's daughter to the Russian crown was backed up by reference to Catherine I's Testament. Ivan Antonovich was declared to be an unlawful ruler, having "no claim, lineage, or right pertaining to the Throne of All the Russias." Coins bearing his likeness were removed from circulation, and large numbers of papers with the oath of loyalty to him were publicly burned in the squares "to the accompaniment of drumbeats."[28]

The new empress began her reign at the age of thirty-two; consequently, her character, views, and habits were already formed. The notion presented in the scholarly literature, that she was completely unprepared for the role of monarch, does not accord with the facts. That Catherine I had involved her daughter in practical concerns could hardly fail to leave its traces on Elizabeth. In addition, the princess had had her own Estate Office and skillfully directed operations on her various holdings.[29] All this gave her the opportunity to acquire experience that she could apply to state activities in the future.

Contemporary assessments also indicate that Elizabeth possessed the qualities necessary for a successful ruler. According to Münnich, she was "endowed by nature with the highest qualities, in terms of both appearance and spirit. . . . She had a lively, penetrating, cheer-

Elizabeth I

ful, and ingratiating mind and great abilities." In April 1743 the English diplomat C. Wich noted that "no other princess in Europe has ascended the throne with better promise of being a great personage, and Providence has abundantly endowed her with all the qualities and all the talents necessary to ensure that she will be beloved and respected by her own subjects and by other nations." Some contemporaries even asserted that hers was "an exemplary monarchy combining all the qualities of a great sovereign and a ruler worthy of praise."[30] There is considerable testimony, however, that these qualities of Elizabeth's were not applied as they should have been. Münnich himself acknowledged that "the empress did not govern anything, and the form of state administration during her reign was the high-handed work of her favorites." Wich canceled out his assessment of Elizabeth by concluding: "But her fondness for pleasures ruins everything." Another foreign diplomat stated that her "intellectual laziness ... prevents her from carrying out many of the duties that are an inseparable component of her high station. She has only mastered two of the qualities of the art of governing a nation—the ability to maintain her dignity, and secretiveness."[31]

Many contemporaries concurred in their opinions of Elizabeth's other character traits. A.T. Bolotov, I. Poze, and Joanna Elizabeth of Anhalt-Zerbst (Catherine II's mother) spoke in almost identical terms of the empress's goodness, philanthropy, and mercy. Catherine II thought that "she was endowed by nature with a good heart, she had lofty sensibilities and, at the same time, much vanity." The French diplomat J.-L. Favier, however, stated that "through all her goodness and humanity ... one can frequently perceive pride, arrogance, and sometimes even cruelty, but suspiciousness most of all." Elizabeth's nature was, indeed, complex and contradictory, and a female contemporary rightly noted that "nobody can read what is in her heart."[32]

Elizabeth manifested real cruelty on only one occasion, in 1743, when she signed a sentence "with most fearful severity" regarding the Lopukhin family. As P.I. Panin rightly commented, the Lopukhins' alleged plot consisted of "the empty talk of two unhappy ladies and the immodest speeches of the son of one of them." The participants in the "plot" were flogged with the knout and sent to Siberia, and four of them—including two women—had their tongues cut out. One contemporary has stated, rightly, that "this cruel punishment, which is more characteristic of barbaric times, does not, of course, redound to the credit of a sovereign whose magnanimity and compassion toward mankind have been so assiduously extolled."[33] The unusual cruelty manifested by Elizabeth in this case support the view held by several authors that Elizabeth reacted out of feminine revenge. It was said that one of the "plotters"—N.F. Lopukhina—outshone the empress by her beauty. In addition, Elizabeth harbored a secret dislike toward the entire Lopukhin family, who were relatives of her father's first wife.

The Lopukhins' punishment may seem especially strange considering Elizabeth's religious nature. One contemporary said that "she was pious without hypocrisy and greatly favored public worship."[34] She strictly observed the fasts, performed the church rituals, made lengthy pilgrimages, and particularly sought to build new churches and monasteries. At the same time, a French diplomat commented, not without irony, that Elizabeth's religious feelings "by no means prevent her from enjoying life. Quite the contrary: these deeds serve, so to speak, to counteract sin and enable her to maintain the soul balanced between good and evil. Such are the teachings of the monks and priests, and Empress Elizabeth conforms to them." Kliuchevskii pointed out that "from vespers she went to a ball, and after the ball she had time to make it to matins." Ukrainian choristers and Italian singers summoned to the court, "in order not to disrupt the integrity of the artistic impression, . . . s[a]ng both mass and opera."[35]

The empress whirled in a dizzying round of amusements, interrupted only by fasting. Many contemporaries, in particular foreign diplomats, wrote about the laziness, negligence, and frivolity of Peter I's daughter, who could not even find the time between amusements to sign papers. Later, M.M. Shcherbatov also noted that "not only domestic affairs of state . . . but even foreign affairs of state, such as treaties," would lie neglected for months "because of the laziness" of the empress.[36] Catherine II likewise attested to Elizabeth's "congenital sloth."

Catherine reported in her memoirs that Elizabeth "had the habit, whenever she was supposed to sign something especially important, of placing the paper, before signing it, under a representation of the Christ shroud, which she particularly respected. After leaving the paper there for a while, she would sign it or not sign it depending on what her heart told her."[37]

Elizabeth's chief quality, both as a person and as a politician, was caution. In all her life, Peter I's daughter never made a single hasty or unconsidered move. She made decisions only after thoroughly considering her advisers' various opinions. S.M. Soloviev suggested that it was this circumstance that subjected Elizabeth to accusations of laziness and negligence that were not always fair. The great historian noted that

> she listened to one opinion, accepted it, and because of the liveliness of her character she could not refrain from expressing her approval; being in no hurry to decide the matter on the basis of a first impression, she listened to another opinion and focused on a different aspect of the matter; placed in a difficult position, comparing and considering, she naturally took her time, and thereby she tended to annoy people who wanted their ideas implemented as quickly as possible. They loudly complained that the empress was not taking care of state business and was devoting all of her time to pleasure.[38]

It is true that Elizabeth was not known for her asceticism, but that was not the main reason for her difficulty in getting things done.

The empress knew how to evaluate her associates soberly and objectively and chose advisers who were genuinely intelligent and competent. The inevitable rivalry among them in their efforts to subject the empress to their influence did not bother her in the slightest. According to Soloviev, "Elizabeth's chief virtue . . . was her impartial and calm treatment of people; she knew their conflicts, hostilities, and intrigues, and never paid the slightest attention to these, as long as they were not detrimental to their work; she impartially protected people who were useful, firmly maintained balance among them, and did not let them destroy one another."[39]

She made no exception for members of her retinue, and she placed no one above the rest. Favier emphasized that "she never, in any way, allows any person, minister or favorite, to control her, but she always makes a show of distributing her favors and pretended trust among them." One of Elizabeth's characteristic traits was her extraordinary fussiness in regard to her autocratic rights. A French diplomat stated that the empress, "who is supremely jealous of her majesty and supreme power, . . . is easily frightened of anything that may threaten to diminish or divide that power. She has manifested extraordinary ticklishness in this regard more than once."[40]

It is worth mentioning that Elizabeth's favorites were distinguished by their modesty and unpretentiousness. None of them ever attempted to become co-ruler with the empress, as Biron did, for example, under Anna Ivanovna or G.A. Potemkin under Catherine II. Razumovskii was content to have Elizabeth's favors; he hardly ever interfered in affairs of state and was noteworthy only in that he protected the Orthodox Church, the Little Russian [Ukrainian] people, his younger brother Kirill, Vice Chancellor (later Chancellor) A.P. Bestuzhev-Riumin, and the poet A.P. Sumarokov. Razumovskii did not pester Elizabeth with his jealousy; as she herself acknowledged, she was "happy only when she was in love."

A highlight of her personal life was having to "indulge and reconcile the delicate feelings of four favorites simultaneously."[41] Two of these (Beketov and Kachenovskii) soon left the scene, and only Razumovskii and Chamberlain I.I. Shuvalov, a cousin of people who helped Elizabeth take the throne, remained. Even more modest than the old favorite, refusing the title of count, a high rank, and large monetary and land grants, Shuvalov was known as a patron of science, culture, and education and a friend of M.V. Lomonosov. Among themselves, Elizabeth's lovers were on extraordinarily good terms. Foreign diplomats noted that Razumovskii "lived in complete harmony with his rival, whom he viewed rather as a comrade. . . . The empress placed equal trust in them and was happy only in their company."[42]

One of Elizabeth's first significant acts was to resolve the issue of the heir to the Russian throne. Her nephew Karl Peter Ulrich, the son of Princess Anna Petrovna, lived in the German Duchy of Holstein; by then he was an orphan. The empress summoned the thirteen-year-old boy to Russia, took good care of him, and promised to be a second mother to him. On 7 November 1742 he was christened Petr Fedorovich (Peter III) and declared heir to the throne. A short while later, Elizabeth deemed it essential to arrange his marriage and after lengthy diplomatic discussions she chose as his betrothed Sophia Augusta Frederika, princess of Anhalt-Zerbst, who converted to the Orthodox faith under the name Ekaterina Alekseevna (Catherine II). Peter and Catherine's wedding took place on 21 August 1745.

The personal relationship between the empress and the heir ultimately did not turn out well. Catherine II recalled that Elizabeth's papers, which she had found, contained two comments: "That confounded nephew of mine irritated me no end," and "That nephew of mine is a monster, the devil take him." In addition, another note by Elizabeth has survived: "I regret to say that this nephew of mine not only lacks intelligence but is forgetful as well"; this note was made after Peter and his wife attended one of the court celebrations unsuitably dressed.[43] It is probable that relations between nephew and aunt were spoiled after Peter began to stay away from the court and spend time at Oranienbaum, which the empress had given him, where he conducted military exercises and abused alcohol and tobacco in the company of officers. According to a contemporary, in 1755 "the grand duke drank a lot and occupied himself exclusively with training soldiers. The empress, who had been extraordinarily fond of her nephew before that, was extraordinarily unhappy with him."[44]

For a long time, one of the empress's biggest worries and concerns was the fact that the grand duke and his wife did not have children. When, at long last, little Pavel Petrovich (Paul I) came into the world on 20 September 1754, the joyful Elizabeth took him away from his mother and began to care for him herself. There were also fundamental differences between Elizabeth and her heir concerning foreign affairs. Elizabeth proclaimed one of the basic principles of her policy to be that of returning to Peter I's course, which had been changed by the hereditary nobility and "German opportunists." An edict signed by the empress on 12 December 1741 declared that during the reigns of preceding rulers "affairs of state were greatly neglected" as a result of abolishing regulations that had existed under Peter I and Catherine I.[45] E.V. Anisimov has correctly defined two basic ideological conceptions of Elizabeth's reign: the political canonization of Peter the Great and an extremely negative view of the period between the death of Catherine I and the ascent of Elizabeth herself.[46]

In the same edict, Elizabeth reinstated "Peter's brainchild"—the Senate, in its capacity as the supreme state body—and dissolved the Cabinet of Ministers, a special institution with extraordinary powers that had overseen the Senate during the two preceding reigns. The edict ordered the cabinet replaced by "a cabinet attached to Our Court, having the same status it did under . . . Peter the Great." This served to restore the personal Imperial Chancellory created by Peter I—the cabinet, the duties of which included receiving documents addressed to the monarch, drawing up edicts for the ruler's personal signature, announcing spoken "imperial orders," and managing the financial side of palace operations. Placed in charge of the restored institution was I.A. Cherkasov, who had once served in the cabinet under Peter and was well acquainted with its organization. That is why Peter I's and Elizabeth's cabinets were almost identical in terms of organizational structure.

The creation of the personal Imperial Chancellory was linked to Elizabeth's desire to take all the reins of government into her own hands and reinstate the importance of autocratic rule. The Supreme

Privy Council and the Cabinet of Ministers that had existed under her predecessors had had the right to pass edicts in the monarch's name. Now, however, the cabinet drew up imperial edicts only for Elizabeth's personal signature. In addition, the former practice of "oral imperial edicts" (imperial orders) was preserved; by the empress's command they were announced to the Senate and to other institutions by persons authorized to do so. Thanks to this reform of the highest state bodies, the monarch continued to dominate the absolutist system. L.G. Kisliagina has rightly commented that "Elizaveta Petrovna's government was marked by the further centralization of power. In practice, the empress personally decided not only important state matters but also very trivial ones."[47]

To make important decisions, however, the empress needed to consult with those whom she had placed in charge of the state apparatus. For this reason, she resurrected yet another of Peter's "institutions"—extraordinary convocations of top officials to discuss the most complicated problems, primarily those of foreign policy. Under Elizabeth these convocations were officially called conferences, and their participants were called "conference ministers." Foreign diplomats called this body the "Grand Council," and scholars have called it the "Extraordinary Council" or the Imperial Council. The conferences had an established procedure for collecting written opinions from the ministers regarding the issues being discussed, and minutes of the meetings were kept. The "opinions" and the minutes were sent to the empress for examination and approval.

Peter I had held similar conferences in association with the College of Foreign Affairs. Elizabeth, however, commanded that they be held "in the Imperial home in special chambers"; meetings of the Senate were also to be moved there. The empress expressed her intention of personally attending the conferences and the Senate "at appropriate times and as business requires."[48] Later, she really did appear at sessions of these bodies, although not very often.

Comparing Elizabeth's notes and remarks that have been preserved with the texts of the signed imperial edicts reveals the mechanism by which supreme authority was exercised. The empress communicated her decision orally or in writing to Cherkasov, who drew up the appropriate legislative or executive document and submitted it "for the imperial signature." It was probably difficult for him, at times, to convert Elizabeth's flow of ideas into clear and precise documents. Here is an example of the creative thinking of Peter the Great's daughter:

Write an edict whereby the court quartermaster's office is placed under the commander in chief to be responsible only to him, namely the chief steward, and nobody must be in command besides him. And write in particular that things must not be as they were under the emperor of blessed memory, namely, the palace servants used whatever they pleased, and so explain that the sovereign's servants are not to be sent out to homes or to work anywhere, nor is any material to be given out, and end it by saying that not a stick of wood goes out without my orders, and the chief steward himself is to see to it that all of the servants are used to run the household, not for anybody else, and once you have written the edict, bring it to me to be signed.[49]

Whenever Elizabeth visited Tsarskoe Selo or Peterhof, Cherkasov stayed behind in St. Petersburg and the empress was accompanied by one of the cabinet secretaries. On 24 January 1746 one of them composed this order for Cherkasov:

Ivan Antonovich! From the report that We received on this date from Field Marshal General Count Lesia concerning the regiments stationed in Courland We have determined that they are understrength and many are shown absent; in regard to this, in confirmation of Our previous edicts please prepare an edict concerning this for the Army College and send it here to Us for Our signature.

Before placing her signature on this letter, Elizabeth added the following to the text: "immediately."[50] This definitely showed that the empress was by no means always lazy or slow to act.

In addition to drafting edicts for the imperial signature, Cherkasov also received documents addressed to Elizabeth—reports and messages from the Senate, the Holy Synod, the College of Foreign Affairs, the Army and Admiralty Colleges, and other institutions, and also numerous petitions "for favors and mercy." Cherkasov reported the content of all these papers to the empress. The petitions were examined selectively, but the principle by which they were selected is not clear. V.I. Demidov, the second most important member of the cabinet, was occupied chiefly with the personal financial-management affairs of the empress. It was through him that she issued orders to have dresses made, bills paid, and money issued for other necessities.[51]

Elizabeth's fastidiousness over matters of power was manifested in the following characteristic episode. After Cherkasov died in November 1757, Demidov undertook vigorous measures to impose order on the operation and management of the cabinet. Demidov's orders testified to this statesman's unusual organizing abilities. But when

Elizabeth found out about the initiative he had shown, she ordered that he be "served with an edict signed by Her Imperial Majesty [inquiring as to] why he was involved in the cabinet's business and routines without instructions from Her Majesty and [stipulating that] from this time on he, Demidov, is not to involve himself in any of the cabinet's business and routines."[52] The post of head of the cabinet on which Demidov had evidently counted was taken by A.V. Olsufiev, a member of the College of Foreign Affairs.

The Senate also experienced the empress's defensiveness over the prerogatives of autocratic rule. In October 1742 Elizabeth became angry because, without her knowledge, the Senate had ordered Field Marshal P.P. Lassy to deploy troops in their winter quarters.[53] Nevertheless, the Senate did assume most of the job of internal administration. It issued legislative acts on its own (Senate edicts), appointed local governors, and dealt with numerous particular matters of state "without troubling Her Majesty with reports." It was believed that the empress exercised control over the Senate's activities through Procurator-General N.Iu. Trubetskoi (whose position was actually called "the Sovereign's eye"). In addition, many Senate members enjoyed Elizabeth's personal confidence and good will.

The Senate's importance was very great during her reign. A.D. Gradovskii went so far as to claim that "Elizaveta Petrovna's rule might be called an administration by the most important officials convened in the Senate."[54] A different point of view was expressed by S.O. Shmidt, who commented that under Elizabeth this body

> did not become the focal point of important state affairs. From the very beginning of the new reign, some matters came to be the personal purview of the empress. . . . The Senate depended on various manifestations of the personal factor in state administration, both in the form of the empress's own actions and in the form of directives and powers which trusted persons and institutions were able to obtain from her.[55]

A quantitative analysis of documents of the highest state institutions confirms the notion that the Senate depended on imperial authority to a significant extent. In November–December 1741, Elizabeth gave the Senate fifty-one edicts (including both written and "oral" edicts) and received from it fourteen reports for "imperial approval." In 1742 these figures were 183 and 113, respectively; in 1743 the figures were 129 and 54; in 1744, 164 and 38; and so on. Hence the highest governmental body functioned under the empress's control and sometimes, in fact, under her immediate supervision. On 10 January 1743 Elizabeth forbade the Senate to undertake any action "on the basis of written or oral proposals" without an edict signed by her personally. On 4 April, however, this decision was violated by the empress herself, when she submitted an oral command to the Senate through Police Chief General F.V. Naumov.[56] Later, the empress's "oral" edicts, rather than disappearing, actually increased in number.

Among the empress's directives to the Senate was one to review the edicts passed since Peter I's time in order to repeal those in conflict with his laws. The Senate began its work, but in eight years it managed to examine edicts only through 1729. On 11 March 1754, at a Senate session with the empress in attendance and with the participation of representatives of the central institutions, P.I. Shuvalov stated that it was not useful to review the legislation of previous reigns, because "although there are many edicts, there are not many actual laws which would be clear and understandable to all." He proposed that the government's efforts be channeled into drawing up a new law code and creating a special commission for the purpose. Elizabeth approved the idea and stated that "manners and customs do change over time, and hence changes in the laws are necessary."[57]

The idea of replacing the long-obsolete Law Code of 1649 with a new code of laws was not new: from 1700 onward, five different legislative commissions labored over it unsuccessfully. Now the Senate created a sixth, which by the summer of 1755 had drawn up two parts of the new code, the "judicial" and the "criminal." Work on Part Three, "On the Status of Subjects," dragged on for a long time and was not completed under Elizabeth. But even after the legislative commission was created, she did not abandon her idea of revising previous legislative acts. On 14 September 1760 the Senate was served with "an imperial command" to submit for her examination "detailed registers of all imperial edicts of the Emperor Peter the Great and subsequent rulers."[58] Actually, that was as far as things went. The "Elizabethan" Legislative Commission continued to function under Peter III and Catherine II until it was dissolved in 1766; the materials it had prepared were turned over to the "Catherinian" Legislative Commission.

The creation of the code of laws formed only a part of P.I. Shuvalov's vast program for the state; he was the actual manager of Elizabeth's government from the late 1740s onward. The program included many important measures in the economic, social, military, and administrative spheres. In particular, it involved the abolition (at

Shuvalov's initiative) of internal customs duties, which were a relic of the country's medieval fragmentation. Shuvalov submitted the draft of the edict abolishing some internal customs fees to the Senate in September 1752. After the document had been revised and reworked by the following August, Shuvalov turned in a new draft to the government for examination, one that called for "eliminating internal customs altogether" and increasing import duties to take their place. On 18 August 1753 the Senate approved Shuvalov's draft and submitted it to the empress for approval; she examined the document in December of the same year. She made one change in it, eliminating the paragraph that authorized foreign merchants to engage in retail trading of certain goods. Elizabeth's edict "On Eliminating Internal Customs and Small Fees" was published on 20 December 1753.[59]

This measure served to promote the development of domestic trade and speeded up the process of forming an all-Russian market. Foreign observers commented on the importance of abolishing internal customs dues, noting that "this institution will do a great deal to promote commerce within this empire." Under Bestuzhev-Riumin's leadership, the members of the Senate hastened to the empress's palace "to declare to her their sincere gladness and the people's appreciation." In response, Elizabeth stated: "Nothing can give me more joy or provide more satisfaction than the opportunity to foster the well-being and prosperity of my dear subjects." She also received a delegation of merchants and promised them "my special protection."[60] The act of raising duties on imported goods not only compensated for the treasury's loss because of the abolition of internal customs fees—it actually resulted in increased revenues to the treasury. In addition, Shuvalov's protectionist measures in foreign trade benefited the interests of entrepreneurial members of the nobility and Russia's emerging bourgeoisie.

Elizabeth's social policies somewhat alleviated the tax burden. In December 1741 the empress forgave arrears for the period between 1719 and 1730 and liquidated the Senate's Arrears Office, which had been trying unsuccessfully to collect them. In December 1752 arrears were forgiven for the period before 1747. The poll tax for 1742 and 1743 was reduced by ten kopecks per head, and in 1750–54 and 1757–58, the poll tax was systematically reduced at the rate of three to five kopecks per year. At the same time, however, at Shuvalov's initiative there was an increase in indirect taxes and in prices for salt and alcohol, the sale of which was a state monopoly.

Another major development during Elizabeth's reign was the Second Revision, a census of the population subject to the poll tax (the first such census was conducted in 1719–21). In September 1742 the empress approved the Senate's report on organizing a census, and on 16 December 1743 she signed the edict that prepared for it. In the course of the census conducted in 1744–47, a 17-percent increase in the population subject to the poll (or soul) tax was recorded. The census not only served to increase treasury revenues from the poll tax but also benefited taxpayers who had had to pay for those who had died or who had run away since Peter I's census.

The act of imposing order on taxation was especially beneficial for serfowners: it was no accident that the Senate commented in its report to the empress that the census would serve to "gratify all landowners."[61] Other measures were also taken on their behalf. In 1742 Elizabeth, contrary to her own father's laws, prohibited landowners' serfs from entering military service at their own initiative. In 1747 nobles were granted the right to sell their serfs as conscripts, which definitively legalized trading in human beings. In 1760 landowners received the right to send objectionable peasants to Siberia at their own initiative; the government counted these as recruits. The expansion of the nobility's rights was accompanied by the concentration of central and local authority in their hands. Representatives of other segments of society could not take part in administering the country and did not even have essential legal guarantees during "Elizabeth's purely autocratic reign."[62]

Elizabeth's reign represented another stage in the consolidation of the ruling class, from which, during preceding reigns, representatives of the hereditary nobility, Baltic Germans, and foreigners invited into Russian service had stood apart. Now, the differences between these noble groups were all but eliminated. The only criterion for determining a nobleman's status in the social hierarchy was his position according to Peter's "Table of Ranks"; the titled nobility merged into the general system of the higher bureaucracy. On 2 August 1748 Elizabeth had an edict issued ordering "that counts and princes . . . who have not earned their ranks shall neither have nor demand any primacy or precedence over those who, while not being princes and counts, have by their merits been granted ranks higher than the former."[63]

In regard to foreigners invited into Russian service, Elizabeth held to the principles of the cadre policies of Peter I, who tried to appoint Russians to the major positions in the state apparatus and the army, keeping foreigners, as much as possible, in subordinate positions.

Whenever someone recommended foreigners for vacant positions, the empress inevitably asked whether there was not a suitable candidate among the Russians. Nevertheless, capable people from other lands continued to be valued. During Elizabeth's reign, Russia became the second homeland for hundreds of outstanding foreign specialists—army and navy officers, engineers, scientists, artists, and musicians.

In December 1751 the empress issued an edict "On the Acceptance of Serbs Desiring to Move to Russia as Subjects and for Service to Russia." This measure was dictated in part by her concern for the Orthodox peoples who had been subjected to national and religious oppression in Austria and Turkey. Altogether, twenty-five thousand South Slavs moved to Russia. Immigrants fit for military service formed special Hussar and Pandour regiments. In doing so, Elizabeth was implementing an idea of Peter I, who in 1723 had intended to "maintain several regiments of cavalry made up of Serbs . . . who enter our service voluntarily."[64]

Elizabeth's nationality policies depended totally on her religious principles, which were far from tolerant. In December 1742 she issued an edict requiring the deportation of Jewish persons from Russia. The Senate tried to explain to the empress that this measure would result in the disruption of the Ukrainian and Baltic German trade, which was primarily in the hands of Jews, and would consequently lead to a reduction in revenues to the treasury. But she affixed this resolution to the Senate's report: "I do not desire mercenary profit from the enemies of Christ."[65] At the beginning of her reign, edicts were passed calling for the conversion of "Lutheran kirks" into Orthodox churches and the closing or demolition of Armenian churches and Moslem mosques. Measures were also undertaken to combat religious dissenters and strengthen Orthodox missionary activity. People of other faiths who converted to Orthodoxy gave the empress special satisfaction. On 20 January 1742 she became godmother to "three Persians and two Turks" when they were baptized at Tsarskoe Selo.[66] Whenever Protestants and Catholics were reported converting to Orthodoxy, Elizabeth ordered the news announced all over the country.

The empress monitored worship procedures and the correctness of the church environment. Once she reprimanded the procurator-general of the Holy Synod, Ia.P. Shakhovskoi, because in one of the new churches "on the iconostasis where angels should be vividly depicted, various idols resembling cupids have been placed."[67] Elizabeth instructed the Synod to correct the Russian text of the Bible and to censor any theological books imported from abroad.

Elizabeth's piety led her to depart from the course of secularizing church and monastery lands set by Peter I, who had succeeded in introducing state control over the economic life of church estates. The creation in 1726 of the College of Ecclesiastical Estates (Economic College), which oversaw the business affairs of the church, had continued Peter's reform. Partial secularization had been implemented in 1740 by introducing secular administration on several church estates, revenues from which went to the treasury. On 15 July 1744 Elizabeth abolished the College of Ecclesiastical Estates and again placed the revenues from monastery lands under the Synod's jurisdiction. On 31 October 1753 these estates returned to the jurisdiction of the clergy.[68]

Elizabeth's departure from Peter's policies was also reflected in the administration of Ukraine. In 1722 Peter I had prohibited the election of hetmans, and in 1734 hetman rule had been abolished. Elizabeth visited Kiev in 1744 and received a deputation requesting the restoration of the hetmanship. The request was granted and in 1750 the younger brother of the empress's favorite, K.G. Razumovskii, became the hetman of Ukraine. Highlights of Elizabeth's reign and the last hetmanship included the granting of many benefits to Little Russia.[69]

One of the most remarkable features of Elizabeth's reign was her attitude toward the death penalty. At the crucial moment on the eve of the coup, she had promised "not to execute anybody." Once she ascended the throne, however, she did not have the courage to abolish the death penalty, and she approached the implementation of that decision slowly and cautiously. As S.I. Viktorskii wittily remarked, Elizabeth's actions reflected "a purely feminine logic in the form of preferring to get her own way without coming out openly and excessively against established views." In addition, the empress was evidently afraid of increasing the number of crimes [by] "remov[ing] the fear of the supreme penalty."[70] It is also important to note that the empress was alone in her desire to abolish the death penalty. The Synod expressed willingness to release her from her promise, and the Senate approved the "criminal" part of the new code, which, in addition to the usual forms of the death penalty, also recommended "hanging by the rib" and an even more horrible form of execution, "tearing a living person into pieces by five horses in the case of more important political crimes."[71] Elizabeth refused to approve that law.

On 10 May 1744 she approved the Senate's report "On Not Abol-

ishing the Death Penalty for Thieves, Bandits, Murderers, and Coun-
terfeiters," but she ordered that all death sentences be submitted for
"imperial approval."[72] None of the sentences was sanctioned by her;
in this way, then, the death penalty was abolished, not de jure but de
facto. Meanwhile, the courts continued to hand down death sentences, and the condemned persons accumulated in the prisons "until
further orders." On 29 March 1753 Elizabeth approved the Senate's
report calling for "criminals sentenced to death" to be sentenced to
hard labor after being flogged with the knout, branded, and placed
in foot shackles for life. But on 30 September 1754 the Senate again
passed an edict ordering that "the death penalty not be carried out . . .
until reviewed." N.D. Sergeevskii summarized this position as follows:
"The death penalty was completely abolished; but from the standpoint of the time and the procedures of the day it was only temporarily halted."[73] Nevertheless, under this "merciful sovereign" torture
was still widely used, as was "old-time punishment by flogging, cud-
geling, and breaking [of bones]," which frequently resulted in the
death of those undergoing the ordeal.

The empress believed that one of her duties was to be concerned
about her subjects' morals. When she found out that there was a
"house of ill repute" in St. Petersburg, Elizabeth, on 28 June 1750,
ordered Cabinet Minister Demidov to find the proprietress of the
house, A. Felker (who was known by the nickname "Drezdensha"),
and "put her and all her retinue in jail under guard." More than fifty
"procuresses and loose women" were caught. On 1 August that year,
Elizabeth had Demidov transmit an order to the Chief Police Office
to "take measures to round up . . . all women and girls of ill repute."
She assigned the supervision of this effort to a special commission
headed by Demidov; in the years 1750 and 1751 alone, the commission investigated about two hundred cases concerning houses of ill
repute, prostitution, rape, pandering, extramarital liaisons, and marital infidelity.[74]

In December 1742 the empress banned the wearing of costly
clothing interwoven with gold and silver, also lace more than three
fingers in width. Old dresses were allowed to be worn until worn out,
but it was stipulated, in order to prevent the sewing of new ones, that
they be brought into state offices and marked with sealing wax in
concealed places. The price of costumes was also set: it was regulated
by the rank of their owners, and ladies wore dresses regulated by the
ranks of their husbands.[75] Edicts were passed in 1743 and 1748 that
confirmed adherence to Peter I's social policies. They ordered that

German clothing be worn and that everybody shave their beards and mustaches "except for the ranks of the clergy and peasants on the land." In St. Petersburg and Moscow it was forbidden to stage fist-fights, maintain taverns on major streets, raise tame bears, ride around on "fast horses," use "curse words" in public places, collect alms, and spread the streets with juniper during funeral processions.[76]

In December 1750 the empress granted the inhabitants of St. Petersburg the right to "have parties in their own homes for amusement, with decent music and Russian comedy." This established the tradition of the home theaters that later became familiar. In the early part of that year, cadets of the Nobility Infantry Corps, an officers' school, performed the first Russian play for Elizabeth, entitled *Khorev*, written by a graduate of the corps named A. Sumarokov. On 30 August 1756, by order of the empress, the first Russian theater was established in St. Petersburg; Sumarokov became its director, and the nucleus of the troupe was composed of actors from Iaroslavl headed by F.G. Volkov.[77] Troupes invited from Italy and France also performed in St. Petersburg. The empress adored the theater and usually attended performances at least twice a week. According to contemporaries, she "loved the arts and sciences, and especially music and painting."[78] It was her tastes and interests that largely promoted the development of Russian science, culture, and education. The second half of Elizabeth's reign witnessed the flourishing creativity of M.V. Lomonosov, the construction of the Winter Palace by the architect B.F. Rastrelli, the opening of Moscow University and gymnasia in Moscow and Kazan, and the creation of the Academy of Art. Among the capital's nobility, education in the home under the supervision of tutors, primarily French, became widespread. From then on, French language and etiquette gained a firm place in St. Petersburg society, and the empress's court, in the words of a contemporary, became "the most splendid in Europe."[79]

Elizabeth was sympathetic to France, but she never let her sympathetic feelings guide her foreign policy. France was not one of the powers that was friendly toward Russia at that time. At the time Elizabeth ascended the throne, the Russo-Swedish war was under way. The new empress asked Chêtardie, the French envoy, to help to arrange a truce, and he did so. But during the course of Russo-Swedish negotiations it became clear that the conflict could not be resolved by diplomatic means. Through a French intermediary, Sweden insisted that the Baltic lands be returned, but that was met by Elizabeth's definite refusal. She stated:

What will the people say, knowing that a foreign princess [Anna Leopoldovna—V. N.], who did not concern herself much with Russia's good and who became the ruler only by accident, preferred war to the shame of giving up something, while Peter's daughter, in order to stop that war, agrees to terms that are as contrary to Russia's well-being as they are to the glory of her father.[80]

When the negotiations reached an impasse, military action continued and ended with the defeat of Sweden, which, according to the terms of the Treaty of Abo in August 1743, ceded part of Finland to Russia.

When Elizabeth ascended the throne, almost all of Europe was caught up in the War of the Austrian Succession, in which dynastic interests and the reciprocal territorial claims of the leading powers were curiously intertwined. The Austrian and Hungarian–Bohemian queen, Maria Theresa, was defending the integrity of her possessions and the right to the German imperial title against France, Prussia, Bavaria, and Spain and in league with England and Holland. Each of the warring coalitions was trying to lure Russia to its side, but Austria had the least chance, because Elizabeth knew that the Austrian ambassador Botta-Adorno had tried to open Anna Leopoldovna's eyes to the plot in November 1741. When foreign diplomats started arguing over seniority at Elizabeth's coronation, she declared: "Botta does not have the slightest reason to think well of himself: when he starts putting on airs he can go back where he came from, because I value more highly the friendship of those who did not abandon me in the past than the good favor of his miserable queen."[81]

Only Chêtardie could be Elizabeth's friend; consequently, Austria's enemies were given obvious preference. But the empress lost faith in the friendship of the French court during the peace talks with Sweden. In August 1742 Chêtardie left Russia without having succeeded in influencing Elizabeth. After his departure, she expressed her attitude toward France thus: "We can manage without Chêtardie if we have no better experiences than her [France's] friendship, and until now it has been a very poor and distressing friendship. If he is to be rewarded for the way he served me during that time, I hope it is not very pleasant for him."[82]

The cooling of relations between Russia and France helped to bring about the Anglo-Russian alliance treaty in December 1742. English diplomacy was also trying to bring about a rapprochement between Russia and Austria, but Elizabeth refused. On 10 December 1742 the empress was read a letter from the English ambassador proposing that the treaty of alliance include an article calling for friendship between the two courts and Maria Theresa, and she ordered that "the article be written as before, without any mention of the Hungarian queen."[83]

Simultaneously, negotiations were under way concerning an alliance with Prussia, which had left the war in June 1742 after seizing Silesia from Austria. In 1743 Elizabeth and the Prussian king, Frederick II, exchanged their two countries' highest orders. But favorable relations with Prussia and enmity toward Austria did not compel the empress to abandon her concepts of justice. At the time of the Russo-Prussian alliance in March 1743, Elizabeth refused to guarantee Prussia's annexation of Silesia.

The War of the Austrian Succession was still going on, and Russia had yet to determine its own foreign policy orientation. Elizabeth was influenced by two groups at her court. One was headed by Bestuzhev-Riumin, who opposed rapprochement with France and Prussia and favored alliance with Austria, Saxony, and the "maritime powers," England and Holland. He was opposed by the Franco-Prussian party headed by Lestok, whom Chêtardie was again sent to help in late 1743. The struggle ended with the victory of Bestuzhev-Riumin, who made skillful use of the practice of opening and reading the French diplomat's correspondence. His reports were found to contain unkind comments about the empress. In June 1744 the enraged Elizabeth expelled Chêtardie from Russia and changed her previous attitude toward Lestok. Another success by Bestuzhev-Riumin was Russia's alliance, concluded that January, with the elector of Saxony and Polish king, Augustus III.

Developments in Europe demanded that Elizabeth clearly state her position. In August 1744 Prussian troops invaded Saxony and Bohemia, and later that year Austria, Saxony, England, and Holland formed an alliance against Prussia. Russia found itself in alliance with belligerent powers. Frederick II and Augustus III appealed to the Russian empress for help against each other. On 19 September 1745 Elizabeth convened a "conference" to discuss the question, "Is it now advisable to permit the king of Prussia, who is our closest and strongest neighbor, to gain more power?" The next day, participants in the conference submitted to the empress a written exposition of their opinions; they unanimously opposed Prussia. On 3 October that year, at the next "conference," these opinions were read aloud, as was the Prussian ambassador's letter containing a request for military aid on the basis of a treaty of alliance.

After she heard the reports, Elizabeth stated that "the occasion for an alliance cannot be acknowledged," inasmuch as Frederick II was a disrupter of the peace. For that reason, it was "more just to offer aid to Saxony. Moreover, any strengthening of the Prussian king is not only useless to Russians' interests—it is actually dangerous." It was decided to move troops into Courland and to inform Prussia that if it continued to commit aggression it would be stopped by the force of Russian arms. After signing the appropriate declaration, Elizabeth declared that she was "acting in accordance with [her] conscience and justice."[84] This determined Russia's foreign policy for more than the next fifteen years. During that period its dominant orientation was diplomatic and military opposition to Prussia.

Unfavorable weather conditions prevented Russian troops from becoming involved in the conflict, but the empress's declaration did expedite the peace treaty between Prussia and Austria and Saxony. Russia's foreign policy orientation was definitively established when the Russo-Austrian treaty of alliance was signed in May 1746. The agreement between the two imperial courts contained a provision stating that in the event that Frederick II attacked Austria, Russia would help Austria to regain Silesia by force of arms. From then on, friendship was established between Elizabeth and Maria Theresa, reinforced by their enmity toward the Prussian king, who made up epigrams about both empresses and indulged himself in obscene jokes at their expense.[85]

After Prussia withdrew, the War of the Austrian Succession continued between Austria, England, and Holland, on one side, and France and Spain, on the other. Opponents of the Austrian House of Habsburg were gaining the upper hand, and England appealed to Elizabeth for help. In November 1747 what was known as the subsidy convention was signed between Russia, England, and Holland, according to which a 30,000-strong corps of Russian troops was to be placed at the disposal of the "maritime powers" for a large sum of money. The corps's arrival at the Rhine the next year led to the conclusion of a European peace treaty. Russia put an end to the eight-year war without firing a shot. But the peace did not last long. The Seven Years War began in 1756, and Russia became involved after coming to Austria's defense against Prussia. This move was determined, to a considerable extent, by Elizabeth's attitude toward Frederick II. In June 1756 the English diplomat C. Hanbury Williams wrote: "the empress's personal animosity toward the Prussian king is so ill concealed by her that it flares up almost every minute." The empress even stated her intention of leading Russian troops in a crusade against Prussia.[86]

Was Russia's entry into the war a political mistake? At the time, the country had to choose between two alternatives: strengthening and enlarging its positions on the shores of the Baltic Sea through struggle against Prussia, or resolving the "Polish question" (the annexation of right-bank Ukraine and Belorussia), which would be possible only if there were a Russo-Prussian alliance. Elizabeth took the first option, while her successors preferred the second. In the course of the Seven Years War, Russian troops occupied East Prussia, and its inhabitants took an oath of allegiance to the Russian empress. Six years of heavy warfare inflicted enormous losses on the country, yet it gained no appreciable benefits. The future Peter III considered himself a friend of Frederick II, and when he ascended the throne he returned to Frederick all the territories Russian troops had conquered. Nevertheless, the war was not entirely without benefits: the victories of Russian arms over the best army in Europe enhanced Russia's international prestige.

To direct the war against Prussia on 14 March 1756, Elizabeth created an extraordinary higher institution—a conference at the imperial court. Its membership included participants in the previous "conferences" on foreign affairs which had been convened on an occasional basis. Because the empress was afraid of reviving the Supreme Privy Council or the Cabinet of Ministers, the new body was not given precisely defined powers. The Conference did not have the right to issue edicts in the empress's name, but in practice it did so anyway. On average, Elizabeth attended meetings of the conference ministers about once every three months; the rest of the time she had her associates transmit her spoken orders to them. The Conference decided most cases on its own, because during the final six years of the empress's life her health frequently prevented her from involvement in state activities. But the most important diplomatic and military issues were reported to her, and she handed down her resolutions regarding them.

The Conference also dealt with numerous matters of domestic politics, which included the secularization of monastery lands. The immediate problem was that monastery authorities were refusing to take in retired military officers and men and provide for their "subsistence," which had been the practice since Peter's time. On 18 January 1757 Elizabeth ordered that the retired military men be assigned to monasteries and that "their support not be stinted in the slightest, under pain . . . of severe wrath and penalty."[87] The conference ministers took advantage of the empress's manifest displeasure and contrived to tie the question of veterans left without shelter to the necessity of introducing secular administration on monastery estates. At a meeting of the Conference on 30 September that year, the empress decided to institute control over church revenues and withhold from these revenues funds for the creation of "invalids' homes." She also ordered that monastery lands be placed under the administration of retired officers "in order that the clerical orders not be burdened by worldly cares."[88] These orders were never implemented while Elizabeth was alive, but they served as the juridical basis for the resolute secularization measures of her successor, Peter III.

The next-to-last year of the empress's life was marked by an attempt to eliminate widespread official abuses and impose order in the selection of high officials. The Conference was given the order to nominate candidates for vacant positions in the state apparatus, and it prepared the appropriate report. In eleven of the fifty-eight cases, Elizabeth did not agree with the recommendations of the conference ministers.[89] She refused to make her favorites A.G. Razumovskii and I.I. Shuvalov members of the Conference and, as was her custom, she appointed a Russian to the position of vice president of the Manufactures College instead of the German whom the Conference had recommended. In addition, she removed N.Iu. Trubetskoi and A.I. Glebov from procuracy posts in the Senate; these men had joined P.I. Shuvalov's court clique and with him were the chief perpetrators of the increased corruption. Ia.P. Shakhovskoi, who was well known for his high principles, was appointed to Trubetskoi's place; simultaneously he became a member of the Conference.

The edict for these shifts was signed by Elizabeth on 16 August 1760 at the same time as another edict demanding that the Senate stop official abuses. That very day, the Conference submitted to the empress a report calling for the promotion of several people, including governors A. Pushkin and P. Saltykov. But Elizabeth ordered that the activities of both men be investigated, for they had "ruined or plundered their provinces."[90]

These were Elizabeth's final bursts of active involvement in the affairs of state. In late 1760 and 1761, the empress's sturdy body engaged in an anguished battle with numerous grave ailments. In addition to asthma and, very likely, diabetes, she suffered from frequent attacks of epilepsy, after which she lay in an unconscious state for several days. On 12 December 1761 "she was suddenly afflicted with severe nausea, coughing, and spitting up blood." Her doctors resorted to bloodletting and saw that "there was already considerable inflammation throughout her blood." During the subsequent weeks, Elizabeth underwent terrible torment, which she endured with stoicism and resignation, saying that "these sufferings [were] too mild in comparison with her sins."[91]

The dying empress still sometimes found the strength for affairs of state, and one of her final decisions was dictated by her concern for the common folk. On 16 December she declared amnesty for persons guilty of bootlegging salt, and she ordered the Senate to find funds to substitute for the salt tax that was such a burden to the population.[92] Sensing death's approach, Elizabeth made confession, received communion and extreme unction, and on the evening of 24 December ordered that the prayer for the dying be read over her twice, as she repeated the words after the priest. She died on Christmas Day.

Any underestimation of Elizabeth's role in Russian history is evidence primarily of a failure to understand the monarch's personal role in an absolutist state system. Peter I's daughter was the pivotal figure in the life of the state during her reign, and it was she who brought Russia into the channel of unhurried and measured development after the vast upheavals of Peter's epoch, the short-sighted experiments of the members of the Supreme Privy Council, and the terror of the "Biron era." The anecdotal image of the dancing and costumed empress must not be allowed to overshadow the figure of the real ruler, who bore the heavy burden of authority to the extent of her powers and abilities.

Notes

1. V.O. Kliuchevskii, *Sochineniia* (Moscow, 1958), vol. 4, p. 339.

2. *O povrezhdenii nravov v Rossii kniazia M. Shcherbatova i Puteshestvie A. Radishcheva* (Moscow, 1984), p. 100 (references are given according to M.M. Shcherbatov's original text as cited in appendices to this edition).

3. E.V. Anisimov, *Rossiia v seredine XVIII veka: Bor'ba za nasledie Petra* (Moscow, 1986), pp. 13–14.

4. RGADA, f. 142, op. 1, d. 560, l. 1.

5. B.-Kh. Münnich, *Zapiski fel'dmarshala* (St. Petersburg, 1874), p. 87; C. Rondeau, *Pis'ma ledi Rondo* (St. Petersburg, 1874), pp. 51–52.

6. J. de Liria, "Pis'ma o Rossii," in *Osmnadtsatyi vek*, vol. 2 (Moscow, 1868), p. 115; Rondeau, *Pis'ma*, p. 52; P.P. Pekarskii, "Elizaveta Petrovna," *Russkii arkhiv*, 1911, no. 1, p. 7.

7. "Shest' pisem A.P. Volynskogo k tsesarevne Elizavete Petrovne," *Russkii arkhiv*, 1865, no. 1, 338–39.

8. N.I. Pavlenko, *Ptentsy gnezda Petrova* (Moscow, 1984), p. 215.

9. *Polnoe sobranie zakonov Rossiiskoi imperii: Sobranie I* (PSZ) (St. Petersburg, 1830), vol. 7, no. 5070.

10. *Sbornik Russkogo istoricheskogo obshchestva* (Sb. RIO), vol. 63 (St. Petersburg, 1888), p. 509.

11. M.I. Semevskii, "Elizaveta Petrovna do vosshestviia svoego na prestol," *Russkoe slovo,* 1859, no. 2, p. 230.

12. de Liria, *Pis'ma,* p. 32.

13. *Russkii dvor sto let tomu nazad: Po doneseniiam angliiskikh i frantsuzskikh poslannikov* (St. Petersburg, 1907), p. 4.

14. N.S. Stromilov, *Tsesarevna Elisaveta Petrovna v Aleksandrovoi slobode* (Moscow, 1874), pp. 9–14.

15. *Russkii dvor sto let tomu nazad,* p. 6.

16. K.-G. Manshtein, *Zapiski o Rossii* (St. Petersburg, 1875), p. 21.

17. *Istoricheskie bumagi, sobrannye K.I. Arsen'evym* (St. Petersburg, 1872), p. 231.

18. N.N. Firsov, *Vstuplenie na prestol imperatritsy Elizavety Petrovny* (Kazan, 1888), p. 124.

19. *Russkii dvor sto let tomu nazad,* p. 41; "Ekaterina II. Antidot (Protivoiadie): Polemicheskoe sochinenie ili razbor knigi abbata Shappa D'Oterosha o Rossii," in *Osmnadtsatyi vek,* vol. 4 (Moscow, 1869), p. 303.

20. *Russkii dvor sto let tomu nazad,* p. 33.

21. Anisimov, *Rossiia v seredine,* pp. 28–29.

22. *So shpagoi i fakelom. Dvortsovye perevoroty v Rossii. 1725–1825* (Moscow, 1991), pp. 224–25; Pekarskii, "Elizaveta Petrovna," p. 10.

23. P.I. Panin, "Russkii dvor v 1725–1744 godakh: Zamechaniia na Zapiski generala Manshteina o Rossii," *Russkaia starina,* 1879, no. 12, p. 594.

24. Manshtein, *Zapiski,* p. 218.

25. *Markiz de la Shetardi v Rossii: 1740–1742 gg.* (St. Petersburg, 1862), p. 264.

26. M.D. Khmyrov, *Istoricheskie stat'i* (St. Petersburg, 1873), p. 141; Manshtein, *Zapiski,* p. 232.

27. Münnich, *Zapiski fel'dmarshala,* p. 82; Manshtein, *Zapiski,* p. 251.

28. *PSZ,* vol. 11, nos. 8473, 8476, 8494, 8641.

29. *Arkhiv kniazia Vorontsova* (AKV) (Moscow, 1870), vol. 1, p. 4; A.N. Benua [Alexandre Benois], *Tsarskoe Selo v tsarstvovanie imperatritsy Elizavety Petrovny* (St. Petersburg, 1910), pp. 21–26.

30. Münnich, *Zapiski fel'dmarshala,* p. 87; *Russkii dvor sto let tomu nazad,* p. 72; A.T. Bolotov, *Zhizn' i prikliucheniia* (St. Petersburg, 1871), col. 162.

31. Münnich, *Zapiski fel'dmarshala,* p. 90; *Russkii dvor sto let tomu nazad,* p. 73; J.-L. Favier, "Russkii dvor v 1761 g.," *Russkaia starina,* 1878, no. 10, p. 193.

32. Bolotov, *Zhizn',* col. 162; "Kniaginia Angel't-Serbskaia Anna Elizaveta, mat' Ekateriny Velikoi: Ee pis'ma," *Russkii arkhiv,* 1904, no. 8, p. 470; I. Poz'e, "Zapiski pridvornogo bril'iantshchika o prebyvanii ego v Rossii," *Russkaia starina,* 1870, no. 2, p. 90; Catherine II, *Zapiski* (Moscow, 1989), p. 547; Favier, "Russkii dvor," p. 191; Rondeau, *Pis'ma,* p. 76.

33. Panin, "Russkii dvor," pp. 613, 614.

34. Bolotov, *Zhizn',* col. 162.

35. Favier, "Russkii dvor," pp. 190–91; Kliuchevskii, *Sochineniia,* p. 339.

36. *O povrezhdenii nravov v Rossii,* p. 100.

37. Catherine II, *Zapiski,* p. 55.

38. S.M. Solov'ev, *Istoriia Rossii s drevneishikh vremen,* bk. 11 (Moscow, 1963), p. 167.

39. Ibid., bk. 12 (Moscow, 1964), p. 34.

40. Favier, "Russkii dvor," p. 191.

41. Münnich, *Zapiski fel'dmarshala,* p. 88; Catherine II, *Zapiski,* p. 187.

42. *Russkii dvor sto let tomu nazad,* p. 71.

43. Catherine II, *Zapiski*, p. 443; "Pis'ma i zapiski imperatritsy Elizavety Petrovny," *Chteniia v Obshchestve istorii i drevnostei rossiiskikh* (ChOIDR), 1867, no. 4, sect. 5, p. 28.

44. A.G. Brikner, "Zhizn' Petra III do vstupleniia na prestol," *Russkii vestnik*, no 2 (1883), p. 728.

45. *PSZ*, vol. 11, no. 8480.

46. Anisimov, *Rossiia v seredine*, p. 45.

47. L.G. Kisliagina, "Kantseliariia shtat-sekretarei pri Ekaterine II," in *Gosudarstvennye uchrezhdeniia Rossii XVI-XVIII vv.* (Moscow, 1991), p. 170.

48. *PSZ*, vol. 11, no. 8480.

49. "Pis'ma i zapiski imperatritsy Elizavety Petrovny," pp. 30–31.

50. RGADA, f. 5, op. 1, d. 75, l. 19.

51. "Imperatritsa Elizaveta Petrovna i ee zapisochki k Vasiliiu Ivanovichu Demidovu," *Russkii arkhiv*, 1878, no. 1, pp. 10–13.

52. RGADA, f. 1239, op. 1, d. 51975, l. 10.

53. B. D'Allion, "Pis'ma iz Rossii vo Frantsiiu v pervye gody tsarstvovaniia Elizavety Petrovny," *Russkii arkhiv*, 1892, no. 10, p. 153.

54. A.D. Gradovskii, *Vysshaia administratsiia Rossii XVIII st. i general-prokurory* (St. Petersburg, 1866), p. 167.

55. S.O. Shmidt, "Vnutrenniaia politika Rossii serediny XVIII veka," *Voprosy istorii*, 1987, no. 3, p. 49.

56. *PSZ*, vol. 11, no. 8695; P.I. Baranov, *Opis' vysochaishim ukazam i poveleniiam, khraniashchimsia v S.-Peterburgskom Senatskom arkhive, za XVIII vek* (St. Petersburg, 1878), vol. 3, p. 120, no. 9012.

57. Kliuchevskii, *Sochineniia*, p. 331.

58. P.I. Baranov, *Opis'*, p. 444, no. 11690.

59. *PSZ*, vol. 13, no. 10164; M.Ia. Volkov, "Otmena vnutrennikh tamozhen v Rossii," *Istoriia SSSR*, 1957, no. 2, pp. 92–94.

60. *AKV* (Moscow, 1871), vol. 3, pp. 650–51, 654.

61. *PSZ*, vol. 11, nos. 8619, 8835; Anisimov, *Rossiia v seredine*, p. 53; Solov'ev, *Istoriia Rossii*, bk. 11, p. 153.

62. Iu. V. Got'e, "Sledstvennye komissii po zloupotrebleniiam oblastnykh vlastei v XVIII veke," *Sbornik statei posviashchennykh V.O. Kliuchevskomu* (Moscow, 1909), p. 145.

63. RGADA, f. 9, op. 5, d. 39, ll. 5–5 ob.

64. *PSZ*, vol. 13, no. 9919; A.P. Bazhova, *Russko-iugoslavianskie otnosheniia vo vtoroi polovine XVIII v.* (Moscow, 1982), pp. 118, 125, 128–29.

65. *PSZ*, vol. 11, nos. 8673, 8840.

66. Benois, "Tsarskoe Selo," 228.

67. Ia.P. Shakhovskoi, *Zapiski* (St. Petersburg, 1872), p. 64.

68. A.I. Komissarenko, *Russkii absoliutizm i dukhovenstvo v XVIII veke* (Moscow, 1990), pp. 106–7.

69. S.V. Eshevskii, *Sochineniia po russkoi istorii* (Moscow, 1900), pp. 114–16.

70. S.I. Viktorskii, *Istoriia smertnoi kazni v Rossii i sovremennoe ee sostoianie* (Moscow, 1912), p. 223; Solov'ev, *Istoriia Rossii*, bk. 11, p. 527.

71. *AKV*, vol. 3, p. 650; Viktorskii, *Istoriia smertnoi kazni*, p. 225.

72. P.I. Baranov, *Opis'*, p. 147, no. 9235.

73. N.D. Sergeevskii, "Smertnaia kazn' pri imperatritse Elizavete Petrovne," *Zhurnal grazhdanskogo i ugolovnogo prava*, 1890, no. 1, p. 59.

74. For more detail, see *PSZ*, vol. 13, no. 9789; M.V. Danilov, *Zapiski artillerii maiora* (Kazan, 1913), p. 44–45; Pekarskii, "Elizaveta Petrovna," p. 24; P.I. Baranov, *Opis'*, p. 232, no. 9968; M.M. Bogoslovskii, "Imperatritsa Elizaveta Petrovna," in *Tri veka* (Moscow, 1913), vol. 4, p. 161; RGADA, f. 8, op. 1, d. 2, ll. 1, 8a, 92; d. 7, 12 ff.

75. A.I. Veidemeier, *Tsarstvovanie Elisavety Petrovny*, 2d ed. (St. Petersburg, 1849), pt. 2, p. 63.

76. *PSZ*, vol. 2, no. 9479; vol. 11, nos. 8701, 8640, 8754; vol. 13, nos. 9959, 9992, 10065; vol. 15, nos. 10824, 10904, 10915 ff.

77. *PSZ*, vol. 13, no. 9824; vol. 14, no. 10599; V.N. Vsevolodskii-Gerngross, *Russkii teatr. Ot istokov do serediny XVIII v.* (Moscow, 1957), pp. 225, 227.

78. Bolotov, *Zhizn'*, col. 162.

79. Münnich, *Zapiski fel'dmarshala*, p. 88.

80. Anisimov, *Rossiia v seredine*, p. 81.

81. Solov'ev, *Istoriia Rossii*, bk. 11, p. 190.

82. RGADA, f. 5, op. 1, d. 75, l. 23 ob.

83. *AKV*, vol. 4 (Moscow, 1872), p. 211.

84. Solov'ev, *Istoriia Rossii*, bk. 11, pp. 368–70.

85. "Zapiski de la Messel'era o prebyvanii ego v Rossii," *Russkii arkhiv*, no. 4 (1874), cols. 1011–12; N.A. Polevoi, *Stoletie Rossii s 1745 po 1845 g.* (St. Petersburg, 1845), p. 74.

86. *Russkii dvor sto let tomu nazad*, p. 99; "Perepiska velikoi kniagini Ekateriny Alekseevny i angliiskogo posla sera Charl'za Uill'iamsa," *ChOIDR*, 1890, no. 2, sect. 1, pp. 121–60.

87. RGVIA, f. 2, op. 113, d. 44, ll. 12–12 ob.

88. RGADA, f. 178, op. 1, d. 3, ll. 245, 256–57 ob.

89. See RGADA, f. 16, op. 1, d. 108, ll. 30–33 ob.; P.I. Baranov, *Opis'*, pp. 438–40, no. 11660.

90. RGADA, f. 178, op. 1, d. 17, l. 376; *PSZ*, vol. 15, no. 11092.

91. Bolotov, *Zhizn'*, cols. 126–27; Veidemeier, *Tsarstvovanie*, pt. 2, pp. 51–53.

92. *PSZ*, vol. 15, no. 11899.

Emperor Peter III, 1762

Although he occupied the Imperial throne for only 186 days, Peter III and his reign merit serious reconsideration. Traditionally depicted as a crude and often violent individual who managed during his brief rule to unleash a vicious attack on everything Russian, Peter has always had a few dissenting admirers, both among contemporaries and among later observers. They have been in the minority, however, because any serious attempt to rehabilitate him entails a reassessment of the reign of his disaffected wife, and successor, Catherine II (the Great).

The grandson of Peter the Great, Peter III (Holstein) had been brought to Russia in 1742 by his aunt, Empress Elizabeth I, and eventually designated as her heir. Shortly after becoming tsar, Peter was murdered in a palace coup engineered by Catherine, who needed to cast him—and his policies—in a negative light in order to strengthen her own tenuous claim to the throne. As emperor, Peter had clearly overstepped the political interests of the elite; otherwise Catherine would not have been able to muster enough support to become his successor. But is there more to his reign than the tendentious accounts of Catherine and her admirers suggest?

Aleksandr Sergeevich Mylnikov thinks so. Taking up the case of the much-maligned Peter III and, echoing the recent labors of American historian Carol S. Leonard,[1] Mylnikov calls for a reappraisal of the man and his reign. "There is no reason to idealize Peter III. . . . But neither is there any reason to condemn him unequivocally and to examine his every action in the spirit of ill will, without regard to the circumstances and motives which dictated them." Distancing himself from generations of Soviet historical writing that took a critical view of Peter, the author presents a plausible alternative. His revisionist account calls for a more sober, less sympathetic evaluation of Catherine, whose unbridled ambition doomed Peter, the victim of "unfortunate circum-

stances." Carefully reconstructing Peter's accomplishments as tsar, Mylnikov challenges the depiction of Peter presented in the manifesto Catherine issued upon her becoming empress. This document charged Peter with undermining the Orthodox Church, with violating Russia's interests by concluding peace with Prussia's Frederick II, and with compromising the state administration. Mylnikov's understanding of Peter's policies and efforts suggests that he failed perhaps as a politician, but not as a statesman.

The reader will note that the author does not agree with Naumov's assessment of Elizabeth I (whom Mylnikov sees as "an empty-headed woman") or with Anisimov's depiction of Biron (whom Mylnikov depicts as "odious").

D.J.R.

Note

1. "The Reputation of Peter III," *Russian Review*, vol. 47, no. 3 (1988), pp. 263–92, and *Reform and Regicide: The Reign of Peter III of Russia* (Bloomington, 1993).

Peter III

Aleksandr Sergeevich Mylnikov

Truly, this was a man unlucky both during his lifetime and after his death. Consider all the epithets bestowed on Petr Fedorovich (Peter III) by historians and writers: "A dull-witted, crude soldier" and "a lackey of Prussia's Frederick II," "a hater of everything Russian" and "a chronic alcoholic," "a narrow-minded, petty tyrant" and "a failure as a husband." Such descriptions represent merely a partial list of the assessments that even today usually accompany any mention of this Russian emperor. Perhaps this unanimous view of Peter III's personality and activities is found in its most magnified form in this recent depiction of him:

Even before this monarch ascended the throne he managed to make himself notorious by his buffoonish pranks, his crude drinking bouts, his total inability to cope with affairs of state, and, something that was especially offensive to his subjects, his disdain for everything Russian. The emperor commanded that the Guards be outfitted with new uniforms after the Prussian model, and he commanded Orthodox priests to shave their beards and wear German clothing similar to that of

Protestant pastors. The future of his reign was predetermined. Five months after Peter III ascended the throne, a plot against him was hatched.[1]

Although there are "no 'puzzles' concerning Petr Fedorovich's personality and habits,"[2] the question [of his reign] is not as simple as it might seem at first glance.

First of all, under Peter III there was discord in the overall orientation of government policy, which developed in the context of the concept "enlightened absolutism." Noting that many of its aspects were linked to a series of "hare-brained schemes" developed by the nobility during the 1750s, S.O. Shmidt emphasized: "The features typical of the policy of 'enlightened absolutism' were revealed most effectively during Peter III's short reign. . . . The so-called Catherinian Age actually began several years before she ascended the throne." To be sure, following the tradition that began with S.M. Soloviev and V.O. Kliuchevskii, Shmidt conceded that "this policy reflected not so much the tastes and intentions of the emperor himself as those of his co-rulers, who had become involved in statesmanship during the preceding reign."[3]

Secondly, the question of Peter III's personal participation in state administration cannot be dismissed on that account. As is well known, such eminent representatives of Russian culture as V.N. Tatishchev, M.V. Lomonosov, and Ia.Ia. Shtelin—who knew him personally—evaluated the grand duke, later emperor, positively. We can hardly ignore [Russian writer] G.R. Derzhavin, who hailed Peter III's abolition of the repressive Secret Office as one of the "monuments of mercy."[4] Nor can we pass over in silence the fact that F.V. Krechetov, imprisoned for life in the Peter and Paul Fortress in 1793 for freethinking, had intended "to clarify the greatness of Petr Fedorovich's deeds," and that in 1801 the poet A.F. Voeikov ranked the late emperor "alongside the names of the greatest lawgivers."[5] If we agree that Peter III was not a mysterious figure, an examination of the principal milestones of his life seems appropriate, if only because it will, to some extent, enable us to understand the falsifications which have unfortunately arisen so frequently in treatments of Peter's reign.

The future emperor came into the world in the port city of Kiel, the capital city of the German Duchy of Holstein. His father was Duke Karl Friedrich; his mother, Peter the Great's eldest daughter, Anna Petrovna. The family's first-born had been eagerly awaited. That is why, at eight o'clock on the day the princess safely delivered her child, Holstein's minister, G.F. Bassevich, dispatched a special courier to St. Petersburg with an urgent, laconic, businesslike message: "He was born between twelve and one o'clock [daytime] on 21 February 1728, healthy and strong. It has been decided to name him Karl Peter."[6] The date is given in New Style; the Old-Style date is 10 February.

The newborn's fate had been predetermined several years before his birth. In the nuptial agreement drawn up in 1724, both husband and wife renounced any claim to the Russian throne, although the tsar retained the right to name as his successor "one of the issue, if God so blesses, from this marriage of princes."[7] Incidentally, as Karl [Charles] XII's nephew, the duke of Holstein also had a claim on the Swedish throne, as did his heirs. The newborn had been named deliberately: Karl, in honor of the Swedish king whose military glory had waned at Poltava, and Peter, in honor of Russia's first emperor, who had converted Russia into a great European power. In this ingenious way, the future duke of Holstein effected a posthumous reconciliation between victor and vanquished. But at the same time, this meant that from the moment of his birth the hereditary duke of Holstein was a potential pretender to both the Russian and the Swedish thrones. This heritage left its mark on Peter III's personality, psychology, and behavior.

Peter's mother died soon after he was born. The father in his own way loved his son, but all his thoughts were directed toward regaining Schleswig, which had been taken by Denmark early in the eighteenth century. Having neither the military nor the financial means to accomplish this, Karl Friedrich could only hope for aid from either Sweden or, and particularly, Russia. Strictly speaking, Karl Friedrich's marriage to Anna Petrovna had reinforced his Russian orientation.

After the death of Peter II, Karl Peter's cousin, and Anna Ivanovna's elevation to the Russian throne, Karl Friedrich's former alignment become impossible. The new empress tried to deprive her cousin Elizabeth of her rights to the throne so as to keep these in her own family, and Peter the Great's grandson, growing up in Kiel, posed a constant threat to the childless empress's plans. She constantly repeated with great hatred, "the little devil is still alive." (These words are sometimes erroneously attributed to Elizaveta Petrovna.)

Karl Friedrich placed all his hopes for the recovery of his lost possessions on his son, whom he began to groom for possible accession to the Swedish throne. The father planted vengeful thoughts in the boy's head, and instructed his son from early childhood in the military Prussian manner. "This manly boy will avenge us," Karl Friedrich used to say, although a "manly boy" was exactly what Karl Peter was not. While he was physically strong at birth, in childhood he was often sickly. At age ten, nevertheless, his father conferred on him the rank of second lieutenant, which produced an enormous impression on the boy and kindled in him a love for military parades and exercises.

After the duke died in 1739, Adolph Friedrich, his cousin once removed, became the orphan's regent (Adolph was later elected king of Sweden). He did not interfere in his nephew's day-to-day education, which proceeded in accordance with established procedure but without supervision. His teacher, a crude and ignorant Swede named O. Brummer, subjected his pupil to refined humiliations, choice curses, and physical violence, even in front of courtiers. Later, in Russia, Peter recalled with a shudder "the cruel way his mentors treated him"; to punish him they would often make him kneel on peas, with the result that his legs would grow "red and swollen."[8]

The doors to Russia, closed under Anna Ivanovna, were locked tight, apparently forever, when she died in 1740. In accordance with her will, the throne went to Ivan Antonovich, a two-month-old baby, her grand-nephew and the son of Prince Anton Ulrich of Braunschweig. Only the route from Kiel to Stockholm remained open to Karl Peter: he received intensive instruction in Lutheranism and was taught to have anti-Russian feelings. But 25 November 1741 marked the beginning of a new chapter in the duke of Holstein's life: Peter I's daughter came to power in St. Petersburg. Childless like her predecessor, Elizabeth hastened to summon her nephew from Kiel in order to reinforce her own dynastic rights, insufficiently strong by that era's standards.

The fourteen-year-old duke arrived on the banks of the Neva on 5 February 1742. Thus, when a delegation from Stockholm appeared in November to report that Karl Peter had been chosen heir to the Swedish crown, it was too late. No one by that name existed any longer; he had been baptized in accordance with Orthodox ritual and officially declared heir to the throne of Russia. From then on, he was known as Petr Fedorovich.

While not herself distinguished for her learning, Elizabeth was astonished by her nephew's ignorance. Teachers were immediately selected for him, and the tutor's duties assigned to Academician J.

von Staehlin. The story often encountered in the literature that the pupil was exceptionally dull-witted, and his tutor unable to find a common language with him, is based on an obvious misunderstanding. Quite the contrary: Staehlin's memoirs note Peter's abilities and superior memory, although they also acknowledge that the humanities did not especially interest the boy and that "he often asked for a lesson in mathematics instead of the humanities."

The heir's favorite subjects were fortifications and artillery, and "watching the soldiers' formations during parades gave him greater pleasure than any ballet."[9] But his lessons took place sporadically, by fits and starts, despite any effort by Staehlin, who had established an affectionate relationship with Peter—an affection Peter retained toward Staehlin for the rest of his life. The empress was largely to blame for this lack of order. An empty-headed woman with a penchant for amusements and frequent travels, she demanded that the heir always accompany her. During one such journey (Elizabeth often traveled not only to Moscow but also to Kiev), he contracted smallpox, the traces of which remained on his face.

On 7 May 1745, after Peter came of age, he was declared ruling duke of Schleswig-Holstein by Augustus III, who was vicar of the Holy Roman Empire, king of Poland, and elector of Saxony. On 25 August the heir married Sophia Augusta Frederika, princess of Anhalt-Zerbst, who took the name of Ekaterina Alekseevna (Catherine) in the Orthodox faith. She was one year younger than her husband.

Although they had first met in 1739, the future husband's and wife's personal feelings received little consideration when the marriage was contracted. The bride had been foisted on Peter by Frederick II, who believed that of all the possible candidates this one would be "most advantageous to Russia and in accordance with the interests of Prussia." And his protégée, imaginative and clever beyond her years, understood perfectly how political calculations had influenced her unexpected elevation to eminence. Not long after her arrival in Russia, she not only thanked Frederick in writing but also assured him that in the future she would find an opportunity to convince him of her "gratitude and devotion."[10] Whereas for Peter the king of Prussia was an example of military prowess (an opinion, incidentally, also held by the European public), for Catherine he was primarily the person who had made her ambitious dreams come true. As for Frederick himself, he came out the winner no matter how events developed.

Neglected and lonely from childhood, Peter at first showed his wife (his second cousin) at least sympathy and trust, if not love. But he acted in vain: Catherine wanted not Peter but the Imperial crown. Catherine concealed this neither immediately after her wedding nor in her later *Memoirs*. Her biographers are inclined to take on faith the future empress's stories about how instead of performing his husbandly duties Peter would play dolls with her at night or make her go through the manual of arms at his command. Because of this, Catherine assures us, for perhaps five or even nine years of marriage she "retained her virginity."[11]

One does not wish to delve into the royal couple's bedroom secrets, but neither can they be completely ignored, because this tied one psychological knot in the reputations (Peter's as well as Catherine's) gradually taking shape in the court environment. In contrast to the naturalness and spontaneous childishness of Peter's relations with his young wife, a sense of alienation was created (and much of what Catherine later wrote and said about Peter was influenced by precisely this disparity). As she tried to distance herself from her husband in the consciousness of those around her, Catherine donned the mask of the injured and abandoned wife. This did not conflict in any way with the love affairs to which she abandoned herself quite quickly. Here is the text of a note, preserved by chance, that Peter addressed in French to his wife: "Madame, I beg you not to worry that you will have to spend tonight with me, because the time that you could deceive me is past. The bed was too cramped. After two weeks of separation from you, the afternoon of this day, Your unhappy husband, whom you have never honored with this name."[12] These words, perfectly transparent in meaning, conflict with Catherine's later story of her "virginity"—after all, the note was dated 1746, scarcely a year after their wedding. And after Paul's birth in 1754, relations between husband and wife became purely formal and far from friendly. Not long afterward, E.R. Vorontsova, full sister to E.R. Dashkova, Catherine's devoted ally, became the grand duke's favorite.

The quarrels of their first years of married life could not fail to influence Peter's character: on the one hand, they produced in him a lack of confidence; on the other, they evoked a mocking bravado with which he tried to protect himself. In addition, the grand duke, as Staehlin had emphasized, even in his youth had had "the ability to perceive what was funny in others and mock it."[13] All of this met with condemnation from the dominant influences at court, and in the long run damaged Peter himself. The Prussian envoy Count Finkenstein observed Peter during that period and reported to his king in 1747 that it was unlikely that the grand duke would ever reign. "It is incomprehensible," he wrote, "how a prince of his years can behave so childishly."[14]

It is not surprising that Peter was depressed by the atmosphere of his aunt's court, and that he tried to spend time in Oranienbaum, his summer residence, as far as could be from the intrigues, conventions, and malice. Quite characteristic is his note to I.I. Shuvalov, a favorite of the empress: "I beg of you, please do me the favor of arranging things so that we can remain in Oranienbaum. When I am needed, they can send a messenger for me, because life in Peterhof is unbearable to me."[15] When one reads these lines, one has a different perspective on the grand duke's penchant, often ridiculed in fiction and historiography, for preferring in his youth the company of servants and lackeys assigned to him to that of the aristocracy. When he took command of the Preobrazhenskii Regiment, Peter enjoyed talking with the soldiers, and in Oranienbaum he was always in the company of officers of the Holstein detachment, which had been summoned for him from Kiel. All of this brought disapproval from high society circles and served to confirm their opinion that the heir was a crude, loud-mouthed soldier.

In reality, Peter's interests were incomparably broader and richer. He loved Italian music and played the violin quite well. The grand duke also loved painting, fireworks, and books. In 1746 he ordered his late father's library brought from Kiel, and it was placed in the Art House in Oranienbaum. Supervision of the library, which also included works on engineering and warfare, was turned over to Staehlin. Not contenting himself with his ancestral book collection, the grand duke set out to expand it. "As soon as a new book catalogue came out," Staehlin recalled, "he would read through it and note down books he wanted, enough to constitute a decent library."[16] After he ascended the throne, Peter III appointed Staehlin his librarian and instructed him to draw up a plan to place the books in the newly built Winter Palace in St. Petersburg; he allocated for this purpose "an annual sum of several thousand rubles." Peter likewise had a collection of violins, about which he knew a great deal. Also preserved is a catalogue of his numismatic collection, compiled by Staehlin.

The grand duke's intellectual world, despite Catherine's claims, was not limited—much less confined—to amusements and entertainment, although both of these constituted a regular part of court life.

But this did not satisfy Peter, whose tirelessness and craving for action were noted by many of his contemporaries, even those not kindly disposed toward him. He tried to make a name for himself in the political sphere. The opportunity for this, it seems, presented itself in 1745, when he became the ruling duke. But Elizabeth I did not allow her nephew to leave Russia. For this reason, the duke was represented in Kiel by a viceroy (from 1745 through 1751 the post was held by the grand duke's uncle, Friedrich August), while executive power was exercised by the Secret Governmental Council, created in 1719. Communications between Holstein and Peter were maintained through an office in St. Petersburg, headed between 1746 and 1757 by I. Pekhlin.

In the grand duke's attempts to influence the administration of his far-off duchy one can detect the desire to strengthen discipline among functionaries and impose order on military affairs, jurisprudence, and other administrative features. Peter also had an abiding interest in Holstein's cultural life. It is clear from the correspondence that has been preserved that he involved himself in improving the University of Kiel in various ways, from approving its professors to repairing lecture halls. Peter wrote many of these instructions in his own hand (in French), which testified to his concern for Holstein's administration, although the constant struggle for influence among the upper administrative ranks in Kiel frustrated the efforts undertaken by the duke.[17]

Some opportunity for the heir to exercise his passion for practical activity was afforded by his appointment on 12 February 1759 to the post of "chief director of the Noble Infantry Cadet Corps." This educational institution had been opened in St. Petersburg at the initiative of one of Peter I's comrades-in-arms, Field Marshal B.-Kh. Münnich, in 1731. The Cadet Corps was not only a military school; it played a substantial role as well in the development of Russian artistic culture, as its graduates included A.P. Sumarokov, V.A. Ozerov, M.M. Kheraskov, and F.G. Volkov.

Peter adopted the post of chief director with great zeal. He became personally acquainted with the students, talked with them, and visited the classrooms and the parade ground. The heir acquired a number of privileges for the corps, including the right to print books "in French, German, and Russian," even if their subject matter was not even indirectly related to the syllabi.[18] At his instigation, the first part of the Nominal Roll, a list of all teachers and graduates of the Cadet Corps since its founding, including those who had fallen into disgrace during the reigns of previous tsars, was published in 1761. With Catherine II's accession to power, the publication of this handbook was discontinued.

The chief director's activities were reflected in his reports to the Senate. Just two weeks after assuming his post, Peter asked that funds be allocated to enlarge the building, in order to improve the cadets' living conditions ("according to regulations, each room is to accommodate five or six cadets. Because of crowding, at present more than ten men are living in each room").[19] Many of the reports that Peter signed emphasized the importance of the corps "for the benefit of the Russian Empire," "in order to provide the army with worthy officers."[20]

One might question whether such reasoning really reflected the thinking of the chief director himself. Was he perhaps just placing his signature, without thinking about it, on papers submitted to him by Corps Director A.P. Melgunov? It is true that Peter did not write the reports to the Senate himself; they were prepared for him. Nevertheless, the grand duke's personality reveals itself in the documents. The request contained in the report of 28 September 1760, to "issue free of charge" artillery ammunition for training purposes, was based on ideas regarding this matter "on the part of the former commander of the corps, Field Marshal Count Münnich."[21] Meanwhile, Münnich, who had been demoted in rank and exiled after Elizabeth I came to power, had been languishing in Pelym for two decades. For this reason, the mere mention of his name—let alone all his titles—is something that only one man could afford (and not without a certain risk): the heir to the throne.

The political inexperience for which Peter was reproached by his contemporaries—possibly not without grounds—was not so much his fault as that of unfortunate circumstances: having proclaimed her nephew her heir, Elizabeth never really prepared him to act as the head of a great nation. A certain role was also played by palace intrigue, in particular by Chancellor A.P. Bestuzhev, who placed all his hopes on Catherine. "According to contemporaries," A.S. Lappo-Danilevskii commented, "Bestuzhev inspired in Empress Elizabeth the fear that Peter might seize the throne, and in this way he did a great deal to keep Peter from participating in Russian affairs of state, limiting his activities to just the administration of Holstein."[22] Personal relations between aunt and nephew also took their toll: they had not been cordial for some time, and near the end they became strained and even alienated.

Differences between the heir and the empress primarily affected foreign policy, especially during the Seven Years War. An Imperial Court Conference was instituted in 1756 as the supreme consultative state organ, the membership of which included the grand duke. Like Catherine, Peter adopted a Prussian orientation. He condemned Russia's participation in the war in general, and against Frederick II in particular. According to J. von Staehlin, Peter "said freely that the empress was being deceived in regard to the Prussian king, that the Austrians were bribing us and the French deceiving us."[23] Moreover, he declared to the members of the conference that "in time we will regret that we entered the alliance with Austria and France."

Did Peter have any contacts at all with the Prussian king during that time? Their correspondence when Peter ascended the throne indicate that Frederick II thanked Peter III for favors previously performed, and Peter III, in turn, reminded him that he had risked everything "for earnest services to you in our own country."[24] Exactly what these "services" were is difficult to say, in view of the absence of documentary evidence, but clearly they grew out of the heir's pro-Prussian sympathies, which he never concealed from anybody. This also accounts for his demonstrative resignation from membership in the conference, by way of protest against Elizabeth I's foreign policy.

Peter's judgments regarding Russia's participation in the anti-Prussian coalition were not without grounds. The only person with real interest in the war was the Austrian empress Maria Theresa, who hoped, with the aid of Russian cannon fodder, to regain Silesia, seized by Frederick II in the early 1740s. According to Peter, Russia's withdrawal from the Seven Years War was tied to the resolution of his territorial claims against Denmark: the Prussian king and his ally the king of England, elector of Hanover, were Holstein's closest neighbors. By enlisting their diplomatic aid—and in the case of Frederick II, possible military support—Peter hoped to realize his father's dream—to regain Schleswig and adjacent territories. In Peter's mind, this was fully in accord with Russia's interests. He set forth his views on these matters in a memorandum addressed to Elizabeth dated 17 January 1760. Once again he denounced the Seven Years War as a disastrous conflict that was "tearing Germany apart," expressed confidence that it would soon end, and recalled his "lofty destiny"— thereby hinting that in the future the throne of the duchy in Kiel and the throne of the emperor in St. Petersburg would be combined in one person, his own.[25]

While concerning himself with Holstein's affairs, he was never indifferent to the plight of the country he was destined to rule. As one fond of military precision, there was much to bother him—his aunt's increasing neglect of business, the high-handedness of the grandees, the disorder of the laws, and the despotism and corruption in administrative and judicial organs. The heir was extraordinarily irritated and disturbed by the neglected condition of the Guards. "While he was still grand duke," Staehlin recalled, "he applied the epithet 'janissaries' to the guardsmen who were living with their wives and children in the barracks, and he said, 'They are only clogging the residence; they are incapable of any kind of work or military exercises, and they are a constant threat to the government.' "[26]

Staehlin reported that while still only the heir, Peter contemplated the need to enhance the nobility's liberties, abolish the Secret Investigative Office, and establish religious tolerance.[27] This testimony finds documentary backing in a number of Senate reports relating to the Cadet Corps. On 2 December 1760 the heir sent a request to the Senate that localities respond to inquiries regarding a geographical description of Russia that the corps had devised. Objectively this reflected endorsement of a similar initiative that Lomonosov had set forth at the Academy of Sciences in 1758. In Peter's report, the pedagogical usefulness of such a description was supported by patriotic arguments: "so that the young men being trained in this corps might not only gain a thorough knowledge of the geography of the foreign lands about which they are presently being taught but also have a clear understanding of the condition of their own fatherland."[28]

Another of his reports, dated 7 March 1761, contained a plan for having the Cadet Corps train the children of soldiers and the lower orders as cadres of "good national tradesmen": blacksmiths, mechanics, harness-makers, shoemakers, farriers, gardeners, and other qualified specialists. Along with these trades, they would be taught reading, writing, arithmetic, geometry, drawing, and German, because, the report stated, "there are as yet no handbooks in Russian." From an estimate appended to the report it turned out that with an annual graduating class of thirty men, "such a tradesman would cost the treasury only two hundred rubles." They would disseminate experience in the army, and after the tradesmen were discharged, "by means of this, good national tradesmen will spread throughout the country."[29] The Senate approved the project and on 30 April 1761 authorized the training of 150 soldiers' and merchants' sons in the Cadet Corps.[30]

That such projects reflected Peter's political orientation is corroborated not only by the accounts of Staehlin, who was well disposed toward Peter, but also by those of Ia.P. Shakhovskoi, who held the post of procurator-general of the Senate under Elizabeth I and did not wish Peter well. With obvious disapproval he recalled how the heir, through his favorite I.V. Gudovich, often transmitted "from himself to me requests or (begging your pardon) demands in favor of manufacturers, tax farmers*, and other matters basically relating to that kind of business."[31] But it was exactly "that kind of business" (so arrogantly disdained by Shakhovskoi) that met the country's real developmental needs and was perfectly in tune with the range of ideas that the grand duke was formulating by the early 1760s.

Once he became emperor, Peter attempted to implement many of his ideas. He ascended the throne on 25 December 1761 (old style), at three o'clock in the afternoon, when Peter I's daughter Elizabeth died. Her successor did not know that fate had granted him an unusually short reign—only 186 days. While paying tribute "to the munificences and mercy" of the deceased empress, in his first manifesto Peter III promised that in every way he would "follow in the footsteps of that wise sovereign, our grandfather, Emperor Peter the Great." From the very first weeks of his reign he paid special attention to strengthening order and discipline in high-level offices, to limiting their powers, and to improving the administration's efficiency.

In emulation of Peter I, he decided to take charge of all this personally, and in order to accomplish it he established a precise daily schedule. The emperor generally rose at seven o'clock in the morning and listened to reports from his high officials between eight and ten; at eleven o'clock he personally directed the changing of the guard, and before or after that he sometimes inspected governmental offices or industrial enterprises. Generally the emperor had lunch at one o'clock—either in his own apartments, where he invited people who interested him regardless of the position they held, or while visiting diplomats or persons close to him. The evening hours were devoted to court amusements and games. He especially loved concerts and often joined in by playing the violin. As night approached, guests and members of the court (diplomats were also present, as a rule) convened to partake of a lavish and merry supper, accompanied by abundant libations. Peter III himself preferred English beer, for wine made him ill. Gossip and joking alternated with discussions of important issues, and diplomats eagerly picked up on things the emperor said—not always

---

*Persons granted exclusive rights to some economic activity—D.J.R.

Peter III

cautiously—and scrupulously reported them to their own governments. Sometimes Peter III left the assemblage, secluding himself with his advisors to discuss urgent matters.[32]

The former Imperial Conference was disbanded, and the examination of issues in its charge was turned over to the Senate, headed by A.I. Glebov. Special departments were created under the Senate, the Justice College, the Patrimony College, and the Judicial Department to handle applications and complaints accumulated from previous years. In May, under Peter III's chairmanship, a council was instituted, the purpose of which, as set forth in the decree, was to ensure that useful reforms "might be put into action as quickly and as effectively as possible." Among the members of the council were eminent statesmen such as Chancellor M.I. Vorontsov, Chairman of the Army College General Field Marshal N.Iu. Trubetskoi, Cadet Corps Director General A.P. Melgunov, and Field Marshal B.-Kh. Münnich, recalled from exile. A leading role was played by D.V. Volkov, who had been appointed the emperor's private secretary in January. Among Peter's closest aides was I.I. Shuvalov, one of the most educated men in Russia, a philanthropist and patron of Lomonosov.

But, the onslaught of reforms, though it had been well planned by Peter III and his advisers, misfired at the end of June 1762. On 29 June, the day assigned by the Church calendar to St. Peter and St. Paul, a solemn ceremony was scheduled. On the morning of the previous day, the emperor and his close associates had left Oranienbaum for nearby Peterhof, where Catherine was supposed to be waiting for them. But they found that she had hastily departed for St. Petersburg several hours before the cavalcade was supposed to arrive. Not long afterward, alarming reports began to come in that with the support of the Izmailovskii Regiment and Guards troops attached to it, Catherine had proclaimed herself monarch and dethroned her husband. After attending worship service in the Kazan Cathedral, Catherine II, leading troops who sided with her, launched a march on Oranien-baum that ended with the seizure of the deposed emperor.

Although Peter III had evidently not ruled out a conspiracy against him in principle—and, in fact, he had received warnings—the events caught him unaware. Had he been more decisive, he might have taken control of the situation: the rank-and-file Guards troops and some of the officers wavered, the army was generally opposed to the conspiracy, and General-in-Chief P.A. Rumiantsev, who had commanded the expeditionary corps in East Prussia, was among the military commanders faithful to the emperor. But, while he at first decided to resist, Peter let slip the opportunity and could not make use of the opportunities available to him—to entrench himself in Kronstadt and, from there, go by sea either to Rumiantsev or to Kiel. He had never in his life been prepared to struggle for power, and his understanding of Russia was limited to the courtiers and the top officers of the Guards, who at the critical moment turned against him. "The sovereign was pathetic," as N.K. Zagriazhskaia said, recalling the hours of the coup.[33] The despairing Peter III decided to enter into negotiations with Catherine II in an attempt to get permission to go to Kiel. After hearing this decision, the emperor's servants began to wail: "Dear Little Father! She is going to order you put to death."[34]

The result of Peter's capitulation was a renunciation of the throne, dated 29 June. It is an irony of fate that that occurred on the Feast of St. Peter and St. Paul. The document of renunciation was truly humiliating: the deposed emperor had to acknowledge publicly his inability "to rule the Russian state not only as an autocrat but also in any other form of government whatsoever."[35] The history of this document is in many ways contradictory and beset with doubts. It was appended to the so-called Manifesto of Particulars, dated 6 July, published on 13 July, and later excluded from *The Complete Collection of Laws of the Russian Empire*.

Contrary to official statements, it is naive to think that Peter III signed his renunciation voluntarily: after his arrest in Oranienbaum he was taken to Ropsha and placed in one room of the suburban palace under the watchful eyes of F.S. Bariatinskii, A.G. Orlov, P.B. Passek, and a few other persons whom Catherine trusted. It was there, on 6 July, that Peter the Great's own grandson was strangled by A.G. Orlov, the brother of the new monarch's latest lover.

The manipulations of the dates of the signing and announcement of the Manifesto of Particulars suggest that it was either composed after Peter III's murder or represented his death sentence. It is also worth noting that Peter III's renunciation was anonymous; it did not say to whom power was transferred. According to the logic of the times, the rightful successor should have been his young son Paul, with his mother as regent until he came of age. A number of grandees—for example, the young tsarevich's tutor N.I. Panin—counted on this. Having seized power, Catherine had for a time to reckon with such sentiments and perform certain maneuvers. This notion is suggested by three letters that Peter III sent from Ropsha.

The first two letters, dated 29 June (one in Russian, the other in French), reflected the prisoner's deep depression and are imbued with a spirit of humility and pleading. The third letter, dated 30 June, was altogether different in tone. In it, the sarcasm so characteristic of Peter comes to the fore. He repeats his request to be allowed to go to Holstein, begs his wife not to treat him "like an arch-criminal," and promises not to "act against your person or your reign"—a declaration of fundamental importance that was made almost in passing, in a postscript. One gets the impression that something had changed in just twenty-four hours. It is most likely that in exchange for acknowledging her rights to the throne, the empress hypocritically promised to allow Peter to go to Kiel. In any case, Catherine II readily reported that ships had begun to be prepared in Kronstadt for this purpose.

But in actuality none of this existed—neither an intention to free the prisoner of Ropsha, nor preparations for his departure, nor ships in the port of Kronstadt. Instead, the tsaritsa had the firm intention to rid herself of her dangerous rival by any means, but in such a manner that she would appear decent to both her contemporaries and posterity. In this, Catherine II succeeded. The final link in the chain of the subsequent discreditation of the deposed, deceived, and murdered monarch was the first brief manifesto, dated 28 June 1762, which informed her loyal subjects of the change on the throne.

The manifesto set forth three principal charges against Peter III—who was, incidentally, not named. Peter was accused of, first, causing "the undermining and destruction" of the Church by the "supplanting of the ancient Orthodox faith in Russia and the acceptance of the laws of another faith"; second, concluding a peace treaty with Frederick II, called a "villain" in the manifesto; and third, being a poor administrator, as a result of which "domestic order, constituting a precious possession of our whole fatherland, has been totally disrupted." These charges, supplemented by governmental announcements in the days following (especially the Manifesto of Particulars), have constituted the nucleus of the myth of Peter III, which became entrenched in the old historiography and then, after 1917, migrated into the Soviet literature as well. The extent to which this myth accorded with the facts has not particularly interested scholars or authors of fiction, and especially not the latter.

To what extent did the charges correspond to reality? First, let us consider the "disruption" of state order. The actual facts testify that vigor and intensity distinguished the activities of the government and of Peter III personally. A total of 192 documents—manifestos, resolutions, and decrees signed by the tsar and the Senate—were recorded in *The Complete Collection of Laws of the Russian Empire* between 25

December 1761 and 28 June 1762 alone. Moreover, these documents do not include edicts dealing with specific issues such as promotions in rank, the leasing of state holdings, and monetary payments. The archival register of extant decrees signed by Peter III includes 220 entries.[36] In addition, Peter III made extensive use of "spoken imperial decrees," the effect of which was regulated by a law dated 22 January. In order to avoid any abuses or misunderstandings, the Senate was instructed to submit to the emperor every week copies "concerning all our verbally announced decrees."[37] Two days before the coup, on 26 June, Peter III signed fourteen edicts.

What is important, however, is not the quantity of laws passed but rather the content and the overall direction of the lawmaking activity. From this standpoint, too, Peter III's reign is remarkable in many ways. Among the acts he signed were many of fundamental, organic importance, such as the February manifestos "On the Granting of Liberty and Freedom to All the Russian Nobility" and "On the Abolition of the Secret Investigation Office." Both manifestos represented the practical realization of ideas that Peter had held for some time: as early as the 1750s, he had been favorably inclined toward reform plans advocated by P.I. Shuvalov and allies of his such as Volkov and Glebov. The intent behind this course of action was to protect the nobility's interests while offering certain benefits and privileges to the merchant class.

On 17 January it is recorded in the chamberlain's journal, "on Thursday, at ten o'clock in the morning," the emperor "expressed his Imperial desire to appear before the Government Senate."[38] There he set forth his intention to exempt the members of the nobility from obligatory state service; this was greeted by an outburst of delight by those who heard him. The next day, Procurator-General Glebov proposed to the Senate that a gold statue be erected to the emperor as a token of gratitude. When he heard about that, Peter III answered: "The Senate can use the gold for a better purpose; I hope by my reign to erect a more long-lasting monument in the hearts of my subjects."[39] One month later, on 18 February, the emperor approved the manifesto emancipating the nobility. The authorship of the text is attributed to either Volkov or Glebov.

It is commonly believed that the manifesto, while reinforcing the nobility's privileged position, reduced its obligations to the state almost to nothing. Indeed, granting to members of the nobility rights to enter freely into military or civil service or not to enter at all, to resign at their own discretion, and to travel abroad and enter the service of foreign sovereigns, did constitute the purpose of this "liberty and freedom." But the bravura tone of the preamble to the manifesto was muffled by various provisos and conditions. Members of the nobility could resign only during peacetime, and service abroad was permitted only in "the European powers that are our allies," with return to Russia being compulsory "when such should be required." The question of noble service in the Senate and its office, which required thirty and twenty men, respectively, was handled in a peculiar manner. The membership of the bodies was left to the discretion of the noblemen themselves by stipulating elections "every year in accordance with the proportion living in the provinces." Parents were held strictly accountable for their sons' education. When their children reached the age of twelve, parents had to inform the authorities as to what their children had been taught and whether they were to further their schooling in Russia or abroad.

Another innovation was the establishment of a kind of "minimum subsistence" for the families of the nobility: those which had fewer than a thousand serfs were obliged to enroll their sons in the Cadet Corps. "However," the manifesto warned, "let no one dare, under pain of Our grievous wrath, to bring up their children without teaching them the sciences befitting a nobleman." Repeated appeals to the power of public opinion and to the nobility's sense of personal duty to the fatherland constituted a remarkable feature of the manifesto, which represented a kind of contract between supreme authority and its main bastion—the nobility.

During a routine visit to the Senate on 7 February, Peter III announced his intention to liquidate the Secret Office. By 21 February he had signed the manifesto prepared by Volkov. It was a remarkable document for its time. While justifying the necessity of this repressive organ under Peter I, the monarch acknowledged that by its very existence the system of secret denunciations had begun to corrupt society, because "evil, cowardly, and idle people were afforded the means either to delay the penalties and punishments they deserved through false maneuvers, or to inflict the most malicious slander upon their superiors or enemies." For this reason, the manifesto emphasized, on the basis of principles of humanity and mercy, "any hateful denunciation—namely, 'word and deed'*—shall not henceforth mean anything." Those who uttered this formula while intoxicated or in a fight

*By decree of Peter I, anyone hearing or overhearing a criticism of the tsar was obliged to proclaim the fact by crying out, "the sovereign's word and deed!" If the accusation was

were subject to punishment as "troublemakers" and "offenders against decency."

The abolition of the Secret Office did not mean that repressive laws were repealed. But from then on their application was subject to strict regulation, and any subject who discovered another's intent to betray the state or act against the monarch was obliged to submit a written denunciation "to the nearest judiciary or report it immediately to the nearest military commander." Throughout, the good intentions of the nobility, to which the "high-ranking merchant class" had been added, were taken for granted. At the same time, the manifesto provided for specific measures designed to rule out slander by "base people of any rank" against their superiors, masters, or other "enemies." The manifesto laid the foundations for replacing nonjudicial tyranny with a normal system of judiciary investigation in cases of political accusations. This served to inculcate a sense of dignity among members of the nobility and representatives of the "third estate" that was taking shape in Russia.

Was there any special legislation designed to reinforce the latter's rights? The question is appropriate, because it arose during the discussions concerning the draft of a new law code being prepared in the 1750s, especially Part Three—"On the Status of Subjects." Deputies from the nobility and the merchant class began to convene in the capital to discuss the draft in January 1762—that is, not long after Peter III came to power. He did more than simply promote this discussion. Along with decrees on urban development (encouraging the construction of stone buildings and organizing fire fighting, sanitation, medical services, and so on), the emperor managed to promulgate a law to establish the State Bank and issue paper banknotes, as well as a number of other acts designed to encourage trade, industrial activities, and merchandising.

These were evidently parts of a broader plan. Staehlin described Peter III's concerns: "He is reviewing all the estates in the country and intends to order the compilation of a plan to elevate the bourgeois estate in Russia's cities, so as to place it on a German footing and encourage their industry." Staehlin commented on the emperor's agreement with his suggestion to "send a number of tal-

---

proved, the accuser received half of the accused's property as a reward. Whatever the decree's intent, it produced an "informer" mentality and mutual distrust, especially among the higher nobility, who were both closest to the tsar and had most to lose by a casual comment.—D.J.R.

ented sons of the merchant class to commercial offices in Germany, Holland, and England, where they could study bookkeeping and commerce and organize Russian offices on the foreign model."[40] Staehlin's reliability is affirmed by the fact that during his talks with Peter III they discussed the idea mentioned above, of training "Russian national tradesmen" with the help of German experts.

A number of Soviet researchers (S.N. Kashtanov, N.L. Rubinshtein, and S.O. Shmidt) and foreign investigators (Marc Raeff, for example)[41] have detected in Peter III's legislation certain new tendencies, such as the encouragement of trade, industry, and handicrafts and the rejection of the nobility's monopoly on entrepreneurial activity, among others. Rather remarkable in this context was a decree on commerce prepared by Volkov and signed by the emperor on 28 March. The decree devoted considerable space to measures designed to expand grain exports ("the state will be able to conduct a massive grain trade, and in this way grain farming will be encouraged") as well as other agricultural exports. Attention was focused on the necessity of taking good care of the forests, which "we consider to be one of the state's most essential and important assets." At the same time, it was forbidden to import sugar, raw materials for the textile mills, and other goods the manufacture of which could be organized in Russia.

Another remarkable Senate decree, dated 31 January, authorized the organization of a mill to manufacture sailcloth in Siberia, "in particular for the port of Okhotsk," in order to eliminate the need to haul it long distance from Moscow and "thereby avoid that loss to the treasury." Several decrees were designed to expand the use of free hired labor, and working men were admonished "not to indulge in vain animosity . . . inasmuch as other men seeking to be hired for the same work can henceforth be reliably found."

The logic of his legislative activity led Peter III to the peasant issue, a question so crucial to the country. In January a woman landowner named E.N. Golshtein-Bek was stripped of her rights to her estate, inasmuch as "the administration of the villages under her disposition could lead not to the benefit but to the ruination of the peasantry." For the first time in Russian legislation, a decree dated 25 February categorized landowners' killing of their peasants as "tyrannical torment," punishable by exile for life. A series of decrees signed by Peter III stipulated the superior social status of state peasants over estate peasants. In accordance with laws proclaimed in February through April, peasants resident on Church and monastery estates were released from their former servitude, given land allotments, and transferred to the state's jurisdiction on payment of an annual poll tax, which for 1762 was set at one ruble per male soul.

While demanding humane treatment of the peasants, however, Peter III and his government put a resolute stop to any forms of "disobedience" or "willfulness" on their part, dispelled rumors of the possible abolition of serfdom, and firmly protected landowners' rights. To a certain point, to be sure, the authorities tried not to advertise repressive measures that it undertook; according to a note from Volkov, the emperor on 31 May instructed the Senate "pursuant to all the above, to implement immediately the suppression of peasants who have become disobedient to certain landowners, but not to make any publication of the same."[42]

Rumors that peasant emancipation might be forthcoming, however, soon forced him to change his tactics; this was announced in a manifesto of 19 June regarding serf rebellions in the Tver and Klin districts. "It is with the greatest anger and dissatisfaction," the manifesto stated, "that We have learned that the peasants of some landowners, having been tempted and blinded by the false rumors spread by indecent people, have refused to be properly obedient to their owners." In order to put a stop to this "blinding" of the peasants and appease the nobility, Peter III assured them: "We intend to preserve the landowners and their estates and holdings intact, and to keep the peasants properly obedient to them." This was the gist of this "wrathful" manifesto. Based on these points, it could hardly have been Peter III's legislative activity that gave Catherine II grounds for accusing him of "disrupting domestic order."

Added to this accusation was another one—namely, that the peace treaty with Prussia "in fact surrendered . . . Russia's glory for total enslavement." The accusation that Peter III was a traitor to the state's interests has proved to be unusually persistent in Russian and Soviet historiography, although it is not only disputable but has long been in need of revision. In actuality, the Seven Years War, with its senseless casualties, had evoked growing criticism in the country. None other than Lomonosov wrote a letter to I.I. Shuvalov in November 1761, in which he said: "The present unhappy warfare in Europe is forcing not only individual people but entire disrupted families to leave their fatherland and look for places far away from the violence of war."[43] Incidentally, these lines coincided almost word-for-word with the aforementioned memorandum sent by the grand duke to Elizabeth I in 1760.

The transition from confrontation to peaceful cooperation with

Prussia proved to be mutually beneficial. For one thing, it prevented Vienna from concluding a separate peace with Prussia (negotiations along these lines had been under way since 1759), which would have isolated Russia.[44] The initiative manifested by Peter III literally from his first hours in power eliminated that danger. Naturally, the sharp turn in Russia's foreign policy proved to be Frederick II's salvation, something he himself did not deny. But for all Peter III's worship of the Prussian king, the steps he had undertaken were no manifestation of altruism.

Peter III concluded peace with Frederick II on terms that partially anticipated Panin's "Northern System." As a matter of fact, in the treaties of 24 April and 8 June and in secret appendixes to them, Frederick II promised Peter III, among other guarantees, that first of all, he would, "effectively and using every means," including military aid, help to liberate Schleswig from Danish occupation; second, that he would promote the election of the emperor's uncle, Prince George Ludwig, to the throne of Courland (in anticipation of the forthcoming negotiations with Prussia, the odious Ernst-Johann Biron, who remained the legitimate duke of Courland, had been brought back from exile); and third, that he would act with Russia to guarantee the rights of the Orthodox and Lutheran populations in Poland and support the elevation to the Polish throne of a candidate friendly to Russia. Had this program been realized, Prussia would have joined the circle of political allies favorable to Peter III.

While establishing friendly relations with Frederick II, Peter III was not inclined to make unlimited concessions. In a message dated 14 April, the Austrian envoy Mercy d'Argenteau relayed the emperor's words to him: "He has already done much for the king of Prussia's benefit; now he, the sovereign of Russia, needs to think about himself and be concerned with how to advance his own affairs and intentions. He will not abandon the Kingdom of Prussia, but only if the king helps him financially." That this was not merely an offhand remark is demonstrated by documents. The treaties that Peter III signed with Frederick II called for halting the withdrawal of Russian troops from Prussia if the international situation worsened. In accordance with this, on 14 May Peter III ordered Rear Admiral G.A. Spiridov of the Reval Squadron to "cruise from the Gulf of Riga to Stettin to escort transport ships"[45]—ships that were supplying provisions and ammunition to the Russian expeditionary corps stationed there.

On 12 February the foreign envoys in St. Petersburg were handed a declaration proposing that all territorial acquisitions during the

Seven Years War be annulled and universal peace established in Europe. But even as it called for an end to military operations, the Russian government undertook measures to improve the fighting capability of its army and, especially, its navy, which by that time had fallen into decline. In February and March, under Peter III's chairmanship, special commissions were instituted to "bring our armed forces into the best condition possible, one more deserving of our friends' respect and more frightening to our enemies."

Finally, there is the accusation that Peter III intended to "undermine" and "destroy" the Orthodox faith, replacing it with Lutheranism. To this day the grounds for such an assertion remain unclear. A document from the Schleswig archives, describing the summer of 1762, contains a reference to "a certain report in the French language" and asserts that Peter III was consulting with Frederick II concerning the introduction of Lutheranism in Russia.[46] The authors of several German pamphlets published immediately after the events of 1762 also wrote about plans for church reform. But nothing in Peter III's legislation reflects any of this, except perhaps for a few decrees relating to specific matters, such as a ban on building private chapels, since the construction of churches was not a personal but a community matter. Even the apocryphical "Opinion," supposedly written by Peter III in his own hand and submitted to the Synod on 25 June, emphasizes that any person has a right to choose his own religion and voluntarily observe its rituals. Strictly speaking, there was nothing unexpected in this—the emperor, who had always been rather indifferent toward religion, believed in the principle of freedom of conscience.

On 29 January he had stopped the persecution of the Old Believers, having directed the Senate "not to effect any prohibition in the law with respect to their customs." The resolution Peter III submitted to the senators emphasized that in addition to Orthodox believers in Russia there were "persons not of that faith, like Mohammedans and idol-worshippers, and that the Christian schismatics are so firm in their inveterate superstition and stubbornness that they ought not to be deterred through compulsion and persecution because they would only flee abroad and in their multitudes live useless lives in the same condition." The rights of the Old Believers were reinforced in the manifesto of 28 February. Until 1 January 1763 "Great Russians and Little Russians of all ranks" who had fled abroad, "and also schismatics, merchants, landless peasants, household serfs, and military deserters" would be permitted to return "without any fear or penalty whatsoever." In the manifesto, freedom of conscience was linked to economic considerations.

The pragmatism and enlightened rationalism expressed in not only these but also a number of other documents signed by Peter III reflect something heretofore unnoticed in the literature—they were textually in tune with Lomonosov's recommendations in his treatise *On the Preservation and Propagation of the Russian People.* Maintaining that the schismatics who had fled to "foreign states, but especially Poland" were like "living dead," the scholar emphasized the economic damage to the country that resulted from this. He believed it essential to revise ineffective methods of combating schism with coercion and to replace them with the kind "which afford the opportunity to correct people's manners and enlighten them more."[47] Peter III not only followed this path, but decided on a more radical step.

After proclaiming freedom of religion, he thought about placing the church hierarchs under state control, not only politically (which Peter I had already done) but also economically, by secularizing church and monastery holdings (something his grandfather did not manage to do!). Having assigned the practical side of the reform to Volkov, the emperor personally took part. Staehlin reported: "He is working on Peter the Great's plan to confiscate monastery holdings and appoint a special Economic College to administer them. . . . He is taking this manifesto into his office to reexamine it and add comments to it."[48] Because the idea was explosive, the reform was not announced in one manifesto but in a series of decrees.

In the first decree, signed on 16 February, tactical considerations dictated the emphasis that the government was merely implementing the will of the late empress, who had wished to combine "piety and usefulness to the fatherland." As a matter of fact, the new procedure had been approved by the Conference in Elizabeth's presence in 1757, although it had not been put into effect. For all the bombastic style of the preamble, Voltairian touches kept creeping into the text of the decree. It noted, in particular, that the empress, wishing to eliminate violations and strengthen "the true foundations of our Eastern Orthodox Church, had deemed it imperative to release monks who have renounced this temporal life from the mundane cares of the world." The decrees of 21 March and 6 April, relating to the administration of former monastery and church holdings and the peasants living there, established the Economic College and transferred the clergy to state maintenance "according to roster."

One can only speculate whether Peter III intended to supplement political and economic control of the Church with changes in Orthodox ritual, although plans of that sort did exist. Specifically, these stipulated the lifting of restrictions on the number of times people could marry and a ban on taking monastic vows before age fifty for men and forty-five for women; they suggested that babies be baptized in warm rather than cold water and that Lent be shifted in time to match the country's climate—to late spring and early summer, for "fasting has not been instituted to commit suicide through [the consumption of] harmful foods but for restraint from excess." The drunkenness, public fighting, and ignorance among certain portions of the clergy were contrasted with the way of life of Lutheran pastors, who "do not go to banquets, christening parties, birth celebrations, weddings, and funerals," and who teach children reading and writing and so on.

All the plans can be summarized as "Let Germany serve as the example." However, they did not belong to the "Russophobe" Peter III but rather to the great Russian scientist and patriot Lomonosov, who wanted to bring the internal regulations and social functions of the Orthodox Church into conformity with the requirements of the spirit of the times.[49] The claims of certain contemporary authors that Peter III made Orthodox priests wear pastors' clothing and shave their beards are obviously dubious. Incidentally, there were some relatively shrewd people among his contemporaries. They included Bishop Ambrosius (A.S. Zertis-Kamenskii), the eminent church writer and lover of books. Addressing Catherine II in 1763, he inquired with concealed sarcasm (though outwardly in a completely loyal manner) as to whether a memorial service for Peter III as a "pious" person might not tempt the people to think that the "vices attributed to him" in the manifestos "might be wrong and that some other type of overthrow had taken place."[50]

In her memoirs, written early in the nineteenth century, E.R. Dashkova stated: "Peter III reinforced the revulsion people felt toward him and evoked disdain by his legislative measures."[51] But this was by no means the case. The emperor's policies were not only in keeping with the interests of broad segments of the nobility, but also evoked support and satisfaction. Many of the laws signed by Peter III and the plans he developed, as evident in extant sources, were within the mainstream of the Shuvalov group's projects. To a large extent they matched Lomonosov's recommendations. The most likely intermediary between the scholar and the emperor was I.I. Shuvalov, to whom Lomonosov dedicated his treatise *On the Preservation and Propa-*

gation of the Russian People. It can be no accident that Catherine disliked Lomonosov. In any case, the overthrow of Peter III, which surprised most of the population, shocked not only the lower orders but also the nobility, especially the Moscow and provincial nobility. On the whole, the situation on the eve of the coup looked different from Dashkova's portrayal.

Naturally, in assessments of this sort a great deal depended on personal relations at court. Reminiscing about her youth, the aged lady-in-waiting Zagriazhskaia (according to A.S. Pushkin) once said of Peter III: "He did not look like a sovereign."[52] This placed him at a disadvantage then and afterward. Indeed, many contradictory qualities coexisted in him: keen observation, zeal and sharp wit in his arguments and actions, incaution and lack of perspicuity in conversation, frankness, goodness, sarcasm, a hot temper, and wrathfulness. All of this was manifest in his behavior after he became emperor. He did not like to follow the strict rules of court ceremonies, and he often deliberately violated and mocked them. To a large extent this accounted for the rumors that Peter III was "hated by Russians" (Count Finkenstein), that he "constantly offended the people's self-esteem" (J.L. Favier), and that he held "hatred and scorn for Russians" (Bolotov).

There were indeed certain grounds for such opinions: a sense of having dual origins (a German father and a Russian mother) engendered in Peter after his arrival in Russia an unstable complex of double identity. Nevertheless, the reports cited above, and others like them, applied not to the people as a whole but rather, as A.T. Bolotov specified, to "our high-ranking grandees."[53] And that was true. Peter III deliberately shocked members of high society who were unkindly disposed toward him, yet he was happy dealing with ordinary people; it was a habit he had acquired in his early years. After he became emperor, he rode or walked around St. Petersburg all alone, without guards, and dropped in at the homes of his former servants. By an oral decree, dated 25 May, he authorized "people of all stations" to take walks in the Summer Garden and on the Field of Mars unimpeded "every day until ten o'clock at night in decent but not vulgar attire."[54]

His directness and simplicity, while evoking a sympathetic response in the people, caused increasing indignation among the upper crust; symptomatic of this were the outrageous rumors and jokes that became widespread in the summer of 1762. They portrayed Peter III as an extravagant half-wit and drunk, ready to sign any paper shoved at him without even looking at it. Thus, the Manifesto Freeing the Nobility was supposedly drawn up by Volkov, whom the emperor, leaving for a secret love tryst, had locked up in his office for the night and commanded to concoct some important law by morning. Again, during a merry banquet, K.G. Razumovskii, who had conspired in advance with his drinking buddies, supposedly yelled "word and deed" at a person who failed to empty his glass in drinking to the emperor's health. Embarrassed over the practice of denunciations, Peter III immediately signed the manifesto abolishing the Secret Office that Volkov had obligingly brought to him.

It is not impossible that Volkov, who, after the coup, did everything he could to distance himself from his erstwhile sovereign, was the source of many of these unlikely stories, believed by generation after generation.[55] After the coup, Catherine II also participated in propaganda of this sort, thus giving it state authority. In the Manifesto of Particulars, for example, the deposed emperor was accused of intending to kill her and prevent [their son] Paul from succeeding to the throne. In addition, credence was given to rumors that Peter III wanted to marry his favorite Elizaveta Vorontsova, but first to marry "forty to fifty fashionable ladies to Prussians and Holsteiners."

Critically evaluating the flow of salacious reports coming from St. Petersburg via Warsaw, a diplomat from Holstein wrote to Kiel in the summer of 1762: "These stupid things are being discussed solely to influence the people after the runaway empress, asking for protection, incited them to rebellion."[56] Even four decades later, Bolotov, then a captain serving at court, recalled with horror Peter III's passion for smoking and a time in Oranienbaum when the emperor and his merrymaking friends "all began to jump up and down on one leg, while others kneed their comrades in the buttocks and yelled."[57]

Examined dispassionately, amusements of this sort seem quite innocent compared to the entertainments of monarchs who ruled before and after Peter III. Like them, he might well have been forgiven these things had he not infringed on the political and material interests of the ruling elite, that "fistful of schemers and mercenaries" who, in A.I. Herzen's apt expression, actually "ran the state."[58] These circles became increasingly irritated not only by Peter III's many far-reaching plans (for example, the plans to expand merchants' privileges or reform the administration of Church holdings) but also by their implementation in practice. Peter III's unexpected and energetic visits to the Senate and, especially, the Synod, into which none of the reigning monarchs had even looked for a long time, frightened and irritated the high-ranking bureaucracy, which had become accustomed to lack of supervision and which shunned actual work.

The emperor's attempts to strengthen military discipline in the Guards units were also greeted without enthusiasm, especially since he did not conceal his negative attitude toward them nor that in time he intended to abolish them altogether, and in the meanwhile proposed to send them against Denmark in a war (to regain Schleswig) that he discussed as if it had already been decided. At the same time, new ways of issuing spoken military commands were being introduced, and uniforms modeled on the Prussian pattern were being made ready. Several units stationed in Prussia were sent against Austria—a recent ally—to aid Frederick II. Among the aristocracy of the capital and among the Guards, worried about their immediate future, measures of this sort were greeted with anxiety and criticism.

Despite the warnings he was receiving, Peter III failed to take measures to protect himself. He was firmly convinced of the stability and naturalness of his rights as monarch—so much so that, in spite of Frederick II's insistent advice, he postponed his coronation until the end of the Danish campaign, which he was convinced would be successful. Later, the Prussian king said, with a soldier's bluntness, "The poor emperor wanted to emulate Peter I, but he did not have his genius."[59] If we accept this at all, it is only in part: there are few examples in which people of no genius at all last long at the helm of state.

Another factor ultimately determined the fate phenomenon of Peter III: the growing detachment of the vehicle of power from the elite, which was striving to preserve the stability of the autocratic regime and, in addition, had an alternative in Catherine. The forces unhappy with Peter III placed their hopes in her just as she placed her hopes in them. This happened, moreover, before Peter ascended the throne, not afterward.

This immediately contradicts the version, taken from Catherine II's own assurances, that in the summer of 1762 she faced the dilemma of "either perishing together with the half-wit or saving myself with the crowd who craved to get rid of him."[60] Here again, however, the empress was being hypocritical. It is well known that during the final years and months of Elizabeth's life, a narrow circle of courtiers discussed the possibility of exiling the grand duke to Holstein and declaring the underage Paul emperor under Catherine's regency. Many were unhappy with this plan, in particular Catherine, who craved more. But the possibility of eliminating the legitimate heir had been formulated.

Catherine took this into account and chose—given the complicated atmosphere of intrigue around the dead empress's bed—the tactic of caution. When, in late 1761, Guards Captain M.I. Dashkov suggested to the grand duchess that she be put on the throne, he heard in response the words that Catherine II would reproduce in her *Memoirs*: "I commanded that he be told, 'For God's sake, do not talk nonsense; what God wills will be, but your undertaking is a premature and unripe thing.'"[61] Incidentally, she did draw the appropriate conclusions. She must be on the alert and provoke Peter to act rashly, while simultaneously winning influential aristocrats and guardsmen over to her side, to wait for a suitable time and, having chosen it, strike the blow. In this sense, Peter III was doomed even before he ascended the throne.

Later as well, however, having had her husband removed and murdered, Catherine II did everything necessary to discredit him not only as a ruler but even as a person. This purpose was served by the grotesque and monstrous characterizations of him in the empress's manifestos of late June and early July 1762, and elaborated in her *Memoirs*, on which she spent a large portion of her long reign, repeatedly rewriting and changing the text. It is worth noting that people immediately recognized the falsity of Catherine's manifestos, evaluating them in a moral light that became the basis of the legend of the miraculous salvation of the "Third Emperor."

One manifestation of this legend was the string of impostors who in the 1760s and 1770s adopted the name of Peter III throughout the vast expanses of Russia and neighboring countries, from Siberia and the Urals to the Adriatic and Central Europe. The denigrating accusations made against Peter III gave rise to similar doubts among high-placed contemporaries as well, as can be seen from the example of Ambrosius, mentioned above. Incidentally, Catherine herself confirmed the shakiness of these accusations not long afterward. On taking power, she had intended to rescind the decrees on the secularization of church and monastery holdings, the peace treaty with Prussia, the Manifesto Freeing the Nobility, and others of Peter III's acts. This was meant to confirm the accusations against him contained in the Manifesto of 28 June.

But in 1764 a new treaty was concluded with Frederick II and the secularization of church holdings was resumed. Although considerably delayed, in 1785 charters were issued for the nobility and the towns. S.S. Tatishchev remarked with some surprise: "However great the difference in the political systems of Peter III and his successor may appear at first glance, it must nevertheless be acknowledged that in some instances she served merely as the continuator of his initiatives."[62] More surprising still is that this historian's shrewd observation has never been properly appreciated by scholars.

Meanwhile, the continuity that Tatishchev noted not only convincingly refutes the principal "vices" of Peter III as listed in Catherine II's introductory manifesto; it also objectively testifies that, despite its costs, his government's course of action was neither reckless nor traitorous. Circumstances forced Catherine to continue some of the reforms begun during his reign; however, as has often happened in Russian history, these were much delayed, undertaken half-heartedly, and stripped of their boldest ideas.

To be sure, there is no reason to idealize Peter III, glossing over his personal shortcomings or awarding his activities higher marks than they deserve. But neither is there reason to condemn him unequivocally and examine his every action in a spirit of ill will, without regard to the circumstances and motives that dictated them. It is even more risky to use Catherine II's *Memoirs* as the principal source for evaluating Peter III. After reading them, Senator F.P. Lubianovskii exclaimed: "It is hard to believe that one who lived so many years with an invincible faith in her future lofty destiny could bring herself to write such a testimony to herself and leave it to posterity—and not in a spirit of remorse, either."[63]

The reasoning that once led historians to justify Catherine II's accession to the throne has long since lost its persuasive power and political meaning. For the sake of establishing the truth, one must reevaluate the tradition that has become entrenched in historical consciousness. To accomplish this, it is essential to enlarge the documentary base, and not simply with archival materials concerning Peter III's affairs of state. Some time ago, scholars noted the necessity of critically analyzing the memoirs of Catherine II, of Dashkova and Bolotov, who were in sympathy with her, and of several foreign eyewitnesses to the events of 1762, including French diplomat C.C. de Rulhière's book *History and Anecdotes of the Revolution in Russia.*

In these and other sources, valuable and reliable information about Peter III and his times is often found alongside distortions, mistakes, crude juggling of the facts, and information that is salacious but essentially unverifiable. Repeating such misinformation uncritically serves only to foster faulty perception of one of the most falsified periods of

Russian history. As early as 1797, N.M. Karamzin called for a fair evaluation of Peter III: "More than thirty years have passed since Peter III, of unkind memory, went to his grave. And in all that time, a deceived Europe has judged this sovereign by the words of his mortal enemies or their base allies."[64] I would say that it is high time this eminent historian's opinion received the attention it deserves.

Notes

1. A. Gavriushkin, "Ozabotias' blagom otechestva," *Mezhdunarodnaia zhizn'*, 1988, no. 12, p. 107.

2. E.V. Anisimov, *Rossiia v seredine XVIII v.* (Moscow, 1986), p. 214. The most recent survey of the historiography on the question is Carol S. Leonard, "The Reputation of Peter III," *Russian Review*, 1988, no. 3, pp. 263–92.

3. S.O. Shmidt, "Vnutrennaia politika Rossii serediny XVIII veka," *Voprosy istorii*, 1987, no. 3, pp. 57–58.

4. G.R. Derzhavin, *Izbrannaia proza* (Moscow, 1984), p. 266.

5. See Iu.M. Lotman, *A.S. Kaisarov i literaturno-obshchestvennaia bor'ba ego vremeni* (Tartu, 1958), p. 30.

6. Russian National Library. Manuscripts Department (OR GPB), f. 73, no. 84, l. 1.

7. P.K. Shebal'skii, *Politicheskaia sistema Petra III* (Moscow, 1870), p. 12.

8. Ia.Ia. Shtelin, "Zapiski o Petre Tret'em, imperatore Vserossiiskom," in *Chteniia v Obshchestve istorii i drevnostei rossiiskikh*, 1866, bk. 4, otd. 5, p. 69.

9. Ibid., pp. 76–77.

10. A.G. Briukner, "Zhizn' Petra III do vstupleniia na prestol," *Russkii vestnik*, 1883, no. 1, pp. 195, 197.

11. A.B. Kamenskii, "Ekaterina II," *Voprosy istorii*, 1989, no. 3, p. 66.

12. RGADA, f. 4, no. 109.

13. Shtelin, "Zapiski o Petre Tret'em," p. 71.

14. S.M. Solov'ev, *Istoriia Rossii s drevneishikh vremen*, (Moscow, 1964), bk. 12, p. 343.

15. *Russkii arkhiv*, 1875, bk. 2, p. 490.

16. Shtelin, "Zapiski o Petre Tret'em," pp. 71, 110; OR GPB, f. 871, nos. 68, 69.

17. R. Pries, *Das Geheime Regierungs-Conseil in Holstein Gottorp, 1716, 1773* (Neumuenster, 1955), p. 74.

18. D.D. Shamrai, "Tsenzurnyi nadzor nad tipografiei sukhoputnogo shliakhetnogo korpusa," in *XVIII vek* (Moscow–Leningrad, 1940), vol. 2, p. 301.

19. RGIA, f. 1329, op. 1, d. 101, l. 3.

20. Ibid., ll. 4, 64.

21. Ibid., l. 64.

22. A.S. Lappo-Danilevskii, "Rossiia i Golshtiniia," *Istoricheskii arkhiv*, 1919, no. 1, p. 275.

23. Shtelin, "Zapiski o Petre Tret'em," p. 93.

24. *Russkii arkhiv*, 1898, bk. 1, pp. 7, 9.

25. RGADA, f. 1261, op. 1, no. 367.

26. Shtelin, "Zapiski o Petre Tret'em," p. 106.

27. Ibid., p. 98.

28. RGIA, f. 1329, op. 1, d. 101, l. 77.

29. Ibid., ll. 87, 88 ob.

30. A.V. Viskovatov, *Kratkaia istoriia pervogo kadetskogo korpusa* (St. Petersburg, 1832), p. 31.

31. Ia.P. Shakhovskoi, *Zapiski* (St. Petersburg, 1872), pp. 157, 176.

32. Ia.Ia. Shtelin, "Zapiski o Petre Tret'em," p. 97; P. Bartnev, "Dnevnik statskogo sovetnika Mizere o sluzhbe pri Petre Tret'em," *Russkii arkhiv*, 1911, bk. 2, vyp. 5; *Zhurnaly kamer-fur'erskie 1762 goda* (n.d., n.p.).

33. A.S. Pushkin, *Polnoe sobranie sochinenii*, vol. 12 (Moscow, 1949), p. 175.

34. K.-K. Riul'er [Claude Carloman de Rulhière], "Istoriia i anekdoty revoliutsii v Rossii v 1762 g." [Histoire, ou, Anecdotes sur la révolution de Russie en l'année 1762] in *Rossiia XVIII v. glazami inostrantsev* (Leningrad, 1989), p. 304. English translation: *A History, or, Anecdotes of the Revolution in Russia* (New York: Arno Press, 1970).

35. "Manifesty po povodu vosshestviia na prestol imp. Ekateriny II," in *Osmnadtsatyi vek* (Moscow, 1869), bk. 4, p. 221.

36. RGIA, f. 1329, op. 1, d. 96.

37. *Polnoe sobranie zakonov Rossiiskoi imperii*, vol. 15 (St. Petersburg, 1830); all other official acts mentioned are cited according to this edition.

38. *Zhurnaly kamer-fur'erskie 1762 goda*, pp. 9–10.

39. Solov'ev, *Istoriia Rossii s drevneishikh vremen*, bk. 13, p. 12.

40. Shtelin, "Zapiski o Petre Tret'em," p. 103.

41. M. Raeff, "The Domestic Policies of Peter III and His Overthrow," *American Historical Review*, no. 5 (1970) pp. 1289–1310.

42. RGIA, f. 1329, op. 1, d. 97, l. 94.

43. M.V. Lomonosov, *Polnoe sobranie sochinenii*, vol. 6 (Moscow-Leningrad, 1952), p. 402.

44. E. Prister, *Kratkaia istoriia Avstrii* (Moscow, 1952), p. 274.

45. Central State Naval Archive, f. 227, op. 1, d. 17, l. 12.

46. Schleswig-Holsteinisches Landesarchiv, 8. I. S. II. No. 12.

47. Lomonosov, *Polnoe sobranie sochinenii*, pp. 401–2.

48. Shtelin, "Zapiski o Petre Tret'em," p. 103.

49. Lomonosov, *Polnoe sobranie sochinenii*, pp. 386, 387, 390, 394, 395, 407–8.

50. "Zatrudneniia pri pominovenii Petra III. Iz bumag M.D. Khmyrova," *Istoricheskii vestnik*, 1881, vol. 4, p. 452.

51. E.R. Dashkova, *Zapiski, 1743–1811 gg.* (Leningrad, 1985), p. 37.

52. Pushkin, *Polnoe sobranie sochineniia*, p. 177.

53. A.T. Bolotov, *Zapiski*, vol. 2 (St. Petersburg, 1872), pp. 164–65.

54. RGIA, f. 1329, op. 2, d. 52, l. 12.

55. G.V. Vernadskii, "Manifest Petra III o vol'nosti dvorianskoi i zakonodatel'skaia komissiia 1754–1766 gg.," *Istoricheskoe obozrenie*, vol. 20 (1915), pp. 51–53.

56. Schleswig-Holsteinisches Landesarchiv, 400. 5. No. 316. Bl. 66.

57. Bolotov, *Zapiski*, p. 205.

58. A.I. Gertsen, *Sobranie sochinenii* vol. 12 (Moscow, 1957), p. 365.

59. N.N. Firsov, *Petr III i Ekaterina II* (Petrograd-Moscow, 1915), p. 23.

60. *Perevorot 1762 goda: Sochineniia i perepiska uchastnikov i sovremennikov* (Moscow, 1908), p. 6.

61. Ekaterina [Catherine] II, *Sobranie sochinenii*, vol. 12, ch. 2 (St. Petersburg, 1907), p. 100.

62. *Sbornik Russkogo istoricheskogo obshchestva*, vol. 18 (St. Petersburg, 1876), p. vi.

63. F.P. Lubianovskii, *Zapiski* (Moscow, 1872), pp. 176–77.

64. Quoted in Iu.M. Lotman, "Cherty real'noi politiki v pozitsii Karamzina," in *XVIII vek*, vol. 13 (Leningrad, 1981), p. 126.

Empress Catherine II, 1762–1796

Described by poet Alexander Pushkin as "a Tartuffe in a skirt and crown," Catherine II (the Great) has long captured the historical imagination. Because Soviet historians had neglected her reign or else characterized it in abusive terms, Aleksandr Borisovich Kamenskii's sketch of Russia's other eighteenth-century "great" ruler attracted considerable attention when it appeared in the Soviet Union in 1989.

Kamenskii's rich essay touches upon many of the historiographical issues associated with Catherine's years in power, and treats the matter of personality in some detail. Unprincipled like other eighteenth-century rulers, skilled in the art of dissembling, Kamenskii's Catherine continued Peter's course in regard to problems of state, but in many ways was prisoner to the country's past that Peter helped shape. Since it was not in Catherine's power to mitigate the ills of serfdom or to abolish the institution ("she would have been swept away by an enraged nobility"), Catherine designed her domestic policies to reinforce the absolutist state—and her own position. Insofar as her various reforms did not alter the status of Russia's social estates, Kamenskii sees "movement forward" when she was empress, but only within the framework of the "feudal structure," which, he argues, actually reached its apogee under Catherine.

Avoiding the ambiguous evaluations of Catherine often encountered in the historical literature, Kamenskii provides a sober assessment that is sympathetic but not uncritical. He more than admits her unbridled ambition, concluding that "her primary goal was to stay in power by any means." Although he disparages her expansionist foreign policy, he sees her sincere interest in discussing civil liberties and humanism as what made her a dangerous topic of *discourse for Soviet historians. In fact, her dabbling in intellectual pursuits makes her rare among Russia's emperors and empresses: "she stands out among the Russian tsars (both before and after her)," writes Kamenskii, "in terms of the breadth of her intellectual interests and inquiries." The author also discusses her amorous attachments with sensitivity, but ultimately doubts that her favorites were worthy of her. "It may be that the tragedy of Catherine the woman is precisely the fact that they were not" [worthy of her].*

Once again, readers will note that the author's observations about earlier Romanov rulers deviate from the revisionist conclusions presented in some of the essays that precede this one. For example, Kamenskii remarks that Anna Ivanovna "farmed Russia out to the Germans," and he more or less accepts Catherine's depiction regarding the immaturity and incompetence of her husband, Peter III.

D.J.R.

Catherine the Great

Aleksandr Borisovich Kamenskii

"Catherine sat there, sad and in tears, or at least trying to look that way. Her hour had not yet come, but it was approaching." Thus E.V. Anisimov concludes the final chapter of his book *Russia in the Mid-Eighteenth Century*, the only popular work to appear in recent decades concerning the social and political history of Russia after Peter I. Catherine's time—a reign that would last for more than thirty years, an epoch that bears her name—was approaching. The date on the calendar read 25 December 1761; the future Catherine II, then still Grand Duchess Ekaterina Alekseevna, née Princess Sophia Augusta Frederika of Anhalt-Zerbst, was almost thirty-three.

When citing the maiden name and title of this Russian empress, some modern fiction writers (historians have not written about her for quite a while)[1] take it upon themselves to assert that the interests of the Russian people were alien to this German woman. Without attempting to dispute this notion, let me comment that Empress Anna Ivanovna, who farmed Russia out to the Germans, was a full-blooded Russian. Another "commonly held" assumption associated with Catherine is her "non-noble" origin. Certain authors of historical novels write about this matter with unconcealed disdain. Incidentally, as is well known, Catherine I was not distinguished in any way by her nobility. However, for some reason people usually do not become upset by this but rather find it touching. More, of course, is involved than mere origins.

When examining the activities of any tsar, emperor, or empress, it is essential to keep in mind that this person was a political figure who, by the will of fate, was invested with unlimited autocratic power. It therefore is necessary to determine the person's preparation for this laborious mission, her views, interests, sympathies, and antipathies, as well as the personal qualities that, in one way or another, were reflected in her activities. Of considerable importance, too, are the autocratic sovereign's attitude toward her "work," whether she had any pronounced intentions and endeavors, and which among these she implemented, successfully or unsuccessfully, and for what reasons—ultimately, what the results of her activities were. This is, roughly, the range of questions this essay attempts to answer—with varying degrees of detail, to be sure, for the history of Catherine II's reign comprises several important problems that merit special examination. The extent to which these problems have been studied, in both prerevolutionary and contemporary historiography, varies. Many questions still require the identification and analysis of new archival documents; hence conclusions drawn today can only be preliminary in character.

* * *

When Empress Elizabeth died in 1761, Catherine was thirty-two years old; she had spent seventeen of those years in Russia. Just what kind of person was this woman at perhaps the most critical moment in her life?

The future empress was born on 21 April 1729 in the city of Stettin (now Szczecin). Her father, Prince Christian August, was a general in the Prussian service and the commander of a regiment stationed in that city. Her mother, the Princess Joanna Elizabeth, born a princess of Schleswig-Holstein, was the younger sister of Prince Karl August, Elizabeth's betrothed, who had died in St. Petersburg. This may have been the decisive circumstance in Elizabeth's choice of a bride for the heir.

Princess Sophia spent much of her childhood in Stettin Castle, but her mother frequently took her on trips to Zerbst, Hamburg, Eutin, Braunschweig, Berlin, and elsewhere. When one considers that in the eighteenth century people did not go visiting for just a day, one must assume that these trips occupied an important place in the life of little Sophia Augusta Frederika (for convenience we will call her Catherine). For whatever reason, she never felt nostalgia either for a particular city or locality, such as Peter III later experienced toward Holstein, and by age fifteen she was ready to like any place on earth where fortune smiled upon her. Nevertheless, even in her childhood, many invisible threads bound the princess to Russia. The theme of Russia occupied an important place in the conversations of the people around her, because since Peter I's time Russia had become an influential power in world politics. Many of Catherine's compatriots went to that very nation to seek their fortunes, and many did find their fortunes there, as the future empress's childhood coincided with the reign of Anna Ivanovna [1730–40]. Moreover, Catherine's mother was the aunt of Karl Peter Ulrich, the grandson of Peter the Great and Charles XII. His fate could hardly fail to excite the members of the House of Holstein, who in 1739 had gathered together in Eutin in order to make their young relative's acquaintance. It was then that Catherine met her future husband for the first time.

She grew up a vivacious, sociable girl who loved to excel in games. But whereas the future, given favorable circumstances, promised Peter Ulrich either the Russian or the Swedish crown, the princess had nothing for which to hope, something her mother, who had brought her daughter up very strictly and tried to suppress any manifestations of pride or arrogance in her, understood very well. For the young girl had more than enough of both qualities, and the need to conceal her feelings taught her the art of dissembling, which she mastered completely and utilized successfully all her life. The suppression of natural qualities—and by extremely crude means at that (in order to quell any excessive pride in the young girl, her mother forced her to kiss the dresses of the noble ladies who visited their home)—evoked in the reflective child a desperate resistance. Later Catherine wrote, "All my life I have retained the custom of yielding only to reason and gentleness; I have responded to any argument with an argument."[2] An interesting characterization of Catherine was offered by Baroness von Prinzen, who had known her in childhood:

> I . . . might think that I knew her better than anyone else, yet I would never have guessed that she was destined to acquire the renown that she sought. When she was younger, I merely noted in her an intellect that

was serious, calculating, and cold, yet one that was just as far from being outstanding or brilliant as it was from everything that is considered to be deluded, capricious, or light-headed. In short, the opinion of her that I formed for myself was that she was an ordinary woman.[3]

But how can anyone call a woman ordinary who was distinguished at the age of fifteen by "a serious, calculating, and cold" intellect, one who was not inclined to be capricious or frivolous? Are these not qualities that are essential in politics?

Thus this proud, ambitious girl, who was inclined to make independent judgments, who possessed a calculating mind, and who considered herself homely,[4] from her early childhood listened to conversations that portrayed Russia as a land of great opportunities. Conversations of this sort increased when Elizabeth was elevated to the Russian throne, since members of the House of Holstein pinned certain hopes on her ascent. In addition, the princess of Anhalt-Zerbst's imagination could hardly fail to be excited by the fact that this vast and wealthy country was ruled by first one, then another, and finally a third, woman. When her mother received an invitation from Elizabeth in December 1743 to visit Russia with her daughter, there was no hesitation. Both the mother and the daughter knew why they were going: Elizabeth had chosen a young woman whom she knew only from her portrait to be the bride of her nephew, the heir to the throne. The princess was fifteen years old, an age which in an eighteenth-century context made her most suitable for marriage; she had evidently not yet experienced any attachments of the heart, and she gave no thought to marriage for love.

They wasted no time arranging the trip. On 31 December the family arrived in Berlin; on 5 January they left the Prussian capital, and on 6 January Prince Christian August said goodbye forever to his daughter. Several years later, when the news of his death reached St. Petersburg, Princess Catherine was informed by Empress Elizabeth that she had no special need to grieve, inasmuch as her father had not been a king. On 25 January 1744 the princess of Anhalt-Zerbst arrived in Riga with her daughter. The travelers were greeted with pomp and circumstance. When they departed from there on 29 January they were accompanied by a squadron of cuirassiers and a detachment of the Livland Regiment as well as a large number of grandees and officers. They rode in the Imperial sleigh, which was lined inside with sable, and the princess's shoulders were covered with a luxurious sable coat—the empress's first gift. On 3 February they were welcomed to St. Petersburg, and on 6 February they were received in Moscow, where the court was located.

Catherine's impressions of her first meeting with Elizabeth were so strong that she never forgot them. In her memoirs Catherine not only mentions the empress's beauty but also gives a detailed description of her attire, which evidently staggered the princess's imagination. Her dream of happiness had become a reality: she was surrounded by honors and luxury, the future promised her an imperial crown, and Catherine could hardly fail to thank fate for this. Fate was personified by Elizabeth, and the payment for this happiness was marriage to Peter, by then proclaimed Grand Duke Petr Fedorovich.

We must assume that at first the princess sincerely venerated the empress and was ready to serve her faithfully and truly, especially since Elizabeth herself was kind to her. As far as her future husband was concerned, the princess had no special affection for him. While two years older than she, he was clearly inferior to her in development. From the evidence it appears that he considered her to be not so much a young woman who needed to be courted as a potential playmate. Instead of speaking to her "in the language of love," he talked to her "about the toys and soldiers that occupied him from morning to night." She yawned and listened patiently.[5]

The princess began to study the Russian language the moment she arrived in Russia, and on 28 June she was christened in accordance with Orthodox ritual and given the name Ekaterina Alekseevna (interestingly, she became Catherine II eighteen years later, also on 28 June). The next day, on Peter's nameday, they were betrothed (eighteen years later, also on his nameday, Peter was stripped of his crown). Catherine became the wife of the grand duke on 21 August 1745. Peter's behavior had not changed throughout the preceding year. It is true that he had begun to pay more attention to women—but not to Catherine. He continued to play with dolls and, to his young bride's horror, even brought them to the marriage bed. It is easy to imagine the despair of the grand duchess, whose strict mother had forbidden her any toys from the age of seven onward.

During the first months she spent in Russia, Princess Joanna Elizabeth managed to spoil relations with the empress and even with her own daughter, and soon after her daughter's wedding she quit Russia. Catherine was left with the capricious, suspicious, inconstant Elizabeth and her rather stupid, childish husband. It was essential, however, to endure and not to spoil the chance that destiny offered. Catherine endeavored with all her might. Later, quite frankly, if also rather arrogantly and cynically, she acknowledged:

> This is the judgment or, more accurately, the conclusion I reached as soon as I saw that I was firmly established in Russia, a conclusion I have never lost sight of for a minute: (1) to please the grand duke; (2) to please the empress; (3) to please the people. . . . I never neglected to accomplish this: modesty, obedience, respect, the desire to please, the desire to do the right thing, sincere affection; I used everything from 1744 through 1761.[6]

Catherine held no delusions regarding her marriage. While she tried to maintain excellent relations with Peter, she rejected any thought of falling in love with him:

> I would have loved my new husband very much if only he had had the desire or the ability to be lovable, but a cruel idea about him occurred to me during the first days of my marriage. I said to myself: If you fall in love with this man you are going to be the unhappiest creature on earth; because of your character you are going to desire mutual affection, but this man does not even look at you, he talks only about dolls . . . and pays more attention to every other woman than to you.[7]

Catherine's life at court was strictly regimented. Specially appointed people kept track of every step she made; she could not even go for a walk without the empress's permission; letters to her parents were written for her in the College of Foreign Affairs; and, of course, she was not permitted involvement in politics. Reminiscing in 1791 about Elizabeth's court, she said:

> There was no conversation whatsoever. . . . We cordially hated one another. . . . Back-biting replaced wit, and . . . the slightest matter-of-fact word was considered an offense to Her Majesty. Clandestine intrigues were considered cleverness. We avoided talking about the arts or science, because everybody was an ignoramus: one might wager that barely half of society, if that, knew how to read, and I am not at all certain that even one-third knew how to write.[8]

For the sake of fairness it should be noted that although there was plenty of jealousy, intrigue, and back-biting in Catherine's court as well, as there is in any court, education was held in high esteem.

For Catherine, reading became a refuge. At first she read French novels, but soon works on the political history of Germany, France,

and England reached her hands. At the same time she became acquainted with Voltaire's works. Later, in the second half of the 1750s,
books of certain other French Enlightenment figures also found their
way to her desk, including Diderot's and Jean le Rond d'Alembert's
Encyclopédie. Thus the solitary young woman, unloved by anyone, isolated from her kind, and deprived of friends (anyone to whom she
managed to form an attachment was removed), led a rather reclusive
life and occupied herself mainly by reading serious books.

Year after year passed, and nothing in her situation changed;
moreover, the empress became increasingly dissatisfied with her, because her marriage to Peter remained childless. Here we come to a
delicate question over which the novelists love to smack their lips but
over which historians generally pass in silence. We are referring to
Catherine's favorites, or, to put it more simply, her lovers. The first of
these, Sergei Saltykov, appeared after she had already endured her
marriage for seven years. Is there anything surprising about the fact
that a young woman wanted to experience genuine love? And why
should we not presume that she was in love with Saltykov? We might
add that she was pushed into marital infidelity at Elizabeth's instigation by people among her closest associates.

In 1754 Catherine gave birth to a son, the future Emperor Paul I.
The question of his paternity is also of great interest to the literati.
Catherine herself was primarily to blame for this; in her memoirs she
insinuates that Saltykov was Paul's father. It must be remembered,
however, that she wrote this at a time when she found it convenient
for Paul not to be considered the legitimate heir to the throne.[9]
During the first years of her marriage, she wrote, Peter not only
played with dolls in the marriage bed and forced his wife to listen to
endless monologues on military themes,[10] but also concocted all
kinds of fantastic stories about himself,[11] drank heavily, and openly
chased other women. He was simply less than a man. In 1750, when
M.S. Choglokova, who had been assigned to keep track of her, denounced her in the empress's name for not having children, Catherine answered that, although she had been married for five years, she
retained her virginity.[12] But Catherine let the cat out of the bag.
While revealing that Peter had proved incapable of performing his
husbandly duties on the first night of their wedding, she remarked:
"And the situation remained that way, without the slightest change,
for a period of nine years."[13] Hence she also afforded Peter the
chance to consider himself Paul's father. Catherine made no attempt
in any way to conceal her liaison with Saltykov, nor did she directly

mention his being Paul's father. When discussing Saltykov's infidelity, she was unable to maintain her ironic tone totally; through it one can perceive hurt and disillusionment, but she accused Saltykov only of indifference to her, and she did not even hint that he show interest in her son. In addition, Paul's character included several features that clearly indicate his kinship with Peter III.

The list of Catherine's "favorites" compiled by M.N. Longinov between 1753 and 1796—that is, a period of forty-three years—lists fifteen men; moreover, she had three in the first nine years prior to her ascent to the throne, of whom the first two were forcibly removed, while the third promoted the coup of 1762. When he published this list, P.I. Bartenev saw fit to remark that "her contemporaries completely forgave her her passions."[14] Indeed, by the time Catherine ascended the throne empresses' "favorites" had long since become the norm, one that did not particularly upset anyone. But whereas Anna Ivanovna turned all the country's reins of government over to her favorite, and Elizabeth's favorites ruled in her name, Catherine's favorites, while wielding enormous influence, never became all-powerful. She always participated directly in foreign and domestic politics. An Englishman who was her contemporary remarked: "The minute you look at her you can see that she was able to fall in love, and that loving her would constitute the happiness of an admirer worthy of her."[15] But were her favorites worthy of her? It may be that the tragedy of Catherine, the woman, is precisely that they were not.

As mentioned, Catherine gave birth to a son in 1754. In the literature we frequently come across reproaches directed at her, namely, that she was a bad mother or even that she did not love her first-born. These reproaches are hardly fair. How could a young woman develop her maternal instincts if her child was taken away from her immediately after birth, after which in order to see him she had to request the empress's permission? Elizabeth tended the baby herself, and any inquiries as to the state of his health might be taken as an expression of doubt in her abilities. Moreover, what Catherine saw on first meeting her son horrified her: "He was being kept in an extremely hot room, swaddled in flannel and placed in a cradle lined with dark-brown fox fur; they had him covered with a satin quilt stuffed with cotton, and on top of that they had placed yet another velvet cover. . . . All this caused him, when he grew up, to catch a cold and fall ill when the slightest breeze touched him."[16] Nor did future events foster any closeness between mother and son. In Paul's presence, Empress Catherine always felt that her claim to the throne was only semi-legitimate.

People's treatment of Catherine after she gave birth reinforced her sense that they looked upon her only as a means of continuing the dynasty. Now that her mission had finally been accomplished, they could easily rid themselves of her. Increasingly, Elizabeth was ill during those years, and this compelled the grand duchess to contemplate her own future. It was not promising, because her relations with the grand duke had become increasingly hostile. Catherine knew that at best she might be deported from Russia after Elizabeth died, or at worst find herself in a convent prison. That meant she had to fight, and for that she would need allies. In this regard, circumstances favored her.

Elizabeth's illness compelled others besides Catherine to view the future with anxiety. Increasingly, the courtiers turned their gaze toward what was known as the little court. Among these was the attentive gaze of Chancellor A.P. Bestuzhev-Riumin. At one time, Aleksei Petrovich had done everything he could to thwart the choice of Catherine as grand duchess; she had then begun to see the chancellor as her worst enemy. Eventually, however, she became convinced that Bestuzhev was the most talented Russian politician of the day, the one who would most consistently protect Russia's interests. On the threshold of the new reign, the chancellor was looking for allies. The fundamental principle of Bestuzhev's foreign policy activities was opposition to Prussia. He was the main promoter of the Seven Years War [1756–63], then under way. The grand duke, on the other hand, spoke openly of his own sympathies toward Prussia and her king, Frederick II, and this evoked considerable annoyance among Russian patriots.

Catherine was wiser. While she believed in her heart of hearts that the war was senseless,[17] she nevertheless demonstrated her support for it in every way. In general she did all she could to gain sympathy: she was modest, pious, kind, polite, and she sincerely tried to be Russian in every way. While perhaps she had not fallen in love with the country during the seventeen years she spent in Russia, Catherine at least had some affection for it. Peter's dislike of anything Russian was incomprehensible to her. She possessed a lively and inquiring mind, and she strove to improve her knowledge of Russian history, customs, and noble families. Recognizing the people's piety, Catherine meticulously performed Orthodox Church rituals and prayed and fasted constantly. All this was in sharp contrast to her husband, who ate meat on fast days and talked and laughed loudly in church. The grand duke behaved in such a manner that many in Russia began to think that his ascent to the throne might be disastrous.

It reached a point where Bestuzhev-Riumin discussed with Catherine a plan for her to ascend the throne and her husband to abdicate. The grand duchess took a cautious approach to the plan, as she did not yet feel confident enough. Meanwhile, little by little, she became involved in politics. This was fostered by growing interest in her among Russian grandees and foreign diplomats, by the fact that Peter was turning over to her certain affairs relating to the administration of Holstein, and by a romance with Stanislaw Poniatowski, a good-looking young Polish diplomat. Evidently, the romance started in the winter of 1755–56 and continued until Poniatowski was expelled from Russia in 1759 after having played an important role in Catherine's life. First, Poniatowski had served as her connection to high-level politics, and, second, he had introduced her to the world of tangled Polish affairs. Later, the expelled Poniatowski's place at her side was taken by Grigorii Orlov, the hero of the Battle of Zorndorf, who had won glory through his reckless bravery and was ready to fight like a lion for her.

Her interest in politics nearly proved fatal to Catherine when the thunderstorm burst upon Bestuzhev and he was sent into exile. However, the investigation uncovered no papers dangerous to Catherine—Bestuzhev had managed to burn them, and incriminating letters to Field Marshal S.F. Apraksin, who had also fallen into disgrace, proved to be completely innocent. Nevertheless, it was a trying experience. By that time, incidentally, the seemingly cautious and meek Catherine was increasingly mastering the laws of political and court battle and was able to oppose her adversaries skillfully.

There was yet another aspect to Catherine's involvement in politics. Everything that she observed during Elizabeth's final years could hardly fail to trouble her. Later, Catherine wrote about her predecessor with unconcealed scorn:

> Her day-to-day activities composed a solid chain of caprice, sanctimony, and indulgence, and because she had not a single firm principle and was not involved in a single serious or solid endeavor, in spite of her great intellect she became so bored that in the final years of her life she could find no better way to amuse herself than to sleep as much as she could; the rest of the time, a woman specially assigned to her would tell her stories.[18]

Indeed, Elizabeth had virtually ended any involvement in state affairs and had turned these over to her retinue. Catherine understood that the empire's luxurious façade of apparent prosperity concealed poverty, misery, and ignorance. She was energetic and vigorous, and it seemed to her that she could govern the country considerably better, because in contrast to Elizabeth she followed definite principles, which she had derived from books, chiefly those written by figures of the French Enlightenment. Such was Catherine's frame of mind on 25 December 1761, the day Elizabeth died.

Concerning Peter III's six-month reign, Catherine subsequently had this to say: "In all the Empire he had no more ferocious enemy than himself."[19] Indeed, Peter seemed to be deliberately acting in a way that would set as many people as possible from all segments of society against him. After all, one may speak of public opinion even in regard to eighteenth-century Russia. V.A. Bilbasov was certainly correct when he wrote: "It is a big mistake to think that there is no public opinion in Russia. Because there are no proper forms for the expression of public opinion in Russia, it is manifested in improper ways, by leaps and bounds, in fits and starts, solely at crucial historical junctures, with a force that is all the greater and in forms that are all the more peculiar."[20] Of what did this public opinion consist during Peter III's reign, and who expressed it?

The enormous importance of the Guards in the palace coups of the eighteenth century is well known. There is no doubt, moreover, that the Guards expressed the interests primarily of the ruling class— that is, the nobility. Yet E.V. Anisimov's study of the social composition of the Life Cuirassiers that elevated Elizabeth to the throne shows that only 17.5 percent of them were of noble birth. He notes that, first of all, "the Guards were characterized by a typical praetorian mentality"; secondly, "the mindset of the Guards . . . was dominated by a feeling that had become a vital component of the public mentality of that time, especially in the capital—patriotism"; in the third place, "the lower orders of the Guards . . . were closer to the broad strata of the capital city's population, where patriotic feelings predominated."[21] Twenty years later, the patriotic sentiments of the capital's population were unquestionably offended by the unwarranted cessation of the victorious war against Prussia and Peter III's open adulation of Frederick II.[22] These sentiments, which had been transmitted to the Guards, were further aroused by the introduction of uniforms of the Prussian type and by the prospect, totally unacceptable to the guardsmen, of having to leave their St. Petersburg quarters to take part in a war with Denmark.

Peter III also did everything possible to provoke opposition among so influential a segment of society as the clergy. While still a grand duke he never concealed his disdain for the Orthodox Church and its rituals, and once he became emperor he troubled himself even less in this regard. Peter demanded that icons depicting Russian saints be removed from churches and that priests shave their beards and, like the Evangelical pastors, wear frock-coats instead of cassocks. Peter also tried, using the "cavalry charge" approach, to solve a problem with which his predecessors, from Ivan the Terrible onward, had wrestled—the secularization of church lands. Finally, on 25 June 1762—three days before the coup—he sent the Synod a decree sanctioning religious tolerance.

Even though the patriotic and religious sentiments of individual courtiers were offended, another issue was much more important to them: under Peter III's administration, no courtier could be assured of his future.

This accounted for the public mood that led to the coup of 28 June 1762, a mood that united the aspirations of members of various social strata. It is easy to see, nevertheless, that some of Peter III's initiatives were progressive. The war with Prussia was indeed something that Russia did not need, and in fact Catherine later turned toward alliance with that state. The secularization of church lands had long been a necessity, and in short order Catherine carried out that reform as well. Nor can we deny the wisdom of the attempt to remove the Guards from St. Petersburg and thereby deprive them of opportunities to influence the country's political life. Finally, the attempt to proclaim religious tolerance deserves approval.

Special mention must be made about what was probably Peter III's most noteworthy legislative act—the Manifesto Freeing the Nobility, which unquestionably reflected the ruling class's aspirations and was received with enthusiasm. The promulgation of the manifesto had important social and political consequences. Despite her own negative attitude toward it, Catherine was compelled, in the final analysis, not only to endorse the act, but also to continue the policies that it proclaimed. Why, then, did the manifesto not guarantee Peter the backing of the nobility, generally considered the throne's main support? Precisely because this document was important primarily to the broad mass of the rank-and-file nobility rather than to the courtiers, the soldiers of the Guards regiments, or the residents of the capital city. And it was the sentiments of these very groups that led to Peter III's downfall. The progressive character of some of his initiatives (from the modern standpoint) was canceled out by the methods by which he attempted to carry them out, methods suggesting he lacked an important political quality: realism. Catherine learned well the lessons of her hapless husband's rule.

There is no need to recount the coup of 28 June, so graphically described in numerous historical works, contemporaries' memoirs, and fiction. Events might have developed quite differently had Peter III's attitude toward his wife merely been one of indifference rather than hostility and aggression. By observing the proprieties and conventions while allowing each to live his own life, they might have coexisted even longer on the Russian throne. But Peter, from the first days of his reign, expressed hostility toward Catherine publicly. This was reflected, for example, in the manifesto elevating Peter III to the throne, which made no mention of either Catherine or Paul. For Catherine, all of the subsequent months were essentially a chain of insults and humiliations, the final link of which was an episode at dinner on 9 June when Peter publicly called her a "fool." For Catherine this episode served as a kind of signal to take action. It was not easy to take the desperate step that her retinue had been urging on her for so long, but she would be doomed if she failed to act or if she were defeated. Contrary to all expectations, the coup was amazingly easy and bloodless. On 28 June 1762 she became the autocratic empress.

The first thing one notices when studying Catherine's reign is the sharp contrast between the programmatic declarations of the "enlightened" monarch, abundantly strewn throughout her official documents and in her personal papers, and her actual policies. "A Tartuffe in a skirt and crown," is how the young A.S. Pushkin described Catherine II. In just a few words the great poet expressed what professional historians require lengthy articles and monographs to set forth. All of these works, whether written by Catherine's apologists or her detractors, show evidence of annoyance: the apologists cannot reconcile the empress's words with her deeds, while her detractors fail to catch her in any especially terrible misdeeds. The former proceed from the basis that all of Catherine's declarations were sincere and that she genuinely tried to act on her words; the latter, convinced that the empress was a liar and a hypocrite, think that she not only did not try to implement her declarations, but actually did the opposite. The truth, evidently—as so often happens—lies somewhere in the middle.

When analyzing Catherine's activity on the throne, it is essential to keep in mind, first, that she was always guided by enormous ambition—even vanity—and, second, that her primary goal was to stay in

Catherine the Great

power by any means. Yet Catherine was sincere in her declarations and her correspondence, indeed, in all her initiatives. Because she did not possess a creative mind, she learned diligently from those who at the time exerted the greatest intellectual influence on Europe's leaders. To be sure, the attention of outstanding philosophes and writers flattered her, but it would be a mistake to think that she corresponded with them only out of vanity: one would have to be genuinely interested in corresponding and, in addition, possess great patience to write almost every day to, for example, Baron Grimm. Moreover, she did this not at the beginning but during the last years of her reign.

It may be that Catherine wanted to enact her teachers' ideas, but that whenever she encountered resistance to her actions or sensed the slightest threat to her own well-being, she would sacrifice everything in order to retain power. Catherine was unprincipled, but in this regard she was no different from most politicians of her day. Another of Catherine's important qualities was her excellent knowledge of people and her ability to take advantage of that knowledge. The perceptive Pushkin also mentioned this: "If ruling requires knowing the weakness of the human soul and how to use it, in this respect Catherine deserves the admiration of posterity. Her magnificence was dazzling, her cordiality was attractive, but her generosity was binding."[23]

Indeed, Catherine's court was distinguished by its magnificence. Although this exemplified considerably more taste and refinement than had characterized the preceding monarch, the ostentatious extravagance of Catherine's grandees and of the empress herself engendered understandable indignation not only in the democratically inclined A.N. Radishchev, but also in the regime's conservative critic M.M. Shcherbatov. However, that was the general tendency in eighteenth-century European aristocratic life, a tendency that had replaced the distinctive asceticism of the Middle Ages and reflected the high developmental level of industry and crafts, which made it possible to supply the market with increasing quantities of a variety of luxury goods. For people of that epoch, the opulence of the European monarchs' courts served as an indicator of the state's power.

Sometimes, Catherine's generosity extended beyond her immediate associates. Quite characteristic, for example, is an episode involving Chief Secretary K.I. Severin: Catherine happened to see Severin walking in the rain and sent him five thousand rubles "for a carriage."[24] Obviously, acts of this sort—and there were many—became widely known. Catherine used this skillfully to improve her reputation. It would be incorrect, however, to see only calculation in her actions: Catherine was not stingy by nature. One might suggest that she was generous at the people's expense. Of course, she was. But she could also have been stingy at the people's expense. The pursuit of luxury required increasing expenditures by high officials, which resulted in a rise in various kinds of abuses of office. It cannot be said that this went unheeded. From time to time throughout Catherine's reign, sensational scandals occurred and functionaries came under investigation; on the whole, however, the fight against corruption was conducted no more intensely than during the preceding period. Catherine understood perfectly that as soon as she started it would greatly offend influential people without whose support she would be unable to retain her throne.

Special mention should be made of the empress's cordiality, noted by Pushkin. All the memoirists, especially foreign memoirists, are unanimous on this point. Catherine developed a definite style of dealing with people. The dissembling that had distinguished her from childhood had become unusually well developed during her seventeen years at Elizabeth's court, and in Empress Catherine it was transformed into something greater, into acting abilities of a high order. Her gift for play acting also greatly furthered the success of her political initiatives. The mask Catherine wore was pleasant to those around her, and to some extent was inseparable from her. But there is another side to the matter as well. During the years of her forced solitude, inactivity, and seclusion, Catherine had no opportunities to choose her associates, and evidently she never became accustomed to that. That is why, once she became empress, Catherine diligently sought people with whom she could converse and readily entered into correspondence with foreign luminaries—preferring foreigners because her immediate associates included few good conversationalists, and even these were her subjects.

At first, evidently, the empress's somewhat untraditional behavior frightened the courtiers, who, accustomed to kowtowing, were ready at any moment to be called "abject slaves." "Whenever I enter a room," Catherine wrote to Madame Geoffrin two years after her coronation, "you would think I was a Medusa's head. Everyone turns into statues and adopts a pompous air. I frequently scream like an eagle against this custom, but screaming will not stop them, and the angrier I get the less relaxed they are with me, so that I have to resort to other means."[25] Years later, Catherine had grown accustomed to this kind of treatment, and, rather than continue to fight it, she actually derived pleasure from it; the court approved the practice and began to appreciate the style of behavior described by A.S. Griboedov in Famusov's story about Maksim Petrovich.*

Any attempt to understand the psychological causes underlying Catherine's particular acts must confront the fact that every day and every hour, while dealing with a multitude of political issues, petty or important, she could not be guided solely by her own whims and her own notions of good and bad. A person who lives in society must constantly compromise. A ruler who wishes to conduct policy, in contrast, is constantly confronted by a choice: she can satisfy one person's interests only at another's expense; she constantly has to betray someone. Once a ruler becomes accustomed to betrayal, she ceases to value the lives of individual human beings, even whole peoples. Something along those lines happened to Catherine.

It was mentioned above that Catherine did not have an imaginative or original mind. At the same time, however, hers was a clear mind that responded quickly to a changing situation. Reading books freed Catherine from many prejudices of her time. While easily rejecting proclaimed principles when dealing with global problems, she readily applied them in cases where this did not impinge upon influential interests. Quite instructive are her resolutions on numerous reports submitted to her, resolutions that constitute an outstanding and barely known source.

Many of her resolutions are distinguished by their accurate formulation, their precision of thought, and sometimes their wit. A Tatar mullah named Murat proclaimed himself a new prophet and wrote a work in which he argued for the establishment of a new world religion with its own appropriate church apparatus, with himself as the head, above all emperors. Murat began to preach his ideas, but this displeased the other mullahs, who denounced him to the authorities. After an investigation, it was expected that Murat and the people he had managed to recruit would be severely punished according to the spirit of the times. The case was submitted to Catherine. This is her decision:

> Order that the new Tatar prophet and his confederates, who are being held in irons in Orenburg, be brought hither, and as they depart from

---

*A reference to playwrite Alexander Griboedov's masterpiece completed in 1824, *Gore ot uma* (The Misfortune of Being Clever, which subjects Russian society to strong criticism.)—D.J.R.

their Tatar dwellings, order that they be unchained, for I see no evil in them but much foolishness, which he has derived from the various fanatical sects of the various prophets. Hence he is guilty of nothing more than that he was born with a feverish imagination, for which no one deserves punishment, for no one creates himself.[26]

Powerful, willful women of strong character who think clearly are often said to have a masculine mind. There is no doubt that Catherine did possess that kind of "masculine mind," but she nonetheless remained a woman, with all the traits characteristic of the "weaker sex." Recounting how the empress, wishing to take a new lover, rid herself of the preceding one, S.B. Rassadin remarks: "The woman in her overpowered the politician."[27] The trouble, however, is that this happened quite often. Catherine sincerely loved her chosen ones, and, although she never turned the reins of state administration over to them,[28] she did, of course, fall under their influence and was bound to carry out their whims. No favorite could be assured of the duration of his "case," but, as long as he lasted, Catherine was a loving, and consequently a dependent, woman. She did not act as commander or autocrat in relation to her lovers. Here is a characteristic scene, as described by F.V. Sekretarev, who as a young boy lived in G.A. Potemkin's home: "The prince and the empress constantly had tiffs. I happened to witness . . . the prince yell in rage at the bitterly weeping empress, jump up from his seat, then quickly, violently walk to the door, open it angrily, and slam it so hard that the windowpanes rattled and the furniture shook."[29] Several memoirists testified to the empress's unfeigned, profound grief in response to the death of another favorite, A.D. Lanskoi, thirty years her junior, toward whom she evidently felt, in part, maternal. Her "masculine mind" and "feminine weaknesses," of course, left their stamp on politics.

The young Pushkin saw in Catherine a generous, affable "Tartuffe in a skirt and crown," knowledgeable about human weaknesses. But he presented her quite differently in *The Captain's Daughter*, written twelve years later. There he romanticized her image in a style typical of the first half of the nineteenth century—making her the wise, compassionate, kindly "Mother Empress." But since the romanticized Pugachev in the story was not portrayed in the traditional way, Pushkin, if he had wished, could have depicted Catherine, too, in an untraditional manner. With maturity Pushkin's judgments apparently became less categorical and unequivocal. The equivocal nature of Catherine's personality, "which so oddly combined the vices and virtues of her time,"[30] is evident in all the above.

"Politics, like chemistry, has its own retorts," Catherine wrote to Madame Geoffrin on 15 January 1766. "Inventions are easy, discoveries are difficult. In the former case, you try things out, add whatever comes to hand; it is quite different in the latter case. In order to reach them it is essential that their subject actually exist."[31] There is a sense of bitterness in these words; Catherine has reigned for three and a half years, time enough to know disappointment.

Authors who have written about the first years of Catherine's reign generally speak of her lack of confidence and her dependence on those to whom she owed her crown. Nevertheless, as one analyzes the empress's actions, one can easily see that she artfully resisted every kind of pressure and almost always managed to get her own way. Catherine was in fact obliged to N.I. Panin, K.G. Razumovskii, A.G. Orlov, and others, and probably, among other considerations, she felt gratitude toward them—a consideration that did not permit her to push them crudely aside, even if they interfered with her.[32] After the coup, however, Catherine had much more confidence than before. Earlier, after all, she had been dealing with just a few conspirators; now she was assured of broader support, and, most important, the possibility of relying on the Guards—that is, military force. She did indeed depend on the Guards, because, as she wrote to S. Poniatowski, "the least of the Guards, when looking at me, says to himself: 'My hands did that.'"[33] It was the Guards for whom she had to perform; it was the Guards she had to accommodate. But the Guards promoted no particular political program; they viewed their work with reverence, and it was necessary only to prevent any ill-considered act that might anger them.

The first period of Catherine's reign—before the peasant war under E.I. Pugachev's leadership [1773–75]—was a time of active reform efforts on her part. Throughout the thirty-four years of her reign she promulgated an average of twelve legislative acts per month, considerably fewer than were enacted during the reigns of her son and her grandson,[34] but these figures are hardly comparable, for Paul's reign was much shorter. Moreover, the intensity of Catherine's lawmaking varied at different stages. The peak was actually reached during the first five years (1762–67), when on average, twenty-two decrees were issued per month. They began to decline after that, and until the early 1780s, on average, thirteen decrees were issued per month. Another increase came in the early 1780s (nineteen decrees per month between 1781 and 1786), followed by another decline, and the 1790s produced only eight decrees per month.

Catherine repeatedly asserted she was continuing Peter I's work. She dreamed of being Peter's equal, and evidently considered herself such. It must be acknowledged, moreover, that although the magnitude, and, most important, the results of her activity bear no comparison with Peter's deeds, which literally changed the face of Russia, she did, nevertheless, continue the course of action he had launched both in domestic and in foreign policy. Which tasks did the empress set herself, and which principles guided her? "If a statesman makes a mistake," Catherine wrote, "if he makes a bad judgment or takes erroneous steps, the whole nation suffers its destructive effects."[35] She proclaimed the people's well-being as her main goal: "I have no concerns other than the greatest well-being and glory of the fatherland, and I desire nothing more than the prosperity of my subjects, of whatever rank."[36] But what did Catherine mean by prosperity? And who were her people, her subjects? Primarily they were the people around her, those who made up her retinue. However, they were divided by their aspirations, constantly advancing various projects that conflicted with one another and that by no means always coincided with the empress's views. Catherine frequently hesitated, and in order not to make a mistake gave her subjects freedom to choose what was best. This was why several commissions were established in the first two years of her reign—one on noble rights, one on commerce, one on the military, one on spiritual matters, and so on. At the same time, Catherine herself gradually became familiar with the state of the country. She once said that her predecessor, having become empress, "saw that the Empire's interests were different from those that Princess Elizabeth had held for a short time."[37] Something like that evidently happened to Catherine too. It was one thing to be indignant over the lazy Elizabeth and the greedy Shuvalovs; it was quite another to handle state problems herself.

In particular, Catherine became convinced that the existing system of administration was ineffective. The governing Senate, created by Peter I as the state administrative body capable, if necessary, of replacing the sovereign, had long since become a purely bureaucratic institution, which took months to deal with the most trivial problem. Local authorities never implemented the Senate's decrees, and the senators themselves often did not know how many or which cities were in the empire. (When she discovered this during a Senate session, Catherine sent five rubles to an academic shop for an atlas.)

Such conditions in the Senate could hardly fail to affect the activities of all offices subordinate to it. Catherine faced two alternatives: either to try breathing new life into Peter's brainchild or to replace it with a different institution, retaining the Senate as merely the supreme judicial authority.

N.I. Panin urged her to take the second route. Catherine appreciated and respected Panin as "the most clever, thoughtful, and zealous person" at the court,[38] but his intentions were at cross purposes to hers. Panin proposed that "an imperial council" be instituted. There was nothing new about the idea itself; similar bodies called by various names had existed under all of Catherine's predecessors since Peter I. But Panin dreamed of conferring considerably broader functions on the council, thus essentially limiting the autocracy. Catherine wavered. She did not want to share power with anybody, but evidently, at first she was unsure of the forces behind Panin. Just as Anna Ivanovna had once signed "conditions" [for ascending the throne], Catherine signed the decree and then tore it up. In this way she nipped in the bud the attempt to impart a more liberal character to Russia's form of government. A sober assessment of the situation, however, reveals that Catherine did not reject the plan solely because it suited her to do so, but also because Panin was isolated. Society was not yet mature enough for ideas of that sort, and the nobility was much more fearful of oligarchy than of a tsar's unlimited or even despotic power. Catherine chose the first route, and in 1763—again, in accordance with Panin's plan—the Senate was reformed. It was divided into six departments, each of which performed specific functions.

Catherine also faced financial problems. When she ascended the throne the treasury was empty, the army had not been paid for a long time, and Russia enjoyed no credit or trust abroad. One way to solve the problem was to secularize church lands, which she did in 1763–64. The Church was stripped of most of its earnings, and a system of "staffed" monasteries, with a set number of monks, was created; it was the culmination of the process started by Peter I to transform the Church into a part of the state apparatus. Having lost its financial independence and become, in effect, a branch of officialdom, the clergy as a class ceased to be a political force. Thus two problems were solved with one blow.

Another important event during the first years of Catherine's reign was the destruction of the hetman system in Ukraine. During the second half of the eighteenth century, several of the empire's provinces enjoyed a status distinct from those of central Russia. This situation derived from a medieval tradition by which special status was conferred upon newly conquered territories, for example Novgorod and Kazan in the fifteenth and sixteenth centuries. Catherine was not inclined to continue this tradition, however; regional autonomy did not match her view of the kind of state she governed. Moreover, "she took no account of the historical, national, or geographical characteristics of individual areas within the vast empire."[39] In a secret directive to A.A. Viazemskii in early 1764, Catherine wrote:

> Little Russia, Livland, and Finland are provinces ruled by the privileges confirmed to them; to violate the latter all at once would be quite indecent; however, to call them foreign countries and deal with them on such a basis is more than a mistake and can with confidence be called stupidity. These provinces, and Smolensk Province as well, must be treated gently so that they become Russianized and stop hunting like wolves in the woods.... Once there are no hetmans in Little Russia, it will be necessary to ensure that even the name hetman disappears forever.[40]

Several months later, Catherine visited the Baltic region, where she issued promises right and left to preserve intact the privileges of the local nobility. In the autumn of that year, she accepted the resignation of Hetman Razumovskii and appointed P.A. Rumiantsev as governor-general of Ukraine; thus the hetman system was ended forever, the heritage of the Cossack freemen was destroyed, and serfdom was extended to Ukraine.

From the very beginning of her reign, Catherine's actions were designed to create a powerful absolutist state—as she herself put it, one "fearsome in itself" and based on "a good and accurate police system."[41] A state of that sort, to Catherine's way of thinking, would ensure its subjects' prosperity. But in that case, why is there a hint of disappointment in her letter to Madame Geoffrin? More than twenty years later, in a letter to another of her foreign correspondents, Doctor I.G. Zimmerman, Catherine wrote: "My desire and my happiness would be to make everyone happy, but inasmuch as everyone wishes to be happy in accordance with his own character or understanding, my desires have often encountered obstacles of which I could understand nothing."[42] And so, the implementation of Catherine's projects was hampered by her subjects' ingratitude and lack of understanding. What were these projects? In the "fearsome" state she was carefully creating for her people's prosperity Catherine also intended to incorporate some of her teachers' and correspondents' ideas.

Nevertheless, she soon reached the same conclusion as her predecessors: the vices of the system of state administration were the vices
of legislation. In force in the country were a great many legislative
acts issued in the eighteenth century by all the tsars from Peter I
onward, as well as what we would today call legally binding acts. Many
of these contradicted one another, and all of them taken together
could not ensure the efficiency of the state apparatus, much less the
prosperity of its subjects. Yet the philosophes assigned the law a vital
role. Catherine knew that in an ideal state the alliance of the people
and the ruler would rest on the law, with which both sides would
comply. While promoting the prosperity of both the state and the
people, the law should also provide a guarantee against despotism—
that is, arbitrary rule by the sovereign. But how could such a system of
law be created?

Catherine was perfectly aware that the dignitaries whom she had
placed on various commissions were inadequate. For the most part,
they did not read French books, and, in their activities, they pursued
not only class (noble) interests but also narrowly estate-oriented (aristocratic) ones. Catherine probably saw this as the reason for the failure of past legislative commissions. Thus she decided upon a bold and
unusual step—that of convening the elected representatives of the
various estates, who would draw up a legal code that met the interests
of all the people. The idea evidently took shape as early as 1764–65,
and for more than two years Catherine was occupied in drawing up
guidelines for the deputies, later known as the Great Instruction.

The work's progress can be judged from Catherine's letters to
Madame Geoffrin. On 28 March 1765, for example, she wrote: "For
two months now I have been spending three hours every morning
working on the laws of my empire. . . . Our laws are no longer suitable
for us, but it is no less certain that just forty years ago [that is, after
Peter I's death—A.K.] they were made vague and given the meaning I
mentioned because of a badly understood craving for power." Three
months later:

> Sixty-four pages of the laws are now ready; the rest will be completed as
> soon as possible. I will send this manuscript to Mr. D'Alembert. I have
> said all I have to say in it, and I will not say another word about it the
> rest of my life. . . . I did not want any assistants in this matter, fearing
> that every assistant would go in a different direction; what is necessary
> here is to draw just one line and stick to it."

And again: "The manuscript is a profession of my common sense," while Montesquieu's work *The Spirit of Laws* should serve as "the prayer book of monarchs with common sense."[43]

The importance Catherine attached to her creation is clear from this; she sincerely hoped, by means of the Great Instruction, to offer "Russia's inhabitants the happiest, most peaceful, most beneficial situation they could have."[44] The Legislative Commission was to establish the law, and Catherine to remain in the people's memory as the kind of lawgiver depicted in D.G. Levitskii's well-known portrait. This reflected her political naiveté and inexperience, remnants of which persisted during the first years of her reign.

It is unnecessary here to analyze the Great Instruction,[45] but it is clear, considering Catherine's intentions and the basis on which she created it, that even edited drastically by her retainers it sounded unfamiliar to the Russian ear. Catherine's political naiveté was rooted in a specific type of soil: she had very vague notions about the country and the people she led. This situation was not improved by her trips from St. Petersburg to Moscow nor by the travels in the Baltic region and along the Volga that she undertook in 1767. Catherine saw only what people showed her and what she wanted to see: "The people all along the Volga here are rich and well-fed. . . . I do not know of anything they might need."[46] It did not disturb her that during this trip more than six hundred petitions were submitted to her, chiefly from landowners' peasants. The Legislative Commission was forthcoming, and it would resolve all misunderstandings.

Sessions of the commission, to which 570 deputies had been elected from all estates except the clergy and the serfs, commenced in July 1767 and continued for almost one and a half years. The commission's activity resulted only in revealing, with the utmost clarity, the aspirations of the various social groups and the conflicts among them over almost every issue discussed. The commission's debates reflected, as in a mirror, both the degree of self-awareness of the individual estates and the overall state of public consciousness, primarily still feudal in character. The ideas of the New Era so dear to Catherine's heart had as yet barely penetrated that consciousness. This was most obvious in attitudes toward serfdom.

The empress's confidence that the peasants were living well and in need of nothing was combined, in this worshiper of Voltaire and Montesquieu, with the conviction that slavery in and of itself was an evil that had to be eradicated. Nothing about this could be said directly in the Great Instruction, but even that which appeared in the edited text sounded "revolutionary." In commenting on Catherine

II's attitude toward serfdom, Soviet historians assert almost unanimously that she had no thought of abolishing the institution and that her declarations were intended only to pull the wool over the eyes of gullible foreigners. If that had been her only purpose, Catherine would hardly have undertaken such an enormous enterprise as the convening of the Legislative Commission; she must have understood that the failure of this undertaking would not enhance her authority. Let us keep in mind, however, that for all her naiveté Catherine was a realist in politics, and she knew that a reform of that magnitude was possible only with the support of a particular social force. She obviously counted on finding that support in the Legislative Commission.

As autocrat, she sought support primarily among the nobility, but this revealed itself to be a reactionary force on the Legislative Commission, one ready to defend serfdom by any means. Nor did Catherine find sympathy among the town representatives, who dreamed of purchasing serfs for their factories. It is instructive to note that Prince Shcherbatov, the brilliant advocate of retaining serfdom, was not treated indulgently by the empress and was not among those closest to her. (Wounded self-esteem shows through quite clearly in Shcherbatov's famous essay "On the Corruption of Morals in Russia.") Many years later, writing the following lines, Catherine was full of bitterness—an emotion the sincerity of which one need hardly doubt:

> You barely dare to say that they are people, the same as we are, and even when I say that myself I risk having stones thrown at me. Oh, what I had to go through because of this unreasonable and cruel society, when the Legislative Commission began to discuss certain aspects of this subject and when ignorant noblemen, whose numbers were immeasurably greater than I could ever have imagined, because I had too high an opinion of those with whom I associated every day, began to conjecture that these matters might result in some improvement of the state of the tillers of the soil. . . . I think there were not even twenty persons who thought about this matter humanely, like human beings.[47]

If Catherine had attempted to act decisively to moderate serfdom, she would have been swept away by an enraged nobility, as all the disputes and conflicts between the rank-and-file nobles and the aristocracy were immediately forgotten. Attacking serfdom would have meant losing her crown, and Catherine had no interest in suffering Peter III's fate. It is hardly reasonable, then, to blame her for not fulfilling a promise that was not in her power. But it would also be a mistake to assume that the empress's opinions, albeit formed under the influence of the Enlightenment, were the same as the views of those who stormed the Bastille for the sake of their ideas. Though she might consider the peasants "the same kind of people as we," Catherine denied the people any possibility of a spiritual life, much less any participation in political life. One of her letters to D. Diderot eloquently reflects this attitude:

> The bread that feeds the people and the religion that consoles them— these are the extent of their ideas. They will always be as ordinary as their [the people's] nature; the flowering of the state, the passing centuries, the coming generations are all words that cannot concern them. . . . Of all the vast space that we call the future the people never see more than the coming day; by their destitution they are deprived of the opportunity to extend their interests into the future.[48]

In late 1768, taking advantage of the start of the Russo-Turkish War [1768–74], Catherine dismissed the Legislative Commission. It was not, as is sometimes asserted, that she was afraid of the excessively liberal speeches of certain deputies; rather, it was that she was convinced of the fruitlessness of her undertaking: the commission was incapable of drawing up a law code. One lesson had been learned, however: "The Legislative Commission, once assembled, brought me light and information from all over the Empire, with whom we are dealing and against whom we must guard ourselves."[49] The commission's protocols, indeed, were much more instructive than trips around the country.

The boundary of the next stage in Catherine II's reign[50] was the peasant war under Pugachev's leadership (1773–75), a central event that undoubtedly marked a turning point. The empress was frightened. She was faced by a genuine threat, compared with which, for example, V.Ia. Mirovich's conspiracy in 1764* looked like child's play. She could save herself only by repressive military means, and the magnitude of the movement defined the character of the repressions. It could no longer be a question of liberalism. It should be noted that Catherine had always dealt unmercifully with personal enemies. She had done so with P. Khrushchev and S. Gurev, who were virtually innocent, and with Mirovich, although the people had expected him

---

*That year a young officer named Vasilii Mirovich made an ill-fated attempt to free Ivan VI from his confinement, during which Ivan was killed. Catherine had Mirovich executed for his role in the attempted coup.—D.J.R.

to be pardoned; she treated Pugachev and his comrades-in-arms the same way. There is no doubt that Catherine saw them as personal enemies who had dared to encroach on her power. Pugachev, moreover, had the effrontery to pose as her dead husband.

For Catherine, despite the cynicism she had acquired over the years, Peter III's death remained a perpetual reproach. She knew, of course, that her participation in the murder of Peter III, and later Ivan VI, was apparent to all those around her, and that consequently the invisible brand of the murderess lay upon her. But she did not see herself that way at all. Although it was true that she had not actually ordered either murder, her henchmen knew how to act in her interests, and so the guilt lay with her as well. Now Peter had come back to life and was waging war against her. One may speculate that, especially in the early stages of the Pugachev uprising, the empress felt an animal fear and a mystical horror, for she was, after all, a child of her times. She had not witnessed Peter's actual death, nor had she attended his funeral. Thence came her mercilessness and cruelty in putting down the uprising. In such cases, incidentally, monarchs never hesitate.

Catherine's reign, properly speaking, began at this point, after she sent A. Viazemskii to the Urals, where the mining and metallurgy workers were creating disturbances. Having settled accounts with them by means of cannon fire, the empress began to sort out the reasons for the troubles and undertook a number of steps that, in her opinion, ought to forestall similar excesses in the future.[51] An investigation into the Pugachev affair was also launched, but it proceeded in a way that clearly indicates that Catherine did not understand what had happened. Her conviction that her subjects had no cause for complaint prevented her from seeing that more was involved than the machinations of noble conspirators, dissenters, or outside adversaries: this was a popular movement, the largest in eighteenth-century Russia.[52] One lesson, however, she learned very well: she could rely completely only on the nobility. Her recognition of this fact made the next twenty years the "Golden Age" of the Russian nobility.

This became evident as early as 1775, with the publication of *The Provincial Reform*, one of the most important legislative acts of the era: its fundamental provisions remained in force until the second half of the nineteenth century, and in some cases until the October Revolution. Many investigators, following V.O. Kliuchevskii, claim that to a considerable extent this act owed its existence to the peasant war, which demonstrated the inability of the local organs of administration either to prevent the uprising or to fight it. The problem of local administration was long-standing. The system of local institutions, set in place by Peter I, had been subject to repeated changes by those who succeeded him, making it the most vulnerable spot in the state apparatus. The reform, consisting of 28 chapters and 412 articles, was developed with the empress's direct participation, and, in Kliuchevskii's opinion, "represents the first attempt Catherine ever made to apply her political theories to the existing state structure."[53] By "political theories" the noted historian meant the ideas of the Enlightenment. Enlightenment ideals were reflected primarily in the introduction of an improved administrative-territorial division with a precise system of local institutions and in the effort to separate administrative and judicial functions. Peter I had made a similar but less successful attempt. Catherine was more consistent. The new judicial bodies, however, were established in accordance with the estate principle, which, while fully consistent with noble aspirations as expressed by the Legislative Commission, conflicted with Enlightenment ideals. This reflected the change in Catherine II's political course after she had put down the peasant war. The nobility's demands to participate in local administration also received consideration.

The nobility's demands, however, were considerably broader. From Peter I's reign onward, there had been an ongoing consolidation of the ruling class, accompanied by legislative formalization of its rights and privileges. Peter I made the first contribution to the legal corpus concerning the nobility with his decree on primogeniture, the Table of Ranks, and certain other acts. Anna Ivanovna then abolished unogeniture while continuing to treat conditional and inherited estates as identical. Peter III took a major step with the Manifesto Freeing the Nobility. The final "little brick" was set in place by Catherine with the provincial reform, followed by the Charter to the Nobility of 1785. This last document praised the nobility in lavish terms, defined the nobleman, and offered a list of privileges that applied uniformly to the Russian nobility, the Baltic Knights, and the Polish and Ukrainian nobility. Among other things the document stipulated that nobles could not be sued by non-nobles nor subjected to corporal punishment, that they were "free and at liberty," that they could buy, own, and sell serfs, that they could establish factories, markets, and fairs, and so on. To put it briefly, the document demonstrated that it was the nobility that supported the throne and constituted the class that above all "must be tended."

Another important act was passed on the same day as the Charter to the Nobility—the Charter to the Towns. The towns represented the second political force that could no longer be ignored. While working on the Great Instruction, Catherine had once dreamed of creating a "third estate" in Russia, like that in France, and had made a solemn promise of it to Madame Geoffrin. The creation of a "third estate" would have meant offering broad opportunities to those engaged in trade and industry. It was hampered in Russia by the absence, given serfdom, of a free labor market. The noble deputies on the Legislative Commission demanded monopoly rights to serf ownership, while town deputies wanted to share this right. At the same time, the town dwellers considered trade and industry to be their own monopolies, while the nobility did not wish to give up their own share of the profits. This tangle of contradictions could be unraveled only by eliminating serfdom, something that was not in Catherine's power. The Charter to the Towns represented a partial attempt to solve the problem. The rights of the "middle segment of the people" were defined, and the title of members of the petite bourgeoisie, like that of the nobility, was declared hereditary. Unlike the nobility, however, the petite bourgeoisie was not exempted from personal taxes and various services. The upper crust in the towns, however, were offered certain benefits that objectively promoted the development of trade and industry.

The Charter also led to the creation of a new system of town administration and self-government, another problem that Peter I had struggled to resolve. Peter's attempt to give self-government to the towns according to the example of medieval European towns had been unsuccessful, and the rights of the town councils that were ultimately created were extremely limited. Although Catherine apparently expanded the powers of the organs of self-government, in fact these organs were hampered by rigid supervision from provincial bodies and the police. Indeed, it could not have been otherwise. In a state that was "fearsome in itself," any form of self-government was inevitably extremely narrow and strictly controlled by the state apparatus.

On the whole, Catherine's domestic policies were designed to reinforce the absolutist state with its elaborate state apparatus (and, consequently, its bureaucracy), including its apparatus of suppression. All of the projects relating to the implementation of the ideas of the Enlightenment proved to be unfeasible,[54] and the foundations of serfdom remained unshaken. In this sense, Catherine II did continue Peter I's cause: she fought against regional autonomy and the independence of the Church, while struggling to improve the system of state administration and formalize by law the rights and privileges of particular classes, thus essentially reinforcing the feudal system.

What did the reforms of Catherine's reign mean? Movement forward? Stagnation? Marking time? There was indeed some forward progress, but only within the framework of the feudal structure. Catherine's reforms were not radical, did not change the essence either of the political system or of social relations, and had not even the slightest effect on the actual position of any social group. The search for "bourgeois tendencies" in Catherine's political reforms is a waste of effort.

Catherine's economic policies look considerably more progressive, because there she was much more successful in enacting the achievements of Western European thought. Guided by the physiocrats, Catherine opposed any state intervention in trade (mercantilism). As an advocate of free industrial and trade activity, she battled trade monopolies and abolished tax farming. None of this, however, lay beyond the bounds of the existing system, and even when it conflicted with the interests of a particular segment of the nobility, it promoted the interests of the ruling class as a whole.

In that case, then, where was the progress? During Catherine II's reign Russian feudalism attained its highest level (as enlightened absolutism), one that finally exhausted its internal resources. In subsequent decades, with the apparent exception of the initial stages of Alexander I's reign, progress in the same direction—that is, within the framework of the feudal system—ceased, while crises increased, ending in the Crimean War catastrophe.

Despite the peasant war of 1773–75, which was a major social upheaval, Catherine's reign on the whole was a time of internal political stability. During Peter's administration, in addition to a vigorous foreign policy that imposed a colossal strain on the country's resources, the system of tax levies was changed, military reform was carried out, and St. Petersburg was constructed, causing constant turmoil in the country and preventing any segment of the population from being sure of its future. The decades that followed saw frequent changes in government (and, accordingly, changes in the course of domestic policy), a string of out-of-control and short-term favorites, and the lack of any specific program. In comparison with all this, Catherine's reign was "calm."

In the sphere of domestic reforms, Catherine bowed to circumstances and showed restraint, for which she compensated by the vigor of her foreign policy. The meaning and importance of

Catherine's foreign policy can be understood only by considering Russian society's ideas regarding foreign policy in the second half of the eighteenth century. As is well known, in the eighteenth century Russia forced her way to the Baltic, secured for herself the right to take part in European affairs on an equal footing, and became a full-fledged European power. The role Russia played in the world arena was fully consistent with the spirit of "Moscow the Third Rome," a theory that had secured an important place in public consciousness. Whereas in the sixteenth and seventeenth centuries Russians had understood this theory primarily in terms of their religious—that is, spiritual and ideological—heritage, in the eighteenth century the theory also came to be perceived in terms of political heritage. Russia should no longer be simply the focus or repository of the one true faith, but should also, by virtue of its political might and importance, be equated with the ancient Roman Empire. In complete accordance with this view, Peter I assumed the title of emperor and proclaimed Russia an empire.[55] Whereas Siberia's annexation had once been seen as the Orthodox Church's victory over the pagans, and Ukraine's annexation as the defense of brothers in the faith, after Peter the right to the political and spiritual heritage of the Byzantine emperors had to be defended in battle not with the Orthodox but with the [Western] Christian world, within which one sovereign bore the title of Holy Roman Emperor.

In the medieval consciousness (and public consciousness in eighteenth-century Russia was primarily medieval), the might of the state and the power of its ruler were demonstrated on the battlefield, and the annexation of conquered territories was viewed as the natural result of military victory. This was precisely how contemporaries perceived Peter I's victory in the Northern War and the annexation of the Baltic lands. The basis of the imperial consciousness lay in the conviction that Russia—the heir to Byzantium—had the right to administer the destinies of other peoples. Examples are the proposals made to Elizabeth to annex Prussia and the plan advocated by Platon Zubov, Catherine II's last lover, to create a Russian empire with St. Petersburg, Moscow, Berlin, Vienna, Constantinople, and Astrakhan as capital cities.

No particularly brilliant military or diplomatic successes were noted for several decades after Peter I's death. Catherine did not consider herself merely Peter's heir, but also wanted to be his equal. And whereas Peter assumed the title of emperor in 1721 and was called "Father of the Fatherland" and "the Great" after having accomplished his most important deeds, Catherine accepted similar titles ("Mother of the Fatherland" and "the Great") from her "grateful subjects" during the first years of her reign. Having become Peter's "equal," she felt unburdened even by the role of heir to the emperors of Byzantium. Incidentally, the religious aspect of the matter concerned her least of all: naturally, she felt no inborn hatred either toward the "Latins" (Roman Catholics) or toward Luther's followers. Moreover, she perceived Europe as something whole, as a "Christian republic" united by a single faith.[56] As the years passed, however, the German Catherine became a Russian patriot who thought that the Russian people were God's elect and believed in Russia's special historical mission.[57] Her subjects' prosperity, as she understood it, would be incomplete unless their elect status was realized in the foreign policy arena. The most immediate goal was that of reuniting all the lands of the Eastern Slavs that had at one time been part of Kievan Rus. This sentiment was fully shared by those around the empress, who were considerably more united in matters of this sort.

In the sphere of foreign policy, Catherine took a strong position from the beginning, treating foreign diplomats in a proud and arrogant manner which also served to enhance her popularity among her subjects. She took firm control of foreign policy from the first days of her reign and did not let go of it until the day she died. The empress paid close attention to the advice of those whose advice she considered worthy, but she herself had the final say.

In 1762 Stanislaw Poniatowski was elected to the Polish throne through her efforts, and in 1763 a treaty was signed with Poland in which Russia pledged not to allow any changes in the structure of the Polish state—that is, Russia secured the right to intervene in Poland's domestic affairs. One answer to this was the formation by Polish patriots of the Confederation of Bar [a Ukrainian town—Trans.], with which France and Austria sided. To neutralize Russia these states goaded it into a war with Turkey. The war was successful for Russia and ended in 1774 with the Treaty of Kuchuk-Kainardji, by which Russia was given Azov and Kerch, while the Crimea was declared independent. Although Russia's acquisitions were small considering its victories, they were supplemented in 1773 by its participation, together with Prussia and Austria, in the first partition of the Polish commonwealth. In 1783 Potemkin conquered the Crimea, and in 1787 a new war with Turkey began, ending in 1791 with the Treaty of Jassy. Russia was ceded the northern Black Sea littoral and Ochakov. A second partition of Poland occurred two years later, making it, finally, a dependent state. This provoked an uprising in Poland, brutally suppressed by troops led by A.V. Suvorov. A third partition followed in 1795 that destroyed Polish statehood until 1918. As a result of the Polish partitions, all of the Eastern Slavic regions that had been part of it found themselves under Russian rule.

At first glance, Catherine's successes in foreign policy were dazzling. The southern steppes, which had represented a constant threat to Russia, became Novorossiia [New Russia], the Crimea joined the Russian Empire, and Russia became firmly established on the Black Sea. Poland, with possessions that had extended to the Dnieper River at the beginning of Catherine's reign, ceased to exist. Russia annexed western Ukraine, Belorussia, Lithuania, and Courland. In fact, however, the successes in the fight against Turkey proved to be incommensurate with the material and human losses, and the attempt to restore the Byzantine Empire was unsuccessful. As for Poland, the consequences of the "successes" of Catherine's policies toward this country can still be felt today.

Special mention should be made of the Eastern Slavic lands newly annexed to Russia. There is no doubt that the liberation of their peoples from national and religious oppression was a progressive phenomenon, but it must also be kept in mind that the social and political development of these territories was somewhat higher than that of Russia. In particular, several towns won by the Russian scepter lived under Magdeburg Law. The extension of the Russian serf system to these lands represented a step backward.

Yet another problem relating to Catherine's foreign policy was that of nationality. As a result of the Russian people's acquisition of the Volga region, the trans-Urals, and Siberia in the sixteenth and seventeenth centuries and the annexation of Ukraine and the Baltic region, Russia became a multinational state. Catherine's military victories considerably augmented the ethnic diversity of the empire and exacerbated the nationality problem. In addition, Catherine specially recruited foreigners to Russia, hoping with their help to settle the expanses of Novorossiia. Judging by the evidence, she was not concerned with the national affiliation of the colonists, but Germans were the most convenient.

It is appropriate at this point to cite two statements indicating that Catherine saw close relations with other peoples as yielding mutual benefits. "There will be no more danger," she wrote, "in allowing our young people to travel (it is often feared that they will run away) once their fatherland is made congenial to them. . . . To be sure, the state would not much suffer at any time from the loss of two or three empty-heads, but if our fatherland were to become what I would like to see it, we would have more recruits than deserters."[58] For foreigners, moreover, the empress thought, Russia would be "the touchstone of their worth":

> Anyone who succeeds in Russia may be assured of success anywhere in Europe.... Nowhere but in Russia are there such masters skilled in noticing the weaknesses, the laughable features, or the shortcomings of the foreigner; you can be assured that they will not allow him to get away with anything, because, naturally, every Russian, in his heart of hearts, does not like any foreigner.[59]

In being guided by this consideration, Catherine was comporting herself in a manner designed not to offend the national sentiments of the Russian people and to make it impossible to accuse her of favoring any nation.

The Jewish question first appeared in Russia during Catherine's reign. Strictly speaking, there was hardly any Jewish population in Russia before the partitions of Poland. According to Russian statesmen, however, the interests of trade demanded that Jewish merchants be permitted to enter the country, and during the first days of Catherine's reign the senators submitted the appropriate bill to the newly crowned empress. Catherine apparently had no prejudices concerning Jews, but, inasmuch as she was playing the role of champion of Orthodox Christianity at the time, she considered it inappropriate to approve the bill, even though she did not want to refuse the senators. As a result, the decision was postponed for an indefinite period. Documents testify that Jewish merchants did visit Russia in subsequent years and enjoyed Catherine's protection. After the first Polish partition, lands with substantial Jewish populations became part of the empire. At first, Catherine declared the full equality of all her subjects. Later, however, the Russian merchant class began to protest vigorously against competition from Jewish traders. As a result, the Pale of Settlement was established in 1791.*

All these, one may say, constitute the political consequences of Catherine's foreign policies. In terms of their moral aspect, it is obvious that these policies can be defined only as expansionist. No account was taken either of the "natural justice" mentioned in the

---

*Urban areas located in western Russia to which the country's Jewish population was confined.—D.J.R.

rescript of 1770, cited above, nor of the fate and interests of other peoples. The role tsardom played in the destruction of the Polish state[60] constitutes a shameful blot on its history. Catherine's expansionism can hardly be justified in this case by the "noble" motive of uniting the lands of the Eastern Slavs. To equate, as she did, Kievan Rus and the Russian Empire of the second half of the eighteenth century is ahistorical, to say the least. The picture would be incomplete, however, if this review of Catherine's foreign policy failed to mention that hers was an age of military victories and achievements, the time of P. Rumiantsev, A. Suvorov, and E. Ushakov. Successes in foreign policy and remarkable victories on land and sea played an important role in the development of Russian national consciousness. It is worth noting, however, that the most powerful impetus in this regard was provided not by these victories but by the Patriotic War of 1812, which involved not the conquest of someone else's lands but the defense of our own.

When discussing Catherine II, mention must be made of her attitudes toward science and the arts. This concerns not merely a basic trait of the empress's personality, without which she cannot be either understood or evaluated, but a factor of fundamental importance to the development of Russian culture in the second half of the eighteenth century.

Catherine took great pains to ensure that her reign would be remembered as a time of enlightened absolutism. She was "an enlightened" monarch, and it is hardly fair to attempt, as some authors have done, to disparage her education and her enthusiasm for "intellectual" pursuits. It can be stated with confidence that she stands out among the Russian tsars (both before and after her) in terms of the breadth of her intellectual interests and inquiries. Not only was Catherine an attentive and sometimes enthusiastic reader, but she herself tried her hand at science and literature. Though she was sometimes carried away by a person, an idea, a book, or a scientific discipline, she always knew that her main task was to rule; hence she never turned any intellectual pursuit into a profession. She was a dilettante both in literature and in the sciences.

Her historical essays, if not brilliantly distinguished by their discoveries or depth of thought, constitute a respectable compilation and are not inferior in any way, for example, to the historical works of M.V. Lomonosov. Her comedies and journalistic works, though they may not bear the stamp of genius, are likewise written with wit and talent. To be sure, Catherine's creative endeavors also reflected her inherent vanity. No problem ever arose, of course, in regard to the publication of her works—which were, incidentally, published anonymously. Compared with modern times, nevertheless, this royal authoress was rather modest. Thus, five years passed after the publication of her play about Rurik before Catherine complained to A.I. Musin-Pushkin and I.N. Boltin about the work's lack of popularity among readers. Yet she could easily have advertised her works with fanfare and evoked positive critical response.

Another essential facet of Catherine's personality was her extraordinary industry. While she adored balls, shows, and all kinds of entertainments, she spent whole days reviewing current papers, reading books, and writing. Nor did she shun translation work. Being well educated and well read were highly valued at her court, a circumstance that could hardly fail to benefit Russian society. Catherine's era produced A.P. Sumarokov, Ia.B. Kniazhnin, D.I. Fonvizin, G.R. Derzhavin, N.I. Novikov, A.N. Radishchev, D.G. Levitskii, A.P. Losenko, F.S. Rokotov, V.L. Borovikovskii, D.S. Bortnianskii, F.I. Shubin, V.I. Bazhenov, M.M. Shcherbatov, I.N. Boltin, I.P. Elagin, A.T. Bolotov, and others. It was a time when Russian culture flourished, and the empress's attitude toward culture did much to promote that.

There is one other significant consideration: neither in science nor in literature did Catherine pretend to a monopoly. Quite the contrary: her interest in history, for example, fostered the development of historical science; she aided Novikov in the publication of documents, Shcherbatov in the writing of his *History*, and Müller in the publication of V.N. Tatishchev's works. The empress's enthusiasm for journalism had an important impact on the number of journals published in Russia, which increased by several times. Catherine did not hesitate to engage in polemics with her subjects in the pages of journals. To be sure, she did not consider Novikov or Fonvizin her equals, and she tolerated no lectures or reproaches from them, but the polemics themselves are noteworthy.

On the whole, Catherine's cultural policies were liberal until the late 1780s. That was probably one of the most serene periods in the history of Russian literature. Much progress was also made in education during those years: the openings of a school attached to the Academy of Art, the Smolnyi Institute, orphanages in Moscow and St. Petersburg, the Society for the Daughters of the Nobility in St. Petersburg, with a department for daughters of the petite bourgeoisie, and a commercial school. Schools were reformed, including military schools. Attempts were made to base curricula on the introduction of the latest achievements in European pedagogical thought. And although the educational system accommodated only a small part of the population, it represented an important step forward. The first Russian charitable institutions also appeared during Catherine's reign. The history of Russian charity, in fact, dates to that era.

From the late 1780s onward, the situation began to change. According to most historians, this resulted from the impression the bourgeois revolution in France had on Catherine. In fact, the revolution constituted a realization in deed of the ideas of which Catherine was so fond, one that allowed her to see how these ideas affected monarchs. In addition, the empress had grown old. She was sixty years old in the year of the French Revolution, which made her an old woman in eighteenth-century terms. In contrast to Elizabeth, Catherine did not become a recluse and did not cease to concern herself with affairs of state, but she was no longer in a mood for reforms or for playing at liberalism with the literati. She became more irritable and considerably less tolerant. During those years of stagnation, certain phenomena of Russian life to which she had formerly turned a blind eye—corruption, favoritism, obsequiousness, and serfdom—took on monstrous forms. "What luck it is for a man to die at the right time, if he cannot leave the scene in good time nor advance forward," A.I. Herzen exclaimed in his *My Past and Thoughts*.[61] Alas, Catherine was not so lucky. During the last years of her reign, when she no longer had either Panin or Potemkin by her side, the final two partitions of the Polish commonwealth, the fight against revolutionary France, and the persecution of Novikov and Radishchev took place. The latter affected more than the history of the eighteenth century, because these persecutions, to quote N.A. Berdiaev, "marked the beginning of the martyrology of the Russian intelligentsia."[62]

Novikov and Radishchev—the great enlightener and the first revolutionary—are familiar to all Russians from their school days. Novikov is known as a publisher and journalist who protested the injustices of serfdom. That he was an active figure in Russian freemasonry, which was why Catherine persecuted him, is hardly ever mentioned except in passing. Now, when affiliation with freemasonry is viewed by some as an activity hostile to Russia and her people, this affiliation seems especially ominous. Yet in the eighteenth and early nineteenth centuries, freemasonry was a religious and philosophical movement that played a definite role in the formation of Russian social thought. Let me quote Berdiaev, whom today's fighters against freemasonry are unlikely to accuse of antipatriotism: "The Russian cultural soul was formed in freemasonry, which provided ascetic discipline for the soul and formulated the moral ideal of the personality. . . . The cultural souls of Peter's era were formed in freemasonry and opposed obscurantism and the despotism of the authorities."[63]

It was for this opposition to despotism, the attempt to create an alternative ideology, that Catherine could not forgive Novikov.

Any discussion of Radishchev includes Catherine's characterization of him as "a rebel worse than Pugachev." Herein lies the key to unraveling the causes of the writer's persecution. It was not his criticism of serfdom nor his condemnation of slavery—which she herself disliked—that bothered Catherine. She saw in Radishchev's book an analogy to Pugachev's rebellion. Pugachev was a menace to her personally; he threatened her power. Radishchev dared to say that her subjects were living badly and the people not in fact prospering. Like Hans Andersen's little boy, he spoke the truth that no one else would say, although everyone knew it—everyone except Catherine. She was convinced that it was a lie. Her subjects could not be unhappy. Only a rebel would have such effrontery.[64]

Potemkin's death, the partitions of Poland, the destruction of Voltaire's works printed by I.G. Rakhmaninov, the aid given to reactionary French émigrés, and the arrests of Novikov and Radishchev are all events of Catherine's final years. She died in November 1796, in the sixty-eighth year of her life. Her antagonist Paul I ascended the Russian throne. As one contemporary put it, "it was as if the palace had been turned into a barracks."[65]

Under Catherine, certain tendencies in Russia's development that had emerged during Peter's time strengthened: centralization of authority, bureaucratization, strengthening of feudalism and serfdom, and foreign expansionism. All this had the objective effect of slowing the country's development and enhancing its sociopolitical and economic backwardness. The sharply pronounced pro-nobility character of Catherine II's social policies served to strengthen feudal exploitation in its most brutal forms. Nevertheless, Catherine's era was a period when Russian culture flourished, an important stage in shaping Russian national consciousness, and an age in which democratic and antifeudal elements combined with elements of an imperial identity.

It may seem surprising that in the conception of the history of feudal Russia developed in the 1930s and 1940s, which persists to this day in its fundamental postulates, kind words can be found to assess the activities of only two monarchs—Ivan the Terrible and Peter the Great. Catherine, on the other hand, who was also dubbed "the Great" by her contemporaries, is, with few exceptions, characterized mostly in abusive terms that scarcely differ from those heaped upon her by Prince M.M. Shcherbatov in his denunciatory essay "On the Corruption of Morals in Russia." The reason for this is expressed in Boris Pasternak's letter to O.M. Freidenberg dated 4 February 1941, in lines astonishing for the depth of their perception of what was happening: "Our benefactor [Stalin] holds that we have been too sentimental until now and that it is time to rethink. Peter I seems to be a parallel that is no longer appropriate. The new enthusiasm, openly confessed, is [Ivan] the Terrible, the *oprichnina* [terror under Ivan the Terrible], and brutality. These are now the themes of new operas, dramas, and screenplays. No kidding."[66] Catherine was much more "sentimental"—that is, more liberal—than not only Ivan the Terrible but Peter as well, and in addition she loved to discuss themes of civil liberties and humanism. There was also, obviously, a psychological factor. While he could measure himself for Peter's uniform and Ivan's coat, Stalin could not, of course, equate himself with a woman.

Also of some interest is the question of historical alternatives. Russia could have taken a different route in the eighteenth century, but by the time Catherine was crowned, evidently, the chance had slipped away. One cannot seriously entertain the idea that an alternative path would have been followed had Catherine been overthrown and replaced by the young Paul or Ivan VI. Certain events might have been otherwise, because different people would have taken the helm of state, but it is difficult to imagine fundamental differences, because the direction of development had been set in Peter's time. Nonetheless, the second half of the eighteenth century is rightly called the Catherinian Age. By the will of fate, a brilliant and extraordinary person who has left a noteworthy mark on Russian history ascended the Russian throne at that time.

Notes

1. Strictly speaking, only Soviet historians have not written about her; in the West a number of monographs have appeared in the last ten years.

2. *Zapiski imperatritsy Ekateriny Vtoroi* (*Zapiski*) (St. Petersburg, 1907), p. 7. This work is especially useful, a source that has not yet been properly appreciated. Excerpts cited from it here, as well as those from Catherine's letters, have been translated from the French and German. It must be noted, however, that the widespread notion that Catherine was unable

to express herself in Russian is a concoction of novelists. This legend is rebutted by numerous extant drafts of her papers. Catherine wrote quite fluently in Russian and fairly grammatically.

3. Quoted from V.A. Bil'basov, *Istoriia Ekateriny Vtoroi* (St. Petersburg, 1890), vol. 1, p. 12.

4. "Until I was fourteen or fifteen years old, I was convinced that I was ugly" (*Zapiski*, p. 12).

5. Ibid., pp. 44–45.

6. Ibid., pp. 58–59.

7. Ibid., pp. 74–75. Meanwhile, Catherine herself had become quite pretty by age eighteen.

8. Ibid., pp. 90–91.

9. Concerning which, see E.V. Anisimov, " 'Fenomen Pikulia' glazami istorika," *Znamia*, 1987, no. 11, p. 219.

10. "I was often very much bored by his visits, which lasted for several hours, and I got tired, because he never sat down and I had to pace back and forth with him in the room. It was difficult keeping up with him while maintaining a conversation about details in the military units, very trivial ones, about which he talked with pleasure.... Never have minds been less similar than ours; we had nothing in common in terms of taste" (*Zapiski*, p. 104).

11. Ibid., pp. 400–401.

12. Ibid., pp. 178–79.

13. Ibid., p. 72.

14. "Liubimtsy Ekateriny Vtoroi," *Russkii arkhiv*, 1911, no. 7, pp. 319–20.

15. I. Redkin, "Graf Dzhon Bekengkhemshir pri dvore Ekateriny II," *Russkaia starina*, 1902, no. 2, p. 442.

16. *Zapiski*, pp. 363–64. Many years later, when her grandson Alexander was born, Catherine took his upbringing into her own hands, and it was different. In a letter to Sweden's King Gustav III the empress said: "Immediately after he was born I took the child into my own hands, and after they bathed him I carried him into another room, where I placed him on a pillow and covered him lightly.... Special care was taken to see that he had clean, fresh air.... He lies on a leather mattress covered with a blanket; he does not have more than one pillow and a very light English coverlet.... Special care is taken that the temperature in his rooms does not exceed 14 to 15 degrees" (*Russkii arkhiv*, 1871, no. 1, cols. 1521–22).

17. See *Zapiski*, p. 92.

18. Ibid., p. 548.

19. Ibid., p. 505.

20. Bil'basov, *Istoriia*, vol. 1, p. 437.

21. E.V. Anisimov, *Rossiia v seredine XVIII veka* (Moscow, 1986), pp. 25–29.

22. Peter wore a ring on his finger with a portrait of Frederick II, and he sported a Prussian uniform decorated with the Prussian Order of the Black Eagle.

23. A.S. Pushkin, *Polnoe sobranie sochinenii* (Leningrad, 1978), vol. 8, p. 91.

24. See *Russkii arkhiv*, 1866, no. 1, cols. 657–58.

25. *Sbornik Russkogo istoricheskogo obshchestva* (Sb. RIO), vol. 1 (St. Petersburg, 1867), p. 258.

26. RGADA, f. 248, op. 113, d. 281, l. 40.

27. S.B. Rassadin, *Satiry smelyi vlastelin* (Moscow, 1985), p. 109. This author has made the most successful recent attempt to understand Catherine II.

28. One of the memoirists noted: "Her weaknesses were those associated with her sex, and, although some of her lovers did abuse her kindness, no appreciable damage

was done to the state." "Zapiski kniazia F.N. Golitsyna," *Russkii arkhiv*, 1874, bk. 1, cols. 1278–79.

29. Ibid., 1882, no. 1, p. 164.

30. Rassadin, *Satiry*, p. 73.

31. *Sb. RIO*, vol. 1, p. 280.

32. Catherine richly rewarded the participants in the coup: by a decree of 9 August, 40 persons received 18,000 peasants and 526,000 rubles (Bil′basov, *Istoriia* [London, 1895], vol. 2, p. 83). In eighteenth-century terms, there was nothing unusual in these actions.

33. *Zapiski*, p. 577.

34. N.Ia. Eidel′man, *Gran′ vekov* (Moscow, 1986), p. 61.

35. *Zapiski*, p. 647.

36. "Instruktsiia general-prokuroru A.A. Viazemskomu," in *Chteniia v Obshchestve istorii i drevnostei rossiiskikh* (ChOIDR), 1858, vol. 1, p. 101. The directive was secret, so Catherine had no need to dissemble in it.

37. *Zapiski*, p. 47.

38. Ibid., p. 575.

39. Ia. Zutis, *Ostzeiskii vopros v Rossii v XVIII v.* (Riga, 1946), p. 290.

40. Quoted in Bil′basov, *Istoriia*, vol. 2, p. 418.

41. *Zapiski*, p. 647.

42. Ibid., p. 610–11.

43. *Sb. RIO*, vol. 1, p. 268, 275–76, 283.

44. Ibid, p. 283.

45. An analysis of the mandate is to be found in numerous works by both prerevolutionary and Soviet-era historians. I am most in tune with N.M. Druzhinin's position (N.M. Druzhinin, "Prosveshchennyi absoliutizm v Rossii," in *Absoliutizm v Rossii* [Moscow, 1964]).

46. Quoted in V.A. Bil′basov, *Istoricheskie monografii* (St. Petersburg, 1901), vol. 3, p. 244.

47. *Zapiski*, p. 175.

48. *Russkii arkhiv*, 1880, bk. 3, p. 19.

49. *Zapiski*, p. 546.

50. Many important events were occurring in the country, to be sure, but a description of them would not add anything fundamentally new to the characterization of Catherine's personality.

51. Factory owners were forbidden to buy peasants for their factories, and later the major private enterprises were gradually transferred to state ownership. In the metallurgy industry, for example, a state monopoly in effect emerged, which soon had a destructive effect on the development of this sector of the economy.

52. See, for example, A.G. Orlov's letter dated 12 November 1774, in *Sb. RIO*, vol. 1, p. 104.

53. V.O. Kliuchevskii, *Kurs russkoi istorii*, pt. 5 (Moscow, 1937), p. 92.

54. Preserved among Catherine's papers is a plan prescribing that peasants be granted their freedom when estates were sold. She thought that in this way serfdom would end in one hundred years (*Zapiski*, pp. 626–27).

55. Concerning which, see Iu.M. Lotman and B.A. Uspenskii's interesting but controversial article "Otzvuki kontseptsii 'Moskva—tretii Rym' v ideologii Petra Pervogo," in *Khudozhestvennyi iazyk srednevekov′ia* (Moscow, 1982).

56. See the rescript dated 19 July 1770, in *Sb. RIO*, vol. 1, p. 41.

57. It is instructive to note, for example, that in her historical works Catherine argued for the Slavic origin of many European and American geographical names and customs, and, enthusiastic about the idea that a proto-language existed, she became involved in compiling a comparative dictionary of all languages on the basis of Russian.

58. *Zapiski*, pp. 639–40.

59. Ibid., pp. 376–77.

60. In fairness, it should be noted that Prussia, not Russia, initiated the partitions of Poland. Incidentally, the real history of the partitions remained a forbidden zone to Soviet historians for quite a long time. The elimination of this "blank spot" will serve to strengthen Soviet–Polish friendship.

61. A.I. Herzen, *Sobranie sochinenii*, 30 vols. (Moscow, 1964), vol. 8, p. 64.

62. N.A. Berdiaev, *Russkaia ideia* (Paris, 1971), p. 22.

63. Ibid., p. 21.

64. Evidently Paul perceived Radishchev's book the same way, because he allowed Radishchev to return from exile. He would hardly have done this if he had seen the book not as a personal attack against his mother, but as an attack against the autocracy in general.

65. *Zapiski kniazia F.N. Golitsyna*, col. 1306.

66. *Druzhba narodov*, 1988, no. 8, p. 252.

Emperor Paul I, 1796–1801

As we have seen, Peter the Great's decision to change the succession law by allowing the reigning monarch to select his or her successor contributed to the unstable system of succession to the throne that characterized eighteenth-century Russia. Perhaps because there was widespread speculation that Catherine would bypass her son Paul and pass on the crown to her grandson, Alexander, Emperor Paul I changed the law of succession by restoring a system of primogeniture in the male line. Be that as it may, this did not save Paul from conspiracy: he was murdered in a palace coup in early 1801.

Generations of historical writing indicate there was good reason to remove Paul, for his policies and personal tastes, particularly his penchant for undoing, changing, or attacking much of what Catherine stood for, alienated important strata of the ruling elite. And it was this elite that, in justifying regicide, colored later historical evaluations of Paul and his years in power. Neglecting Paul's brief reign, Soviet historians did not produce a single monograph devoted exclusively to the "Russian Hamlet." Outside Russia, several serious attempts to present a more balanced assessment of the emperor have appeared in recent years,[1] and it is in the context of this revival of writing about Paul that Iurii Alekseevich Sorokin's reappraisal needs to be placed.

After characterizing Paul as "intelligent" and his nature as "complex and contradictory," Sorokin provides a succinct discussion of how generations of Russian historians have viewed Emperor Paul. The author highlights the major influences in his formative years and early adulthood, focusing on the ambivalent relationship between Catherine and her son and on Paul's growing rift with Catherine. Recognized during a tour of Europe as Catherine's heir, Paul returned home with clear ideas in regard to how his country should be ruled. His various writings, in particular his so-called Instruction, argues Sorokin, represented "a concrete, well-developed program . . . for the develop-

177

*ment of Russia." Moreover, unlike many authors, Sorokin dismisses the no-
tion that there was a major turning point in Paul's life, arguing that there
was "merely a slow evolution of Paul's personality." Why did others see some
sort of rupture? "An emperor's qualities, habits, and characteristics are more
pronounced in his subjects' eyes than the qualities of a grand duke," the
author maintains.*

*Sorokin also rejects the reports of Paul's purported mental illness. On this
issue he is in agreement with historian Mikhail Pokrovskii who quipped that
Paul was no more unbalanced or jealous of his power than the other Romanov
tsars that succeeded Peter the Great. Paul fell because he violated tradition;
greed led to the conspiracy to remove him, not principles. "It was dissatisfaction with his policies that evoked dissatisfaction with his personality rather
than the reverse." To Paul's credit, he subordinated these policies to the needs
of the empire and centralization of the state apparatus (and to the strengthening of his own personal power). Paul's reign was not an aberration, but "a
logical stage in the development of Russian absolutism, one in which the
monarch implemented the only possible policy (from the standpoint of absolutist interest) using the appropriate methods."*

D.J.R.

Note

1. See Roderick E. McGrew, *Paul I of Russia, 1754–1801* (New York, 1992) and Hugh
Ragsdale, ed., *Paul I: A Reassessment of His Life and Reign* (Pittsburgh, 1979).

Paul I

Iurii Alekseevich Sorokin

General Ia.I. Sanglen, a man who had witnessed and endured much
in his life, wrote: "Paul will forever remain a psychological problem.
Despite his kind and sensitive heart, his elevated soul, his enlightened intellect, his passionate love of justice, and his knight-of-old
spirit, he was an object of horror to his subjects." The former chief of
the secret police under Alexander I turned out to be right. Paul I's
complex and contradictory nature has never been fully understood,
either by his contemporaries or by later generations of historians.

Those who were close to the emperor and intimately involved in his affairs, even though they did not sympathize with Paul, treated him more gently than those who observed him fleetingly, did not take part in major governmental work, and wrote about him on the basis of casual, superficial impressions or even second-hand reports. It is interesting to note that aristocrats spoke of him more kindly than did people from more modest noble families. All in all, the memoirists' assessments of Paul I proved to be very persistent and influenced more specialized studies.

Before the Revolution of 1917, the official historiography concerning Paul's reign underwent substantial changes: it began with favorable assessments, but by the late nineteenth century it evaluated the emperor more soberly and offered unequivocally negative characterizations (N.K. Shilder). During the first Russian Revolution [of 1905], however, it once again became apologetic (E.S. Shumigorskii).[1] Bourgeois historiography, which began by affirming Paul's madness and assessing him nihilistically (V.O. Kliuchevskii), subsequently characterized him more and more harshly, especially during the first Russian Revolution.[2] But World War I and the revolutionary crisis radically altered these assessments. Liberal historian M.V. Klochkov's book reiterated the conservative official version: Paul, a man of great intelligence, of fiery temperament, and of high and rationally founded principles, deserved to be counted among the host of Russian saints.[3]

Conversely, Soviet historiography never evidenced particular interest in Paul's reign or personality. Soviet historians, on the whole, went beyond prerevolutionary historians in evaluating his domestic and foreign policies, but in evaluating his personality they never rose above M.N. Pokrovskii, who wrote before the revolution.[4] The works of S.B. Okun and N.Ia. Eidelman were the exceptions that proved the rule.[5] In and of themselves, the conclusions these scholars produced were not new, having already appeared in the literature (if one includes the overall assessment of Paul's personality), but Paul was not their main topic. They were more interested in clarifying features of Russia's sociopolitical development from the late eighteenth to the early nineteenth centuries. As a result, Soviet historians have yet to produce a single monograph on Paul's reign.

The parents of the future monarch, Crown Prince and Grand Duke Petr Fedorovich and Grand Duchess Ekaterina Alekseevna (later Emperor Peter III and Empress Catherine II) remained childless for more than nine years. The birth of an heir was impatiently awaited by his grandaunt, Elizabeth I (1741–62). The boy's birth secured Peter

I's line of succession and gave a certain stability to the ruling dynasty. Grand Duke Peter took his heir's birth indifferently, spending only a few minutes of the day, 20 September 1754, alone with his wife, all the while making advances to her lady-in-waiting E.V. Vorontsova. The birth of Grand Duke Pavel Petrovich (Paul) was celebrated lavishly with court balls and masquerades, fireworks, and spectacles. The empress bestowed 100,000 rubles on Catherine for giving birth to a son. The celebrations continued for about a year.

To be sure, rumors circulated that Grand Duke Peter could not have children because of his chronic alcoholism and that Empress Elizabeth, who wanted an heir, closed her eyes to Catherine's intimacy first with Choglokov and then with S.V. Saltykov, the chamberlain of the grand duke's court. Several historians treat Saltykov's paternity as an indisputable fact. Some later asserted, in fact, that Paul was not even Catherine's son. In *Materials for a Biography of the Emperor Paul I* (Leipzig, 1874) it is alleged that Saltykov's child was born dead and that a Finnish baby was substituted for him—in other words, Pavel Petrovich was not only not his parents' child but not even Russian. By this it was insinuated that no Russian could ever possess such a character, conduct such policies, or apply such methods as the future emperor. Consequently, the Romanov dynastic succession was compromised, and Emperor Alexander II, like his father and grandfather, had no right to the Russian throne.

The young grand duke was completely separated from his parents and brought up in the old-fashioned way—that is, he was turned over to a whole staff of nannies who were totally ignorant of how to care for a child. These same women scratched the empress's heels during the night, entertained her with frightening stories about ghosts and goblins, and silently endured her slaps in the face. It was small wonder that Paul almost died of thrush on the second day of his life. At times they dropped him from his cradle onto the floor; later they frightened him so much with old wives' tales that he hid under the table whenever he heard a door slam. When Paul was four, he began to learn arithmetic and Russian grammar, but his proper education and training started only in the summer of 1760, when Count N.I. Panin, one of the most important Russian statesmen in the second half of the eighteenth century, was assigned as his chief tutor. Well-known European scholars were also invited to serve as teachers to the heir to the throne. Catherine even negotiated with D'Alembert, but he refused the appointment.

One of the most important sources concerning Paul's upbringing is the memoirs of his tutor S.A. Poroshin. With enviable meticulousness, he recorded in his diary everything relating to the crown prince. Paul was taught the Scriptures, Russian, French, German, history, geography, and physics. Particular attention was paid to French literature, and he was made to read Corneille, Voltaire, Rousseau, and others. Paul attended palace spectacles at which French comedies and ballets were performed. The grand duke's instruction was not neglected, but it was unsystematic. He might acquire profound knowledge in one subject and quite superficial knowledge in another—it all depended on the teacher. Overall, however, his upbringing had a "French" character, with all the merits and shortcomings thereof. Paul learned easily, manifested keen intelligence and seriousness, but, of course, was not above skipping his lessons or pleading illness. In order to encourage him, a manuscript newspaper was published at court, and Paul received assurances that it was being distributed all over Russia.

The crown prince achieved his greatest success in the Scriptures. His religious teacher, Father Platon, made Paul write compositions on particular themes. One can only be astonished at the intelligence and knowledge of the ten-year-old child who wrote, for example:

> It is true that access to the sciences is somewhat difficult and unenticing. But the patience and diligence that are employed in overcoming the initial difficulties are soon rewarded with unimagined pleasure and evident benefit. I know this from my own efforts. I must confess that at the beginning of my studies there was a certain amount of boredom for me, but by following kindly advice I overcame it and can now see that it was as nothing compared to the satisfaction that followed it.[6]

Poroshin noted and described certain personal qualities of Paul's that were to develop later. While remarking on the grand duke's exceptional intelligence and abilities, Poroshin complained that "he simply will not apply himself and meanwhile thinks about the pettiest trifles." Paul invariably insisted on his own way, even when his desires were quite "unreasonable." The diary entries attest to the crown prince's extraordinarily well-developed imagination: he dreamed of commanding a detachment of noblemen and performing great feats, then of rising from corporal to captain. "He has fun at such times, incessantly bobbing up and down and flinging his hands backward in that way he has." Paul was always in a hurry, and if dinner or bedtime were even a few minutes late, it brought him to tears. He did not lie in bed in the morning. Incidentally, according to Poroshin, the grand duke was fully aware of his own shortcomings (prankishness, impatience, and inconstancy) and sincerely tried to correct them. All later authors commented on these qualities.

From infancy Paul was brought up to be a future ruler: he granted audiences to foreign ambassadors, and major dignitaries of Elizabeth's time dined at his table so that he might listen to their conversations and master the difficult skills required of a tsar. Panin had been given strict orders "not to allow Paul to acquire a taste for petty details but to try to get him used to general affairs."[7] Only very rarely, on holidays, was the boy permitted to play with children his own age. He was most friendly with A. Kurakin (Panin's nephew) and A. Razumovskii.

Catherine reported that in the last year of her life Empress Elizabeth seriously considered transferring the throne to her grand-nephew rather than her nephew. Catherine herself nurtured ambitious dreams of becoming empress and tried to ensure that the crown went to her husband rather than her son lest the throne be lost to her forever. Elizabeth died after securing Peter III's promise to love his son. After he became emperor, however, Peter refused to acknowledge Paul as his heir for a long time; in any case, Paul is not mentioned in the manifesto marking Peter III's accession to the throne, and only through a church ceremony did he receive the title of crown prince.

The consensus of opinion is that Panin played a key role in Peter III's overthrow. But he wished his pupil to become tsar and Paul's mother to serve as regent until Paul came of age. Catherine was not altogether displeased with this program, but she wanted more, and for this reason felt reserve toward Panin's plans. On the night of the coup, 27 June 1762, Panin and the seven-year-old Paul were escorted to the Winter Palace by soldiers, and early in the morning of the following day, in Kazan Cathedral, he swore an oath of fealty to the new empress and was again declared the heir. These events proved to be his first great shock, and he began to suffer severe seizures. The doctors even feared for his life.

Having been raised apart from his mother, among adults who were "men of officialdom"—indeed, Paul saw his mother primarily as the empress—he always approached her ceremoniously, accompanied by his mentor. Catherine was cold to her son, chiefly because those who opposed her rule rallied round him. (The assertion that the throne by rights belonged to Paul was surely not without foundation.) There was very little change, however, in the crown prince's daily life. Meanwhile, he turned fourteen; according to Panin's program, Paul was to begin instruction in the "direct science of the state"—politics. Senator G. Teplov was assigned to teach this science, but he inspired a ghastly boredom in the young man. Strictly speaking, Teplov's instruction amounted to reviewing papers brought in from the Senate. Consequently, Paul turned his interest to military matters, trying to learn all their details and subtleties, which very much frustrated both Poroshin and Panin. Nonetheless, the latter invited his brother, General P.I. Panin, to teach the crown prince the arts of war and, under the general's supervision, Paul received a thorough military training.

Paul turned eighteen on 20 September 1772 and thus came of age. The diplomatic corps—and certain Russian dignitaries as well (in particular, N.I. Panin)—expected that the crown prince would at least share the "burden of power" with his mother. But Catherine II allowed her son only the post of Fleet Admiral of the Russian navy and colonel of the Cuirassier Regiment—a post already granted him in 1762. Panin remained high master of the court—that is, he continued to play the role of Paul's mentor. The grand duke took on his new duties with great diligence. He had a thorough knowledge of naval affairs. In his order to the Admiralty Board on 22 October 1774 he stated: "Someone has assigned to Kronverkskaia harbor a Lieutenant Polianskii, retired, a drunk who has received bad evaluations. Be more careful in the future and do not submit any more choices like that to me."[8] The sources do not indicate that Paul was oppressed by his unenviable lot (Panin, on the other hand, was very disgruntled and wove a network of subtle intrigues designed to elevate his pupil). In agreements on 21 May and 14 July 1773, Paul renounced the Duchy of Schleswig-Holstein (his father's legacy), retaining for himself only the title and right to award the Holstein Order of St. Anne.

Shumigorskii informs us that in August 1773 Panin, together with his trusted secretaries D.I. Fonvizin and P. Bakunin, concocted a plan that would have concentrated the entire administration of the state in Paul's hands, but Bakunin reported it to Count G.G. Orlov, a favorite of Catherine's. A nasty scene took place between the empress and the crown prince, during which Paul handed his mother lists of the participants in the intrigue. Catherine threw them into the fire without a glance (she had already learned the names from Bakunin). After this confrontation, Paul made timid but not entirely successful attempts to become closer to his mother.

Meanwhile, negotiations for Paul's marriage were in full swing. As early as 1768, Catherine had directed Asseburg, the Danish envoy to Russia, to evaluate some of the German princesses. Panin, who was inclined to be pro-Prussian and who had already succeeded in introducing Paul to Prince Heinrich of Prussia, supplied his friend Asseburg with appropriate recommendations. King Frederick II of Prussia also took an active part in the matrimonial endeavors. Catherine's choice fell on Princess Wilhelmina of Hesse-Darmstadt. She and Paul were joined in wedlock on 29 September 1773 (after converting to Orthodoxy she took the name Natalia Alekseevna). Showered with favors, Panin was retired from his post as mentor, although he maintained his influence over Paul.

The grand duke and grand duchess, having no court of their own, began to appear at Catherine's court frequently. Careful observers who knew Paul well noticed that he was then extremely impetuous, inconsistent, suspicious, and unable to withstand others' influence, so that someone else usually directed him in all his actions. In his sincere desire to repair his relations with his mother, he did not shrink even from informing on his mentor and willingly told her all the court gossip, causing resignations and banishments from the court. For example, Count Matiushkin hinted to Paul that N.I. Saltykov had been instructed to observe his behavior; the crown prince told his mother, and Matiushkin was forced to leave the service.

The Pugachev uprising made an enormous but mixed impression on Paul. With all his heart he hated the "people's inconstancy" and experienced fear in the face of the uprising, which shocked the empire. According to N.A. Sablukov, the image of Pugachev on horseback, unsheathed saber in his hand, at the head of the mob, haunted Paul all his life. Moreover, Pugachev campaigned as Peter III, and the crown prince worshiped his father, all the more so because he had hardly any knowledge or recollection of Peter. According to unconfirmed reports, Paul even intended to join the pretender. Once he became emperor, Paul is known to have sent Senator Runich to the Urals, where the surviving Pugachevites were kept, with a declaration granting them a royal pardon.

In 1774 Paul was hard at work on a draft of his *Reflections on the State in General*, which he gave to Catherine. While working on it, the crown prince took counsel with the Panin brothers, who directed it and discussed the details. This work by Paul is extremely important to our understanding of his political sympathies and also serves to clarify his attitude toward the policy of Catherine II, who at the time was preparing to implement the provincial reform.

To preserve Russia's "happy position," Paul proposed that the country renounce wars of aggression and prepare solely for wars of defense. Toward this end, four armies were to be concentrated at the frontiers of the empire—one against Sweden, one against Prussia and Austria, one against Turkey, and the fourth in Siberia. All other regiments were to be quartered inside the country in permanent positions, receiving recruits and provisions from the local inhabitants. In time, it was proposed to end recruitment and to replenish the army with soldiers' sons. The regiments were given identical staffs and precise charters and instructions that spelled out the rights and duties of all military personnel, from field marshal to private. The *Reflections* stipulated the strict regulation of military life, from "official matters" to formations. Iron discipline and personal responsibility were to be instilled. Paul suggested that soldiers would be "incomparably happier and more willing to serve, because they will not suffer or perceive themselves to be subject to the caprices and brutalities of particular commanders who defile the service and drive people out of it rather than expounding its virtues."

Many historians are inclined to view this document as Paul's political credo. In fact, they treat the *Reflections* as a kind of political program, one that he used as a guide after he became emperor. There are, however, no solid grounds for such conclusions. There can be no doubt, though, that Paul did try to instill greater discipline in the Russian army, even in regulatory details, to counter the uncontrolled behavior of Catherine's regimental commanders, who frequently viewed the formations entrusted to them as a source of additional earnings. The idea of having permanent regimental stations and replacing recruits with soldiers' sons is in keeping with Alexander I's policy of "military settlements" (a policy linked to A.A. Arakcheev, a favorite of both Paul and Alexander). But only faint echoes of the *Reflections* may be heard in Paul's actual policies.

Catherine II read her son's work with something less than enthusiasm, for it contained a veiled criticism of her own policies. It may be that this is why Paul was not given a seat either in the Senate or on the Imperial Council. He was, in fact, kept out of state business and always suffered from G.A. Potemkin's antagonism. On 21 April, her birthday, the empress gave Paul a cheap watch as a gift, while she gave her favorite fifty thousand rubles. The crown prince felt hurt. He saw Potemkin not only as his mother's favorite but also as his own political rival, a man occupying a place in the government that Paul considered his by right. Thus began the many years of grave enmity between Paul and Potemkin, who was supported in every instance by Catherine II. Not long afterward, Paul suffered a terrible blow, made worse by family discord. Despite Catherine's calculations, Natalia Alekseevna proved to be a proud and strong woman with a firm character. She completely subjected her nervous, impressionable husband to her influence. At the time, the crown prince's childhood friend Razumovskii was close to the grand duke's family. Together, he and Natalia Alekseevna tried to neutralize both Catherine II's and N.I. Panin's influence on Paul. To some extent they succeeded in this. In one of his letters to Razumovskii, Paul confessed:

> Your friendship has performed a miracle in me: I am beginning to get rid of my former suspiciousness. But you are fighting a decades-old habit and wrestling with something that fearfulness and ordinary inhibitions have implanted in me. Now I have made it my rule to live as agreeably as possible with everyone. Away with hobgoblins, away with anxious concerns! Behavior that is equable and in harmony with circumstances—that is my plan. I am curbing my intensity as much as possible: every day I choose projects that force me to think and to develop my thoughts, and I am gaining more and more from books.

The crown prince's pro-Prussian sympathies were replaced with pro-French ones. But people (according to one version, Catherine; according to another, Prince Heinrich of Prussia) were insinuating to him that his wife was overly close to Razumovskii. Natalia Alekseevna managed to convince her husband that she and Razumovskii were being slandered for political reasons. Paul withdrew into himself, and his relations with his mother became even more strained. Yet matters never reached the point of open conflict between mother-in-law and daughter-in-law, and on 15 April 1776 Natalia Alekseevna died in childbirth. Paul was stricken with grief. In order to "heal" her son and show him that the deceased woman was not worth his tears, Catherine II gave him the love letters between his wife and Razumovskii, who by that time had been removed from the court. At the same time, efforts were under way to marry the crown prince to the seventeen-year-old Princess Sophia Dorothea of Württemberg. The spiritual trauma left a deep mark: not a trace of Paul's former cheerfulness remained, and his character became morose and withdrawn.

On 13 June 1776 the crown prince visited Berlin to meet his future wife. Frederick II tried to use the proffered opportunity to establish friendly ties with Paul, greeting him with rather heavy-handed Prussian pomp and circumstance. He was accorded the most solemn honors, of which he was often deprived at home, and the Prussian king entertained the grand duke with a variety of festivities, maneuvers, parades, and spectacles. Paul was enchanted with Frederick, his fiancée, and Prussia. He tried to emulate Frederick in the way he dressed, walked, and even rode on horseback. The Prussian state system as a whole, and the Prussian army in particular, pleased him with its orderliness, based on centralization, regulation, and iron discipline. On top of everything else, he fell in love with his fiancée. The secretary of the French Embassy in St. Petersburg, the chevalier de Corberon, rightly noted in his diary that Paul was pleased with Berlin, whereas people there were not pleased by his stinginess. He gave the overseer of the Summer Palace, Prince Heinrich, only forty gold coins and did not tip the lackey and the guards at all.[9] But this is almost the only accusation of stinginess; it is quite likely that Paul simply had no money, for he very seldom did.

Catherine received her son's betrothed kindly but without any special warmth, as the latter recalled even in her old age. The wedding was celebrated on 26 September 1776. The new grand duchess, who was baptized under the name Maria Fedorovna, had received a strict upbringing in the German hinterlands; she seemed reserved and unpretentious and tried to adjust to Russia as quickly as possible. With rare unanimity, both her contemporaries and the prerevolutionary historians rated her "an angel incarnate."

The crown prince's Prussian sympathies, which had strengthened while he lived in Berlin, were met with understanding and empathy both by his wife and by Panin. In the context of his Prussophile inclinations, Paul did not hesitate to subject his mother's policies to sharp criticism. His letter to K.I. Saken has been preserved: "For me there are no [political] parties or interests aside from the interests of the state, and, given my character, it is hard for me to watch while things just slide as a result of negligence and personal views. I would rather be hated for doing right than loved for doing wrong."[10]

At court, the heir was treated with studied indifference and even disdain, his title openly disregarded. The growing rift with his mother worsened as his first-born, Alexander, and his second son, Constantine, were brought up by Catherine herself. She regarded them as the "property of the state" and wanted to raise them herself. Paul could not conceal his sense of humiliation, and sometimes spoke rather harshly of both his mother's policies and her favorites. Because of this tension, it is difficult to separate the personal from the political. Paul criticized the very essence of Catherine's policies.

He developed his ideas in private letters, in particular to Panin. In his opinion, the government should have been concentrating not on acquiring new territories, but on improving the internal organization of the state—developing trade and industry, promulgating new laws that would be binding on everyone, creating an administration responsible to the law, and so on. The main task was to organize the army so as to define precisely the nobility's rights and obligations to the empire. Paul believed that the nobility were discouraged from service, above all because nothing was steadfast, hence everything depended on the temporary disposition of the powers that were, which generated abuses. Second, exemption from compulsory service was not reinforced by necessary education. Third, "local commanders" had the authority to alter the old rules of service and institute new ones, as well as to advance people in rank and confer awards on the basis not of seniority but of whim.[11]

Paul considered it of paramount importance to concentrate all legislative initiative in the monarch's hands, so that the nobility would merely serve and be generously compensated. How sharply these plans contrasted with Catherine II's measures! Eidelman suggests (without offering evidence, incidentally) that Paul was not merely under the Panins' influence but even shared their constitutional plans until 1789.

The Imperial family's conflict, however, was not resolved, and Catherine II suggested to her son and his wife that they travel "incognito" throughout Europe. On 19 September 1781 Paul and his wife, under the name of Count and Countess Severnykh, embarked on a journey that lasted fourteen months. They visited Austria, Italy, France, The Netherlands, Switzerland, and southern Germany. The journey's outcome surprised Catherine somewhat: in Europe, Paul was received as heir to the Russian throne, and he managed to make himself liked everywhere. A memoirist describes crowds of people near the hotel where the grand duke and grand duchess took up residence. Paul walked around Paris without any formalities, accompanied only by one of the members of his retinue. He visited Les Invalides, the Academy of Sciences, and hospitals, comporting himself everywhere with simplicity and dignity. "He was gracious, courteous, and dignified . . . and he failed at nothing in a country where amiability is valued above all. He spoke little, but his speech was always appropriate and simple, and nothing complimentary that he said seemed in any way contrived."[12] Moreover, in Europe's courts Paul managed to win sympathy for his ambiguous position in Russia.

As a token of special favor, Austrian Emperor Joseph II acquainted Paul with the secret pact between Russia and Austria, about which the crown prince had had no knowledge. It was in Europe that he received the sobriquet "the Russian Hamlet," later adopted by Russian memoirists and historians.

Catherine II was pleased with the political results of his travels (in particular the strengthening of her alliance with Austria), but this brought no improvement in her relations with her son. Having been shown such favor in Europe, Paul increasingly wished to participate in governing the country. Catherine, however, allowed him only to attend reports twice a week and to dine with her on Sundays. N.I. Panin, cast from favor, died on 31 March 1783. Although risking his mother's displeasure, Paul attended Panin's death and closed his mentor's eyes.

After that, the crown prince showed no dissatisfaction with his position. The English ambassador, James Harris, remarked: "The behavior of the grand duke and the grand duchess . . . is more reasonable than might have been expected. They live almost completely on their own; they have excluded their former favorites from their company and say that they now wish to be guided only by the desires of the empress."[13] This kind of behavior brought a response from Catherine II. On 12 May 1783 she discussed with Paul (for the first time!) certain important foreign policy problems—Polish affairs and the question of annexing the Crimea. A frank exchange of opinions evidently took place, ending in a final break because it revealed the total dissimilarity in their views. At about this time the first rumors circulated concerning the possibility that not Paul but his eldest son, Alexander, would inherit the throne. The general consensus was that Catherine worshiped Alexander.

On 6 August 1783 Paul received the estate of Gatchina, which had previously belonged to G. Orlov. From then on, a qualitatively new stage in his life began. All his illusions about taking part in governing the empire, or even influencing governmental policy, disappeared, and Paul confined himself to Gatchina and its interests. In this little world, he could arrange everything as he saw fit. Crown Prince Paul now had his own court, including people whom Catherine also received. Thus, in St. Petersburg there were reports of the grand duke's "shenanigans." People often severely ridiculed Paul's courtiers, and those who enjoyed his special favor were openly snubbed in the empress's court.

The upkeep of the grand duke's court was more than modest: Paul suffered constantly from a shortage of money, and either had to plead with his mother through third parties or borrow (generally from his wife's German relatives). The Vadkovskii family preserved notes from Maria Fedorovna in which she asked for loans of twenty-five and fifty rubles for everyday expenses.[14] Meanwhile, one of Catherine II's ex-favorites, Zavadovskii, received a payment of fifty thousand rubles, a lifetime annuity of five thousand rubles, forty thousand rubles to pay off his debts, and four thousand souls in Ukraine—and tore his hair in vexation because it was too little.

As Fleet Admiral of the Russian navy, Paul won the right to keep three battalions at Gatchina, which he trained to suit himself. According to the rolls of 1796, the troops at Gatchina consisted of 2,399 men, including 1,675 infantry (74 officers), 624 cavalry (40 officers), and 228 artillery (14 officers). Outfitted in uniforms extraordinarily similar to the Prussian ones, like Frederick II's units they were constantly engaged in changing-of-the-guard drills, inspections, and so on. This was all under the command of Paul himself, who did not miss a single mounting of the guards. At Gatchina Paul wrote new military regulations for combat, garrison, and camp service. He also penned numerous instructions to officials and new rules governing economic support of the troops. He focused special attention, however, on improving the artillery. Cannon and rifle exercises were conducted using plans drawn up by the crown prince, and a fortress was stormed.

Maria Fedorovna attended these exercises frequently. Grand Dukes Alexander and Constantine also took part in them, commanding battalions. They were extremely proud of their Gatchina uniforms. A. Czartoryski states that Alexander wanted to settle permanently at Gatchina with his father. Generally, the sons arrived on Friday, took part in maneuvers on Saturday, and returned to St. Petersburg on Sunday.

The military way of life at Gatchina was a target of universal derision. Even so thoughtful and serious an observer as Colonel Sablukov allowed himself to wax malicious: "Among ourselves, we officers often made fun of the Gatchinites. Some officers they were! What strange people! Such mannerisms! And how strangely they spoke! All the new procedures and new uniforms were freely subjected to criticism and almost universal condemnation."[15] The officers who served at Gatchina were primarily poor noblemen, not of high birth, for whom a career in the Guards was almost impossible. They bore Paul's extraordinary demands with resignation and would do anything to gain favor. Later, A.A. Arakcheev recalled that at the time he had only one pair of white buckskin breeches, which he laundered every evening and put on, still wet, in the morning.

The lax morals of Catherine's Guards regiments had no place at Gatchina. The grand duke demanded iron discipline and, fully in the spirit of Frederick II, did not tolerate "smart alecks." At the same time, he took care of his subordinates. He knew every man's family situation and petitioned St. Petersburg on their behalf; he might give someone's daughter a dowry, for example.

A circle of persons close to Paul emerged in Gatchina. Gatchina officers such as Arakcheev, Obolianinov, Kologrivov, Lindener, Kannabikh, and others later became grandees during his reign. Among his close associates, Paul dropped his reserve and became merry and charming. He was not above playing a game of blind man's buff or badminton, and he liked dancing. But his main activities were concealed from outsiders.

Paul was not an idle observer of Catherine's reforms; rather, he tried to develop his own ways to resolve the problems that the country faced. On 4 January 1788, while preparing to take part in the war against Sweden, he wrote three letters to his wife, a letter to his eldest sons, a testament, and a special Instruction—or, as he called it, a "prescription"—on how to govern the empire. These papers show clearly that he assessed quite soberly his place in the state hierarchy, and he did not deem it necessary to embellish his position. "God has seen fit to bring me into the world," Paul wrote to his wife, "for that condition which, although I have not attained it, is one for which I have endeavored to make myself worthy all my life."[16] It is not by chance, also, that Paul did not sign the testament, addressed to Catherine II, as crown prince or heir to the throne, but only as grand duke. Of special interest, however, is his Instruction.

Like Catherine II, Paul believed that the best form of government was absolute monarchy, because it "combines in itself the force of laws and the speed of one person's authority." The empire needed laws, most importantly a law on succession to the throne that would guarantee stability and order. No other new laws were needed; all that had to be done was to amend the old ones to reflect the present "internal state situation"—that is, to publish a collection of existing laws, to eliminate contradictions among them, to separate decrees from laws, and so on. Paul viewed the nobility as "the bulwark of the state and the sovereign," and, in contrast to his mother, wished not to allow "superfluous members or unworthy persons" into the privileged estate. As for industry and industrialists, "it is well to be concerned, especially in our country, where that aspect is neglected." Paul focused special attention on the financial system. Starting with the proposition that "the revenues of the state belong to the state rather than the sovereign" (Catherine quite frequently confused them), Paul condemned the newly initiated issuance of paper money and the devaluation of coins.[17]

We have here a concrete, well-developed—however briefly formulated—program, based on the *Reflections*, for Russia's development. Paul himself implemented part of it, thirty-eight points, once he became emperor, and his sons Alexander I and Nicholas I implemented another part. Therefore, the view expressed in the nineteenth century (by A. Czartoryski, N.A. Sablukov, D.A. Miliutin, M.I. Semevskii, and M.V. Klochkov) that Paul had a program of sorts governing his activities when he became emperor, turns out to have been true.

During Paul's long tenure, Gatchina changed radically. A hospital and a school were built there, as well as four churches—Orthodox, Lutheran, Catholic, and Finnish (while very pious, Paul was extremely tolerant in matters of faith). The Gatchina library acquired thirty-six thousand volumes. The porcelain and glass factories, the fulling mill, and the hat shop, set up using Paul's own funds, looked more Prussian than Russian. The duchess of Saxe-Coburg, who visited St. Petersburg in 1795 accompanied by her daughters, described Gatchina: "As soon as you ride onto the estate, tricolor (black, red, and white) gates appear, and Guards challenge the travelers in the Prussian manner. The worst thing, however, is that these soldiers are Russians who have been turned into Prussians, and they are dressed in Frederick II's old-fashioned uniforms."[18]

Naturally, being kept out of affairs for a long time affected the crown prince's character. Away from Gatchina he was stern, morose, taciturn, and caustic, and he knew how to save face, as the saying goes. He bore the favorites' jibes with dignity, although some went beyond the bounds of decency (once Platon Zubov publicly remarked to the crown prince, "Have I said something so stupid, that you should agree with me?"). Only rarely did he hint that his hands were still tied, but that on ascending the throne he would act differently. Although outwardly he showed deep respect for his mother, it is unlikely that Paul experienced sincere feelings for her. At home in Gatchina, however, he was frightening in moments of rage. Officers who were late for the mounting of the guard—Major Freygang, for example—fell into a dead faint at Paul's reprimands. His slightest whims were immediately carried out.

No one, not even Maria Fedorovna and the children, dared to violate procedures that he had set. At the same time, Paul was forgiving, and he acknowledged his own mistakes, apologized and asked forgiveness, and tried to be fair and generous. The debaucheries of Catherine's court were alien to him. To be sure, he became infatuated with women (E.I. Nelidova, for example), but according to Sablukov, "he was not an immoral man. . . . He hated depravity and was very much devoted to his wife."[19] Friction between Maria Fedorovna and her lady-in-waiting soon gave way to a lifelong friendship. Many people assumed that Paul's love for Nelidova was platonic.

All the memoirists state that Catherine II treated Paul unfairly and that this spoiled his character. In 1784 the crown prince wrote to N.A. Rumiantsev:

> Here I am, thirty years old, and I have nothing to do. . . . My serenity, I assure you, does not depend on the circumstances that surround me; it is based on my clear conscience and the realization that there are some virtues not subject to the action of any earthly power, and it is toward them I must strive. This serves to console me in many times of trouble and raises me above them; it teaches me patience, which many perceive to be a sign of sullenness in my character. As far as my behavior is concerned, you know that I strive to make it agree with my moral concepts and that I cannot do anything against my conscience.

Irritation and even bitterness, which Paul suppressed, increasingly ate at the crown prince's soul. He was also noticeably influenced by his dealings with French emigrants. One of these, Count Esterhazy, vehemently preached the "iron rod" as a reliable tool against revolution and met with understanding and responsiveness from Paul. While accepting many historians' opinion concerning the deterioration of his character as a result of the solitary life at Gatchina and other factors, we must emphasize that there was no abrupt turning point whatsoever, merely a slow evolution of Paul's personality.

During her final years, Catherine II considered transferring the throne to her grandson, her beloved Alexander, rather than her son. But in late 1795 and early 1796, Alexander became very close to his father. The empress demanded that Maria Fedorovna help her with her plans: it would be necessary to persuade Paul to abdicate in favor of his son and sign the appropriate documents. But Maria Fedorovna refused, just as Saltykov and La Harpe had before her. On 16 September 1796 the empress discussed the subject with her grandson. Alexander, who evidently had become accustomed to maneuvering between his father and his grandmother, gave his verbal consent to Paul's removal, but at the same time he wrote a number of letters (one of them to Arakcheev, his father's favorite) in which he used the title "His Highness" with respect to Paul—that is, he acknowledged Paul as the legitimate heir. Nevertheless, there were rumors at court and in St. Petersburg that preparations were under way on a manifesto of succession, according to which Paul would be placed under arrest in the remote castle of Lode and Alexander named as successor.

However, these expectations were never realized. On 5 November 1796 Catherine II had a stroke, after which she lived twenty-two hours but never regained consciousness. Immediately, various persons each dispatched five or six couriers to Gatchina. The first to arrive was Nikolai Zubov, the brother of Catherine's last favorite. Paul and his wife were having supper in the mill that he had ordered built at Gatchina. Forgetting etiquette, Zubov almost ran in, fell on his knees, and informed them of the empress's hopeless condition. Paul turned crimson and burst into tears; he commanded a team to be hitched immediately, then became angry because it took so long to bring the horses. He was very excited and feverishly embraced his wife and Zubov. Finally, at about five o'clock in the afternoon, the crown prince set out. Along the way, he met a large number of couriers (around twenty-five persons) hastening to Gatchina with the news, among them Count F.V. Rostopchin, a Gatchinite dispatched by Alexander.

At about eight o'clock in the evening, Paul entered the Winter Palace, where he was received as emperor. First he visited the dying woman. Countess V.I. Golovina, who had been granted many favors by Catherine and for that reason did not especially like Paul, was astonished by the sincerity and depth of his feelings: he wept and repeatedly kissed his mother's hands—in short, he comported himself like a dutiful son. He settled down for the night in the "corner" office, right next to the room where Catherine lay. All night people passed by the dying woman's bed, people to whom Paul wished to give orders of various kinds. Malicious tongues immediately accused him of insulting his mother.

At 9:45 A.M. on 6 November, Catherine passed away. Paul called for the deceased's papers. Sanglen reports that Platon Zubov conducted Paul into the empress's office and there gave him four pack-

Paul I

ets. The first two contained sealed documents concerning his abdication and banishment to Lode Castle, the third a decree transferring G. Orlov's estate [Gatchina] to Count A.A. Bezborodko, and the fourth Catherine II's last will and testament. Paul allegedly tore up the first two packets and put the will in his pocket without reading it. This account of the events is found only in Sanglen's report. This, along with Paul's subsequent relations with Zubov, casts doubt on the veracity of the memoirist's version.

Rostopchin reports that Paul, in the presence of his sons Alexander and Constantine as well as Bezborodko and Procurator-General Samoilov, personally piled all the papers together on a prepared tablecloth, which a valet sealed with the emperor's seal. Most memoirists, however, assert that Bezborodko informed Paul that there was a will in favor of Alexander, after which they secluded themselves in the empress's office and spent a long time burning papers in the fireplace. The latter account seems more probable and is confirmed indirectly by the favors that Paul showered upon Bezborodko (in particular, granting him about thirty thousand souls, as well as other gifts). Historians agree that there was a document transferring the throne to Alexander, but hold that Paul destroyed it while Catherine was in her death throes.

At twelve midnight on 6 November 1796, the upper clergy and the court took an oath of allegiance to the new emperor and his heir, Grand Duke Alexander. Russia was then confronted with numerous difficult problems. After Pugachev's rebellion and the revolution in France, Catherine's government had conducted a systematic policy to combat "revolutionary contagion" and "popular inconstancy." The empire's finances were in disarray, and the issuing of paper money continued (a paper ruble was worth sixty-six silver kopecks). Embezzlement and graft had reached unprecedented levels and become virtually legal. "Never before have crimes been so blatant as now," Rostopchin wrote to Count S.R. Vorontsov. "Impunity and brazenness have reached their limit. Ribas alone has been stealing more than 500,000 rubles per year."[20] "The official riffraff" (as K. Mason termed them) shirked their duties. In the Senate, about twelve thousand legislative matters lay neglected.

But the army was in the worst situation of all. Of the 400,000 men on the rolls, the army was short at least 50,000; maintenance funds were plundered by regimental commanders, and three-quarters of the officer corps existed only on paper. Officers were commissioned or promoted to the next higher rank only on the basis of favoritism.

Many men received ranks without serving at all. Desertion was a widespread phenomenon. About two thousand Russian turncoats served in the Swedish army alone.[21] Although Catherine's musketeer regiment was supposed to have 1,726 men, rarely were more than 800 assembled on the parade ground. The general in St. Petersburg had about a hundred officers, while regimental companies were commanded by warrant officers. Army combat officers served fifteen years in rank, while ignoramuses from the Guards who had entered the army regiments with double promotions were foisted on them as commanders. Rifles were kept in service for as much as forty years, and the fleet was equipped with guns cast in Peter I's time.[22]

Meanwhile, in Europe the anti-French coalition was collapsing. Catherine II had intended to support it with Russian bayonets. For this purpose, a 60,000-man corps was prepared, despite the fact that no funds existed for such an endeavor. The new emperor tried to address the most crucial and urgent problems. The second decree he signed rescinded the recruitment of ten thousand men for the war with France, and this was soon followed by an order halting the issuance of paper money. The new monarch needed reliable servitors and counted primarily on Gatchinites. On 10 November the Gatchinite battalions were merged with the Guards, which caused unhappiness among the old Guards officers.

All the memoirists acknowledged that the emperor's first steps had a certain validity, but they interpreted them differently. Thus Czartoryski characterized as useful "the ban on serving in the army as one pleased, amateurishly," and also the young courtiers' obligation to choose a branch of service. Czartoryski thought that one of Paul's most magnanimous acts was the release of the Polish prisoners (T. Kociuszko, I. Potocki, and others). From the standpoint of Semenovskii [Regiment] officer M. Leontiev, among the best actions of Paul's government were the establishment of the Loan Bank, the promulgation of the "bankruptcy charter," and the exemption of the Lomonosov family from the poll tax. Sablukov had high praise for Paul I's extensive granting of estates. A.T. Bolotov described in detail how Paul honored the late empress and praised Paul because "he immediately made both his sons his associates in handling his affairs." E. Dumont asserted that one of the true merits of the new reign was that it strengthened army discipline, improved officer morale, and "made the administration of justice less corrupt."

However, contemporaries are unanimous on one point: the motivation behind all Paul's innovations was his desire to act contrary to

Catherine II's policies. G.R. Derzhavin compared St. Petersburg after the arrival of the Gatchinite battalions to a conquered city. "Never before have all the decorations been changed so quickly at the sound of a whistle as happened when Paul ascended the throne. Everything was changed in a day—costumes, hairdos, looks, manners, and occupations," Czartoryski wrote.[23] It was for this "metamorphosis," this "wrecking" of Catherine's system that Paul I's contemporaries could not forgive him, to say nothing of the historians, who as often as not merely reproduce the memoirists' assessments.

Although there was a virtual avalanche of new decrees, regulations, and ordinances promulgated during the first months of Paul's reign, the new emperor had a system. He focused most of his attention on the army and the Guards, and this was only natural considering their pathetic state at the end of Catherine II's reign. Regulations governing cavalry and infantry service appeared on 29 November 1796, and naval regulations were issued on 25 February 1797. The Guards and army regiments received new uniforms modeled on Prussian ones, perukes, and other accoutrements. Paul took part in all the mountings and changings of the Guards and paid attention to even the smallest details of army life. The soldiers' pay was improved, strict regulations governing promotion in the service were introduced, and for administrative convenience the armed forces were divided into eleven districts and seven inspectorates.

The status of the Guards was transformed. "Our way of life, the officers' way of life, has changed utterly," wrote Adjutant E.V. Komarovskii of the Izmailovskii Regiment. "Under the empress we thought only about going to the theater and to parties and walked around in coats and tails; now we have to sit from morning to evening in the regimental yard and be instructed in everything, like recruits."[24] The unaccustomed burdens of service led to mass resignations. In the first three weeks of Paul I's reign, between 60 and 70 of the 132 officers in the Horse Guards contrived to resign. The vacancies that this opened made possible rapid movement through the ranks. The aforementioned Komarovskii, in fact, rose from sergeant to major general in seven years!

Although Paul I at first dealt gently with Platon Zubov and others among Catherine's grandees, he could not trust them, and thus he tried to surround himself with people on whose loyalty he could rely. He summoned Prince Repnin from Lithuania and promoted him to field marshal general; from Moscow he summoned his childhood friend A.B. Kurakin, whom he named a privy councillor. As his secretary, Paul appointed N.V. Lopukhin, who had been summoned from Kishinev. Contrary to the view expressed in much of the historical literature, Paul did not persecute Catherine's grandees: those who retired generally did so with promotions, awards, and grants of money or land. All the presidents of boards of directors and heads of departments who had served under Catherine retained their posts.

Simultaneously, all prisoners of the Secret Expedition were released; N.I. Novikov and A.N. Radishchev were freed; and Kociuszko received permission to go to America. All those of lower ranks who had been under investigation were pardoned. Contemporaries noted Paul's kindness to Catherine's son by G. Orlov, A.G. Bobrinskii, who was granted the title of count and vast estates in Ukraine. Even those who took part in the coup of 1762 suffered no punishment other than banishment from court and being forbidden to enter the capital (this ban, incidentally, was soon rescinded). A.G. Orlov-Chesmenskii (who, it is commonly believed, murdered Peter III) dined informally with Paul I throughout the latter's reign!

Paul I also took pains to expand the aura of legality surrounding his rule. Contemporaries laughed at the coronation of Peter III's remains and their burial alongside Catherine II. But the political sense of this action was clear: he was acknowledging as his father the person who had refused to acknowledge Paul as his son. This probably explains Paul's wish to be crowned as soon as possible: on 5 April 1797 he was crowned in the Kremlin by Metropolitan Platon, once his teacher and mentor.

As his foreign policy, Paul I declared that he desired peace with all countries and that he renounced all military actions, a stance that grew directly out of the *Reflections* and the Instruction (although he also lacked funds to continue the war).

Paul I's first acts, therefore, did not generally appear to conflict with the country's interests, nor did they in fact embody anything qualitatively new. Why, then, did they encounter such irritation and even hostility among his contemporaries, in particular the nobility and Guards of the capital? A major factor was the increased burden of service, to which the Guards were totally unaccustomed. "Service under Catherine was easy," V. Selivanov recalled. "It used to be that when you went on guard duty (and the men had guard duty for weeks at a time), you took your featherbed and some pillows, a nightshirt, a nightcap, and a samovar. After retreat was sounded, you had supper, undressed, and went to sleep; it was just like home. Once Paul ascended the throne, the service became burdensome and strict."[25]

During Paul's reign an officer was personally responsible for his unit, and the endless inspections and changes of the guard that tested the soldiers' training might end in unpleasantness, up to and including arrest and expulsion from the service. Officers' furloughs, which had lasted for years, and the practice of assigning noblemen's sons to regiments on the day of their birth, which allowed them to attain officers' rank by the time they came of age, were ended. All the court titles (such as chamberlain and gentleman of the bedchamber) were eliminated from the regiments because it was permitted to serve only in a military or a civilian unit.

The Gatchina officers, who had less claim to nobility than the St. Petersburg officers—many came from Germany, Courland, and Ukraine—sometimes had more rapid and significant careers than the old hands in the Guards. This offended the St. Petersburg nobility.

The new regulations evoked universal disdain because of their similarity to the Prussian system. Indeed, little attention was paid to shooting and bayonet combat; it was concentrated instead on battlefield maneuvers. The new uniform provoked unprecedented animosity. Sanglen attests that "the destruction of the uniforms struck some as scornful and others as criminal. Changing Guards officers from denizens of the tsar's court to soldiers in the army, introducing strict discipline and, in short, turning everything upside down, amounted to spurning the public consensus and suddenly violating an order sanctified by tradition."[26]

The demands of service were also extended to civil servants. Whereas under Catherine, senators did not appear in the Senate for years at a time, Paul I had candles burning in every chamber and work in full swing at five o'clock in the morning. Bribe-taking—indeed, corruption in general—was rigorously prosecuted. Nonetheless, people generally believed that civil service was much easier than military service, so scions of eminent families no longer disdained it. Although he curtailed many official posts, Paul I continued the salaries of dismissed persons. D.B. Mertvago attests: "The government's severity produced fear. . . . Dismissed judges and scribes who had no estates scattered to the dachas that they had received as gifts."[27]

St. Petersburg underwent astonishing changes. The barriers, milestones, and sentry boxes were painted black and white (which at the time was considered the height of ugliness). City dwellers were strictly regulated. Round hats and tail coats were forbidden; instead, German vests, cocked hats, wigs, and buckled boots were prescribed. The lights went out everywhere at 10 P.M., and everyone in the capital was supposed to go to bed. Everyone was even supposed to eat lunch at the same time—one o'clock in the afternoon. Officers were not to ride in enclosed carriages but only on horseback or in open carriages. On meeting the emperor one was supposed to alight from the carriage and bow (only ladies were permitted to remain on the footboard)—otherwise, one would be arrested. The contrast with the preceding reign was so great that the grumbling, mingled with sarcastic mockery, reached even the emperor himself. The petty regulations governing trivial everyday situations were especially burdensome to the nobility, accustomed to considerable personal liberty.

Finally, the sheer number of new laws and regulations boggled people's minds. New decrees were issued so frequently that people could not assimilate them; they violated them and were subjected to penalties, so that even people high in rank developed a sense of insecurity regarding their future. During the four years of Paul I's reign, 2,179 legislative acts were promulgated—an average of 42 per month (under Catherine II, the average was 12 per month).[28] Public opinion saw Paul I's first acts as reflecting his hatred of Catherine II and his wish to obliterate her memory, and linked this to the emperor's personal qualities. Dissatisfaction with his policies evoked dissatisfaction with his personality, and not the reverse, as the memoirists and prerevolutionary historians thought. Naturally, as Paul attempted to concentrate all authority in his own hands, his personal qualities became an increasingly important social factor. Individual, isolated acts of his, recorded in numerous anecdotes, can be explained only by his personality. It is possible, of course, to blame the emperor's personality for certain domestic and foreign policies adopted by his government. But the basic thrust of these policies could not change radically under the influence of his personality: Paul I systematically implemented the policies of the nobility.

Many memoirists ascribe the deterioration of Paul I's character to bad company. This is a common theme, but opinions differ as to the specific personalities involved. Named most often are I.P. Kutaisov, P.Kh. Obolianinov, the Kurakin brothers, Arakcheev, and N.A. Arkharov; A. Gagarin, F.V. Rostopchin, and Procurator-General Lopukhin are named less frequently. These were the people who, out of greed or base impulses, took advantage of Paul's "evil" moments to inform on people, evoke his wrath, and cause the disgrace of innocent people, among other things. However, the most thoughtful observers have acknowledged that Paul I was surrounded by people who, in moral terms, were superior to the closest associates of Catherine II. It is unlikely that Paul's character underwent such substantial changes after he ascended the throne that one can speak of some kind of turnaround or abrupt deterioration. Rather, an emperor's qualities, habits, and characteristics are more pronounced in his subjects' eyes than the qualities of a grand duke.

It is also true that Paul I did not surround himself with courtiers who had their own opinions on particular issues. He selected his top officials primarily according to the following criteria: performance of duties (often blind); the ability to carry out an assignment without argument in the shortest possible time—that is, speed in carrying out orders; honesty and incorruptibility; and "knowledge of the service." These qualities were hardly sufficient to produce important statesmen. Paul needed conscientious performers of tasks, bureaucrats in the proper sense of that word, persons who acknowledged their su-periors' will and instructions. It is no accident that none of Paul I's associates became eminent figures in Russia's history. Arakcheev and Rostopchin are the exceptions that merely prove the general rule.

The emperor transferred the Gatchina way of life to St. Petersburg. He regulated his own personal life just as strictly as he did the lives of his subjects—and he never deviated from a daily routine once he had adopted it. Generally he rose very early and drank his coffee. By 6 A.M. he had received the governor-general of St. Petersburg with his report, and at 7 A.M. he listened to reports on foreign affairs. Around 9 A.M. he attended the changing and mounting of the guard, both generally performed before large numbers of people. If the crowd interfered, Paul I politely asked them to draw back. In general, inspections of the Guards lasted two hours, and at all times and in any weather, even frost or rain, the emperor was in attendance. After that came an outing, generally accompanied by Kutaisov, and official visits. Lunch was at precisely 1 P.M. At Gatchina, Paul and his wife had often lunched at others' houses, but in St. Petersburg etiquette demanded a special ceremonial and a lavish table, although Paul I ate and drank moderately.

A.A. Bashilov, a page, describes the "sovereign's inordinate forbearance": lunch was a little pure Neva water and two or three of the very simplest and healthiest dishes. After his meal he drank only a glass of burgundy or claret (among the Guards, officers drank two or three bottles of champagne after lunch). Sterlet, truffles, and other foods were served, but Paul never touched them.[29] His favorite dish was sausages and cabbage. A second outing after lunch, on horseback or in a carriage pulled by six white horses, always had a purpose: a visit to a hospital or a charitable institution, or simply an inspection of the St. Petersburg streets. At 6 P.M. the emperor returned home to his wife, and at 7 P.M. spectacles were performed at court. He preferred French plays (Molière, Corneille, Racine). At 9 P.M. came supper, and by 10 P.M. the emperor was already asleep.

He tried to impose this way of life on all St. Petersburg. But after ten in the evening, behind tightly pulled blinds with double linings (in court residences), a frenzied merriment took place. Incidentally, gentleman of the bedchamber D.V. Vasilchikov recalled at the end of his life that "things were never so merry as at his court. Everyone seized the moment, everyone lived for the present, and therefore they partied till they dropped and really lived it up." Paul I himself, however, was not averse to merry-making and dancing.

M. Leontiev described Paul I's appearance:

> This sovereign was small in stature, not more than 5' 3" tall. Because he was sensitive about his height, he always stood erect and never bent his legs while walking but rather lifted them as if he were marching and came down on his heels, so that his feet pounded loudly. His hair was light brown, with a touch of grey. He had a high forehead—or, more accurately, a bald spot at the top of his head, but he never covered it with hair and would not tolerate anyone else doing so. He had a large but lean face and a snub nose, with creases running from the nose to his chin. He also had large, grey, extraordinarily menacing eyes. He was somewhat swarthy, had a rather husky voice, and spoke with a drawl, always dragging out his final words. When silent he had the habit of puffing out his cheeks and suddenly releasing them, and as he did so he opened his mouth a bit, so that his teeth showed; this he did often when he was angry, which happened almost every day. Sometimes when he was merry, he would hop up and down on one foot. He wore a dark green uniform, single-breasted, with two rows of buttons, a low collar made of red cloth, and aiguillettes, and a black hat—at present a tricorn—with no decorations at all.[30]

It is said that as Paul aged, he resembled Peter III more and more. He loved frugality, at least in regard to himself, and he refrained from overindulgence. Potemkin could lose diamonds and not even notice. A.B. Kurakin, nicknamed "The Diamond Duke," wore vests studded with precious stones. A parade uniform worn by one of Catherine's pages cost a thousand rubles. Paul had one greatcoat, which he wore autumn and winter; depending on the weather it had a lining of either cotton or fur, sewn in the day he went out. But even people who were not Paul I's friends acknowledged his extraordinary generosity. The "buying-up of estates" during his reign can be explained by his principles: the emperor believed that it was better for a peasant to be privately owned (he had written and spoken about this at Gatchina). In the four years of his reign he distributed about 600,000 souls; on his coronation day alone he granted 82,000 souls (Catherine II, in her thirty-four years, distributed 850,000 souls). Awards of this sort were easily won by an officer who distinguished himself during an inspection, or even by a petitioner.

His contemporaries commented on Paul's romantic elation, his unusual chivalry. A.I. Herzen called him "a Don Quixote with a crown." Eidelman saw this quality of the emperor, first of all, as a reflection of misunderstood medieval chivalric codes, second, as a peculiar interpretation of Masonic rites, and, third, as part of the general development of reactionary romanticism in Europe in response to the French Revolution.[31] In Eidelman's opinion, Paul I's "chivalry" defined his world view and influenced both his domestic and his foreign policies.

It would be wrong, however, to see Paul's romanticism as either the quintessence of his personality or the basic ideological substantiation of his activity. Quite the opposite is true: neither the romantic flair of his letters nor his private conversations and actions, which might make sense to medieval knights (during maneuvers at Gatchina, Maria Fedorovna was supposed to stand in a tower while the battalion, commanded by Paul, defended her against "enemy" attacks), ought to conceal the essence of his policies or overshadow his personality. Paul was by no means inclined to look at the world through rose-colored glasses, nor did he attempt to joust with windmills. His policies were subordinate to the tasks of the empire and designed to reinforce absolutism, to ensure the greatest possible centralization of the state apparatus, and to strengthen the monarch's personal power.

The content of his policies, therefore, should not be considered "utopian." Those methods used to implement them that favored the "iron rod" and required extraordinary speed in turning ideas into realities, methods based on a certain disdain of the nobleman's personal liberties and rights, could not have succeeded by themselves. But they were utopian only to the extent that any central authority's efforts are utopian when it attempts, through repression, "tightening the screws," and suppressing personal liberty, to achieve political stability and dynamic, vigorous state development. The form in which Paul cloaked his initiatives was traditional to Russia, and it did not differ noticeably from that used in either the preceding or the subsequent reigns.

Paul's attachment to chivalric romance by no means defined his nature. He was more a gentleman than a medieval knight. Paul's courtesy toward and affection for the ladies, his ability to remember his promises, and his effort to act in accordance with the laws and regulations that he himself had established are facets of Paul's behavior that many of his contemporaries noted and treated as a manifestation of the "chivalry of times past." Probably, however, they were generated by his French upbringing, court etiquette, and his particular character rather than by mystical knightly rites. In other words, Paul's romantic, chivalrous world view is attested only by the memoirists' claims and a few offhand remarks. Even the fact that he took the Order of Malta under his protection can be explained entirely by political circumstances.

Paul's membership in the Masons[32] has never been proved. Arguments adduced have included the following: (1) Panin, Paul's tutor, belonged to several Masonic lodges; (2) people who were close to Paul were Masons (N. Lopukhin, S. Pleshcheev); (3) the Mason Novikov was released from prison; and, probably the main argument, (4) Paul did possess a chivalrous romanticism. These do not seem to be very convincing arguments.

According to his contemporaries, Paul was extraordinarily intelligent and observant; he had a brilliant wit and a powerful memory. While traveling around Russia, he spoke with an officer named Engelgardt in Kazan, and during the conversation he recalled the man's origins and service, that he had a sister named Barbara, and even her age. A.P. Khvostova tells the story of a Moscow merchant's wife who presented Paul with a cushion embroidered with a sheep. To it she attached a little verse: "To the father of his loyal subjects I present this sheep / In hopes that he will give my husband a title." Paul I's resolution stated: "I am the father of my loyal subjects / But there are no titles for sheep."[33]

In general, Paul would forgive any prank and even a serious gaffe if it came with a witty answer. He strove to make his own actions comply with legality, which he understood in his own particular way: as not only obedience to written laws but also unconditional obedience to higher authority—the emperor, of course, most of all. He wanted to impart a certain aura of sacredness and infallibility to the monarch's authority. Anyone who dropped a complaint in a special box could appeal to him. Paul went through the complaints personally, and his answers were printed in the newspaper. In this way, some major abuses were exposed. Here Paul I was adamant. No type of personal service or origin could save the wrongdoer from punishment. Thus, Prince Sibirskii and General Turchaninov were demoted and sentenced to life in exile in Siberia for corruption. Under Paul, a junior officer could demand judgment against a regimental commander and count on an impartial hearing. Kotlubitskii, a favorite of the emperor, struck a merchant with a lash. The merchant threatened to bring suit. Kotlubitskii offered him 6,000 rubles to drop the case, for he knew that the suit would not go well for him.[34]

To his contemporaries, nevertheless, all of Paul's worst qualities loomed large. A.M. Turgenev found in him "a rashness and a character hot-headed to the point of frenzy" that left no room for sound judgment, "and an inclination to apply harsh punishments, which destroyed a man." To the nobility of the capital, the emperor was insufferable because he ascribed a supernatural significance to unswerving performance of ceremonial requirements and loved to appear in public wearing a crown and mantle. S.I. Mukhanov was placed under arrest by him because he failed to genuflect in response to Paul's praise but merely gave a salute with his sword. F.N. Golitsyn perceived the emperor's biggest fault to be that of demanding that his will be executed by the quickest possible means, regardless of the consequences. Paul believed in principle that his subjects' highest virtue was unconditional obedience to the tsar, who must be respected, feared, and honored; no matter how harsh he might be, his subjects must "merely submit obediently."

But the petty oppressions and demands caused the greatest resentment among the nobility of the capital. Arkharov, the St. Petersburg police chief, started tearing round hats off the heads of St. Petersburg residents almost as soon as Paul ascended the throne. But R.S. Trofimovich reports that when Arkharov tore the hat off an Englishman on 26 November 1796, Paul became enraged and "conferred on everyone the freedom to wear round hats."[35] Mukhanov's daughter testified that her father served two and a half years without attracting even a sideways glance from the emperor, although he did whatever he pleased and did not dress as Paul liked, but A.S. Shishkov was horrified because he had to change shoes twice a day. Leontiev considered Paul I a "perfect despot" because he did not like tragedies, and S. Tuchkov was offended by the changing of the color of the sword-knot and the cockade, which he saw as a sign of the army's disintegration.

One can easily see that the memoirists were primarily protesting the most blatant and superficial manifestations of the emperor's will; the deeper, inner sense of Paul's transformations was ignored. Pokrovskii himself remarked that "Paul's love of military regulations and his mania for parades and uniforms were essentially derived qualities, the outwardly most striking forms of his love of regulation and order in general."[36] But who among his contemporaries was in a position to understand this? N.I. Grech wrote:

> The absurdities and trifling insults also overshadowed the genuinely good things in his new reign. The arsenals probably still house the enormous Catherinian cannons on their ugly red carriages. At the very beginning of Paul's reign, both the cannons and the carriages were given a new form and made lighter and more maneuverable than the previous ones. The old artillerymen, including those who were intelligent and knowledgeable about their trade, cried out against the innovation. What!? Abolish the guns that thundered against the enemy on the banks of the Kagul and the Rymnik?! This is sacrilege! The loudest grumbling, mingled with scornful laughter, rang out when they decided to fire the cannons at a target. Whoever heard of or saw such a thing?! Yet it marked the first step toward transforming and perfecting our artillery.[37]

Even more malicious derision was directed against the Prussian-model uniform that Paul I introduced in the army (even the ladies-in-waiting ridiculed it). But Selivanov thought that "the uniforms under Paul were still a great deal more comfortable and convenient than the previous ones. Then the uniforms were broad, spacious, had hems, and were fastened in accordance with the season."[38]

When Paul was eleven, Poroshin told him something that proved to be prophetic: "Even with the best of intentions, you will make yourself hated." A specific manifestation of this hatred was the rumor about Paul's mental illness, reproduced in many memoirs. Among historians, V.O. Kliuchevskii was first to comment on his madness, followed by P. Morane, M.K. Liubavskii, K.V. Sivkov, and others. The psychologist P.N. Kovalevskii decided that psychologically Paul I was not responsible for his actions. Another professor of psychology, V.F. Chizh, stated just as authoritatively that Paul's mind was absolutely normal, although he did consider him a madman politically.[39]

The basic argument in favor of the emperor's illness involved his policies. Not understanding and not accepting Paul I's initiatives, his contemporaries, and historians after them, ascribed the emperor's policies to a mental disorder, while amiably acknowledging his sober intelligence, variety of talents, and so on. M.V. Klochkov analyzed and dismissed as baseless, if not actually falsified, the specific incidents that allegedly certified Paul's madness. Nevertheless, the gossip about Paul I's alleged mental illness served as one motive behind the conspiracy that led to his assassination.

Contemporaries explained the assassination of the tsar on 11 March 1801 by reference to Paul I's policy toward the estates: his violation of the Charter of 1785, his repression of the officer corps, the political instability he created in the country, his erosion of the guarantees of the nobility's freedoms and privileges, the break that he caused in diplomatic relations with England, and, finally, his inability to rule the empire. Formally, indeed, Paul I's government had violated articles of the Charter by forbidding provincial noble assemblies and reintroducing corporal punishment. But the latter was applied only under exceptional circumstances involving political crimes, and only after the persons in question were stripped of their title of nobility.

Precedent had been set by the case of the retired warrant officer Rozhkov on 2 February 1797. The Senate submitted a report to the emperor concerning Rozhkov's "impertinent and corrupting words about the sacred icons and sovereign majesties," recognized as a crime calling for the death penalty. The death penalty, however, had been abolished by decree in 1754, leaving as punishment the knout, slashing of the nostrils, shackles, and penal servitude. Because Article 15 of the Charter prohibited even this ("corporal punishment shall not apply to noblemen"), the Senate decided to strip Rozhkov of his rank and noble status, place him in irons, and send him to penal servitude. Paul added a resolution: "Inasmuch as he has been stripped of his noble status, neither do privileges apply to him. Proceed accordingly."[40]

Corporal punishment was inflicted on Second Lieutenant Fedoseev, Lieutenant Perskii, Ensign Trubnikov, and several other persons. But these actions occurred within a general context of harsh police measures undertaken by the monarchy to combat "revolutionary contagion" after 1789. They represent the logical continuation of Catherine II's conservative policies, but in response to French diplomatic and military victories, which accounted for their great severity. Although no more than a dozen nobles received corporal punishment, all of the cases were well known and were condemned both in the salons of high society and in the barracks of the Guards. Rumor attributed them entirely to the emperor's despotism.

The question of the magnitude of the repressions then remains unclear. Paul's contemporaries were full of recollections about retirements, arrests, executions, nobles stripped of their rank, and banishments, to Siberia and elsewhere. Information about the number of victims is contradictory: according to Valishevskii (Waliszewski), more than 2,500 officers were affected; according to Shilder, more than 700 persons. The most authoritative estimates are Eidelman's; he reports that about 300 noblemen were imprisoned, sent to penal servitude, or exiled, and a great many others were punished less harshly, the total number of victims topping 1,500. Nobles were very rarely banished to Siberia; they were more often sent to their estates, to the provinces, or to an army regiment.

Examining orders in the army and the Guards,[41] we sampled officers' service transfers in November 1800. Three hundred and ninety-six were dismissed from the service at their own request; fifty-three were expelled from the service on orders from above; two were demoted to enlisted rank; three were exiled to hard labor; two were stripped of noble rank by decision of the Supreme Court; and six were banished to Siberia. During the same period, 304 were readmitted to the service, and 520 were promoted to the next rank. The number of those who suffered was considerably smaller than the number of those who benefited—that is, were promoted. Frequently, moreover, an officer who had been expelled from the service was readmitted at the same rank. Those who retired were awarded either the next rank or land. Either at an intercessor's request or simply because he was in a good mood, Paul I either rescinded punishments altogether or substituted lighter ones. Often sentences were deliberately delayed. Officers placed under arrest did not necessarily lose the emperor's regard (immediately after his release from custody, Chichagov was assigned to command the Baltic Squadron); even banishment might not hurt a person's career.

Naturally, being "kicked out of the service" did not foster Guards officers' loyalty to Paul I, but it would be wrong to exaggerate the officers' disgruntlement on this account. During his service, A.F. Voeikov was arrested and forbidden to enter either of the capital cities. Despite this, he considered Paul I "a true tsar in his intelligence, education, generosity, and magnanimity."[42]

None of Paul I's specific measures explain why he was assassinated, because the measures themselves grew out of the general direction of his policies and their ideological substantiation. One opinion that has become entrenched in scholarship, that the fundamental reason behind the conspiracy was Paul I's infringement on the nobility's common interests, explains little, because the autocracy has always to some extent restricted both the personal and the class interests of the nobility. There is no evidence in the literature indicating that Paul I introduced more restrictions of this sort than did, for example, Catherine II. In other words, there was no particular infringement on the nobility's class interests under Paul I, nor was there any political conflict between the ruling class and the emperor. Paul I's despotism remained narrowly personal. The conspiracy against him[43] included no issue of principle (despite subsequent declarations about the necessity of saving the state, the nobility, the Imperial family, and so on). To the conspirators greed alone spoke the desire either to keep or to acquire a comfortable spot. Another factor, probably, was the tradition of the palace coups of 1725–62, although in its nature and, indeed, its technology, the conspiracy of 1801 differed from the eighteenth-century coups.

From 1762 onward, a hostile attitude toward both Paul's abilities and his spiritual qualities, inspired by Catherine II, emerged in Russian society. The sarcastic laughter, gossip, and often outright nonsense were all directed at proving him incompetent. This tradition of belittling Paul's personality was also employed by the conspirators to justify his assassination. And because actually participating in conspiracy was unbecoming to a loyal nobleman, to quote Sablukov, "a great many criminal figures of the time, and their descendents, did their best to distort and conceal [the true picture of Paul's reign—Iu.S.]."[44]

The memoirists list the following as organizers of the conspiracy: St. Petersburg Governor-General P.A. Pahlen, Admiral Ribas, N.P. Panin (the nephew of Paul's mentor, N.I. Panin), and the English ambassador to Russia, [Charles] Whitworth. Obviously, N.P. Panin was the ideal instigator of the conspiracy. In a letter to Maria Fedorovna he confessed to the eminent role he had played in the events of 11 March, and he pointed out the motives for his participation, the most important of which was that "he had nothing for which to be grateful." It was Panin who attempted to involve Alexander in the conspiracy (to his contemporaries, the heir's complicity was an indisputable fact, which is why Alexander's tears and grief inspired first respect for the future emperor's artistic talents, then open indignation). An extant letter from Panin to Alexander I states, in particular, "I will carry with me to the grave the sincere conviction that I have served my country and dared to be the first to reveal to your eyes the lamentable picture of danger that threatened the empire with destruction."[45]

Pahlen assumed the functions of the conspiracy's "technical" supervisor. He developed the plan and selected the necessary people. After Panin was removed, Pahlen negotiated with Alexander, and through his efforts the Zubov brothers—Paul's irreconcilable enemies—were brought back to St. Petersburg. His motive was to preserve his own position, a difficult one given Paul I's unsteady character. Baron Heyking recounts a conversation with Pahlen immediately after Alexander I's ascent to the throne. Proud of his participation in the conspiracy, Pahlen asserted that he had received nothing from Paul I except medals, which he returned to Alexander who then "conferred" them on him again, that he had always hated Paul, and so on.

Lord Whitworth's participation in the conspiracy was reflected in generous financing. Many people saw Pahlen with golden guineas. During a game of cards in March 1801, Pahlen wagered 200,000 gold rubles—a lot of money for a modest nobleman from Courland, even one who had attained the heights of power.

The rank-and-file participants in the plot included the princes Zubov, Generals Talyzin and Uvarov, Iashvil, Bennigsen, Tatarinov, and Skariatin, among others. Altogether there were sixty conspirators, although naturally a larger number of persons knew of the plot. It is interesting to note that with rare exceptions, the high aristocracy, like the rank and file among the Guards, did not take part in it. The social composition of the conspirators and the absence of even a minimal program indirectly confirm the conclusion that each of them had a personal interest in overthrowing Paul I.

Evidently, Paul I suspected that a conspiracy was being prepared against him and correctly linked it to Alexander. Princess D.Kh. Lieven attests that the emperor saw the book *The Death of Caesar* on his eldest son's desk; he found a history of Peter, opened it to the page describing the death of Crown Prince Alexei, and ordered Kutaisov to remove the heir. The matter went beyond hints: at eight o'clock on 11 March, he summoned Alexander and Constantine to repeat their oath of fealty. Paul I also discussed the conspiracy with Pahlen, demanding that appropriate measures be taken, but he succumbed to the hypocritical assurances of his closest associate.

At midnight on 12 March, the conspirators, rather tipsy after supper at Talyzin's place, gained entry to Mikhailovskii Castle, but only ten to twelve persons reached Paul I's bedchamber. The memoirists give differing accounts of the emperor in his final moments. He was demoralized and could barely speak (according to Langeron, Veliaminov-Zernov,

Czartoryski, and von Wedel); he maintained his dignity (according to Sablukov), even meeting the conspirators with sword in hand. He was the first to strike a blow against N. Zubov and resisted until the final moment. They strangled him with a scarf and trampled him with their feet, and even hacked him with sabers (leaving deep wounds on his hands and head). Flushed with wine, the conspirators desecrated the corpse, and Zubov was even compelled to stop them.

On 12 March the manifesto was published. Emperor Alexander I promised to rule "in the mind and heart" of his most august grandmother, Catherine II. In this way, Paul I's reign was consigned to oblivion, as if it had been erased from history. The manifesto of 12 March 1801 marked the beginning of a tradition that surrounded not only the assassination but even the person of Paul with a "conspiracy of silence."

Scholars have characterized Paul's reign as a "military–police dictatorship" (M.M. Safonov) or as "unenlightened absolutism" (A.V. Predtechenskii, N.Ia. Eidelman). The particular conservatism of Paul's system of government, in these authors' opinions, prevented the emergence and development of a Russian Enlightenment and retarded Russia's historical progress. Moreover, they lay the blame for the establishment of such a regime directly on Paul's personality. But could late eighteenth- and early nineteenth-century Russia really have adopted a policy qualitatively different from that which Paul imposed? And was his personality really as great an influence on policy as the scholarly literature would have us believe?

The imperial domestic and foreign policy course that took shape under Paul I, was consistent with the need to preserve the status of the nobility and the interests of the absolute monarchy. The emperor chose means to accomplish this that matched his goals. Many of his contemporaries understood this. G.R. Derzhavin did not like Paul I, but he lamented the fact that, "while condemning the rule of Emperor Paul they began to distort, indiscriminately, so to speak, everything that he did."[47] However, many of his orders could not be rescinded, so necessary were they and so consistent with the objective needs of the empire.

The reign of Paul I, then, was a logical stage in the development of Russian absolutism, one in which the monarch implemented the only possible policy (from the standpoint of absolutist interests) using appropriate methods. As for the influence of Paul's personality on this policy, it seems one must agree with Pokrovskii:

As a person, Paul was no more unbalanced or jealous of his power than any other Russian monarch. Everything that Paul I did would have been done by any normal man of his intellectual development and inclinations who was placed in a similar situation, and even his predilections did not constitute a deviation from the norm but merely an exaggeration of the habits and customs that had emerged from the soil of the Potemkin–Zubov regime.[48]

The basic qualities and properties characteristic of Paul I were by no means exceptional among Russian monarchs of the eighteenth and early nineteenth centuries. His idiosyncrasies and eccentricities never went beyond the procedures and customs that prevailed in his time and in his social milieu. Even the most "notorious" of Paul's qualities were representative of many Romanovs from Peter I to Nicholas II, from their love of uniforms and their mania for parades to their protection and support of noble rights and privileges. Under the specific conditions of the destruction of absolute monarchies in Europe, Paul I did all he could to reinforce absolutism in Russia, to which he ascribed an almost mystical character, and virtually deified his own power. Ultimately, the same route was taken by his older son, the ideological inspirer of the "Holy Alliance."

Contemporary memoirs are full of hypocritical indignation over the bloodshed committed on 11 March 1801. They condemned assassination in general from the standpoint of Christian morality—ultimately condemning the assassination of the "sacred person" of the emperor. Hardly anyone, however, regretted that it was Paul I who fell victim to the violence. His death was considered a lamentable but well-deserved retribution. V.F. Khodasevich emphasized that most of the stories about Paul came from the mouths of people who were trying either to justify his assassination or at least to reconcile themselves to it. By condemning him they justified themselves. This is one way to account for the primarily negative attitude of his contemporaries toward Paul's personality, which then became firmly entrenched in the literature.

Notes

1. *Konchina rossiiskogo imperatora Pavla I* (Moscow, 1802); *Zhizn' Pavla I, imperatora i samoderzhtsa vserossiiskogo* (Moscow, 1805); N.M. Karamzin, *Zapiska o drevnei i novoi Rossii* (St. Petersburg, 1914); D.A. Miliutin, *Istoriia voiny 1799 goda* (St. Petersburg, 1857), vol. 1; N.K. Shil'der, *Imperator Pavel I* (St. Petersburg, 1901); A.G. Brikner, *Smert' Pavla I* (St. Petersburg, 1907); E.S. Shumigorskii, *Imperator Pavel I* (St. Petersburg, 1907).

2. V.O. Kliuchevskii, *Sochineniia* (Moscow, 1958), vol. 5; D.A. Kobelo, *Tsesarevich Pavel*

Petrovich (St. Petersburg, 1887); *Tri veka* (Moscow, 1913), vol. 5; A.A. Kornilov, *Kurs russkoi istorii XIX v.* (Moscow, 1912); and others.

3. M.V. Klochkov, *Ocherki pravitel'stvennoi deiatel'nosti vremeni Pavla I* (Prague, 1916).

4. M.N. Pokrovskii, "Pavel Petrovich," in *Istoriia Rossii v XIX v.* (Moscow, 1908), vol. 1, pp. 21–30; idem, "Istoriia Rossii s drevneishikh vremen do nashikh dnei," in *Izbrannye proizvedeniia* (Moscow, 1965), vol. 3, bk. 2; I.M. Vasilevskii, *Romanovy: Portrety i kharakteristiki* (Prague, 1923); V.I. Samoilov, *Vnutrenniaia i vneshniaia politika Pavla I* (Khlebnikovo, 1946); O.Sh. Gvinchidze, *Brat'ia Gruzinovy* (Tbilisi, 1965); and others.

5. S.B. Okun', *Istoriia SSSR, konets XVIII—nachalo XIX v.* (Leningrad, 1974); N.Ia. Eidel'man, *Gertsen protiv samoderzhaviia* (Moscow, 1984); idem, *Gran' vekov* (Moscow, 1986).

6. Platon, *Pravoslavnoe uchenie, ili Sokrashchennoe khristianskoe bogoslovie* (n.p., 1765) p. 172.

7. Semena Poroshina zapiski, *sluzhashchie k istorii e. i. v. blagovernogo gosudaria tsesarevicha i velikogo kniazia Pavla Petrovicha* (St. Petersburg, 1881) p. 25.

8. *Russkii arkhiv*, 1871, no. 1, p. 149.

9. *Russkaia starina*, 1902, vol. 2, pp. 382–83.

10. *Sbornik Russkogo istoricheskogo obshchestva*, vol. 20, p. 412.

11. *Russkaia starina*, 1882, no. 2, pp. 416–17.

12. Ibid., no. 11, p. 330.

13. *Russkii dvor 100 let nazad* (St. Petersburg, 1907), p. 273.

14. *Ubiistvo imperatora Pavla* (Rostov-on-Don, n.d.), p. 3.

15. *Russkii arkhiv*, 1869, no. 11, p. 1883.

16. *Vestnik Evropy*, 1867, no. 3, p. 306.

17. Ibid., pp. 316–22.

18. *Russkii arkhiv*, 1869, no. 7, p. 1102.

19. *Zapiski generala N.A. Sablukova o vremenakh imperatora Pavla I i o konchine etogo gosudaria* (Leipzig, 1902), p. 6.

20. *Russkii arkhiv*, 1876, no. 4, p. 399.

21. A. Petrushevskii, *Generalissimus kniaz' Suvorov* (St. Petersburg, 1900), pp. 444–45.

22. G. Reimers, "Peterburg pri imperatore Pavle Petroviche v 1796–1801 gg.," *Russkaia starina*, 1883, no. 9.

23. A. Czartoryski, *Memuary* (Moscow, 1912), vol. 1, p. 113.

24. *Russkii arkhiv*, 1867, no. 2, p. 226.

25. Ibid., 1869, no. 1, p. 165.

26. *Russkaia starina*, 1882, no. 4, p. 475.

27. D.B. Mertvago, *Zapiski* (Moscow, 1867), p. 182.

28. Eidel'man, *Gran' vekov*, p. 61.

29. *Zaria*, no. 12 (1871), pp. 203–4.

30. *Russkii arkhiv*, 1913, no. 9, pp. 301–2.

31. Eidel'man, *Gran' vekov*, pp. 72–76.

32. Samoilov, *Vnutrenniaia i vneshniaia politika*, p. 18.

33. *Russkii arkhiv*, 1907, no. 1, p. 45.

34. Ibid., 1868, no. 7, p. 1074.

35. Ibid., 1909, no. 1, p. 203.

36. Pokrovskii, "Istoriia Rossii," p. 162.

37. N.I. Grech, *Zapiski o moei zhizni* (Moscow-Leningrad, 1930), p. 138.

38. *Russkii arkhiv*, 1869, p. 165.

39. P.N. Kovalevskii, *Imperator Petr III, imperator Pavel I* (St. Petersburg, 1906); V.F. Chizh, "Imperator Pavel I," *Voprosy filosofii i psikhologii*, 1907, bks. 88–90.

40. *Ukazy gosudaria imperatora Pavla Pervogo, samoderzhtsa vserossiiskogo* (Moscow, 1797).

41. *Prikazy 1800 g.* (St. Petersburg, 1800).

42. "Iz zapisok A.F. Voeikova," in *Istoricheskii sbornik vol'noi russkoi tipografii v Londone A.I. Gertsena i N.P. Ogareva* (Moscow, 1971), bk. 2, p. 120.

43. Our understanding of the causes of the conspiracy goes back to Pokrovskii ("Pavel Petrovich").

44. *Russkii arkhiv*, 1869, no. 11, p. 1913.

45. *Vremia Pavla i ego smert'* (Moscow, 1906), p. 196.

46. [Missing in original.—Trans.]

47. G.R. Derzhavin, *Sochineniia* (St. Petersburg, 1876), vol. 6, p. 723.

48. Pokrovskii, "Istoriia Rossii," p. 168.

Emperor Alexander I, 1801–1825

Complex, elusive, cunning, shy, insincere, enigmatic, and contradictory are just some of the mystifying appellations that observers and historians alike have used to describe Tsar Alexander I, who came to the throne in 1801, following the deposition and murder of his father, Emperor Paul I. Hailed as a liberal by some and a tyrant by others, Alexander has puzzled generations of historians, because of the unfulfilled promise of many of his endeavors and the psychological paradoxes inherent in so many of his actions. Whereas some of the Russian authors represented in this collection have sought to rehabilitate the tarnished reputations of their protagonists, Moscow University historian Vladimir Aleksandrovich Fedorov presents a disparaging description of Alexander I, "a republican in words but an autocrat in deeds."

Like many writers, Fedorov places great importance on Alexander's formative years, when he was torn between the two worlds of St. Petersburg (Catherine II) and Gatchina (Paul I). The result was an insincere heir to the throne. And one who did not like Russians. "Extremely proud, mistrustful, and suspicious, Alexander took clever advantage of people's weaknesses and knew how to play at 'sincerity' as a reliable way to control people and subordinate them to his will," writes Fedorov. The author supplements this none-too-flattering characterization with flashes of a suspicious Alexander monitoring his subjects' mail, and a cruel ruler who brutally cut down a peasant who dared to cross his path. Fedorov also assesses the emperor's foreign policy, his attempts at would-be reform, and the period of religious obscurantism and mysticism that prevailed during part of his reign.

In Fedorov's view, Alexander's tenure did not mark a return to Catherine's "Golden Age" for the nobility or a total rejection of his father's policies. Not a reformer by nature, Alexander above all else strove to strengthen the autocracy and further bureaucratization of the state administration. Perhaps because of the traditional source base utilized by the author, he eschews drawing a conclusion, opting instead for formulation of an agenda for future research, and making the case that "this monarch's reign still awaits a definitive study."

D.J.R.

Alexander I

Vladimir Aleksandrovich Fedorov

Paul I's eldest son, Catherine II's grandson, was born on 12 December 1777. Catherine II named him in honor of Alexander Nevsky, the patron saint of St. Petersburg. Alexander was her favorite grandson, and she herself took charge of his upbringing. He was taught Russian literature and history by M.N. Muraviev, a writer and one of the most enlightened men of his time (the father of future Decembrists); he was taught the natural sciences by the well-known scientist and traveler P.S. Pallas; and he received religious instruction and spiritual guidance from Archpriest A.A. Samborskii, who, although he was, according to his contemporaries, a "man of the world, devoid of any profound religious feeling," nonetheless managed to inspire this feeling in his pupil. Samborskii had lived in England for a long time and was a passionate Anglophile; as well as religious instruction, he was responsible for teaching Alexander English.

At the recommendation of F. Grimm, the diplomat and writer on public affairs with whom Catherine conducted a friendly correspondence, F.M. La Harpe, a Swiss, was invited to Russia in 1782. A highly educated man devoted to the ideas of the Enlightenment as well as a republican in his views, his job was to act as Alexander's tutor and teach him French. He spent eleven years in this post (1784–95), introducing Alexander to abstract concepts concerning the natural equality of people, the superiority of the republican form of government, and the political and civil liberties and "universal good" toward which a ruler ought to strive. La Harpe nevertheless carefully avoided the sensitive issues confronting Russia under serfdom. He concerned himself chiefly with his pupil's moral upbringing. It is recounted that, at La Harpe's advice, Alexander kept a journal in which he recorded all his misdeeds. Later, he said he owed everything good in him to La Harpe.

Overall supervision of the upbringing of Alexander and his younger brother Constantine was assigned to Count N.I. Saltykov, a limited but clever court intriguer whose chief duty was to report to the empress every step the boys made, and their teachers, too.

Despite the selection of brilliant teachers, Alexander did not get a thorough education. His teachers noted that their pupil had an aversion to serious study, tended to be slow and lazy, and was inclined to idleness. He did not know how to concentrate. He read very little; because he possessed extraordinary intelligence he could quickly grasp an idea, but he just as quickly forgot it. In 1793, when Alexander was not yet sixteen years old, Catherine II had him married to the fourteen-year-old Princess Louisa of Baden, who was baptized into Orthodoxy as Elizaveta Alekseevna. With his marriage, Alexander's schooling ended.

The real school in his upbringing was the feud between Catherine II's "big court" in St. Petersburg and Paul's "little court" at Gatchina. The need to maneuver between them taught Alexander, as V.O. Kliuchevskii said, "to live with two minds, to maintain two façades," and this developed secretiveness and hypocrisy in him. The pomp and refined conversations of the salons could not conceal from him the unseemly life of his imperious grandmother's court. He saw the unattractiveness of the crude procedures at Gatchina and the scornful attitude of Catherine and her courtiers toward the "little court"; he heard his father's unambiguous statements concerning Catherine's "usurpation" of his rights to the throne. This period shaped Alexander's personality and has provoked conflicting assessments and judgments from both his contemporaries and historians.

By 1787 Catherine had decided to bypass Paul and name Alexander as her heir, and in 1794 she revealed this plan to her most trusted associates, justifying it by reference to Paul's "morals and incompetence." It has been said that V.A. Musin-Pushkin opposed Catherine's plan and that the matter of succession to the throne was halted for a time.[1] In September 1796, not long before she died, Catherine again discussed her decision with Alexander and began to compose a manifesto about it. Catherine's intentions were no secret to Paul; he had learned of them from Alexander himself. Alexander assured his father that he had no wish to accept the throne, and in A.A. Arakcheev's presence he took an oath of fealty to Paul as emperor and called him "Imperial Highness," even while Catherine was alive.[2]

To dispel his father's suspicions, Alexander declared for all to hear that he wanted to "renounce this unseemly position" (the succession to the throne) altogether; he also reported this in letters that were undoubtedly opened and inspected on Paul's behalf. In 1796 he wrote to La Harpe (who by then had already left Russia) that he wished to "settle down with my wife on the banks of the Rhine" and "live the peaceful life of a private man, finding my happiness in the company of friends and the study of nature."[3]

After Paul ascended the throne, Alexander was assigned to several important posts. He was appointed military governor of St. Petersburg, chief of the Guards of the Semenovskii Regiment, a cavalry and infantry inspector, and, somewhat later, chairman of the Senate's Military Department. Every morning he had to report to his father and listen to stern reprimands for the slightest mistakes. Various major military appointments also went to Constantine, whom Paul treated as curtly as he did any other officer. Contemporaries attest that Alexander and Constantine were very much afraid of their despotic father.

A friendly, "intimate" circle of young aristocrats formed around Alexander in 1796—Prince A.A. Czartoryski, Count P.A. Stroganov, N.N. Novosiltsev, and Count V.P. Kochubei. At the time, they were enamored with the ideas of the Enlightenment. The most gifted and remarkable among them, Stroganov, tried to influence Alexander. Stroganov's cousin Novosiltsev, who possessed a sparkling literary style, gave an "elegant and relaxed" tone to the circle. The intelligent and talented Czartoryski, a shrewd politician and fiery Polish patriot, cherished the thought of restoring the Polish state and placed his hopes in Alexander as the future emperor. Kochubei, a confirmed Anglophile, had outstanding diplomatic abilities.

Meeting in secret, the members of the circle held frank discussions concerning the necessity of abolishing serfdom, the harm done by despotism, and the superiority of the republican form of government. At such times, Alexander voiced some quite radical views. Czartoryski recalls him saying that he:

> hates despotism ... [and] loves liberty alone, to which all people have identical rights, that he had been following the French Revolution with keen interest, that, while he condemned the Revolution's horrible excesses, he wished the Republic success and rejoiced in it, ... that he wished to see republics everywhere and acknowledged this form of government to be the only one consistent with the rights of humanity, ... that a hereditary monarchy was an unjust and absurd institution, and

that supreme power ought not to be conferred on the basis of the accident of birth but by the vote of the people, who would know how to elect the person most capable of governing a state.

Czartoryski assures us that Alexander said this with complete sincerity.

Around the time of Paul I's coronation, Czartoryski, at Alexander's behest, prepared a draft "manifesto" that described the "embarrassment" of an absolute monarchy and the advantages of the form of government Alexander hoped to install once he became emperor, thus establishing liberty and justice. The manifesto went on to say that Alexander, "having taken on this obligation, sacred to him," intended to "renounce power so that he who was deemed most worthy of it might strengthen and perfect the undertaking the foundation of which he had laid."[4] Alexander was quite satisfied with the draft, thanked Czartoryski for it, and then hid it in a safe place and never mentioned it. That was quite typical of Alexander.

Later, after he became emperor, he often declared his intent to introduce a constitution, "legitimate and free institutions," and representative government; he assigned someone to draft documents in this spirit, approved them, then invariably shelved them. The characteristic gap between his words and his deeds, his demagogic declarations and his actual policies, may be explained by the indubitable influence of the contradictory policies of Catherine II's "enlightened absolutism," where fashionable liberal and enlightened ideas accorded well with reactionary, absolutist, feudal practice.

The "horrible four-year school under Paul," in N.M. Karamzin's words, left its mark. Added to Alexander's secretiveness and hypocrisy was fear of his despotic father, followed later by fear of conspiracy. Constantly haunted by the "shadow of his murdered father," Alexander also feared that he himself would fall victim to a conspiracy. Paul I's government had generated universal dissatisfaction, especially among the nobility, whose interests had been most affected. Given Paul's unpredictable behavior, no one felt safe. One of his contemporaries attests that Paul had already prepared an order to his favorites Arakcheev and F.I. Lindener "to incarcerate the empress and his two sons and thereby get rid of everyone who seemed suspicious to him." Empress Maria Fedorovna was to be banished to Kholmogory, Alexander imprisoned at Schlüsselberg, and Constantine incarcerated at the Peter and Paul Fortress.[5] This also helped the conspirators to win Alexander to their cause.

The conspiracy against Paul I was already being formulated by the middle of 1800. The mastermind behind it was Catherine's grandee N.P. Panin, while the director and executor was St. Petersburg's governor-general, Count P.A. Pahlen. Other parties to the conspiracy were the English ambassador C[harles] Whitworth and a large group of Guards officers. In September 1800, Panin had a confidential discussion with Alexander, during which he "hinted" at the possible use of violence against Paul. After that, Pahlen conducted all talks in Alexander's presence. Alexander gave his consent on condition that his father's life would be spared, and he even forced Pahlen to swear to this. "I gave him that promise," Pahlen said later. "I was not so foolhardy as to vouch for something that was impossible. But it was necessary to soothe my future sovereign's pangs of conscience. So on the surface I agreed with his intention, although I was convinced that it could not be fulfilled."[6] Later, Alexander claimed that the conspirators had "deceived him," and he demonstratively banished all of them to the countryside. Some scholars assert that Alexander demanded this verbal oath from the conspirators, although he himself expected no other outcome from the endeavor.[7]

In early March 1801 Paul caught wind of the conspiracy under way and confided the news to Pahlen. There was no time to lose. The conspirators conferred with Alexander and decided on a time for the deed—the night of 11–12 March, when soldiers of the Semenovskii Regiment, whose chief was Alexander, would be standing guard. At one o'clock in the morning, Pahlen brought him the news of Paul I's "sudden death." It is said that Alexander "burst into tears." Pahlen forced him to appear before the Semenovskii and Preobrazhenskii regiments, which were assembled in the courtyard of Mikhailovskii Castle. "Enough of this childishness. Now act like a tsar and show yourself to the Guards," he said.[8] On 12 March 1801 a manifesto was published, stating: "The fate of the Most High has seen fit to cut short the life of our most beloved father and sovereign, Emperor Pavel Petrovich, who died unexpectedly as the result of a stroke on the night of the 11th–12th of this month."[9]

On receiving the news of Paul I's death, "society in the capital city surrendered itself to unrestrained and childlike rejoicing," one contemporary recalls. "Their ecstasy even crossed the bounds of decency."[10] A harmonious choir of triumphal odes welcomed Alexander I's ascension to the throne. Among these was G.R. Derzhavin's ode entitled "On Emperor Alexander I's All-Joyful Ascension to the Throne." To be sure, the ode was never approved for publication because it contained an unambiguous hint of the palace coup, but Alexander gave the poet who wrote it a diamond ring. Karamzin also greeted the tsar's coronation with poetry. "After Paul's brief and unhappy reign, Alexander's ascension to the throne was welcomed with enthusiastic rejoicing," the Decembrist A.M. Muraviev wrote. "We had never before placed such high hopes on a successor to power. We rushed to forget the mad reign. All the people placed their hopes on the pupil of La Harpe and Muraviev."[11]

Alexander himself impressed the public with his behavior and even his appearance. The emperor, modestly clothed, rode out or walked "informally" through the St. Petersburg streets; the crowd greeted him enthusiastically, and he "graciously responded to this tribute of honor."[12] His very words and actions, as Muraviev noted, "breathed with the desire to be loved."

In August 1801 La Harpe, summoned from Geneva by Alexander, returned to St. Petersburg. But he was no longer the republican "Jacobin" who had once troubled court circles. Now he warned his pupil against the "illusory freedom of people's assemblies and liberal enthusiasms in general." As an example he pointed to Prussia, "which united order with laws" through a firm monarchical authority. He advised Alexander "to retain absolute power intact." "Do not allow yourself to yield to the aversion that absolute power engenders in you; preserve it whole and undivided," La Harpe said. And he advised: "You must instill within your ministers the idea that they are merely proxies," obligated to report to the monarch everything that is going on, "clearly and fully." The tsar must "pay close attention to their opinions but make his own decisions without them, so that all that remains to them is to carry them out." Finally, he demanded that Alexander punish Paul's assassins so that there would be no similar attempts in the future. Although he understood the damage caused by serfdom, La Harpe advised Alexander to approach matters gradually, "without causing any sensation or alarm" and without infringing in any way on the nobility's property rights.[13]

Alexander ascended the throne with his views and intentions already formed, with a definite "tactics" of behavior and running the state. His contemporaries spoke of such traits as secretiveness, hypocrisy, and inconstancy: "an utter fawner" (M.M. Speranskii); "a weak and cunning ruler" (A.S. Pushkin); "a Sphinx who was not divined in his lifetime" (P.A. Viazemskii); "a crowned Hamlet haunted all his life by the shadow of his murdered father" (A.I. Herzen). People also noted in him "a strange mixture of the philosophical infections of

Alexander I

the eighteenth century and the principles of natural autocracy." His boyhood friend Czartoryski later had this to say: "The emperor loved the outward forms of liberty, as one may love an idea, . . . but he wanted nothing other than forms and appearance and was not at all inclined to tolerate their being turned into reality." General P.A. Tuchkov remarked in his own memoirs that "at Alexander's ascension to the throne, certain of his actions clearly showed the spirit of unrestricted autocracy, vengefulness, vindictiveness, mistrust, inconstancy, and deceit." A.I. Turgenev (brother of the Decembrist N.I. Turgenev) called Alexander "a republican in words but an autocrat in deeds" and believed Paul's despotism preferable to the covert and changeable despotism of Alexander.[14]

Alexander I was distinguished by his truly virtuoso ability to take advantage of other people's trusting natures; he possessed "an inborn gift for amiability" and was therefore easily able to win to his side people with various views and convictions—he could talk "liberalism" with the "liberals," speak of "the unshakable foundation" with reactionaries, shed "copious tears" with the religious fanatic Baroness J. von Krüdener, and converse with Quakers about the salvation of the soul and religious tolerance. For his acting ability, his contemporaries called Alexander the "Northern Talma" (a well-known French actor of the day). "The world seldom gives birth to such an artist," wrote S.P. Melgunov of Alexander I, "not only among royalty, but also among mere mortals."[15] "Acting," however, is characteristic of many monarchs, a feature of their positions that is completely excusable.

Extremely proud, distrustful, and suspicious, Alexander took clever advantage of people's weaknesses and knew how to play at "sincerity" to control people and subordinate them to his will. He loved to surround himself with people who did not like one another and made clever use of their mutual enmity and intrigues; he once stated to Ia.I. de Sanglen, head of the chancellory of the Ministry of Police, "Intriguers are just as essential to state affairs in general as honest people are, and sometimes even more so."[16]

M.A. Korf recalled that Alexander, like his grandmother Catherine II, "was supremely able to win over people's minds and penetrate other people's souls, while keeping his own thoughts and feelings to himself."[17] The French writer Madame de Staël, who was greatly impressed by Alexander when she met him in Paris in 1814, described him as "a man of remarkable intellect and knowledge." Alexander spoke to her about the harmfulness of despotism and earnestly recounted his sincere desire to liberate the serfs. In the same year, while visiting England, he showered compliments on the Whigs and assured them that he intended to create an opposition in Russia as well, because then matters could be handled more appropriately.[18]

Alexander's "magnanimity" and "courtesy" conquered the well-known Prussian statesman Baron F. Stein. However, one of the Russian emperor's character traits did not escape the Prussian minister's notice: "He frequently resorts to the weapon of cunning and slyness to achieve his goals."[19]

Napoleon's assessment of Alexander I's character and qualities is unquestionably of interest, for Napoleon was a good judge of people. Reminiscing in St. Helena about his meeting with Alexander at Tilsit in 1807, Napoleon wrote,

> The tsar is intelligent, elegant, and well-educated. He can charm people easily, but one must beware of that; he is insincere. He is a genuine Byzantine from the period of the Empire's decline. He has, of course, genuine or simulated convictions; however, in the end these are only nuances given to him by his upbringing and his tutor.... It is quite possible that he duped me, for he is subtle, deceptive, and adroit; he can go far. If I die here, he will become my true heir in Europe.[20]

This sounds like an acknowledgment of the Russian emperor's unusual abilities, and in fact Napoleon considered Alexander his equal.

Alexander was not fond of people who "rose through their talent." Contemporaries remarked that "he likes only mediocrity; genuine genius, intelligence, and talent frighten him, and he will make use of them only against his will, in the most extreme cases."[21] Naturally, he could not manage without intelligent and talented statesmen and military men, people such as M.M. Speranskii, M.I. Kutuzov, and N.S. Mordvinov. We cannot call untalented even certain reactionary figures of his reign, such as A.A. Arakcheev, A.S. Shishkov, and Metropolitan Filaret. But for the most part, he was surrounded by unprincipled courtiers of no honor or conscience, people like Moscow's Governor-General F.V. Rostopchin, Minister of Religious Affairs and Public Education A.N. Golitsyn, "suppressors of education" D.P. Runich and M.L. Magnitskii, and the bigoted and fanatical Archimandrite Fotii.

Alexander himself had rather unflattering things to say about the dignitaries with whom he surrounded himself. In 1820 he complained to Prussia's King Frederick-Wilhelm III that he was "surrounded by scoundrels" and "would like to expel many, but the same kind of people would come to take their place."[22] He tried to associate with people who had no other ties in aristocratic circles; he attracted those known in society as nobodies, even objects of contempt; he was unwilling to appoint to state posts any representatives of aristocratic lineages who conducted themselves in an independent manner. The feelings of those passed over were especially offended by "the predominance of foreigners" in Russian service, whom Alexander demonstratively preferred. "In order to be liked by the ruler, it was necessary either to be a foreigner or to have a foreign surname," A.M. Muraviev complained.[23]

In the salons, people shared with one another the witticism of General A.P. Ermolov who, when asked by the tsar what reward he wished to receive for his military services, answered: "Sire, make me a German." The Decembrist I.D. Iakushkin recalled: "People constantly heard about statements in which Emperor Alexander expressed open disdain for Russians." While reviewing his troops in 1814 in the French town of Vertu, and in response to the Duke of Wellington's words of praise for the troops' organization, Alexander declared for all to hear that he was obliged to foreigners for this. Once, in the Winter Palace, "while speaking of Russians in general, he said that every one of them is either a knave or a fool." It is not by accident that one of the Union of Salvation's goals was to oppose foreigners in the Russian service.[24]

Alexander's own family called him a "gentle, obstinate person." The Swedish ambassador, Baron Stedingk, had this to say about him: "While it was difficult to convince him of anything, it was even more difficult to get him to give up an idea that had taken hold of him."[25] He manifested special obstinacy and firmness in issues of pride. His obstinacy was wholly linked to a weak will, like the conflict between his "liberalism" in words and the despotism and even cruelty in his deeds. "He is too weak to govern and too strong to be governed," remarked Speranskii, who also noted the tsar's inconsistency ("he does everything halfway").

Alexander never forgot the events of March 1801—not out of "twinges of conscience" but rather as a warning. The suspiciousness that he inherited from Paul I increased as the years went by. This accounted for the system of surveillance and investigation, which expanded especially during the final years of his reign. He himself listened eagerly to denunciations and even encouraged them, demanding that his staffers keep track of one another. He even considered it permissible to read his wife's correspondence.

His contemporaries gained the impression that he was extremely frivolous and unstable. He especially loved "the company of women remarkable" not only for their beauty but for their minds, and he accorded them a "chivalrous courtesy, full of elegance and kindness," as some of his female contemporaries (for example, Madame de Staël, D.F. Finkelmon, A.P. Kern, the countess of Choiseul-Gouffier, and the countess of Edling) expressed it. According to Countess Edling, "Alexander's treatment of women never changed with the years, and his piety never prevented him from having a good time."[26] One must note that Alexander had great success with women, who, as they themselves admitted, were drawn to his "delicate, symmetrical features and light complexion, his clear blue eyes," full of "gentleness and softness," and his witty and gallant speech. Everyone—including his wife—knew all about Alexander's lengthy liaison (more than twenty years) with Maria Antonovna Naryshkina—a woman of rare loveliness and charm. F.F. Vigel recalled that St. Petersburg, "which teemed with beauties," had none equal to her. When he first saw her in the theater, in his own words, "my mouth dropped open; I stood before her box and with the most idiotic of expressions on my face admired her beauty, which was so perfect that she seemed unnatural, impossible."[27] In 1808 Naryshkina bore the tsar a daughter, Sophia, whose death in 1824 Alexander saw as a great personal tragedy.

Police reports to Austria's Chancellor Metternich during the Congress of Vienna, where the European monarchs convened, are replete with reports about the Russian tsar's philandering. It must be said, however, that with Alexander, "playing at love" was subordinated to diplomatic intrigues. In the salons of Vienna, the diplomatic game continued behind the scenes, and Alexander, like French Minister of Foreign Affairs Talleyrand, did not shy away from it.

Plenty of portraits of the emperor have been preserved in which Alexander looks like a well-built young man, rosy-cheeked and blue-eyed, with a pleasant smile. Considered closer to real life is a portrait painted by the English artist G. Dawe. This painting depicts a pensive man of middle years with small sideburns and hair that has thinned. From childhood Alexander was near-sighted, but he preferred to use a lorgnette rather than wear glasses; he was deaf in his left ear, which had been damaged in his childhood when he stood close to an artillery battery while it was firing. Beginning in young manhood, he took a cold bath every day to build up his strength. In his everyday life he was relatively modest and frugal. From springtime until far into autumn he generally lived in Tsarskoe Selo, where he occupied small rooms in the palace. Early in the morning, in any kind of weather, he walked around the palace grounds. After 1816 Karamzin was his constant companion on outings. The emperor and his court historiographer talked about a variety of burning political issues.[28] In the winter, the emperor moved back to St. Petersburg, where he attended the mounting of the guard in the mornings, followed by military exercises.

During the first years of his reign, he rarely left Tsarskoe Selo or St. Petersburg. The final ten years of his reign were characterized by frequent and lengthy journeys. It has been estimated that during that period Alexander covered more than 135,000 miles. He traveled to the north and south of Russia, spent time in the Urals, the central and lower Volga, Finland, and Warsaw, and visited London, Paris, Vienna, and Berlin several times, as well as several other cities in Western Europe.

In the manifesto of 12 March 1801 Alexander I had declared that he would govern the people "entrusted to him by God" in accordance with "the laws and the heart of our most august grandmother, now resting in the bosom of God," thereby emphasizing his adherence to the political course set by Catherine II, who had done so much to expand the nobility's privileges. He also started by reinstating the charters to the nobility and the towns, which Paul I had abrogated, and restored the nobles' elective corporate institutions. He exempted nobles and the clergy from corporal punishment (which Paul had reintroduced), declared amnesty to all persons who had fled across the border to get away from Paul's repressions, and brought back from exile as many as twelve thousand civil servants and military men who had fallen from favor or who had been punished by Paul for political reasons. Noteworthy among them were "Radishchev, the former College Councillor," whom Paul had brought back from Siberia but exiled to Kaluga Province, and "Artillery Lieutenant Colonel Ermolov," who had been banished to Kostroma.

Alexander also abolished others among Paul's decrees that irritated the nobility—for example, the bans on wearing round French hats, on subscribing to foreign newspapers and journals, and on traveling abroad. In the towns, the notices listing persons out of favor disappeared. Free trade was declared, and it was ordered that private printing plants be unsealed and their owners permitted to publish books and journals. The fear-inspiring Secret Expedition, devoted to investigations and reprisals, was abolished. These did not yet amount to reforms, but only rescinded some of Paul I's most tyrannical orders, orders that had provoked universal dissatisfaction. The effect of these measures upon people, however, was exceptionally great, generating hopes for further changes. Not only in Russia did people believe in the sincerity of Alexander's reformist intentions; even American President Thomas Jefferson thought so.

Although Alexander I, in the manifesto on his ascension to the throne, emphasized the continuity between his own rule and Catherine II's, his reign marked neither a return to Catherine's "Golden Age" nor a complete rejection of Paul's policies. Alexander did not like to be reminded of his grandmother's reign, and he was not on friendly terms with Catherine's dignitaries. While demonstratively rejecting the character and methods of Paul's rule, he adopted many of its features, in particular its main direction—the further bureaucratization of administration and strengthening of autocracy. In fact, the "Gatchina system" (adherence to military regimentation) was deeply rooted in him, and he retained his love for parades and the mounting of the guards all his life. By nature, Alexander I was not a reformer. His extremely knowledgeable biographer, Grand Duke Nikolai Mikhailovich, reached this conclusion: "Emperor Alexander was never a reformer; during the first years of his reign he was more conservative than all his counselors."[29]

Alexander could hardly fail to reckon with "the spirit of the times," however—in particular, the influence of the ideas of the French Revolution—and to a certain extent he even adapted these ideas to his own ends. Here is a curious statement of his: "The most powerful weapon that the French used and are still using to menace other countries is the general conviction that they have managed to disseminate, namely, that they represent the people's freedom and happiness," and for this reason "the real interests of the legitimate authorities demand that they tear this frightful weapon out of French hands and, having taken possession of it, turn it against the French themselves."[30] This is the context in which we must examine the tsar's high-sounding demagogic declarations (especially abroad) of his desire for transformation, for ensuring "people's freedom and happiness," and his intention to abolish serfdom in Russia and introduce "legal, free institutions"—that is, constitutional procedures.

In fact, Alexander I strove to strengthen absolutism without changing the basic direction of Catherine II's and Paul's policies, using methods consistent with "the spirit of the times." One of the characteristic features of the Russian autocracy was its ability, in particular circumstances, to be flexible, to make concessions, and to adapt to new phenomena and processes within the country while using these to strengthen its own position.

When he ascended the throne, Alexander I publicly and solemnly proclaimed that the basis of policy would no longer be the monarch's whim but rather strict compliance with the laws. The manifesto of 2 April 1801 concerning the abolition of the Secret Expedition stated that from then on "a reliable barrier [was] erected against abuses," and that "in a well-ordered state all crimes must be detected, judged, and punished to the full extent of the law."[31] Whenever the opportunity presented itself, Alexander loved to talk about the priority of legality. The people were promised legal guarantees against tyranny.

All of these declarations had immense social resonance. The idea of legality, of establishing "the rule of law," was a major one among representatives of various segments of Russian public opinion—Speranskii, Karamzin, the Decembrists, and Pushkin (the idea was expressed most explicitly in Pushkin's ode "Liberty"). To work out a plan for the transformation, the tsar enlisted his "young friends" Stroganov, Kochubei, Czartoryski, and Novosiltsev, who constituted his "intimate circle" or "Unofficial Committee." Although the committee was called "unofficial," many people knew and talked about it. Incidentally, Alexander himself made no secret of it, and he drew on its support in his struggle with the highly placed opposition. His "young friends," however, had already abandoned their former republican enthusiasms and become more moderate in their views. Cautious in their projects and proposals, and despite drawing up plans to reform the state administration and discussing the necessity of issuing a charter to the people, they based their plans on the inviolability of absolutism and the preservation of serfdom.

Between June 1801 and May 1802, the committee convened thirty-five times, but in 1803, after meeting just four times, it was abolished. Alexander I now felt more secure on the throne and had no need to engage in liberal talk. Although the entire exercise was limited to these talks, they frightened the aristocracy of Catherine's time, which christened the committee "a Jacobin gang." Cause for this unflattering epithet was given by the tsar himself, who jokingly called his own "intimate circle" the "Committee of Public Safety."

But the "spirit of the times" did shine through in measures—however secondary they may have been—that Alexander implemented on such burning issues as the peasant question. From the very beginning, the new tsar, without any special decree or manifesto, halted the transfer of peasants to private hands. No such grants followed the tsar's coronation in September 1801, "to the great resentment of many who craved that distinction."[32] When in 1802 a dignitary (Duke A. Virtembergskii) asked Alexander I to grant him an estate, the tsar answered: "The Russian peasants for the most part belong to the landowners; I consider it excessive to demonstrate the humiliation and misfortune of such a state, and that is why I promised not to increase the number of these unfortunates and have made it a rule not to turn the peasants over to anyone's possession."[33]

This by no means signified that state-owned peasants were fully guaranteed that they would not be turned into serfs. Between 1810 and 1817, because of the empire's difficult financial straits, more than ten thousand male peasants were sold into private hands. It was also common to lease state-owned peasants to private persons in Belorussia and western Ukraine (by the end of Alexander I's reign, 350,000 peasants were leased). State-owned peasants were also made serfs by other means: for example, they were transferred to appanage departments, assigned to state-owned plants and factories, and organized into military settlements (the last was the worst form of serf dependency).

The measures designed to alleviate serf status may be judged by an 1801 decree banning the publication of announcements of sales of serfs "without land," although engaging in this kind of sale was not prohibited; instead, the published announcements described the peasants as not "for sale" but "for hire." Decrees of 1808–9 prohibited landowners from selling peasants at "retail" fairs or banishing them to Siberia for petty offenses. Landowners were obliged to feed their peasants during famine years. Another decree with insignificant results was that of 20 February 1803 on "free tillers of the soil"; it allowed peasants to buy their liberty on the basis of a mutual agreement between them and the landowners. The purchase price was so high and the deal accompanied by such enslaving conditions that, as of 1825, less than 0.5 percent of all serfs had managed to take advantage of that right. The first stage of peasant reform in Latvia and Estonia was carried out in 1804–5, but the reform extended only to "individual peasant proprietors." These received individual liberty without land, which they would have to lease from their landowners in exchange for feudal duties—labor services and rent in kind. In principle, such measures by Alexander I did not infringe upon landowners' rights and privileges. To be sure, the decree of 12 December 1801 conferred upon the non-noble free classes—merchants, small traders and craftsmen, and state-owned peasants—the right to purchase land. A manifesto of 1 January 1807, "On the Allocation to the Merchantry of New Benefits and Privileges and of New Means for the Expansion and Strengthening of Trading Enterprises," stimulated the development of national entrepreneurship.[34]

Many of Alexander I's measures concerned education, the press, and the central administration. The censorship charter of 1804 is considered one of the most "liberal" in nineteenth-century Russia. It stated that censorship was being introduced "not to stifle the freedom to think and to write but solely to take proper measures against abuses of it." It recommended that the censors be guided by "a reasonable leniency toward the writer, not indulge in fault-finding, and interpret passages with double meanings in the manner most favorable to the writer rather than prosecute."[35] Censorship practice nullified these benign desires, however, and the years when Alexander I's reactionary policies intensified were characterized by real censorship terror. Nevertheless, it would be wrong to ignore such manifestations of relaxed censorship during the early years of his reign as the expansion in publishing activity, the appearance of new journals and literary collections, and the printing of translations.

Alexander allocated 120,000 rubles from his personal funds for the translation and publication in Russian of the works of such well-known Western European educators, philosophers, economists, sociologists, and jurists as Adam Smith, Jeremy Bentham, Cesare Beccaria, Jean Delolme, and Montesquieu. Later, Decembrists under investigation repeatedly mentioned these authors from whose works they had borrowed "the first freethinking and liberal ideas."

Education reform was implemented in 1803–4. From then on, educational institutions accepted representatives of all classes, and at lower levels instruction was free of charge. Continuity in school programs was introduced. The lowest level was the one-grade parochial school, the second the three-grade district school, the third the six-grade gymnasium in a provincial city, and the highest the university, each of which was placed in charge of a school district and was supposed to supply it with curricula and teaching cadres. Between 1802 and 1804, universities were opened in Dorpat, Vilna, Kazan, and Kharkov and took their place alongside the University of Moscow, which had been in existence since 1755. The St. Petersburg Pedagogical Institute, too, received university status (it was converted to a university in 1819). In addition to training teachers for gymnasia, the universities were to train cadres of office workers for the civil service, as well as doctors. The universities were given rather broad autonomy. Considered on a par with the universities were certain privileged secondary educational institutions such as the Demidovskii Lyceum (in Iaroslavl) and the Tsarskoe Selo Lyceum. The founding of the Institute of Railways in 1801 and the Moscow Commercial School in 1804 marked the beginning of specialized higher education. Between 1808 and 1814, the seminaries were also reformed. Speranskii took an active part in working this out, for he himself was a product of seminary training and was perfectly aware of its shortcomings. At his initiative, the curriculum in seminaries and ecclesiastical academies underwent a complete overhaul in favor of increasing the number of general-education disciplines; ecclesiastical educational institutions were given a certain autonomy; and corporal punishment was abolished.

Of even greater importance was the transformation of the organs of central administration. All the important laws between 1802 and 1812 (and later, under Nicholas I as well) were drafted or edited by Speranskii. This was the acme of Speranskii's career; he simultaneously occupied the posts of assistant (deputy) minister of justice, state secretary, and director of the Commission to Draft Laws and the Commission on Finnish Affairs; he was also in charge of preparing financial reforms. In late 1808 Alexander I directed Speranskii to draw up a plan for the Russian state's transformation, and by October 1809 the latter submitted his document, entitled the Draft Statute of State Laws, to the tsar. These reforms were supposed to be implemented from above, the idea being to strengthen the autocracy by giving it a "legal form."

Speranskii's draft provided theoretical justification and support for class inequality, noble privileges, and the absence of political and civil rights among "the working folk," who included serfs, hired laborers, and domestic servants. The "middle estate" that was introduced (merchants, small tradesmen, state peasants) were given "civil" but not political rights. The draft held to the principle of a "separation of powers"—legislative, executive, and judicial—in which judicial power was independent and executive power was accountable to the legislative authority. The system granted access to the country's administration only to the landowners and the upper layer of the newly risen bourgeoisie, without limiting the tsar's absolute power at all.

Alexander I called the draft "satisfactory and useful," but the attempt to implement it met with strong resistance from high officials, who considered it too radical and "dangerous." The project was reduced to the establishment in 1810 of a State Council, which became a consultative body under the emperor. The new organization centralized legislative business, ensured uniformity of juridical norms, and prevented contradictions between legislative acts, but the legislative initiative itself, like the final approval of laws, remained entirely the tsar's prerogative. Members of the State Council were not elected but appointed by the emperor.

The year 1811 saw the publication of *The General Institution of the Ministries*, prepared by Speranskii; it crowned the reform started in 1802, when the old colleges of Peter's time were replaced with a new, European form of supreme executive authority—ministries. Under the new system, matters in each department were decided by a minister responsible to the emperor alone. The structure and function of the ministries had originally not been precisely defined, but the new law strictly limited the competence of the ministries, established the principle of one-person management, and regulated relations between the ministries and the other organs of supreme state administration—the Senate, the Committee of Ministers, and the State Council. The reorganized central administration continued to exist, with minor changes, until 1917.

Speranskii's changes caused dissatisfaction among reactionary court circles, which began to intrigue against him. Rumors reached Alexander I, fueled by court regulars, that Speranskii was saying "unseemly" things about him. The vain emperor thought he was being insulted, but he did not show it; in fact, he began to make quite a show of giving Speranskii signals of his "good favor," and this, as the courtiers knew from their own experience, constituted a sure sign that a fall from grace was imminent. On 1 January 1812 Speranskii was awarded the order of Alexander Nevsky. But on 17 March 1812 he was summoned to an audience with the emperor. After a two-hour confidential discussion, he emerged from the emperor's office "in great confusion." Once home, he found Minister of Police A.D. Balashov and his aide sealing up his papers. Next to the house was a carriage to take Speranskii into exile. Speranskii was first sent to Nizhnii Novgorod, but soon he was transferred to Perm.

Court circles rejoiced at Speranskii's fall. Some people were even surprised at the tsar's "leniency" in not having punished "this criminal, turncoat, and traitor." Convinced that Speranskii was innocent, Alexander decided to sacrifice him in order to quell rising discontent. On the day following Speranskii's banishment, Prince A.N. Golitsyn, the Procurator-General of the Holy Synod, sought out Alexander with a report and found the emperor pacing around his office "with a very gloomy expression." "Is Your Highness ill?" asked Golitsyn.

"No, I am well," answered Alexander. "But your expression?" Golitsyn continued. Alexander replied, "If someone cut off your hand, you would probably cry out and complain that it hurt you; last night they took my Speranskii away, and he was my right hand!" Golitsyn recalls that "all of this was said with tears in his eyes," and throughout the entire audience the emperor went on about this "loss."[36] A little later, Alexander met K.V. Nesselrode, head of the Ministry of Foreign Affairs. Nesselrode had liked Speranskii and was distressed that the tsar had "rid himself of so loyal and zealous a servant." "You are right," Alexander replied, "but only current circumstances could force me to make such a sacrifice to public opinion."[37] It was typical that the official decree exiling Speranskii was not implemented. Nor was he stripped of his ranks, his decorations, the gentry status he had won through service, or his estates, but merely relieved of the posts he had occupied and sent away from the capital "for a while"—until his "trial," which, however, never took place. Within four years, Speranskii was "pardoned," appointed governor of Penza, then, in 1819, governor-general of Siberia, where he carried out a number of administrative reforms. In 1821 he was returned to St. Petersburg, appointed a member of the State Council and the head of the Commission on Codification, and given substantial land grants.

The beginning of the nineteenth century in Europe was marked by the Napoleonic wars, which involved all the countries and peoples of Europe, including Russia. In 1803 Napoleon began preparations to invade England. The English government promptly established a new European coalition against France, an effort aided by Napoleon's own actions. On his orders, the Duc d'Enghien, a member of the French royal house suspected of conspiring against Napoleon, was seized in Baden in 1804 and later shot. This event caused an explosion of indignation among all the European monarchs, but only Alexander I launched an official protest. An ostentatious period of mourning was proclaimed in St. Petersburg, and a note protesting the "shedding of royal blood" was sent to Napoleon. Napoleon answered defiantly that "royal blood" had also been shed in Russia itself; Alexander I might take the trouble to seize and punish his own father's murderers. This was a transparent and public accusation.

The coalition's military actions against France were unsuccessful. After the allied troops' defeat on 2 December 1805 near Austerlitz, Austria capitulated and concluded a humiliating peace with Napoleon. Russian troops withdrew to Russia, and Russian–French peace talks began in Paris. A peace treaty between Russia and France was concluded on 8 July 1806, but Alexander I refused to ratify it, and Russia formally remained at war with France.

In the summer of 1806, Napoleon seized Holland and the western German principalities. In the autumn a fourth coalition was formed against France (Prussia, England, Sweden, and Russia), but only Prussia and Russia actually fought. On 1 October 1806 the Prussian ambassador to Paris handed Talleyrand an ultimatum: France must withdraw its army from the Rhine. Napoleon refused this demand, and the French army invaded Prussia. On 14 October the Prussian troops were totally routed in two battles. Frederick-Wilhelm III fled to the Russian borders. The French occupied almost all of Prussia and threatened Russia. On 16 (28) November 1806 Alexander signed a decree "On the Beginning of the War with France."[38] This was followed by edicts renouncing the Franco-Russian trade treaty and expelling the French consuls and all French citizens from Russia. A plan to form a people's militia was also announced.[39] For seven months, the Russian army had to wage a stubborn battle alone against superior French forces. Napoleon succeeded in driving Russian troops back to the Niemen, but the French army also sustained such substantial losses that Napoleon could not bring himself to invade Russia at that time.

On 25 June 1807 a peace treaty and a treaty of alliance were concluded between Russia and France at Tilsit. At Alexander I's insistence, Napoleon agreed to preserve Prussia's independence, although its territory was reduced by half. The terms of the Treaty of Tilsit and the treaty of alliance, unfavorable to Russia, forced her to follow Napoleon's lead in politics and restricted Alexander I's independence in international affairs. According to the treaty, Russia recognized all Napoleon's European conquests and acknowledged him as emperor. Russia was obliged to break with England, and in the event that that country refused to make peace, the Russian emperor was to "act as one with France." The Treaty of Tilsit gave Russia freedom to act against Turkey and Sweden. According to Napoleon's calculations, that would "tie the hands" of Russia and guarantee him freedom of action in West European affairs. Especially grave consequences resulted from Russia's joining the continental blockade in 1808, which inflicted substantial damage on the country's economy, because England had been Russia's main trading partner.

Although in the end the Treaty of Tilsit preserved Russia's position as the greatest European power, and although the country suffered no territorial "losses" and was considered France's "ally," its terms severely wounded Russian patriotic sensibilities. Alexander I's popularity abruptly declined. Universal grumbling increased. "In general, discontent against the emperor is increasing more and more," Swedish Ambassador Stedingk reported to his king, "and in this regard people are saying things that are terrible to hear." According to the testimony of a Russian contemporary, "from eminent courtier to barely literate clerk, from general to ordinary soldier, everyone, while still obedient, grumbles with indignation."[40] R. Savary, the French ambassador to St. Petersburg, wrote: "There is clear opposition against everything the emperor does." In 1807 copies circulated of a "Draft Appeal" to the emperor by the nobility, demanding that he exhibit firmness in foreign policy matters.[41] There was even talk of a possible palace coup that would place Alexander I's intelligent and active sister Ekaterina Pavlovna, who lived in Tver, on the throne. According to the French historian A. Vandal, Duke Savary assiduously gathered and spread rumors about a "conspiracy" against the Russian tsar.[42]

Alexander kept close track of the sentiments of the various circles and collected information about them. In 1805, as he was going off to war, he had created the Temporary Committee of Supreme Police to keep track of public opinion and what the public was saying. After the Treaty of Tilsit, this committee was converted into the Committee of Public Security, which was given the duty of opening and reading private correspondence.[43]

People in the ruling circles, however, were perfectly aware that the agreements of 1807 represented only a breathing space before renewed military conflict with Napoleon's France. "The probability of a new war between Russia and France," Speranskii wrote, "arose upon conclusion of the treaty. The treaty itself incorporated almost all the elements of a war. . . . It was not possible for Russia always to adhere to it, or for France to believe that its terms would be kept."[44] Both sides began to prepare for war immediately after the peace and the alliance were concluded in 1807, despite the signing of a secret pact in Erfurt in 1808 that declared, "His Highness the Emperor of France and His Highness the Emperor of Russia wish their alliance to be closer and forever unbroken."[45]

Napoleon had never prepared himself so carefully for any war as he did for the campaign against Russia, since he knew that he would have to face a powerful adversary. He placed 1.2 million soldiers under arms. The approximately 650,000 men who made up the Grande Armée began to march toward the Russian border. In Russia, all the details of Napoleon's preparations for war were known. From 1810 onward, the tsar's ambassador in Paris, Prince A.B. Kurakin, reported twice a month on the numerical strength, armaments, and deployment of French troops; in exchange for large sums of money he obtained valuable information from Talleyrand, Napoleon's minister of foreign affairs.

Russia knew the approximate dates of the French army's invasion. The notion of the "suddenness" of Napoleon's attack, widespread in the literature, is wrong. Equally incorrect is the assertion that the invasion took place "without a declaration of war." Napoleon made such an official declaration on 10 (22) June, two days before the invasion, through his ambassador to St. Petersburg, J. Lauriston.[46] But Russia was not ready for war, even though the rearming of the Russian army had been in full swing since 1810: her western borders had been reinforced, fortresses had been built, and stores of ammunition, fodder, and feed had been set up. The country's difficult financial situation, however, made it impossible to complete this program. The archaic recruiting system was not enough to train the necessary reserves.

Alexander I was not a brilliant military man. His contemporaries noted that wherever he was directly involved, his troops suffered defeat. During the meeting at Tilsit, Napoleon had said frankly to Alexander: "Military affairs are not your strong suit." Sober military men, wise statesmen, and even members of the tsar's family held the same opinion. On the eve of war, Alexander had a long conversation with Speranskii, asking him in particular what he thought about the upcoming war and whether he, the emperor, ought to take a direct hand in supervising military actions. Speranskii advised Alexander not to take personal command, but to create a Boyar Duma and make it responsible for waging the war. He also "had the effrontery" to lavish praise on the "military talents" of Napoleon, thus deeply wounding the tsar's pride.[47]

Alexander's first act on learning that the French troops had invaded was to propose peace to Napoleon, dispatching General A.D. Balashov with a letter to the French leader. Incidentally, Alexander did not believe that this mission would be successful but merely hoped to gain time. The tsar's presence in the army inhibited the actions of the Russian command. Alexander found in himself the courage to heed the arguments of influential persons and members of the tsar's family, but his departure from the army also had another purpose—to lay responsibility on his generals for the first failures and the retreat of Russian troops. Nor could Alexander fail to heed the voice of public opinion that demanded he appoint as commander in chief M.I. Kutuzov, who had been especially out of his favor since Austerlitz. "The public wanted him to be appointed, so I appointed him," he said to Adjutant General E.F. Komarovskii. "As for myself, I wash my hands." Alexander also complained about not having been turned over to Suvorov or Rumiantsev in his youth: "They would have taught me to fight."[48]

Although he was in the capital, Alexander kept abreast of everything that was taking place in the active army and was not content with its commanders' official reports. True to his principle of setting people against one another, Alexander, having turned command over to M.B. Barclay de Tolly, appointed the latter's rival General A.P. Ermo-lov chief of staff with the right to report personally to the emperor. After appointing Kutuzov as commander in chief, he installed as chief of staff Kutuzov's personal enemy General L.L. Bennigsen, who reported to the tsar every step Kutuzov made.

The Russian troops retreated, fighting in well-organized fashion and in full battle order. Some time before reaching Smolensk, Napoleon became convinced that he faced a prolonged and exhausting campaign. From Smolensk he sent captured General P.A. Tuchkov to Alexander I with a peace proposal, but he received no response. Later, when he was in Moscow, Napoleon appealed to the tsar several times with similar proposals, but all of them were rejected. Not long before the war started, seeing that it was inevitable, Alexander had stated: "I will not start the war, but I will not lay down arms as long as a single enemy soldier remains in Russia." Once war broke out, he repeatedly stated his readiness to "exhaust all the forces of the empire and go clear to Kamchatka" before concluding peace with Napoleon. It is said that when Colonel Michaud, sent by Kutuzov, brought the news that Moscow had been captured and burnt, Alexander "began sobbing," but swore to continue the war until complete victory was achieved: "I will let my beard grow long and will consent to eat potatoes with the least of my peasants rather than sign the disgrace of my fatherland."[49]

The War of 1812 was truly a national war, a war of liberation, and it ensured victory over the aggressor. On 25 December 1812 the tsar's manifesto announcing the end of the Patriotic War was issued. Russia turned out to be the only European country capable not only of opposing Napoleon's aggression but of inflicting a shattering defeat upon him. The enormous army, tempered by many battles and led by exceptional commanders, was destroyed. Victory came at great cost: huge human and material losses, the destruction of ten provinces that had been arenas of military action, and the burning of Moscow, Smolensk, Vitebsk, Polotsk, and other ancient towns. Moreover, the victorious conclusion of the campaign of 1812 did not mean that the fighting would not resume. Napoleon himself thought that the war against Russia was not yet over. Military actions, however, continued outside Russia's borders. Soviet historians generally view the Russian army's campaigns abroad in 1813–14 as a continuation of the Patriotic War of 1812. Alexander I saw it as the accomplishment of his goal—overthrowing Napoleon. "I will not conclude peace as long as Napoleon remains on the throne," he stated publicly. One must give due credit to Alexander I's diplomatic skills, for he succeeded in forming a European coalition that led in 1814 to the shattering of Napoleon's empire and the liberation of Europe's peoples from its yoke. Yet the European powers repaid the tsar with extreme ingratitude: not wishing Russia to grow stronger, they concluded a secret military pact against Alexander, and only Napoleon's short-lived return to power in 1815 caused them again to ally with Russia. As a result of these powers' intrigues, and contrary to Alexander I's wishes, the Bourbons were restored to the French throne. Alexander did not like them and was not inclined to restore them to the throne of France. But the leaders of the European powers insisted on this, and the minister of foreign affairs, Talleyrand, and Fouché, the minister of police, joined their cause, betraying Napoleon. Alexander I agreed, on condition that a constitution that he approved be introduced into France. But when Louis XVIII assumed the French throne, he did not fulfill these promises, and this evoked the tsar's anger.

Russia's military triumphs made Alexander the one who decided Europe's fate. His pride was more than satisfied. After the decisive battle at Fère Champenoise (near Paris) he said proudly to Ermolov, "Well, Aleksei Petrovich, what will they say in St. Petersburg now? They used to consider me a simpleton." He went on: "For twelve years I have had the reputation in Europe of a mediocre man: let's see what they'll have to say now."[50] In 1814 the Senate conferred on Alexander I the title of "blessed, magnanimous restorer of sovereigns." Alexander I, however, refused this title, just as he opposed the Senate's decision to erect a monument to him (the famous Alexander Column was raised by Nicholas I). The emperor was at the zenith of his greatness and glory. The Decembrist I.D. Iakushkin recalled the enthusiasm with which Alexander was greeted on his return to Russia. But he was shocked by the following episode during the tsar's inspection of the Guards, who had just returned from France: a peasant, shoved aside by the crowd, ran across the road right in front of Alexander I's horse. "The emperor spurred his horse and bore down upon the fleeing peasant with his sword unsheathed. The police went for the peasant with their clubs. We could not believe our own eyes, and we turned away out of shame for our beloved tsar. For me this was the first disillusionment on his account."[51]

The hopes of the men of the Home Guard—serfs—for the "liberty" that had been promised them as reward for their heroism in the Patriotic War proved to be in vain. On 30 August 1814, the tsar's official name day, a manifesto was announced "On the Liberation of the Russian State from the Attack of the Gauls and the Twelve Nations with Them."[52] The manifesto announced the granting of various awards to the nobility, the clergy, and the merchant class, but for the peasants it stated: "The peasants, our faithful folk, may they receive their reward from God."

The years from 1815 through 1825 are generally considered a time of political reaction, sometimes called the "Arakcheev era." Reaction, however, did not set in all at once. Until approximately 1819–20, despite the implementation of a number of reactionary measures, there was also some "flirting with liberalism": plans for reforms continued to be made, the press and the educational system were not yet subject to the harsh persecution that began later. The years 1818–20 saw the publication of K.I. Arseniev's *Russian Statistics* and A.P. Kunitsyn's *Natural Law*, which set forth enlightened ideas and openly discussed the necessity of abolishing serfdom in Russia. The texts of West European constitutions continued to be published in the journals.

In November 1815 Alexander I signed a constitution for the Kingdom of Poland, which belonged to the Russian Empire. The constitution was quite liberal for its time. On 15 (27) March 1818, during the opening of the Polish Sejm [Parliament] in Warsaw, the tsar gave a speech in which he declared his intention "to extend" the constitutional procedures instituted in Poland "to all the countries that Providence has entrusted to my care," but with this provision: "once they have attained the necessary maturity."[53] This speech made a strong impression on progressive people in Russia and nourished their hopes of the tsar's constitutional intentions. Karamzin remarked that Alexander's speech "resonated strongly in young hearts—they sleep and dream of a constitution."[54] Alexander's other constitutional declarations were circulated. On 25 October 1818 the Decembrist N.I. Turgenev recorded in his diary a statement Alexander I made to Prussian General Meson: "Ultimately, all nations must be liberated from autocracy. You can see what I am doing in Poland and what I want to do in my other possessions."[55]

In 1818 Alexander directed N.N. Novosiltsev to draw up a state constitution according to the principles of the Polish Constitution of 1815. The draft was ready by 1820 and received the "highest approval." Although Novosiltsev's draft, which had been prepared in the utmost secrecy, remained only on paper, its very existence was characteristic of Alexander's policy during those years. Peasant reform in the Baltic region was implemented between 1816 and 1819. In 1817–18 the tsar gave secret orders to twelve high officials to prepare drafts abolishing serfdom in the Russian provinces as well. They included such well-known figures as Minister of Finance D.A. Guriev; Admiral N.S. Mordvinov, a member of the State Council; the rector of St. Petersburg University, M.A. Balugianskii, a professor and lawyer; and A.A. Arakcheev. Fundamental to their drafts was the gradual emancipation of the serfs with compensation to their owners. Thus, in Arakcheev's version the government bought the serfs from the landowners. There was also discussion concerning the creation of a special committee to prepare a peasant reform. In the face of powerful opposition from most noble serfowners, however, Alexander I decided not to follow this path.[56]

During the immediate postwar years, however, Alexander I also imposed a number of reactionary measures. Herzen called the establishment of military settlements in 1816 "one of the greatest crimes of Alexander I's reign." At first, Arakcheev argued against the military settlements and proposed that the term of military service be reduced to eight years, after which discharged soldiers would form necessary reserves. He later said, "The military settlements were the sovereign's own idea, his child." He characterized himself as "merely a loyal implementer of this plan according to my own devoted zeal."[57] But as soon as Alexander I decided on military settlements, Arakcheev became one of the most zealous and persistent executors of the measure. According to Shilder's observation, Arakcheev perceived "this imperial fantasy as a reliable way to reinforce his own position still further and to ensure that in the future he would exert a dominant influence on affairs of state."[58]

Arakcheev had begun his service at the court during Paul I's reign. At first, Alexander did not care much for him, and once, in the company of some Guards officers, the tsar called him a "scoundrel," but later Alexander came to see that Arakcheev possessed such useful qualities as an attention to detail, a truly maniacal devotion to order, an unswerving attachment to duty, and outstanding organizational abilities. Alexander's letters to Arakcheev during those years are replete with assurances of "friendship" and expressions of "heartfelt feelings," exemplified by this letter of 1820: "Twenty-five years have demonstrated my sincere devotion to you and have shown that I am not changeable."[59] Arakcheev's career under Alexander I (like Speranskii's) began in 1803. In 1808 Arakcheev was already minister of war and—to give him his due—in this post (which he occupied until 1810) he did much to provide the Russian army with first-class artillery. But Arakcheev's "hour of glory" really began when he was appointed head of the military settlements and chairman of the State Council Department of Military Affairs. The years 1822 to 1825 were the period of greatest authority for this tsar's favorite, whom the whole country hated. In the position of de facto prime minister he reported to the tsar on all branches of government, even the Senate. All the ministers had to present their reports to the emperor "via Count Arakcheev." Any person, even of the most exalted rank, who wished an audience with the tsar, had first humbly to "present" himself to Arakcheev and, through him, request the tsar's consent to such an audience.

Contemporaries, and later various historians as well, perceived the "serpent Arakcheev" as Russia's main "evil" in those years. As they saw it, the emperor, occupied with foreign affairs and, in later years, experiencing "a profound weariness of life," turned over the administration of the country to his cruel favorite. F.F. Vigel, a well-known memoirist of the time, referred to Alexander I as "a landowner who turned his estate over to the administrator" (Arakcheev) in full confidence that in his hands "the people would not be pampered." Pro-monarchy gentry historians attempted to shift all the blame for the country's troubles onto Arakcheev so as to show Alexander I in the most favorable light. Without denying in the least the favorite's considerable influence on affairs of state, it must nevertheless be emphasized that the tsar himself inspired the reactionary course of political action, and Arakcheev merely implemented his policies zealously. Even when he was abroad, Alexander kept the reins of government in his own hands and was involved in every detail, including those concerning Arakcheev's own "department"—the military settlements. P.A. Kleinmikhel, the chief of staff of the military settlements, testified that many of Arakcheev's orders regarding the military settlements came directly from the emperor.

Through a network of informers, Alexander kept close track of the prevailing mood in Russia and issued the appropriate instructions to the generals in charge of investigation.[60] Alexander was masterful in knowing how to "shift his own unpopularity" onto others. Even Arakcheev saw this; he felt unsure of his position even at the height of his power. He once said to another high official about Alexander I: "You know him—right now I am in, tomorrow you will be, and then I will be again."

The autocracy's reactionary course of action was closely linked to the reaction all over Russia. Alexander's final shift into reaction, shaped in 1819–20, was noted by his contemporaries. "How he has changed!" N.I. Turgenev wrote of Alexander in mid-1819. In the autumn of 1820, the tsar himself told Austrian Chancellor Metternich that he had "changed completely." Observant contemporaries, in particular the Decembrists, linked the tsar's altered course to the political upheavals in Western Europe—the revolutions in Portugal, Spain, Naples, and the Piedmont, and the Greek uprising of 1821. "The events in Naples and the Piedmont, along with the Greek uprising, caused a decisive shift in the sovereign's purpose," wrote V.I. Shteingeil.[61]

Alexander's speech at the opening of the Second Polish Sejm on 1 (13) September 1820 differed markedly from the one given two and a half years earlier. He dropped his promise to grant Russia "legal and free institutions." During this period, revolution had broken out in southern Europe. "The spirit of evil is attempting once more to establish its calamitous dominion," the emperor said. "It is already hovering over part of Europe, already amassing evil deeds and fatal events." The speech threatened the Poles that force would be used to repress any political "disorder among them."[62] At the Congress of the Holy Alliance convened in Troppau in the autumn of 1820, Alexander I spoke of the necessity of "taking serious and effective measures against the conflagration that has encompassed all of southern Europe, the flames of which have already spread to all countries."[63] "The conflagration in Europe" forced the reactionary powers of the Holy Alliance to act together despite their differences.

In Troppau the tsar received word of a rebellion among the Life Guards of the Semenovskii Regiment, who rose up in October 1820 against the brutalities of their commander, E.F. Shvarts. The first to deliver this unpleasant news to Alexander was Metternich, who presented it as proof that there was "unrest" in Russia as well. The regiment was disbanded and its elements assigned to various army units; the First Battalion was court-martialed, most of its personnel were sent to Siberian garrisons without the right to service benefits, and the "instigators" were sentenced to the knout and indefinite penal servitude. Quite instructive for its hypocritical words about "mercy" is the tsar's confirmation of the court's sentence. "The Sovereign Emperor," it states, "having taken into account the long garrison service of the enlisted personnel, as well as their participation in battles, has graciously deigned to absolve them from dishonorable punishment by the knout, commanding that each run the battalion gauntlet six times and·then be sent into the mines."[64]

Alexander was convinced that a secret society had inspired the rebellion by the soldiers of the Semenovskii Regiment. "No one in the world will convince me that the soldiers conceived this rebellion, or that it resulted, as has been claimed, solely from Colonel Shvarts's brutal treatment of them," he wrote to Arakcheev. "... It is my conviction that there are other causes lurking here . . . and I ascribe it [the unrest] to secret societies."[65] Efforts to uncover such societies increased. It was not, however, the police who found the trail of the Decembrist Union of Welfare. Between November 1820 and February 1821, the authorities obtained a series of reports. In late May 1821, after Alexander I returned from abroad, General I.V. Vasilchikov handed him a list of the most active members of the secret society. It is said that the tsar threw the list into the fire, as if he did not wish to know "the names of these unfortunates," because he himself "had shared their views in his youth," and he added: "It does not become me to punish."[66]

But he knew how to punish, and very harshly too. Thus, while he declared in his edicts that human error must not be corrected using force, but through gentleness and enlightenment, Alexander I nevertheless secretly ordered several Dukhobors* shot for refusing to fight during the war. He listened to the homilies of K. Selivanov, a Skopets,† but upheld a court martial's decision to have Skopets soldiers beaten. His refusal to prosecute openly in court by no means stemmed from considerations of "humanity." According to S.G. Volkonskii's testimony, Alexander I did not like to "punish publicly"

---

*A Russian religious sect that refused to recognize the state or serve in the armed forces. Owing to the help of writer Leo Tolstoy, large numbers of Dukhobors emigrated to the United States and Canada during the reign of Nicholas II.—D.J.R.

†Another Russian religious sect persecuted by the Russian government.—D.J.R.

at all. Reflecting on "what might have happened to the members of the secret society if Alexander had not died in Taganrog," Volkonskii wrote: "I am convinced that the emperor would not have allowed such publicity, such disclosure about the secret society. A number of persons would have rotted alive in Schlüsselburg, but he would have considered it shameful to let it be known that there had been an attempt against his rule."[67] In fact, while he did not desire to prosecute publicly, Alexander did punish several people found to be members of the secret society without benefit of trial or publicity; he dismissed them, exiling them under police surveillance.

On 1 August 1822 Alexander I sent V.P. Kochubei, head of the Ministry of Internal Affairs, a rescript prohibiting secret societies and Masonic lodges and demanded that military officers and civil servants pledge in writing that they did not and would not belong to such organizations.[68] During 1821–23 a centralized and elaborate network of secret police began functioning in the Guards and the army. The surveillance system was divided into districts, each with its own center, provisional meeting place, password, and a whole network of lower and higher "correspondents." Special agents kept track of the actions of the secret police itself as well as one another. The "civilian" secret police also stepped up its activities. "There was no shortage of spying at that time," A.I. Mikhailovskii-Danilevskii recalls. "The government was suspicious, and it was the rare society that did not have its spies— most of them, however, were known. Some of them belonged to the old noble families and wore chamberlains' uniforms."[69]

Surveillance was instituted even over senior state officials, including Arakcheev (who, incidentally, had his own secret police). The Decembrist G.S. Batenkov, who had served with him, recalls how, during a walk with him along the Fontanka, Arakcheev pointed to a spy who had been "assigned to watch him."[70] Arakcheev, however, having his own network of spies, treated this as something ordinary. Throughout Alexander I's reign, functioning "black offices" engaged in the opening and inspecting of private letters. It was a "classic" time of denunciations. Denunciatory reports were submitted not only against persons holding progressive views but also against influential reactionaries, for example A.D. Balashov, the minister of police; A.N. Golitsyn, the minister of religious affairs and public education; Metropolitan Filaret; and Arakcheev. M.L. Magnitskii even reported on Grand Duke Nikolai Pavlovich (the future Nicholas I). Despite this, the government did not succeed in neutralizing the activities of the secret organizations.

The onset of a reactionary governmental course of action in 1820–25 was manifest in all areas. All of the decrees promulgated during the first years of Alexander I's reign that had limited to some extent the landowners' arbitrary treatment of their peasants were rescinded. The landowners' right to banish peasants to Siberia "for acts of insolence" was reinstated; peasants were forbidden to complain of their owners' brutality. Persecution of the educational establishment and the press became harsher, as censors mercilessly prosecuted any instance of freethinking. In 1819, Magnitskii was sent to Kazan University to conduct an "inspection." Detecting "a spirit of freethinking and godlessness," he demanded a "public destruction" of the university. Alexander did not agree to this, but he did appoint Magnitskii a trustee in the Kazan Education District.

More than half of the professors were expelled from the university, and all books that Magnitskii saw as exhibiting "harmful tendencies" were removed from the university library. The trustee highhandedly drafted students into the army, introduced a barracks-type regimen in the university, and reported to the emperor: "The poison of free thought has finally been banished from the university, where now the fear of God reigns." In 1821 D.P. Runich, who had been appointed trustee of the St. Petersburg Education District, wrought havoc in the capital city's university. He started by denouncing the sciences—taught "in a spirit contrary to Christianity"—and he instituted court procedures against the best professors, K.I. Arseniev, A.I. Galich, K.F. Herman, and E.V. Raupakh. The trial lasted until 1827, when it was halted because no "crime" had been proved.

It was a time when religious obscurantism and mysticism prevailed, encouraged by Alexander I. The tsar's keen interest in mysticism had been apparent since 1814. Before then, according to Alexandra Fedorovna (Nicholas I's wife), he had been quite "frivolous and lighthearted" in matters of religion. But in 1814, in Paris, he had met Baroness J. von Krüdener, the "European Pythia," and had had long conversations with her about religion. These conversations continued in Russia. He took under his wing the spiritual gatherings of the fanatical E.F. Tatarinova and had dealings with all kinds of "prophets" and "prophetesses." Nikitushka Fedorov, a musician whom Alexander summoned who had a reputation as "a prophet" and "holy fool," was awarded civil servant status. The tsar later cultivated the acquaintance of Archimandrite Fotii, a close friend of Arakcheev known for fanaticism. A.S. Shishkov compiled biblical excerpts for Alexander.

In 1814, after returning from Paris, Alexander took the Bible Society under his patronage. He became a member of it and donated substantial sums of money to it. The "flower" of aristocratic reaction of the time joined the Bible Society. A.N. Golitsyn was appointed its chairman. By 1824 it had eighty-nine branches in Russia and had published 876,000 copies of the Bible in forty languages spoken by the peoples of Russia. The activities of the Bible Society were linked to the Ministry of Religious Affairs and Public Education, which Golitsyn himself headed. The activities of the Bible Society and Golitsyn's department infringed upon the prerogatives of the Orthodox Church, however, which led to dissatisfaction among and resistance from the higher clergy. In 1824, with support from Arakcheev and Fotii, the clergy managed to have the "religious" ministry abolished, Golitsyn dismissed, and the Bible Society disbanded (a decree of 12 April 1826 officially shut it down). Despite the tsar's keen interest in mysticism, he could not tolerate his "prophets'" interference in governing the state, and when Baroness Krüdener, for example, tried to become involved in politics, she was immediately banished from Russia.

In 1819 Alexander I addressed the question of who would succeed him on the throne. His daughters Elizabeth and Maria, born to him and Elizaveta Alekseevna in 1797 and 1806, had died in infancy. The health of the tsar's wife left no hope that she would have more children. Although the coronation manifesto of 15 September 1801 named no heir, the General Act on Succession to the Throne and the Law on the Institution of the Imperial Family, promulgated by Paul I on 5 April 1797, made Constantine, next to Alexander in age and named crown prince by his father in 1799, the tsar's legitimate successor. Constantine, however, was "in the same family circumstances" as Alexander—that is, he was childless—and he in effect had separated from his wife in 1801. The birth of a son, Alexander (the future Alexander II), to another of the tsar's brothers, Nicholas, in 1818 resolved the matter. In the summer of 1819, Alexander I notified Nicholas and his wife that they would "be called in the future to the Imperial throne."

In the same year, Alexander visited Constantine in Warsaw, where the latter was serving as the tsar's viceroy. During their meeting, Alexander gave Constantine verbal permission to divorce his wife and enter a morganatic marriage with the Polish noblewoman Joanna Grudzinska—on condition that he yield his right to the throne to Nicholas. Later, in 1825, Constantine said that he himself had renounced his right in favor of Nicholas. Even earlier, within his family circle, Constantine had reportedly said that he wished never to be tsar ("they'll murder me as they did my father"). The documents relating to Constantine's abdication (and, in fact, his behavior during the days of the interregnum in 1825), however, suggest that his abdication was not an entirely voluntary gesture.

On 20 March 1820 a manifesto was promulgated "On the Dissolution of the Marriage of Grand Duke and Crown Prince Konstantin Pavlovich and Grand Duchess Anna Fedorovna and an Additional Decree Concerning the Imperial Family."[71] The manifesto gave Constantine permission to divorce his wife, and the second decree stated that when a member of the tsar's family marries "a person who is not a member of a ruling house, that member cannot convey any rights pertinent to members of the Imperial family, and any children born of such a union will not have the right to succeed to the throne." The terms of the manifesto forced Constantine to abdicate his right to the Russian throne, which he did. On 2 February 1822 Alexander gave his written "consent" to this, and on 16 August 1823 a manifesto appeared in which Alexander, referring to Constantine's letter, conferred the right to the throne on Nicholas.

All these acts were drawn up and maintained in deep secrecy. The only people who knew about the manifesto were Alexander himself, Golitsyn, Arakcheev, and Metropolitan Filaret, who had composed the text. The manifesto was placed in the Dormition Cathedral for safekeeping, and three copies of it, certified by Alexander I's signature, were kept in the Synod, the Senate, and the State Council, each with the following inscription in the tsar's own hand: "To be kept with state documents until I shall ask for them, and in the event of my death, to be opened prior to any other action." Judging by this note of Alexander's, we may presume that he did not consider his decision final.

The manifesto violated Paul I's Law on the Succession to the Throne, as M.A. Miloradovich, the governor-general of St. Petersburg, noted after Alexander I's death when the manifesto was read to the members of the Senate, the Synod, and the State Council. Miloradovich stated that the emperor's will, "as expressed in the sealed document, cannot constitute the law, because the Russian sovereign cannot dispose of the succession to the throne by testament."[72] Nicholas was first forced to swear fealty to his brother as emperor. Even though Constantine had publicly renounced the throne in his letters, Nicholas could not be proclaimed emperor until Constantine issued an official abdication manifesto. Constantine, however, refused to do this and confined himself to private letters. To this day, his behavior remains a mystery, for it created a dynastic crisis that the Decembrists used to their advantage.

Contemporaries paint a rather unattractive picture of Russian conditions during Alexander's final years. "Constricted education," "inhibited freedom," "corruption in the courts," "complete absence of legality and justice in jurisprudence," embezzlement on an unprecedented scale, and universal complaints about the suffocation of industry and trade—to the Decembrists all of these were examples of "universal wretchedness." "Unhappy faces could be seen everywhere. People in the street shrugged their shoulders; everywhere people were cautiously asking where it would all lead. All the elements were in ferment," the Decembrist A.A. Bestuzhev later wrote to Nicholas I from prison.

Dissatisfaction was mounting against Alexander I himself, who could no longer use Arakcheev as a "cover." D.I. Zavalishin recalled that during the final years of Alexander I's reign "exasperation with him was considerable, and nothing was more obvious than the extent to which the sovereign had lost the people's respect and good will in a short time." P.G. Kakhovskii also commented on the "general indignation" against Alexander I during those years.[73]

Those close to Alexander I noted that in later years he became increasingly morose and began to seclude himself more frequently. Actually, he could not fail to notice the increasing discontent among the common people and various segments of society. Convinced of the existence of secret societies and the preparation of a conspiracy against him, he suspected the involvement of influential military personnel. When the tsar's papers were sorted in 1826, a note was found, dated 1824, in which Alexander described the growth of a "pernicious spirit of freethinking" among the troops and the existence "of secret societies or clubs in various places," organizations that involved such influential military persons as A.P. Ermolov, N.N. Raevskii, P.D. Kiselev, M.F. Orlov, and others.[74]

In the middle of July 1825, Alexander received reliable information that a conspiracy was being developed against him among troops stationed in the south of Russia. I.V. Shervud, a noncommissioned officer in the southern military settlements, happened to uncover a secret society and immediately reported his find to the tsar. By itself, however, a single instance was insufficient cause to launch repressions against participants in the conspiracy. Alexander I personally ordered formulation of a plan to expose individual members and leaders of the secret organization. Arakcheev headed the investigation. Information about the conspiracy compelled Alexander I to cancel a troop inspection that had been scheduled for the autumn of 1825 in Belaia Tserkov.[75] The Decembrists later admitted that they had intended to utilize this inspection to launch their rebellion.

On 1 September 1825 Alexander set out for the south, where he intended to visit the military settlements, the Crimea, and the Caucasus (the journey was undertaken in order to improve the empress's health). By 14 September the tsar had reached Taganrog. Nine days later, Elizaveta Alekseevna arrived. She and Alexander visited Azov and the mouth of the Don, and on 20 October he set out for the Crimea, where he visited Simferopol, Alupka, Livadia, Yalta, Balaklava, Sevastopol, Bakhchisarai, and Evpatoria. On 27 October, on the way from Balaklava to St. George's Monastery, the tsar caught cold because he was riding in only his uniform despite a damp and piercing wind. On 5 November he returned to Taganrog, already gravely ill. His personal physicians noted that he had a fever. Earlier, I.O. Witt, the head of the southern military settlements, had arrived in Taganrog with a new report of a secret society, a report containing the names of the plot's leaders (including P.I. Pestel). Before setting out for the Crimea, Alexander had summoned Arakcheev to Taganrog, but Arakcheev did not arrive because of a personal tragedy (the murder of his lover, N. Minkina, by her house serfs).

From 7 November onward, the emperor's illness worsened. Emergency bulletins were dispatched to St. Petersburg and Warsaw concerning his health, which showed a slight and temporary improvement on 9 November. On 10 November Alexander ordered the arrest of those members of the secret organization who had been discovered. This was Alexander's last order. Soon afterward, he took to his bed for the last time, and I.I. Dibich, chief of the General Staff, took over the job of exposing the secret organization. The tsar's attacks of sickness became increasingly severe and lengthy. On 14 November Alexander fell into delirium. His physicians gave up all hope of recovery. In his delirium, the tsar repeatedly addressed the conspirators, calling them "Monsters! Ingrates!" On 16 November the tsar "fell into a lethargic sleep" that alternated with convulsions and death throes. At eleven o'clock on the morning of 19 November, he died. The next day a post-mortem examination was carried out on the body, and a detailed document was drawn up, with the signatures of nine doctors and Adjutant General A.I. Chernyshev. The tsar's body was then embalmed, dressed in a general's uniform, and placed in a coffin.

The unexpected death of Alexander I, who had rarely been sick before and who had enjoyed excellent health, gave rise to rumors and legends, for he was not even forty-eight years old. Even while his body was on its way to St. Petersburg, it was already rumored among the people that the tsar had not died, but had secretly gone into hiding. (According to one version, he had mounted his horse at night, unnoticed, and ridden off in a direction unknown; according to another, he had embarked on an English ship one night and sailed to Palestine.) They also said that the corpse of a soldier, beaten to death (or that of a coachman, "resembling" the tsar, who happened to die at the same time), and not Alexander, had been placed in the coffin. Fantastic tales about the events of Taganrog appeared in foreign newspapers in 1826.

Among numerous rumors that later circulated, the most widespread was the legend of the "mysterious old man" Fedor Kuzmich, the name under which Alexander I allegedly remained in hiding until 1864. The legend gave rise to a vast literature, including L.N. Tolstoy's story *The Memoirs of Fedor Kuzmich*. (The author himself, however, treated this as an "attractive legend," the subject of which served artistic productions but not historical research.)[76]

At the turn of the century, two famous historians, biographers of Alexander I who had access to the family papers in the royal archive, devoted particular attention to this legend. These were N.K. Shilder and Grand Duke Nikolai Mikhailovich. Shilder concluded that the "metamorphosis" of Alexander I into the elder Fedor Kuzmich was "the fruit of popular fantasy,"[77] and published documents disproving the tale. Nikolai Mikhailovich, who had at first been inclined to accept the story, rejected it after studying these and other materials. In his monograph *The Legend of Alexander I's Death in Siberia as the Elder Fedor Kuzmich* (St. Petersburg, 1907), Nikolai Mikhailovich traced in detail the legend's history and presented arguments against it. The same position was argued even more forcefully by K.V. Kudriashov in his *Alexander I and the Mystery of Fedor Kuzmich* (Petrograd, 1923), in which all the data on this subject were collected and analyzed from all perspectives. Kudriashov demonstrated the implausibility of the view that Alexander I had willingly and secretly renounced the throne.

Notwithstanding all this, the legend finds its way into the literature to this day. It is characteristic of journalists and sensation-seekers to support it, while as a rule professional historians dispute it.[78] Nonetheless, the press makes renewed attempts to establish the "authenticity" of the legend of "the elder Fedor Kuzmich."[79] History, including Russian history, knows numerous examples of similar rumors and the appearance of various legends in connection with the untimely or unexpected death of a tsar or his heir. It is owing to such rumors that we have imposters. Even after the death of Constantine Pavlovich, Alexander I's brother, from cholera in 1831, rumors long persisted among the people that he was alive. Several imposters appeared, pretending to be Constantine.

The history of the life and reign of Alexander I contains controversial and little-studied problems. To this day it is unclear why in 1821 Alexander I refused to prosecute the secret society in open court and why he decided to conceal the manifesto bypassing Constantine and transferring the throne to Nicholas. Also unknown are the causes of the depression that Alexander's contemporaries noted during the emperor's final years. The essence of the "governmental liberalism" at the beginning of Alexander I's reign and the character of his social policy are insufficiently studied; conflicting assessments have been made of his position on the "Polish," "Finnish," and "Greek" questions. This monarch's reign still awaits a definitive study.

Notes

1. *Russkii arkhiv* 1869, pp. 642–43; 1882 (recollections of S.M. Golitsyn and N.A. Sablukov).

2. M.V. Dovnar-Zapol'skii, *Obzor noveishei istorii Rossii* (Moscow, 1912), vol. 1, p. 30.

3. N.K. Shil'der, *Imperator Aleksandr Pervyi: Ego zhizn' i tsarstvovanie*, 4 vols. (St. Petersburg, 1897–98), vol. 1, p. 114.

4. V.I. Semevskii, *Politicheskie i obshchestvennye idei dekabristov* (St. Petersburg, 1909), pp. 31–32.

5. *Istoricheskii sbornik Vol'noi russkoi tipografii v Londone A.I. Gertsena i N.P. Ogareva* (1859; repr. Moscow, 1971), bk. 1, pp. 49–50.

6. S.B. Okun', *Ocherki istorii SSSR: Konets XVIII—pervaia chetvert' XIX veka* (Leningrad, 1976), p. 128.

7. The history of the last palace coup in Russia is investigated in detail in N.Ia. Eidel'man, *Gran' vekov* (Moscow, 1982).

8. S.P. Mel'gunov, *Dela i liudi aleksandrovskogo vremeni* (Berlin, 1923), vol. 1, p. 5.

9. *Polnoe sobranie zakonov Rossiiskoi imperii: Sobranie pervoe* (PSZ), vol. 26, no. 19779.

10. Quoted in Mel'gunov, *Dela i liudi*, p. 11.

11. *Memuary dekabristov: Severnoe obshchestvo* (Moscow, 1981), p. 123.

12. Shil'der, *Imperator Aleksandr*, vol. 2, p. 331.

13. Mel'gunov, *Dela i liudi*, p. 55.

14. Dovnar-Zapol'skii, *Obzor*, p. 25.

15. Mel'gunov, *Dela i liudi*, p. 83.

16. Dovnar-Zapol'skii, *Obzor*, p. 39.

17. Grand Duke Nikolai Mikhailovich, *Imperator Aleksandr I* (St. Petersburg, 1912), vol. 1, p. 24.

18. Dovnar-Zapol'skii, *Obzor*, p. 35; A.N. Pypin, *Obshchestvennoe dvizhenie v Rossii pri Aleksandre I* (St. Petersburg, 1900), p. 44.

19. Pypin, *Obshchestvennoe dvizhenie*, p. 40.

20. A. Valloton, *Aleksandr I* (Moscow, 1991), p. 97.

21. Pypin, *Obshchestvennoe dvizhenie*, pp. 43–44.

22. Ibid.

23. *Memuary dekabristov: Severnoe obshchestvo*, p. 125.

24. *Zapiski, stat'i, pis'ma dekabrista I.D. Iakushkina* (Moscow, 1951), pp. 8–10, 384.

25. Mel'gunov, *Dela i liudi*, p. 64.

26. Ibid., p. 99.

27. F.F. Vigel', *Zapiski* (Moscow, 1928), vol. 2, p. 23.

28. N.Ia. Eidel'man, *Poslednii letopisets* (Moscow, 1983), pp. 112–18.

29. Grand Duke Nikolai Mikhailovich, *Imperator Aleksandr*, p. 24.

30. "Instruktsiia Aleksandra I N.N. Novosil'tsevu, 1804 g." Quoted in Okun', *Ocherki*, p. 119.

31. *PSZ*, vol. 26, no. 19813.

32. Shil'der, *Imperator Aleksandr*, vol. 2, p. 68.

33. M.I. Bogdanovich, *Istoriia tsarstvovaniia imperatora Aleksandra I i Rossii v ego vremia* (St. Petersburg, 1869), vol. 1, pp. 97–98.

34. *PSZ*, vol. 29, no. 22418.

35. *PSZ*, vol. 27, no. 20620.

36. D.N. Seslavin, *M.M. Speranskii* (Kiev–Kharkov, 1899), p. 21.

37. Shil'der, *Imperator Aleksandr*, vol. 3, p. 41–42.

38. *PSZ*, vol. 29, no. 22356.

39. V.G. Sirotkin, *Duel' dvukh diplomatii. Rossiia i Frantsiia v 1801–1812 gg.* (Moscow, 1966), pp. 48–50.

40. Shil'der, *Imperator Aleksandr*, vol. 2, p. 211.

41. *Arkhiv grafov Mordvinovykh* (St. Petersburg, 1901), vol. 3, pp. 615–24.

42. A. Vandal', *Napoleon i Aleksandr* (St. Petersburg, 1910), vol. 1, p. 111.

43. Shil'der, *Imperator Aleksandr*, vol. 2, pp. 362–66.

44. *Russkaia starina*, 1900, no. 1, p. 57. Speranskii's note was given to Alexander at the end of 1811 or the very beginning of 1812.

45. Valloton, *Aleksandr I*, p. 120.

46. Troitskii, N.A. *1812: Velikii god Rossii* (Moscow, 1988), pp. 44–45.

47. Shil'der, *Imperator Aleksandr*, vol. 3, p. 48.

48. Mel'gunov, *Dela i liudi*, p. 65.

49. Valloton, *Aleksandr I*, p. 186.

50. Mel'gunov, *Dela i liudi*, p. 67.

51. *Dekabristy: Izbrannye sochineniia v dvukh tomakh* (Moscow, 1987), vol. 2, p. 382.

52. *PSZ*, vol. 32, no. 25669.

53. *Deviatnadtsatyi vek* (Moscow, 1872), bk. 1, pp. 476–77.

54. N.M. Karamzin, *Pis'ma k I.I. Dmitrievu* (St. Petersburg, 1866) p. 236.

55. Quoted in Semevskii, *Politicheskie i obshchestvennye idei*, p. 76.

56. Cited in ibid.

57. *Russkaia starina*, 1904, no. 4, p. 15.

58. Shil'der, *Imperator Aleksandr*, vol. 4, p. 24.

59. Ibid., vol. 1, p. 180.

60. Mel'gunov, *Dela i liudi*, p. 71.

61. *Vosstanie dekabristov: Materialy* (Moscow, 1976), vol. 14, p. 18.

62. Shil'der, *Imperator Aleksandr*, vol. 4, p. 179.

63. Ibid., p. 186.

64. Grand Duke Nikolai Mikhailovich, *Imperator Aleksandr*, p. 124.

65. *Russkii arkhiv*, 1870, no. 1, p. 63.

66. Shil'der, *Imperator Aleksandr*, vol. 4, p. 204.

67. *Zapiski Sergeia Grigor'evicha Volkonskogo* (St. Petersburg, 1902), pp. 427–28.

68. *PSZ*, vol. 38, no. 29151.

69. *Russkaia starina*, 1890, no. 10, p. 503.

70. *Russkie propilei* (Moscow, 1916), vol. 2, p. 106.

71. *PSZ*, vol. 37, no. 28208.

72. S.P. Trubetskoi, *Materialy o zhizni i revoliutsionnoi deiatel'nosti* (Irkutsk, 1983), vol. 1, p. 233.

73. *Iz pisem i pokazanii dekabristov* (St. Petersburg, 1906), pp. 29–30, 39–40; D.I. Zavalishin, *Zapiski dekabrista* (Munich, 1904), vol. 1, p. 253.

74. Shil'der, *Imperator Aleksandr*, vol. 4, p. 330.

75. M.V. Nechkina, *Dvizhenie dekabristov* (Moscow, 1955), vol. 2, p. 197.

76. L.N. Tolstoy, *Polnoe sobranie sochinenii*, 90 vols. (Moscow, 1956), vol. 77, p. 185.

77. Shil'der, *Imperator Aleksandr*, vol. 4, pp. 445–46, 560–86.

78. L.L. Liubimov, "Taina startsa Fedora Kuzmicha," *Voprosy istorii*, 1966, no. 1; S.B. Okun' and N.N. Belianchikov, "Sushchestvuet li 'taina Fedora Kuzmicha'?" *Voprosy istorii*, 1967, no. 1.

79. See *Uchitel'skaia gazeta*, 1990, no. 23 (June).

Emperor Nicholas I, 1825–1855

Setting the tone for her article in the very first sentence ("It would be difficult to find a more odious figure in Russian history than Nicholas I"), archivist-historian Tatiana Aleksandrovna Kapustina presents a persuasive sketch of Tsar Nicholas I. Although she does not attempt to counter the more or less unanimous assessment found in the historical literature of Nicholas's incumbency as a period of political conservatism, she nonetheless reminds us that "it would be an oversimplification to judge the thirty-year reign of Nicholas I solely as a period of deep reaction." To be sure, Nicholas knew he was ill-prepared for the role of autocrat and this is probably why he showed little enthusiasm for assuming the throne when Alexander I died in 1825. However, Nicholas's response to the rebellion that broke out in connection with the complicated succession, the Decembrist Revolt, reinforced his belief in himself and convinced him he was destined to be sovereign. Critical of Soviet historiography that presents the Decembrists as glamorous revolutionaries in search of a liberal order for Russia, Kapustina reminds us that these misguided individuals sought "to destroy the Imperial family and dismember Russia." She likewise dismisses Soviet historians' depiction of Nicholas's sustained persecution of poet Alexander Pushkin. Taking into account the circumstances in which Nicholas implemented his policies, Kapustina suggests that Nicholas's views were important, but so were real limits to autocratic power. "Life within the framework of the obsolete system went on, quite contrary to the conservative foundations of Nicholas's policies." This is an important and provocative notion raised—but not developed—by the author. Her examples come mainly from the realm of developments in the Russian economy, where changes—ironically enough—resulted in the breakdown of the economic and social foundations on which the autocracy had been founded.

The author argues that Nicholas's administration can be divided into two periods, with 1840 representing the turning point, after which reaction and diplomatic isolation increasingly characterized the Russian state. Ending her account with an evaluation of Nicholas's foreign policy, she shows how diplomatically isolated Russia became embroiled in the Crimean War. In discussing the rumors that surrounded Nicholas's death, she convincingly dismisses the possibility that he might have committed suicide. Kapustina ascribes symbolic meaning to his death: defeat in the Crimean War represented personal defeat, and marked the dawn of a new era in Russia.

D.J.R.

Nicholas I

Tatiana Aleksandrovna Kapustina

It would be difficult to find a more odious figure in Russian history than Nicholas I. Historians unanimously consider his reign a period of deepest reaction. As the eminent liberal historian A.E. Presniakov characterized it, "Nicholas I's reign was an epoch of extreme self-assertion of Russian autocratic rule ... in the most extreme manifestations of its actual domination and fundamental ideology."[1] The image of this "gendarme of Europe," this "snake that strangled Russia for thirty years, this Nicholas of the Stick" looms before us from the pages of the works of Alexander Herzen, N.A. Dobroliubov, and Leo Tolstoy. The name Nicholas I evokes these textbook lines from Herzen's *My Past and Thoughts*:

> He was handsome, but his handsomeness was chilling; no other face could so mercilessly reveal the character of the man as his face did. His rapidly receding forehead, and his lower jaw, which was developed at the expense of his cranium, expressed an unbending will and weak thought, more of cruelty than of sensuality. But the main thing was his eyes, totally without compassion, wintry eyes.[2]

It seems that everything is clear about this singular, straightforward character, that the historical role of Nicholas I has been assessed once and for all. But things are not quite that simple.

Starting in the second half of the nineteenth century, and especially after the October Revolution of 1917, Russian historians and philosophers such as I. Ilin, K.N. Leontiev, and I. Solonevich began to speak up and to offer different evaluations of the personality of Nicholas I and his reign's importance for Russia. They saw him as "a knight of the monarchical idea," the "first autocrat since Peter" who was able to keep the empire on the path of its unique historical development, despite the flames of revolution that had broken out in Europe. This view is expressed most consistently in the works of the philosopher Leontiev, who considered Nicholas I a "true and great legitimist" who "was called upon to hold back for a time . . . the overall disintegration"[3] that went by the name of revolution. Just who was this autocrat whose name is inseparably linked to an entire epoch in the political, social, and cultural life of Russia? Was he "the strangler of liberty" and a despot, or was his personality more complex than this? The answer to this question is closely linked to the dispute over Russia's destiny, Russia's path of development, Russia's past and future, which has not yet subsided even now, well into its second century.

Catherine II's life was coming to a close when she was notified on 25 June (6 July) 1796 of the birth of her third grandson. A son, Nicholas, had been born to Grand Duke Paul and Grand Duchess Maria Fedorovna. From the very first, his physical development astonished those around him: "He has a deep voice and an amazing wail. He is just about twenty-four inches long, yet his hands are only a little smaller than mine. In all my life I have never seen such a knight," Catherine wrote to her regular correspondent Baron Grimm concerning the newborn. In the same letters she accurately foretold Nicholas's future. She wrote: "I have become the grandmother of a third grandson who is also, I think, destined, thanks to his unusual strength, to reign, even though he does have two older brothers."[4]

In contrast to his older brothers, Alexander and Constantine, whose upbringing was taken over entirely by their grandmother, Nicholas and his brother Michael grew up in the atmosphere of the punctilious court of their mother, Empress Maria Fedorovna. According to her contemporaries, she was a good and intelligent woman, but she was extremely strict and pedantic in the German fashion, demanding that her children observe all the niceties of court etiquette. In his early childhood, Nicholas always felt fear and awkwardness in meetings with his mother, and only later, during his young manhood, were warm and cordial relations established between the two. In contrast, Emperor Paul, who had been deprived of parental affection in his childhood, cast off his ordinary sternness when he was in the children's rooms, turning into a father who was passionately attached to his younger children. He pampered his sons and called them "my little rams, my lambkins." But conspirators assassinated Paul on 11 March 1801. At that time Nicholas was barely five, and troubled memories of his father's frightful death haunted him forever.

During his first seven years, Nicholas's nanny was a British woman named Jane Lyon, whom he called [until her death in 1842—D.J.R.] "my lioness" [a pun he coined early—D.J.R.]. She was a woman of bold and resolute character, but at the same time she was tender and kind, and she exerted considerable influence on the grand duke's developing character. Under her unflagging care, Nicholas grew up to be a strapping youngster who astonished everyone around him with his health and resolute character.

The grand duke's schooling began in 1802, when he was removed from the hands of women to the jurisdiction of tutors or, as they were called at the time, "cavaliers." His chief teacher was to be M.I. Lamsdorf, who had neither any pedagogical experience nor any views on general education. He was a stern old trooper, cruel and callous, a typical representative of the system of child-rearing that prevailed at the time, a system that made extensive use of corporal punishment. Later, in his memoirs, Nicholas wrote frankly about himself and his brother Michael:

> Count Lamsdorf knew how to inspire in us just one feeling—fear, so much fear and so much certainty of his omnipotence that our mother's face came to have secondary importance. This state of affairs deprived us completely of the happiness of filial trust in our mother, whom we were allowed to see only rarely; even then it was like being sentenced. From early childhood, the incessant shifting of persons around us inculcated in us the habit of looking for their weak points so as to take advantage of them in order to obtain what we needed and desired, and, I must confess, not without success. Count Lamsdorf and others who emulated him utilized strictness, and his hot temper absolved us even of the feeling of our own guilt, leaving us with only resentment of the harsh treatment that was frequently undeserved. In short, my mind was chiefly occupied with fear and the search for ways to escape punishment. To me, schooling was nothing but compulsion, and I studied unwillingly. I was often accused—and not without reason, I think—of being lazy and easily distracted, and frequently Count Lamsdorf would punish me with the birch, quite painfully, right in the middle of lessons.[5]

Sometimes Lamsdorf did not confine himself to the birch but would wield a ruler or even a gun-cleaning rod. It was as if the grand duke were always gripped in a vise; he did not dare to stand up freely, or to sit down, or to walk, or to speak. He did not dare to romp around and misbehave in the presence of adults, like other children. Because he was impulsive and animated, Nicholas had difficulty enduring that kind of regimen. He became coarse and arrogant. The journals kept by his teachers are full of notations such as "In his games he almost always ends up hurting himself and others"; he had "a penchant for posing and making faces."[6] He would encourage the clever Michael to mock other people around them, but he himself could not take a joke, as this seemed offensive to him. For this reason, his games with friends often turned into fights. Once Nicholas, frightened by the roar of cannon fire, hid behind an alcove, and when his playmate Vladimir Adlerberg finally found him there and started to make fun of him for being a coward, he struck his friend so hard with a gun butt that Adlerberg had a scar for the rest of his life.

In Nicholas's young soul, however, the desire to command, his persistence and stubbornness, were combined with goodness, directness, and honesty. Inherent in him was a spirit of cameraderie that he later expressed in his loyalty to his allies. He was a steadfast friend to his younger brother Michael and his sister Anna. Paul's younger sons were most fond of military games, playing soldiers and building fortresses. Of all the musical instruments, Nicholas liked the drum most of all. The little grand dukes would jump out of their beds in the middle of the night and stand guard for hours with toy guns in their hands.

Maria Fedorovna's chief concern was to combat her younger sons' interest in things military. She insisted that the youngsters wear civilian clothing and spend as much time as possible learning the sciences. But Nicholas's favorite lessons were those given by Colonel Gianotti, a military engineer, and also lessons in physics and drawing, for which the grand duke had a special talent. Later he became so proficient at this art that he taught himself how to engrave his own drawings, which are now in the Russian National Library.

The grand duke had absolutely no interest in the humanities. Writing a composition was a task completely beyond him. He so disliked Greek and Latin that after he became a father he eliminated these subjects from his own children's educational program.

Starting in 1809, the empress mother took her sons away from their friends to prepare them to attend the University of Leipzig. But Alexander I, who had established a lyceum in Tsarskoe Selo, objected; his younger brothers could complete their education there. This idea was never realized, however, and Nicholas and his brother were shut up in the palace at Gatchina, where they were taught the sciences at a university level. Maria Fedorovna tried to load her sons' days with so many activities that they would have no time for military studies. But her efforts produced the opposite effect. Nicholas rebelled against the coercion, and the sciences evoked revulsion in him. Even after he became emperor, he retained sad memories of that time:

> We were tormented with abstract subjects by two men, very good men, perhaps, and very learned, but both of them insufferable pedants: Balugianskii and Kukolnik. One of them would talk to us in a mixture of languages, not one of which he knew very well, concerning Roman, German, and God knows what all laws; the other man would talk of something called "natural law." In addition, we had someone named Storch, with his sleep-inducing lectures on political economy, which he would read to us out of a little book printed in French. During these gentlemen's lessons we would either doze or draw something silly, such as caricatures of them, and then later we would cram for examinations, without future use or benefit.[7]

The Patriotic War of 1812 had an enormous influence on the world view of the future emperor. Inspired by patriotism, he did not entertain the slightest doubt that victory was near, even when the French were right in Moscow. When Nicholas turned sixteen he was itching to join the army, but his mother resolutely opposed this. In 1814, the grand duke's dream finally came true: Tsar Alexander I permitted his brothers to join the active army, but they had no chance to take part in combat.

A meeting with Alexander I took place in Paris, by then occupied by the allies; there the grand duke's attention was drawn primarily to military institutions such as barracks, hospitals, and Les Invalides. On the journey back to Russia, a remarkable event took place in the grand duke's life. While in Berlin he became acquainted with Princess Charlotte, the daughter of the Prussian King Frederick-Wilhelm III, a friend and ally of Alexander I. Nicholas liked the young princess very much, but Maria Fedorovna thought that he was still too young to get married.

After he returned to St. Petersburg, Nicholas devoted himself to military science, studying strategy based on the materials of the military campaigns of 1814 and 1815. Later, after he ascended the throne, Nicholas I personally supervised the drafting of military combat plans. Construction and engineering also appealed to him, whereas classes in jurisprudence and political economy inspired nothing but boredom and confirmed his keen dislike of "abstractions" for the rest of his life. "The best theory of law," Nicholas I said, "is good morality, which should be in the heart regardless of these abstractions, and have religion as its foundation."[8] Nicholas's education was completed, as was the custom at the time, by travels all over Russia and Europe. He spent time in London, where the debates in Parliament interested him least of all; he spent all his time in the company of officers of the British army.

In 1817 the event that Nicholas had been awaiting for so long took place: his wedding in July with Princess Charlotte, who took the name Alexandra Fedorovna and was baptized in the Orthodox faith. "I felt very, very happy when our hands were finally joined; I gave my life with complete trust into the hands of my Nicholas, and he never betrayed that trust,"[9] the empress recalled in the final days of her life. Alexandra Fedorovna was a wonderful woman who truly became a guardian angel for Nicholas—an exemplary wife and a tender mother. In their thirty-eight years of marriage seven children were born to them: Alexander (in 1818), Maria (1819), Olga (1822), Alexandra (1825), Constantine (1827), Nicholas (1831), and Michael (1832). Among her contemporaries, the empress was remembered as somewhat frivolous but absolutely devoid of any desire for personal dominance, a kindly and mild woman. She had no political influence at all and did not strive for it; she devoted herself wholly to her family and to charity. "After the empress's death her papers revealed that she annually spent two-thirds of her personal income on pensions passed out to the sick and the indigent, on the alms house that she had established on Vasilevskii Island, and on occasional aid which she provided at times of fires or other disasters."[10]

A.F. Tiutcheva, the daughter of the poet F.I. Tiutchev and a lady of the court, wrote in her *Memoirs*:

Emperor Nicholas nurtured toward his wife—that fragile, innocent, elegant creature—the passionate and despotic adoration of a strong nature toward a weaker being whose sole owner and ruler he considers himself to be. To him she was a charming little bird whom he kept locked in a golden cage encrusted with precious stones, to whom he fed nectar and ambrosia . . . but whose wings he would clip without any regret if she should ever want to escape from the gilded bars of her cage. But in her enchanted dungeon the little bird never even thought about her little wings.[11]

After his wedding, Nicholas's youthful studies came to an end. His brother, the emperor, appointed him inspector general for engineering affairs and commander of the Life Guards in a sapper battalion. Nicholas worked zealously in the performance of his duties. He focused all his energy, all his powers of command on drilling the units assigned to him. So it was that veterans of the Napoleonic wars ended up under the command of this young officer who had no combat experience at all. The Gatchina system,* which turned soldiers into machines, was not viewed sympathetically by the combat generals to whom Nicholas was subordinate by virtue of his branch of service. "I began to crack down [on them]," Nicholas recalled, "but I was all alone in that, because those things which, as a duty to my conscience, I decried, were permitted everywhere, even by my superiors. It was a most difficult situation."[12]

Alexander I gave the young married couple the Anichkov Palace as a gift; the grand duke called it a paradise. His first child was born in Moscow in 1818, the future Tsar-Liberator Alexander II. One of his contemporaries has left us a revealing portrait of Nicholas at that time:

Nature has endowed him with one of the best gifts she is able to give those whom destiny has endowed with a high place: he has a most noble appearance. His usual expression reflects something stern and even forbidding. His smile is the smile of condescension rather than the result of a cheerful disposition or of fondness. His habit of dominating these feelings has become so much a part of his being that you will not notice in him any sense of constraint, nothing out of place, nothing overly studied, although his every word, like his every movement, is measured, as if he were reading from a musical score. There is something unusual about the grand duke: he speaks with animation, simplicity, and to the point; everything he says is intelligent; there is not a single vulgar joke, never a single funny or inappropriate word. Neither in the tone of his voice nor in the structure of his speech is there anything that would reflect pride or secretiveness. Yet you sense that his heart is closed, that the barrier is insurmountable, and that it would be foolish to try to penetrate to the depth of his thinking or to expect his complete trust.[13]

By 1819 Nicholas had command of the Second Guards Brigade, and from all appearances he was happy with his position. But it was

*That is, the new military order introduced by Paul I (1796–1801), based on the Prussian system.

not long before his family idyll was disrupted. From his youth Alexander I had often felt burdened by the throne and dreamed of abdicating. After the victory over Napoleon, under the influence of the religious sentiments that were growing in him, he returned to that dream more and more frequently. It was necessary to think about a successor. The emperor's daughters had died in infancy. Constantine Pavlovich, whose second marriage was to a Polish woman, also had no children. The most reasonable claimant to the throne, in this situation, was Nicholas.

In the summer of 1819, after reviewing the troops of the Second Brigade in Krasnoe Selo, Alexander I had dinner at his brother's palace, during which they had a remarkable conversation that was recorded in the memoirs of Grand Duchess Alexandra Fedorovna:

> Emperor Alexander . . . was conversing amiably when he suddenly changed tone and, becoming very serious, he began to say to us . . . in the following words that he had been very pleased that morning with Nicholas's command of the troops and was doubly pleased that Nicholas was fulfilling his duties so well, because in time he must assume a greater burden, inasmuch as the emperor looked upon him as his own heir, and that this would take place much sooner than one might expect. . . . We sat there as if petrified, our eyes opened wide, and we could not utter a word. As far as I myself am concerned, the emperor continued, I have decided to give up the obligations that I bear and to withdraw from the world. . . . Seeing that we were on the point of bursting into tears, he tried to console us, and he told us soothingly that this would not happen right away, and that several years would probably go by before the plan was put into effect. Then he left the two of us alone. You can imagine the state we were in. Nothing like that had ever even occurred to me, even in a dream. It hit us like a thunderbolt; the future seemed foreboding to us and not conducive to happiness. It was a memorable moment in our lives![14]

In his own memoirs, Nicholas himself compares his state of mind with that of a traveler: "suddenly a precipice yawns beneath his feet, and an irresistible force is pushing him onward, giving him no opportunity to step away or turn back."[15] Although some of Nicholas's biographers, for example, G.I. Chulkov, believed that the grand duke's conversation with the emperor was not altogether unexpected, inasmuch as Nicholas secretly dreamed of the throne, one may argue that Nicholas was aware that he was not prepared for the role of monarch. Alexander I did not do anything to keep his brother informed of affairs of state, and Nicholas continued to serve as an ordinary general whose acquaintance with society, in the words of Nicholas himself,

> was confined to waiting every day in the anterooms or the secretary's office, where . . . prominent persons having access to the sovereign would gather. . . . Meanwhile, all the young people, adjutants, and frequently even officers were waiting in the corridors, wasting time or amusing themselves . . . and they spared neither their superiors nor the government. That time . . . constituted extremely valuable practice in getting to know people and individuals, and I took advantage of it.[16]

Nicholas's gradual familiarization with the way things were done in the Guards, where "subordination disappeared and was preserved only on the front," led him to believe that behind the free and easy ways of military life at that time lurked something more serious—a plot against the government.

Meanwhile, in the summer of 1823, Alexander I decided to make his decision to turn the throne over to Nicholas legal, and he instructed Metropolitan Filaret to draw up the appropriate manifesto. This important state document, however, was not made public, and in the churches they continued to pray for Constantine Pavlovich as the heir to the throne. One copy of the Manifesto of 16 August 1823 was placed in the Dormition Cathedral in the Moscow Kremlin, while others were stored at the Senate, the Synod, and the State Council in St. Petersburg. To this day the question of why Alexander I decided to keep the act of succession secret remains unanswered, but the most likely explanation is that its proclamation was to be directly connected to the emperor's impending abdication. However, the secret was not kept absolutely, in particular by Alexander I himself, who made his intentions known to Alexandra Fedorovna's brother Prince Wilhelm who, of course, talked with his sister about it. Moreover, in the 1824 Calendar of the Berlin Court, Nicholas was named as the heir to the Russian throne.[17]

In early September 1825 Alexander I and Empress Elizaveta Alekseevna left St. Petersburg and went to Taganrog; beginning on 18 November, bulletins began arriving in the capital city concerning the emperor's illness, which became alarming from 25 November onward. On that day, Nicholas found out that there was almost no hope that the sovereign would recover and, after consulting with M.A. Miloradovich, the governor-general of St. Petersburg, he proposed that when the news of Alexander I's death came, Constantine should be proclaimed emperor immediately; Nicholas assured Miloradovich that he would be the first to swear allegiance to Constantine. On the morning of 27 November, during a worship service in the Winter Palace, a courier arrived from Taganrog to announce the tsar's death. Nicholas was shaken, but he maintained his composure and immediately swore allegiance to Constantine Pavlovich and administered the oath of allegiance to the Life Guards Company of the Preobrazhenskii Regiment. This was immediately followed by oaths of allegiance from persons of the entourage and dignitaries of the court. Empress Maria Fedorovna was extremely disturbed by all this and hastened to inform Nicholas that a document existed that made him heir to the throne. At a meeting of the State Council, a packet containing Alexander I's will was unsealed, and this caused high officials to doubt whether they should swear allegiance to Constantine. But Nicholas was obstinate, stating that it was his own adamant will that the legitimate sovereign be his elder brother. By the evening of that day, the entire Guards had sworn allegiance to Constantine.

Soon afterward, however, a letter came from Constantine in Warsaw, declaring that he renounced his rights in favor of Nicholas, and making reference to Alexander I's rescript. Yet Nicholas refused to yield. At a meeting of the members of the tsar's family it was decided that, inasmuch as Constantine's letter had been written before he had received the news of the oath, it could not be definitive. The question of the succession to the throne was becoming more and more confused. Couriers galloped from St. Petersburg to Warsaw and back. Constantine, who in his own words had had a life-long feeling of "natural revulsion for the throne," declared his decision irreversible. He refused to come to the capital, and he threatened "to withdraw even further unless everything was arranged in accordance with the will of our late emperor."[18]

On 12 December the situation became even more complicated. From General I.I. Dibich in Taganrog Nicholas received a packet containing a detailed report on a conspiracy by secret societies aiming to overthrow Imperial rule in Russia. On the same day, Lieutenant Ia.I. Rostovtsev of the Chasseurs, who was personally acquainted with many Decembrists, showed up in the Winter Palace and warned the grand duke about the conspiracy, although he did not name any of the participants. Later, a letter came from Warsaw expressing Constantine's absolute refusal. All of this forced Nicholas to back down and to bring himself to take a step unprecedented in Russian history—to change his oath of allegiance. On 13 December a manifesto was drawn up, relating the recent course of events, Constantine Pavlovich's refusal to assume the throne, and Nicholas's decision to accept it. The manifesto was drawn up by M.M. Speranskii, but the basic provisions were dictated by Nicholas himself. That evening an emergency meeting of the State Council was held. Without waiting for Grand Duke Mikhail Pavlovich, who had been delayed, Nicholas for the first time presided over the meeting and read the manifesto announcing his accession to the throne. The first man to bend his knee to the new sovereign was Admiral N.S. Mordvinov, the very person whom the Decembrists envisioned as the head of their provisional government.

The members of the northern and southern secret societies took advantage of the interregnum. The societies' plan of action was not actually worked out until the very last moment. The arrest of several prominent members (including P.I. Pestel) forced them to act in haste. Rumors of an impending second oath seemed to offer a propitious moment for an uprising. The conspirators decided that the officers would try to persuade the soldiers in their units not to take the oath of allegiance to Nicholas, and that they would march them out onto Senate Square and force the Senate to proclaim a constitution. Nicholas was not well liked among the Guards because of his proud and quick-tempered manner, his rudeness, and his harsh treatment of soldiers and officers. They had much more sympathy for Constantine, an eccentric but easy-going man who had been tempered in battle during Suvorov's Alpine campaign and the campaigns of 1805–14. The Decembrists resorted to deception, telling the soldiers that they were defending the rights of the legitimate heir to the throne against Nicholas's encroachment.

The fourteenth of December turned out to be the darkest day in Nicholas I's life. In the morning the Senate and the Synod convened for the oath of allegiance; simultaneously, the oath was administered to the troops. During the ceremonies in the Moscow Life Guards Regiment, officers D.A. Shchepin-Rostovskii and M.A. and A.A. Bestuzhev managed to persuade a number of soldiers not to take the oath. While attempting to intervene, Regimental Commander P.A. Fredericks, Brigade Commander General V.N. Shenshin, and Colonel Khvoshchinskii were gravely wounded. The regiment was marched out of the barracks and onto Senate Square. At the same moment, the troops began to stir in the Grenadier Guards Regiment, and some of the soldiers joined the rebels. Finally, a Guards detachment marched onto Senate Square. The gathered troops formed a square. But Prince S.P. Trubetskoi, who had been declared dictator of the uprising, did not come out, and this to some extent took the initiative away from the rebels. Having found out that some of the capital city's garrison had stopped obeying orders, Nicholas I swiftly worked out a plan of action. He was in a decisive frame of mind. A day earlier, having been informed of the impending plot, he had written to P.M. Volkonskii: "On the fourteenth I shall either be sovereign or dead."[19] By nature Nicholas had never been a coward, and in his youth he had sought in vain for an opportunity to take part in battle, but he could not have assumed that fate intended him to risk his life in his own capital city.

Amid all the confusion and from the very first hours of his reign, Nicholas I was obliged to assume responsibility for putting down the uprising. Reviewing in his mind the deployment of the opposing forces, he took into account the fact that the largest reserve of loyal troops at his disposal was in the area of Millionnaia Street, Liteinyi Prospekt, and the Tauride Gardens. Nicholas assigned the Preobrazhenskii and Sapper troops the job of guarding the Winter Palace, where his wife and his mother were in their chambers in the grip of hysteria, then walked downstairs to the palace guardhouse, where he addressed the soldiers of a company of the Finland Life Guards on duty there: "My boys! The soldiers of the Moscow Regiment are acting up. You must not do as they are doing; do your job like the fine brave lads you are!" He commanded them to load their guns, and then he gave the order, "Forward, quick step, march!"

When he came out of the palace gates he found that the entire square was swarming with agitated people. "I had to gain time," he wrote in his memoirs,

> in order to permit the troops to assemble. I had to distract the people's attention with something out of the ordinary. These were the thoughts that came to my mind, almost as an inspiration, and I began to speak. I asked them whether they had read my manifesto. Everyone said no. The idea occurred to me to read it then myself. . . . I started out quietly and leisurely, enunciating every word. But I confess that my heart just about faltered, and God alone held me up.[20]

All that day, Nicholas I kept his place at the head of the First Battalion of the Preobrazhenskii Regiment and, in full view of the mutinous formation, placed his life at risk. "The most surprising thing," he said later, "is that they did not assassinate me that day."

Part of the day passed in indecisive actions by both sides; the government did not immediately use force. Metropolitan Serafim and Grand Duke Mikhail Pavlovich were sent out to remonstrate with the rebels, but without success. After Miloradovich was mortally wounded by P.G. Kakhovskii, Nicholas I realized that he faced a battle to the death, and he ordered the cannons to be loaded. The first salvo was blanks, but the rebels did not budge. Then the second salvo hit the middle of the formation with canister shot, and the rebels began to panic and flee. The uprising was put down. The next day, Nicholas I wrote a letter to his brother in Warsaw and related the events of the first day of his reign. Regretfully he wrote: "My dear, dear Constantine! Your will has been done: I am the emperor, but, my God, at what a price! At the price of my subjects' blood."[21]

The fourteenth of December was forever etched in Nicholas I's memory, and it left an indelible stamp on his character and his view of the world. An observant traveler named de Custine, the author of the well-known book *Russia in 1839*, remarks: "He was no longer the taciturn, melancholic, and small-minded person he had been during his youth; he had turned into a hero as soon as he became the monarch."[22] Nicholas came to believe in himself; he believed that Providence had destined him to be sovereign. But at the same time, from the start of his reign he felt that he could count on nobody. He undertook the investigation of the Decembrists' case himself, interrogating those in custody, and by alternating threats with a hypocritical compassion for their bad luck he managed to extract frank test-imony. As he explored patterns of thought so alien to his own and perused the testimony of the Decembrists, Nicholas discovered a Russian reality full of contradictions. He ordered that the Decembrists' opinions concerning Russian affairs be compiled for him. Despite this, the emperor's political views did not become any less conservative.

In order to investigate the Decembrists, the Special Committee was formed on 17 December; it completed its work by 30 May 1826. On 1 June a Supreme Criminal Court was appointed, consisting of members of the State Council, the Senate, and the Synod, presided over by Prince P.V. Lopukhin. As members of the court Nicholas I appointed two figures of state who had liberal reputations, Speranskii and Mordvinov. A total of 121 men were put on trial. The trial went so swiftly and formally, without subjecting the defendants to interrogation or to confrontation, that many of the Decembrists did not even realize that they were being tried.

All the guilty were classified into eleven categories, and those as-

Nicholas I

signed to the first category (thirty-one men) were sentenced to death by decapitation. Five men (P.I. Pestel, K.F. Ryleev, P.G. Kakhovskii, S.I. Muraviev-Apostol, and M.P. Bestuzhev-Riumin) were placed outside the categories and sentenced to an agonizing death by quartering. Hence, the judges proved more harsh than the emperor. The report of the sentence was submitted to Nicholas I, who by an edict of 10 July 1826 granted life to Decembrists of the first category and moderated the degree of punishment for all the rest; but he turned over the cases of those who were placed outside the categories to "the discretion of the Supreme Criminal Court," which sentenced them to be hanged. It is said that when Nicholas I discovered this, he remarked that officers should be not hanged but shot, but A.Kh. Benkendorf insisted on that disgraceful form of punishment.

Carried out on the night of 17 July, the Decembrists' executions made a very harsh impression on society, because there had been no public executions in Russia since the uprising led by E.I. Pugachev was suppressed in 1775.

In contemporary historiography, there has been serious discussion of why Nicholas I preferred not "to rely on the privileged social group" consisting of the revolutionary members of the nobility in order to implement the program of reforms they were proposing. Some researchers believe that "had Turgenev's program, or something like it, been implemented, it could have been completed by the 1840s, and Russia would have been a constitutional state with a free peasantry."[23] But in the first place, Nicholas I faced in the Decembrists not a liberal opposition to the existing government or a group of peaceful reformers, as they are sometimes represented to be, but a military conspiracy the goals of which were to destroy the Imperial family and dismember Russia. Second, he always felt that there was something intolerably false about a constitutional monarch turning his authority over to a governmental oligarchy. Nicholas I always said that he recognized only two forms of government—unlimited monarchy and a republic.

The events of 14 December taught Nicholas to distrust any form of opposition by the nobility. After all, it had not been nobles who saved the Romanov dynasty on Senate Square in 1825; it was, in M.N. Pokrovskii's words, "peasants wearing Guards uniforms." The conclusions that Nicholas I drew under the influence of the tragic circumstances of his accession to the throne were reflected in a manifesto made public after the conclusion of the Decembrists' trial, which had "purged the Fatherland of the consequences of the infection that had festered for so many years in its midst." Nicholas I called upon all the estates to unite in trusting their government, but he especially admonished the nobles to be mindful of their duty to "guard the throne." He promised that the need for reforms would be satisfied—"not because of impudent daydreaming, which is always destructive," but by means of gradual governmental reforms. The public could facilitate this by expressing to the authorities "every kind of modest desire for something better, every thought about strengthening the force of the laws," which would be "received with good grace."[24]

The first step on the path of implementing Nicholas I's "conservative reaction" to the events that accompanied the beginning of his reign was the activity of the Committee of 6 December 1826; this committee was supposed to examine the drafts of reforms mapped out during Alexander I's reign and formulate immediate changes in the structure of state institutions, as well as in the status and rights of individual estates. In the course of examining all these matters, the problem of serfdom, so fateful to Russia, arose. By the time Nicholas I ascended the throne, it was already clear that serfdom was incompatible with the concept of equal civil rights, and that serf labor was less productive than free wage labor. The peasant question occupied a leading place in Nicholas I's domestic policies, but the results achieved during his reign did not match the efforts expended. The reason for this may be sought both in the emperor's personal views and in the conditions under which he was compelled to implement his policies.

The emperor himself disliked serfdom, an attitude that he had acquired from his youthful impressions as he traveled around Russia and encountered the unseemly aspects of the peasants' way of life. The Decembrist affair only served to strengthen his convictions. However, Nicholas I was not by any means an advocate of complete emancipation of the peasants, that is, of conversion to a system without social estates. His views on the peasant question derived from his general views on relations among the estates. If the nobility could not have political independence, inasmuch as that would conflict with the absolutist principle, then the nobility also should not have the right to own another estate—the peasantry—as property. Nicholas I clearly understood this, as well as the idea that that kind of possession was detrimental to the economic interests of the state. This was the origin of his desire to restore to the peasants their civil rights and to confer upon them a special position within the state.

It is evident, however, that Nicholas I could never conceive of a state system in which the people were free of state tutelage. He looked on the nobility as an agent of governmental authority over the peasantry. These views probably account for the indecisive character of the measures regarding the peasant question undertaken during his reign, which amounted to nothing more than particular amendments and changes. Even for this course of action and among the persons closest to him the emperor did not find sufficient support. Count S.S. Uvarov, a theoretician in Nicholas's governmental system and one of the most educated men of his time, said that "the question of serfdom is closely linked to the question of the autocracy." These two parallel forces had developed together, each with the same historical beginning and an identical legitimacy; "therefore, abolishing serfdom would inevitably lead to the collapse of the autocracy."[25]

Practical measures concerning the peasant question during Nicholas I's thirty-year reign can be summarized as follows. In 1833 an edict was issued prohibiting the auction of peasants and the sale of individual members of a family; it also forbade payment of private debts by transferring peasants without land. The "Secret Committee to Seek Funds to Improve the Condition of Peasants of Various Ranks" was formed in March 1835; M.M. Speranskii and E.F. Kankrin played a prominent role in it. But when the committee's activity showed no significant results, Nicholas I turned the job over to General P.D. Kiselev, a moderate reformer from Alexander's reign who was personally acquainted with many Decembrists. In 1834 Kiselev carried out reforms in the administration of the Danubian Principalities and thereby found favor in the emperor's eyes. The special Fifth Section was established in His Imperial Majesty's Chancellery, to which were assigned all matters relating to the administration of state peasants.

All subsequent measures taken by Nicholas I's government either improved the position of the state peasants, or regulated the condition of the landowners' peasants. The state peasants, on whom taxes were levied, were considered a personally free rural estate. In practice, however, the government looked on them as its own serfs: the Ministry of Finance, which was supposed to provide for them, considered the state peasants just a source of revenue for the budget. At Kiselev's insistence, a Ministry of State Domains was set up in 1837 to "exercise guardianship over free rural burghers" and to oversee agriculture. The government also began to buy up landowners' estates for the treasury in order to emancipate the peasants from serfdom (altogether, 178 estates were purchased), and "auxiliary loans" were established for which up to 1.6 million rubles were paid out every year. Attention began to be focused on medical care, and training schools were established.[26] These measures did produce positive results: the state peasants' solvency rose by the end of Nicholas I's reign, and tax arrears declined.

Things did not go as well in the case of privately owned peasants; the Secret Committee was set up in 1839 to discuss that problem. Kiselev spoke out against freeing the peasants without giving them land, because he saw that as a source of constant trouble. He sent Nicholas I a memorandum in which he argued for the peasants' right to receive a personal allotment from the landowner, for which they would owe service but could arrange an agreement for a complete buyout. The discussion of the "Draft Plan on Obligated Peasants" took two years. Because it encountered stiff resistance within the top bureaucracy composed of the nobility, Nicholas I was forced to back down. During discussion of the plan in the State Council on 20 March 1842, he gave a speech that reflected his views on the peasant question. The emperor admitted that "serfdom, as it now exists, is an evil that is palpable and evident to everybody, but of course, to meddle with it now would be a still greater evil." His compromise program was reflected in his statement that "liberty should not be given, but the way should be opened to a different, transitional stage that at the same time preserves inviolable the hereditary ownership of the land."[27]

Taking issue with Prince D.V. Golitsyn's proposal to limit the landowners' power over the peasants by drawing up what he called inventories, Nicholas I acknowledged: "I am, of course, an autocrat and monarch, but that is a measure that I will never take, just as I will never force agreements on the landowners; it must be a matter of good will for them, and experience alone will show to what extent it is possible to proceed from the voluntary to the mandatory."[28] The draft submitted to the State Council incorporated substantial changes, yet lost its meaning because the proviso implementing it was left up to the discretion of the landowners. Kiselev's original plan, therefore, was transformed from a state measure into a new way peasants could be set free at the landowners' discretion.

The attempts to resolve the peasant question during Nicholas I's reign show that not even a tsar who tried to act as an autocrat in the full sense of that word could remain uncompromising toward the nobility, regardless of his own views. Life within the framework of the obsolete system went on, quite contrary to the conservative foundations of Nicholas's policies. The empire's economy embarked upon new paths of development. New sectors of industry were formed, such as sugar-beet processing in the south and machine building and textiles in the central part of the country. The Russian Central Industrial Region emerged, and increasingly fed itself by purchasing grain in the agricultural provinces. In spite of the government's measures, the contingent of educated commoners enrolled in the universities continued to grow, and the middle segments of society became stronger. The authorities had to reckon with the country's new needs. These new and increasingly stronger tendencies were also reflected in Nicholas's personal interests: he became absorbed in matters of technology, entrepreneurship, and financial policy. His government accounted for the construction of half of the entire network of highways built in Russia before 1917. The first railroad, from St. Petersburg to Tsarskoe Selo, was built in 1837, and the railroad from St. Petersburg to Moscow was built in 1851.

The development of scientific thought was successfully under way in Russia. The works of G.I. Gess, N.N. Zinin, and A.A. Voskresenskii were the glory of Russian chemistry; the first refined platinum was produced in 1828. In 1842 K.K. Klaus discovered a metal previously unknown, and it was named "ruthenium" in honor of Russia. The Pulkovo Observatory was opened in the 1830s. The outstanding Russian mathematician N.I. Lobachevskii developed the theory of non-Euclidian geometry. In the field of physics and electrical engineering, remarkable results were obtained by B.S. Iakobi. The network of medical facilities grew more extensive, and Russian surgery, as exemplified by N.I. Pirogov, achieved world renown.

All of this took place against the background of growing crisis in the feudal economy. Nicholas I presided over the final disintegration of the economic and social foundations on which autocracy had flourished. Sharply distrusting social forces—conservative forces because of their degeneracy and progressive forces because of their revolutionary nature—tsarist rule tried to exist in isolation, and the autocracy amounted to no more than the personal dictatorship of the emperor. Nicholas believed that administration of the state in accordance with his own personal will and views was precisely the autocrat's job. This principle was reflected in the central governmental structure due to the preeminent importance of His Imperial Majesty's Chancellery, the agency of the emperor's personal rule.

In the very first year of his reign, Nicholas I placed all legislative matters under the jurisdiction of this chancellery, and for this purpose he established a special Second Section within it. Deep in its recesses, a colossal amount of work had been completed by 1832 under Speranskii's supervision on codifying the laws of Russia. For the first time since the Law Code of 1649, laws that had been scattered among many thousands of documents were brought together into a regular system. The result of this was two publications: *The Complete Collection of Laws of the Russian Empire*, in forty-seven volumes incorporating laws from 1649 through 1825; and *The Code of Laws of the Russian Empire*, that is, the laws in force, in fifteen volumes.

It was no accident that Nicholas I's choice fell upon Speranskii. The emperor realized that the labor of putting together the code of laws would require enormous experience and knowledge, of the sort possessed by this out-of-favor minister from the liberal period of Alexander I's reign, a man who in his plans for transforming the state adhered to views that were the opposite of Nicholas's own. The emperor undoubtedly knew about the Decembrists' plans to include Speranskii in their provisional government, and for this reason he distrusted him at first. With his typical directness, Nicholas told Baron M.A. Korf after Speranskii's death:

> Not everybody understood Mikhail Mikhailovich [Speranskii], and not everybody was able to appreciate him properly; at first I myself may have sinned against him more than anybody else. People told me so much nonsense about his perverse ideas and scheming.... But later, time and experience eliminated the hold of this nonsense on me. I found him to be a most faithful and zealous servant, with an enormous store of knowledge, enormous experience, and an energy that never flagged.[29]

In 1826, however, Nicholas I had thought differently; he had been extraordinarily harsh in his remarks about Speranskii. But to ensure the undertaking's success, he did not hesitate to turn it over to Speranskii, because at the time Speranskii was the only man capable of accomplishing the job of codifying the laws.

Domestic policy successes during the first half of Nicholas I's reign were linked to the names of government figures from Alexander's time—M.M. Speranskii, P.D. Kiselev, M.S. Vorontsov, S.S. Uvarov, and E.F. Kankrin. During the campaigns of 1828–29 and 1831, Russian troops were commanded by generals who had served in the Patriotic War of 1812—I.I. Dibich and I.F. Paskevich. In the words of B.M. Chicherin, Nicholas I:

> inherited from his predecessor a whole phalanx of men who, if not of high character, were at least intelligent and educated. He appreciated

them and tried to make them into obedient tools of his will, something that was not hard to do; they were the glory of his reign. But the more he came to enjoy power and became filled with the sense of his own greatness, the more he came to surround himself with servile nonentities.[30]

Of all the state institutions of the Nicholaevan age, the greatest notoriety went to the Third Section and its corps of gendarmes. The section was created in 1826 under Count Benkendorf's direction as a secret police agency and a source of personal information for the emperor regarding events in the country. Nicholas I delved deeply into reports that concerned not only major events but also the pranks and escapades of individual persons who fell under the gendarmes' surveillance. The Third Section was called upon to maintain a direct liaison between the autocrat's government and his people. By this slippery path, which gave rise to informing and denunciation, Nicholas I sought popularity and trust. A war against social dissatisfaction was being waged under his personal supervision. This was done in two ways: harsh suppression of all its manifestations, coupled with some alleviation of its causes. Even as he put down peasant disturbances, Nicholas I demanded a review of the peasantry's complaints of landowners' cruelty, and in extreme cases he would order the miscreant landowners exiled to Siberia and their estates seized. These cases produced a strong impression, but at the same time they provoked considerable dissatisfaction among the nobility.

Nicholas I endeavored to preserve the mask of an impartial judge, the father of his subjects. He took his role as autocrat seriously, sometimes even risking his own life. In 1830 cholera broke out in Central Asia and spread to Moscow and St. Petersburg. The epidemic affected all strata of the population. Grand Duke Constantine Pavlovich and his wife died from cholera, as did Field Marshal Dibich. The measures taken against the epidemic proved to be ineffective, as they consisted of nothing more than isolating the foci of the infection and forcibly placing people in hospitals, sometimes without sufficient grounds. All of this caused bitter feelings among the population and a number of rebellions. Nicholas I himself visited places in the grip of the epidemic. In 1830, on being informed that cholera had reached Moscow, he immediately hurried there and almost came down with the infection himself. In St. Petersburg on 22 June 1831, a cholera rebellion reached threatening proportions. Troops were called out to Haymarket Square, where a crowd of five thousand were gathered, but they went about their work lackadaisically. Then Nicholas, who was in Peterhof at the time, immediately rushed to the capital, went out among the milling crowd, and gave a speech that did much to calm people down. This incident is depicted in bas-relief in the monument to Nicholas I created by the sculptor Klodt.

After Nicholas I ascended the throne, major changes also took place in the field of public education. One of his first steps was to close the Bible Society in 1825. The cosmopolitan mysticism that characterized the final years of Alexander's reign did not match Nicholas I's sympathies; he was the defender and guardian of the traditional Orthodox faith. Nicholas himself was a fervent believer. When, during his reign, Bishop Mitrofan of Voronezh was canonized, Nicholas sent a golden altar cover to the prelate's shrine, then traveled to Voronezh to worship the saint. The tsar was concerned about the condition of the rural clergy, for he viewed its members as the bulwark of the nation's morality. Under Nicholas I, the government waged a struggle against sectarianism: starting in 1827, engaging in dissidence was declared a capital offense.

During Nicholas's reign, the ideological foundation of the monarchical state was definitively formulated. In 1832 the assistant minister of public education, S.S. Uvarov, in a report to the emperor concerning Moscow University, set down this famous triad: "Orthodoxy, Autocracy, Nationality," which he called the "ultimate anchor of our salvation and the most reliable guarantee of the strength and greatness of our Fatherland."[31] This formula immediately captivated Nicholas I, because it proclaimed a new principle: that the monarchy should rely directly on the patriarchal peasantry, bypassing the nobility that had compromised itself on Senate Square.

The new ideas were implemented primarily in the field of public education, which was imbued with the principle of the estate system. As early as 1827, an edict from the tsar presented educational institutions with this fundamental requirement:

> Everywhere, the subjects taught and the actual methods of instruction shall, as far as possible, be provided with regard to the future destiny of those being taught, so that each one may, along with sound concepts common to all concerning faith, the laws, and morality, acquire the kind of knowledge that is most essential to him . . . so that he, while not being below his estate, will also not strive overly much to rise above that in which, in the ordinary course of things, he is destined to remain.[32]

The fulfillment of these requirements served as the basis for the new charter given to middle- and lower-level educational institutions in 1828, which designated parochial schools for persons of "the lowest orders," district schools for town dwellers, and gymnasia for the children of nobles and officials.

The conservative measures of the first years of Nicholas I's reign also included the publication in 1826 of a new censorship charter consisting of more than two hundred paragraphs, which considerably exceeded in severity the censorship rules of Alexander's time. Among the public this charter was known as "the iron charter." In 1828, however, it was replaced by a more moderate law in which the censors were advised to examine the literal meaning of a speech and not to try to interpret it on their own. At the same time, a secret order was circulated among the gendarmes, according to which persons subjected to censorship fell under secret-police surveillance. All these measures were designed to combat the "spirit of freethinking" that had become widespread during Alexander I's reign.

After the Decembrists' uprising was crushed, Moscow, or, more precisely, Moscow University, became the center of freethinking. During the 1830s the government arrested numerous student revolutionary circles, including those of N.P. Sungurov and the Kritskii brothers. University autonomy was curtailed in every way, and military rules were imposed on student life. But it would be an oversimplification to judge the thirty-year reign of Nicholas I solely as a period of deep reaction. The Nicholaevan era was also a period of genuine flowering of Russian literature and art. The period was marked by the creativity of A.S. Pushkin and V.A. Zhukovskii, N.V. Gogol and M.Iu. Lermontov, and the masterpieces created by K. Briullov and A. Ivanov.

As he strove to place all aspects of national life under his personal control, Nicholas I focused particular attention on Russia's culture and art. In the words of N.P. Vrangel, the emperor fancied himself a connoisseur of art—and, in fact, he was pretty well versed in the styles and schools of painting and sculpture. "But in all things he was primarily a military man—military in his manners and tastes, in all his thoughts and doings."[33] For this reason, anything that went counter to his convictions had no right to exist. It is recounted that once as he was walking through the Hermitage, the emperor's gaze fell upon the statue of Voltaire sculptured by J.-A. Houdon. "Destroy that monkey," came the imperial command, and the masterpiece would have been doomed to destruction had it not been for the intervention of Count A.P. Shuvalov, who gave secret orders to move the statue into the basement of the Tauride Palace, where it remained until Alexander

II's reign. However, if we dismiss such blunders by Nicholas I as his auctioning paintings from the Hermitage in 1851, it must be acknowledged that he made a substantial contribution to Russian culture by setting up the Hermitage and turning it into a museum accessible to all. In 1840 the architect Franz Karl Leo von Klenze built a new Hermitage at the tsar's orders, and the museum's collections were catalogued and enlarged.

Nicholas I's favorite brainchild was the Aleksandrinskii Theater, which flourished in the 1830s and 1840s. The Russian stage at that time was enriched with works by N.V. Gogol, I.S. Turgenev, A.N. Ostrovskii, and M.I. Glinka. The art of the theater reached special heights. During that period, P.A. Karatygin, I.I. Sosnitskii, A.E. Martynov, M.S. Shchepkin, and V.N. Asenkova performed brilliantly on the stages of the Imperial theaters. Russia became a second home to such first-class European performers as ballerinas Marie Taglioni and Fanny Elssler and opera singer P. Viardot. In the palace theater, shows took place twice a week, with all the members of the Imperial family in attendance. Nicholas I's favorite plays were light salon comedies, and he loved the ballet as well. In the Aleksandrinskii Theater he knew each actor, even the most insignificant one, by name; during intermissions he went backstage, where the cast immediately surrounded him. Karatygin enjoyed his particular respect. Once, while he was talking to the performer, who was exceptionally large in stature, Nicholas asked him: "Well now, Karatygin, which of us is taller?" Grand Duke Mikhail Pavlovich stood them back to back and started to measure. The actor turned out to be a little taller than the emperor. "But you're taller than I, Karatygin!" exclaimed Nicholas I. "Merely longer, Your Majesty," the noted tragedian responded. This correction pleased the emperor inordinately.[34]

Soviet studies on the life of A.S. Pushkin expended much effort trying to represent Nicholas I as the persecutor of the famous poet, as the man who suppressed his creativity and was virtually to blame for his death. But the facts paint a different picture. In May 1826, while the investigation of the Decembrists was still ongoing, the poet submitted a petition to the tsar requesting the opportunity to vindicate himself before the government. After his coronation, the tsar summoned the poet to Moscow, where he granted him a two-hour audience. Later, Pushkin recalled:

They escorted me, covered with mud, into the emperor's office. He said to me, "Hello there, Pushkin, are you pleased to be home?" I answered politely. The sovereign spoke with me a long time, and then he asked "Pushkin, would you have taken part in 14 December if you had been in St. Petersburg?" "I certainly would have, Sire: all my friends were in on the conspiracy and I could not have stayed out of it. It was my absence alone that saved me, for which I thank God." "You've been fooling around a bit," the emperor cautioned. "I hope you will be more judicious now and we won't have to quarrel any more. You will send everything you write to me; from now on I myself will be your censor."[35]

In the 1830s Pushkin made a decisive change in his life by marrying and returning to government service. From Tsarskoe Selo he wrote to P.A. Pletnev: "I have some news for you: the tsar has taken me into his service—not his Chancellery, or the court, or military service; no, he has given me a salary and opened up the archives to me so that I can delve in there and do nothing. That's very kind of him, don't you think?" E.V. Fedorova comments, "Pushkin the historian had no quarrel at all with the autocracy."[36] In fact, the tsar loaned him twenty thousand rubles from the treasury to publish his *History of the Pugachev Rebellion*, a work that touched on a theme to which the autocracy was rather sensitive. Regarding Pushkin's duel, Nicholas I showed himself a fair judge: after the poet died, the tsar ordered his family's material needs to be met, and he demoted [his opponent,] D'Anthès, in rank, had him tried, and expelled him from Russia along with [D'Anthès's second,] Baron Heeckeren.

Substantial changes took place in the empire's architectural face: the fading of classicism and its replacement with a national although not very original style was symbolic of the Nicholaevan era. The tsar nourished a special passion for architecture. Not a single public building project passed without his personal approval. His favorite architect was C. Thon, who designed the Grand Kremlin Palace and the Cathedral of Christ the Redeemer in Moscow. To contemporaries these seemed rather mediocre in terms of their artistic significance; in our day, however, they are perceived as important architectural monuments. During Nicholas I's reign, the Alexander Column was erected on Palace Square in St. Petersburg, the construction of St. Isaac's Cathedral was begun and the Winter Palace, damaged by fire in 1837, was rebuilt. During its restoration, the tsar demanded opulent decorations for the ceremonial apartments, but in his private chambers he mostly preferred comfort and simplicity. Peterhof, his favorite summer residence, was a monument to Nicholas I's personal tastes. Located there, not far from the Gulf of Finland, were the suburban homes of the Imperial family—the Alexandria, the Cottage, and little Nicholas House.

In his everyday life, Nicholas I was unpretentious. He was a moderate eater and indifferent to wine. He began his working day early. A contemporary recalls that on winter days, around seven o'clock in the morning, "city dwellers walking along the Neva embankment past the palace, could look in the sovereign's window and see him sitting alone in his office at his desk, reading and signing whole mounds of papers by candlelight." But that was just the beginning. The real work started at nine o'clock when the ministers began to arrive. Each of them had certain days in the week when he was supposed to come with his reports, but sometimes the emperor received several ministers at once.

> At one o'clock in the afternoon, regardless of the weather, the sovereign went out—unless there was a scheduled military exercise, inspection, or parade—to . . . inspect the educational institutions, barracks, workshops, and other official establishments. During these visits Nicholas I inquired into all the details of management and often made comments regarding what needed to be changed or eliminated. He had a remarkable memory and never forgot what he had ordered, and woe unto those in charge if, on revisiting a particular establishment, he found that his orders had not been carried out.[37]

Nicholas I preferred to relax with his family. In the evenings, in the Imperial family's chambers, "the preferred entertainment was music, performed by soloists of the Imperial theaters, and sometimes also famous foreign virtuosi. . . . Often the sovereign himself took part in these home concerts; he was an excellent flute player. When there was no music, they spent the time reading the latest Russian and foreign works; those who wished to do so played cards, and Nicholas was as fond of this activity as anybody else."[38] During his reign court society first began to speak Russian; the emperor himself set the example. Before that, the language of high society had been French.

During Nicholas I's reign, life at the court reached an unusual level of splendor; ceremonies at the Winter Palace were astonishing for their brilliance and magnitude. Especially renowned was the New Year's Masquerade Ball, to which even ordinary citizens were admitted. At the masked ball Nicholas I loved to flirt with a pretty mask. Yet, according to the recollections of contemporaries, "Nicholas I was never known to have any major or especially outstanding infatuations." His only serious liaison was with V.A. Nelidova, who was one of the empress's favorite ladies-in-waiting. This affair was "absolutely justified by the broken health of the empress, whom the sovereign worshiped." When Nicholas I died, the empress summoned Nelidova to her, embraced and kissed her, and, "removing a bracelet with a portrait of the sovereign from her hand, she herself placed it on the wrist of Varvara Arkadievna."[39] But the emperor was known to have other liaisons as well, which he himself called "silly little things." In this regard he was a true son of his time, which was not distinguished for the rigor of its mores.

When he ascended the throne, Nicholas I inherited from his predecessor not only Russia's enormous international prestige but also two unresolved political problems: the Eastern Question (that is, the necessity of acquiring free passage for Russia from the Black Sea and the fate of Turkey's Christian subjects) and the fact that the empire included a constitutional state hostile to it—the Kingdom of Poland. Russia's annexation of the Duchy of Warsaw created multiple difficulties for the tsarist government. Nicholas I's opinion was that the empire's western border was not strengthened, but was actually weakened by the annexation of such an unreliable neighbor. The fact that the Kingdom of Poland had a constitutional system was incompatible with Nicholas I's view that its creation had been a mistake "worthy of regret." Inasmuch as he had inherited the Polish constitution from Alexander I, however, he considered it his duty to comply with that constitution, and he did not deviate from his duties as a constitutional monarch until the Polish uprising of 1831.

Nicholas I was crowned king of Poland in the spring of 1829, but he refused to have the ceremony performed in a Catholic cathedral, and it was only at Constantine Pavlovich's insistence that he attended a worship service there after the ceremony in the royal castle. A meeting of the Sejm, which had not convened since 1825, had been scheduled for 1830. Outwardly, the sessions of the Sejm went well, but they showed that the opposition, with its ideal of national independence, was alive and well and strongly influenced the Polish nobility and officer corps. When the news of revolution in France reached Warsaw, it had an electrifying effect. On 17 November 1830 crowds of university and military-school students broke into Belvedere, Grand Duke Constantine's residence, and wrecked the arsenal. Warsaw, and with it all the Kingdom of Poland, was in the grip of rebellion. The rebels elected a provisional government, which sent a delegation to St. Petersburg to negotiate with Nicholas I. The delegation's principal demand was to reunite Poland with the eastern lands of the country that Russia had annexed, as well as to protect the constitution. The

Polish peasantry, oppressed by the nobility, did not support the up-rising. According to N. Danilevskii's observation, "the uprising could not be explained by anything other than the Poles' annoyance be-cause their plans of restoring Poland's ancient grandeur had not been realized."[40] These plans had been gestating in Polish society since the Napoleonic wars and had received demagogic support from Alexander I.

Nicholas I received the news about the uprising on 25 November. He appointed I.I. Dibich as commander in chief of the army that was dispatched to Poland. On 12 December the government issued a manifesto to the people of Poland, in which the rebels were prom-ised forgiveness provided that they immediately resumed their duties and released their prisoners. However, the Sejm issued its own ap-peal to the people and stated that it would not lay down its arms until Poland gained independence. On 13 January 1831 the Sejm declared that the Romanov dynasty no longer occupied the Polish throne. Nicholas I's response, a manifesto dated 25 January, stated: "This impudent disavowal of all rights and oaths, this obstinacy of evil design has turned criminal; the time has come to use force against those who know nothing of contrition."[41] In a letter to Constantine Pavlovich, Nicholas I said: "Which of the two must perish—for that, evidently, is inevitable—Russia or Poland? You yourself must de-cide."[42] The same sentiments were expressed by Pushkin in his poem "To the Slanderers of Russia."

Combat operations got under way. Near Grochów, Dibich crushed the rebels, but he failed to take advantage of his victory, and instead of storming Warsaw he ordered the troops to withdraw. Soon after that, I.F. Paskevich was appointed to take the place of Dibich, who was dying from the cholera then raging. Paskevich's troops crossed the Vistula, and by July they were at the gates of Warsaw. Before storming the city, Paskevich promised the Poles they would be granted an amnesty and the constitution would be protected, pro-vided that they yielded the city, but his offer was refused. Warsaw fell on 26 August 1831.

After the Polish uprising was suppressed, the idea of correcting the historical injustice caused by the partitioning of Poland in the eighteenth century, an idea that had been in part shared by Paul I and Alexander I, was dead and buried. Russia's policies came to be dominated by the opposite idea, that a deep gulf divided the inter-ests of Poland and Russia. The tsarist government began to view the Kingdom of Poland exclusively as a western part of the empire. Nicholas I revoked Poland's constitution. These words, addressed to Paskevich, resound with unconcealed joy: "I have received the Chest with the remains of the late lamented constitution, for which I thank you greatly; it is to rest in peace at the Armory."[43] In 1832 Nicholas I issued his Organic Statute, which defined Poland's state structure: the name "Kingdom of Poland" was retained, while the crowning of the tsar with the Polish crown, the special Polish troops, and the Sejm were all abolished.

While visiting Warsaw in 1835, Nicholas I addressed representatives of the Polish nobility with this warning: "If you nurture any dreams of . . . an independent Poland and other such chimaera, you will call down upon yourself only great unhappiness. On my command, a citadel is to be erected here, and I declare to you that in the event of the slightest trouble I will give the command to destroy your city; I will destroy Warsaw, and this time, of course, I will not have it rebuilt."[44]

In its policy of Russifying the Kingdom of Poland, Nicholas I's government tried to rely for support primarily on the peasantry. Measures were undertaken to limit serfdom there. The most important measure was the introduction of inventories, designed to give legislative definition to peasant service obligations, into the western district in 1846. Tsarism's struggle against the Polish national liberation movement turned into restrictive and reactionary measures in the field of public education and religion as well. Censorship was introduced, and travel abroad was made difficult. In 1839 the Warsaw Education District was established, and instruction in secondary schools began to be conducted in Russian. Warsaw University was closed. Catholicism was subjected to oppression, and monasteries were shut down. This reactionary policy did even more to complicate the already difficult, conflict-filled Russian–Polish relations and made it impossible to prevent a new revolutionary upheaval in the Kingdom of Poland in 1863.

Nicholas I's character, views, and convictions exerted a major influence on the Russian Empire's foreign policy. During the first years of his reign, he manifested considerable caution in his diplomatic statements. Because he was inexperienced, he felt awkward among ambassadors and when Minister of Foreign Affairs K.V. Nesselrode made his reports. Very soon, however, the emperor perceived Nesselrode to be an ordinary office clerk who knew how to write in French whatever was dictated to him but who was quite incapable of giving advice on his own. Nicholas I kept Nesselrode at the helm of foreign policy and subordinated that branch of state administration completely to himself; soon it became one of his favorite concerns.

In contrast to Alexander I, who never forgot that he was the monarch of a European power and was overly sensitive to the West's opinion of Russian affairs, Nicholas I showed himself a quite different man from the first day of his reign: on 14 December in Senate Square, when a representative of the diplomatic corps approached him and expressed his readiness to support the young tsar's authority by his presence in the tsar's retinue, Nicholas I answered that "this scene is a family affair, and Europe has no part in it."[45]

The dominant thinking behind Nicholas I's diplomatic activity was his conviction of the need to wage an untiring struggle against revolution, no matter where or in which form it was manifested. In this he was consistent; he even stood up for the Turkish sultan against rebellious Christians, and he did not permit agitation on behalf of the Slavs either in the Ottoman Empire or in Austria. "He was unwilling to permit vassals and subjects (even those of the Orthodox faith) to rise up against legitimate authority."[46] At first glance, this attitude may seem contradictory to Russia's own interests. But K.N. Leontiev considered it to Nicholas I's credit that he "realized at the time that a policy of emancipation, even outside the boundaries of his own country, was something that might seem advantageous at first but was in reality extremely dangerous and could, in the event of the slightest carelessness, come home to roost on the head of the emancipator himself."[47]

Nicholas I's first step in foreign policy was an agreement with England concerning the Greek question. The St. Petersburg Protocol was signed on 4 April 1826, calling for the formation of a Greek state with its own government, independent of Turkey only in regard to finances. Russia and England pledged to support one another in carrying out this agreement. It made the Austrian chancellor, Prince Klemens von Metternich, nervous, for he perceived it as a violation of the principles of the Holy Alliance. Frightened by the ultimatum, the Turks signed the Akkerman Convention in October 1826. Meanwhile, France had also joined the agreement. To Austria's horror, three great powers had formed an alliance against Turkey. In 1827 a convention of cooperation among them in regard to defending the Greek uprising was signed in London. The convention called for sending a squadron of the three powers into Turkish waters.

On 20 October 1827 the three powers' squadron destroyed the Turkish–Egyptian fleet in the Bay of Navarino. Even after this, however, Sultan Mahmud II refused to recognize Greek independence. The Russian government decided to go to war to complete the liberation of Greece, an act that would guarantee Russia freedom of trade through the Straits and would strengthen its influence in the Balkans and the Transcaucasus. Military operations began in May 1828. The Russian army, which had only drilled on the parade grounds, could not at first overcome the Turks' resistance, and it looked as if the campaign might end in a draw, to the jubilation of Austrian diplomatic circles. Soon afterward, however, Paskevich took Kars in the Transcaucasian theater of operations, while troops commanded by Dibich occupied Silistria and Adrianople in the Balkans. Naturally, all of Europe was nervous about the Russian troops' resounding success, and Nicholas I realized that not only Austria but his own allies, England and France, were watching with envy the Russian troops' advance toward Constantinople.

Fearing international complications, Nicholas I hastened to finish the war and submitted his demands. A peace treaty was signed at Adrianople on 14 September 1829. Turkey lost its Black Sea coast from the mouth of the Kuban to St. Nicholas Harbor. The islands in the Danube delta were given to Russia, and the southern branch of the mouth of the river became the border. Russian trading vessels received confirmation of their right to free passage through the Bosporus and the Dardanelles. As for Greece, it was declared an independent state linked to the sultan only by the obligation to make yearly payments; the population of Greece was granted the right to elect a monarch from among the reigning dynasties of Europe (but not England or Russia).[48] In this way, Russia's victory in the war granted independence to Greece and autonomy to Serbia, Moldavia, and Wallachia. The Treaty of Adrianople represented an important milestone in the liberation of the Balkan peoples from the Ottoman yoke and was one of the most brilliant victories of Nicholas I's diplomacy.

Having set as the goal of his domestic policy the preservation of the existing social and political structure, Nicholas I also adhered to the principle of legitimacy and the Holy Alliance in his foreign policy. In his eyes, the struggle against the revolutionary movement in Europe was also a struggle for the real interests of Russia as a European power. The principal task of his foreign policy was to establish once and for all Russia's position in the East, to secure its positions on the shores of the Black Sea, and to ensure the Russian fleet free passage through the Straits. Added to this principal task was another one:

maintaining Russia's prestige in Europe by defending the status quo, including those concessions that had been made to the new order by 1815, but with a firm resolve not to make any further concessions.

Both these tasks—a return to the traditional, eighteenth-century Russian policy in regard to the Eastern Question, and a continuation of the policy of the Holy Alliance—took on one and the same legitimist coloration under Nicholas I. When he came out in support of Greece in 1826–27, therefore, he was by no means pursuing the goal of supporting the Greek liberation movement but only conducting a course of action to resolve the Eastern Question that was advantageous to Russia's interests at that time.

Nicholas I attached utmost importance to his alliance with Austria and Prussia, viewing these states as an essential part of his conservative political system. Although linked by family ties to the court of Berlin and kindly disposed toward the Prussian royal family, Nicholas I was nevertheless displeased with Prussia's attempts to head a national movement in Germany, especially after 1840, when Frederick-Wilhelm IV ascended the throne. Nicholas I perceived Prussia's policies, aimed at uniting Germany and achieving hegemony in Europe, as treason against the Holy Alliance. For this reason, despite his Prussian sympathies, he maintained close ties with Austria and always acted as a defender of the Habsburg state whenever anything that threatened to weaken it or break it up emerged in a particular part of Austria's patchwork empire.

Nicholas I anxiously kept an eye on the source of all revolutionary upheavals—France. Because he foresaw an inevitable upheaval in that country, he condemned the overly harsh, ultrareactionary measures of Charles X, but he viewed the latter's downfall and the transfer of power to Louis Philippe in 1830 as a challenge to the "old order." Nevertheless, he was convinced that the monarchy of Louis Philippe was of a conservative, compromising nature, and he consented to recognize the new order in France. But Nicholas I's hostility toward the French king, who had played up to the revolutionaries, was so strong that he took malicious pleasure in the downfall of Louis Philippe's monarchy in 1848.

In response to the Polish uprising of 1830–31 and the revolution in France, Nicholas I began to return to the principles of the Holy Alliance, from which he had deviated at the beginning of his reign. In 1833 he concluded a convention with Austria and Prussia directed against revolutionary forces in Europe. "On mature contemplation of the dangers that continue to threaten the order that was established in Europe by public law and the treaties of 1815," the powers "unanimously decided to strengthen the conservative system that constituted the unshakable foundation of their policy."[49]

The year 1840 divides the reign of Nicholas I into two periods. By the late 1830s he had achieved a number of successes in domestic and foreign policy (the compilation of the Law Code in 1833, provisions for the state peasants in 1837, the financial reform of 1839, and the Treaty of Adrianople in 1829). But in the 1840s the picture started to change. Nicholas I's staff of officials began to diminish in number and decline in quality; after 1842, Kiselev considered the peasant question lost, and financial measures became more risky. The London Conference of 1840, convened to "secure the independence and integrity of Turkey," constituted a direct affront to Russia's prestige and its pretensions to dominance in deciding the Eastern Question. From then on, as the European armies converted to more rapid-fire weaponry and the principal navies of the world converted to steam engines, Russia began to lag behind in military technology.

In February 1848 revolution erupted in France and a republic was proclaimed. Diplomatic relations between Russia and France were immediately broken. Meanwhile, revolution in Europe continued to flare up and spread to Prussia and Austria. Metternich was forced to flee Vienna. These events unsettled Nicholas I. He personally drafted a manifesto, dated 14 March 1848, stating:

> Having arisen first in France, rebellion and anarchy were soon transmitted to neighboring Germany, and as they spread everywhere with an impudence that increased to the extent that the governments gave way, this destructive flood at length came to menace our own allies, the Austrian Empire and the Kingdom of Prussia. Now, recognizing no other boundaries, the impertinence in its madness poses a threat also to our own Russia, which God has entrusted to Us.[50]

A tense standoff developed between revolutionary Europe and tsarist Russia. In an all-out attempt to strangle the revolution, Nicholas I sent Russian troops into the Danubian Principalities and thus provoked protest from England. In an effort to put down the uprising in Italy, large amounts of money were allocated to the Austrian government. When the revolution spread to Hungary in early 1849, the Austrian government appealed to Nicholas I for aid. A manifesto of 26 April announced that a Russian army of a hundred thousand men had entered Galicia. The rebels were routed, and the captured Hungarian generals were turned over to Austria. But when Nicholas I found out that thirteen of them had been executed, he directed Nesselrode to convey to the Austrian Cabinet an expression of "disapproval of that kind of senseless brutality." The suppression of the Hungarian uprising was a triumph of the conservative foreign policy of Nicholas I, who came to be called "the gendarme of Europe."

This policy provoked the displeasure of those European governments that owed their very existence to Russia—Austria and Prussia. They watched with alarm and envy as the Russian Empire's hegemony grew in the East. Nicholas I gained a new enemy in the person of Napoleon III, who proclaimed himself emperor of France in 1852. Nicholas refused to recognize him as a legitimate monarch; in correspondence he called Napoleon "friend" rather than "brother." This offended and irritated the proud and haughty Napoleon III. The aim of his policy, hostile to Russia, was to destroy the European monarchical alliance of 1833. Successfully choosing a moment when relations were cooling between Russia and Prussia and, in part, between Russia and Austria, he directed a strike against Russia, the country that most consistently followed the principle of legitimacy so inimical to Napoleon III. Delighted with his success in 1848, and especially by the fact that revolution had not penetrated Russia, Nicholas I perceived the situation that developed as a propitious moment to regain everything he had lost in regard to the Eastern Question since the late 1830s. He clearly overestimated his own strength in his belief that the European powers, weakened by revolution, would back down before Russia.

Grounds for a conflict were found in the Turkish government's violation of the rights of the Orthodox Church in Palestine. Encouraged by France, Turkey turned over the keys to the Bethlehem Cathedral to the Catholics. As N.Ia. Danilevskii remarked, "France's demand was itself no more and no less than a challenge hurled at Russia, which out of honor and dignity could not refuse it. This dispute over a key, which many would consider to be of rather little consequence . . . , had for Russia—even from an exclusively political point of view—much more importance than any issue over borders."[51] It was a matter of Russia's prestige in the eyes of the Slavic world, a matter of Russia's state interests. So at Russia's insistence, in July 1853 at a conference of representatives of five European powers, the conciliatory Vienna Note was drafted; it satisfied Nicholas I, but was rejected by the Turkish sultan.

Napoleon III and the English ambassador Lord [Stratford] de Redcliffe encouraged Turkey to declare war on Russia. Then Nicholas I sent an army of eighty thousand men to occupy the Danubian Principalities and demanded that Turkey fulfill its treaty obligations. It was not long, however, before he was forced to realize that he did not have a single ally in Europe. England, France, Turkey, and Sardinia all opposed Russia. Finding himself in a face-to-face standoff with a hostile coalition, Nicholas I took a desperate step: he entertained the possibility of turning the war that was brewing into a war of liberation by proclaiming the independence of the nations that had been enslaved by the Ottoman Porte. He outlined this plan in a note to Chancellor Nesselrode in November 1853. But Nesselrode objected to the plan, because it conflicted with the policy to which Russia had adhered for decades. The chancellor's opinion prevailed, and Russia entered the war politically isolated.

Public opinion in Germany was also extremely hostile to Russia. Every success sustained, not only by the Western powers but also by the Turks, was celebrated everywhere as a victory for the common cause of all Europe. But what astonished Nicholas I most of all was the position of Austria, which he had only recently saved from dismemberment. Austria concentrated an enormous army at Russia's borders and threatened to invade, thereby forcing Nicholas I to withdraw his troops from Moldavia and Wallachia, after which the Austrians occupied both principalities.

In early 1854 Nicholas I mapped out a plan of military action. He anticipated encounters with the enemy in the Crimea, the Caucasus, and Bessarabia. Throughout the summer of 1854, the English fleet attacked the Russian coasts on the Baltic and the White Seas and in the Pacific, but these attacks were unsuccessful. Military actions in the Transcaucasus and along the Black Sea coast, in which Russia's troops succeeded at first, soon lost their importance, because an Anglo-French landing force of sixty-two thousand men was deployed in the Crimea. Russian troops on the peninsula numbered no more than fifty-two thousand men. The first encounter with the enemy on 7 September, near Alma, ended in failure, and the Russian troops withdrew. Scuttled ships closed off entry to the Bay of Sevastopol. The siege of Sevastopol began on 11 September and lasted 350 days.

The failure of Russian troops in the Crimea, and the colossal strain on his physical and mental resources, undermined Nicholas I's health. He devoted seventeen hours a day to business, and despite his exhaustion continued to work through the night. On 9 February 1855 he attended an inspection of the Life Guards Battalions of the Izmailovskii and Chasseurs regiments, which were being assigned to the active army; this took place at the riding-ground of Engineers' Castle. His doctors asked him not to go out in the cold, but Nicholas I refused.[52] He rode out of the palace wearing a light raincoat despite the temperature, twenty degrees below zero. His health worsened, and when the emperor returned to the palace around evening he was extremely ill. The next day he again went out to inspect the Guards. That excursion was his last.

Pneumonia developed with terrifying speed. On 17 February Nicholas I's condition became critical. He retained all his faculties, and he took confession and communion. As he blessed his son Alexander, the heir to the throne, he told him: "Serve Russia! I should like to take upon myself all the difficulties and hardships and bequeath to you a peaceful, well-ordered, and happy kingdom. But Providence has decreed otherwise."[53] As he said goodbye to the members of his family, Nicholas I commanded that the Guards, the army, the navy, and especially the defenders of Sevastopol be thanked in his name for their faithful service. He himself chose the site of his grave in the Cathedral of Saints Peter and Paul, and asked that his burial be a modest one and that the period of mourning be as brief as possible.

After Nicholas I's death, rumors circulated in the capital city that the emperor had been unable to bear the disgrace of his defeat and had killed himself by taking poison prepared for him by Mandt, the family physician. These rumors also came to be reflected in the historical literature. Although even today we have insufficient information to judge their reliability, it is hardly likely that a man such as Nicholas I, a believer who possessed a strong will and courage, would ever commit suicide.

But his death was symbolic. Nicholas I's whole being was imbued with the governmental system of which his reign was the embodiment, and he could not endure the defeat of his ideals, the humiliation of Russia, and the treachery of his allies. With the death of this "conservative genius,"[54] as K.N. Leontiev called Nicholas I, a new epoch began in Russia's history.

Notes

1. A.E. Presniakov, *Apogei samoderzhaviia: Nikolai I* (Leningrad, 1925), p. 3.
2. Alexander Herzen, *Sobranie sochinenii* (Moscow, 1975), vol. 4, p. 58.
3. K.N. Leont'ev, *Tsvetushchaia slozhnost'* (Moscow, 1992), pp. 237, 243.
4. B.B. Glinskii, *Tsarskie deti i ikh nastavniki* (St. Petersburg, 1912), p. 226.
5. Quoted in G.I. Chulkov, *Imperatory* (Moscow, 1991), p. 171.
6. N.K. Shil'der, *Imperator Nikolai I. Ego zhizn' i tsarstvovanie*, vol. 1 (St. Petersburg, 1903), p. 22.

7. Quoted in Glinskii, *Tsarskie deti*, p. 256.
8. Presniakov, *Apogei samoderzhaviia*, p. 13.
9. *Zhizn' imperatorov i ikh favoritov* (Moscow, 1992), p. 54.
10. *Russkaia starina*, 1896, no. 10, p. 11.
11. A.F. Tiutcheva, *Pri dvore dvukh imperatorov* (Moscow, 1990), p. 103.
12. Chulkov, *Imperatory*, 176.
13. P.B. Kozlovskii, "Dnevnik," *Russkii arkhiv*, 1892, vol. 2, p. 12.
14. *Zhizn' imperatorov i ikh favoritov*, p. 575.
15. Chulkov, *Imperatory*, p. 176.
16. Ibid.
17. M.A. Polievktov, *Nikolai I. Biografiia i obzor tsarstvovaniia* (Moscow, 1918), p. 44.
18. Ibid., p. 48.
19. Chulkov, *Imperatory*, p. 182.
20. *Mezhdutsarstvie 1825 g. i vosstanie dekabristov v perepiske i memuarakh chlenov tsarskoi sem'i* (Moscow–Leningrad, 1926), p. 23.
21. Ibid., p. 31.
22. *Rossiia pervoi poloviny XIX v. glazami inostrantsev* (Leningrad, 1991), p. 453.
23. B. Anan'ich and V. Chernukha, "Pervyi shag k revoliutsii," *Rodina*, 1991, no. 9, p. 28.
24. Presniakov, *Apogei samoderzhaviia*, p. 25.
25. Ibid., p. 33.
26. Polievktov, *Nikolai I*, p. 309.
27. Ibid., pp. 312, 313.
28. Ibid., p. 315.
29. A. Filippov, *Imperator Nikolai I i Speranskii* (Iuriev, 1897), p. 5.
30. *Russkie memuary 1826–1856* (Moscow, 1990), p. 304.
31. Ia.A. Gordin, *Pravo na poedinok* (Leningrad, 1989), p. 157.
32. Polievktov, *Nikolai I*, p. 83.
33. N.P. Vrangel', *Iskusstvo i gosudar' Nikolai Pavlovich* (Petrograd, 1915), p. 3.
34. *Stolitsa i usad'ba*, 1915, no. 46, p. 11.
35. V.V. Veresaev, "Pushkin v zhizni," *Sochineniia*, vol. 2 (Moscow, 1990), p. 288.
36. E.V. Fedorova, "Gibel' Pushkina," *Vestnik M[oskovskogo] G[osudarstvennogo] U[niversiteta]*, 1991, no. 3, p. 44.
37. P.M. Shiman, "Imperator Nikolai I," *Russkii arkhiv*, 1902, no. 3, p. 163.
38. *Russkii arkhiv*, 1902, vol. 1, p. 462.
39. *Istoricheskii vestnik*, 1910 (January), pp. 109–10.
40. N.Ia. Danilevskii, *Rossiia i Evropa* (Moscow, 1991), p. 37.
41. Polievktov, *Nikolai I*, p. 131.
42. Ibid., p. 132.
43. Presniakov, *Apogei samoderzhaviia*, p. 65.
44. Polievktov, *Nikolai I*, p. 141.
45. Chulkov, *Imperatory*, p. 186.
46. Leont'ev, *Tsvetushchaia slozhnost'*, p. 242.
47. Ibid.
48. *Istoriia diplomatii*, vol. 1 (Moscow, 1959), pp. 542–44.
49. Chulkov, *Imperatory*, p. 214.
50. Presniakov, *Apogei samoderzhaviia*, p. 73.
51. Danilevskii, *Rossiia i Evropa*, p. 14.
52. *Zhizn' imperatorov i ikh favoritov*, p. 582.
53. Ibid., p. 589.
54. Leont'ev, *Tsvetushchaia slozhnost'*, p. 243.

Emperor Alexander II, 1855–1881

"I turn over my command to you, but unfortunately not in the good order that I would wish. I am leaving you many worries and troubles." Such was Nicholas I's legacy to his son and heir, Alexander II, who ascended the throne during Russia's defeat in the Crimean War. Trounced by a military alliance of the great powers, Russia faced broad-scale disaffection at home and growing calls for reform. These were the circumstances in which the new Romanov emperor took power. The tsarist government soon relaxed censorship, lifted restrictions that had been placed on universities and on foreign travel, encouraged economic ventures, emancipated the peasantry, and introduced several other "great reforms" in the judiciary and in local government. More reforms followed. But on 1 March 1881 the Tsar–Liberator fell to an act of political terror. His murder dashed hopes that Russia would take a step toward instituting a constitutional order and ushered in a period of conservative reaction.

Alexander II's rule has attracted its share of attention, but Soviet authors did little to shed light on the significance of this crucial turning point in Russian history: his life and reign were in need of reassessment. Larisa Georgievna Zakharova of Moscow State University succeeds admirably in this regard, penning one of the most penetrating, thoughtful, and subtle accounts of the tsars to appear in Voprosy istorii. Drawing on a vast array of archival material, contemporary sources, and historical works, Zakharova offers a convincing portrait of Alexander's personality and reevaluation of his reforms. Despite the best efforts of his tutors, Alexander was shaped as a military man "in his habits, his world view, and his environment." Understanding this is key to making sense of his behavior as statesman. The author emphasizes that prior to his becoming tsar, Alexander did not exhibit any liberal

*inclinations. Yet "without any general program whatsoever," he and his offi-
cials embarked upon a program of reform, which Zakharova accounts for in
clear, forceful language. Although she accepts the argument found in the
literature that Alexander became more conservative following the first attempt
on his life, she notes that the overall trend toward reform continued throughout
his years in power.*

    *More emperor and autocrat than reformer or liberator, Zakharova's Alexan-
der is a tragic figure. As she so aptly puts it: "The tragedy of the Tsar–Liberator became the tragedy of Russia." Maintaining that the time has come to
balance the ledger, she concludes that Alexander II's reforms were designed not
to "improve the life of the people, develop the principle of elective representation,
or lay the foundations of a state ruled by law . . . [but] to entrench the
autocracy, strengthen military power, and expand the empire for the sake of
Russia's greatness as Alexander II and his closest associates understood it."*

D.J.R.

Alexander II

Larisa Georgievna Zakharova

During a moment of panic on 30 July 1835, Nicholas I, on his way to
Prussia to visit his ailing father-in-law, King Frederick-Wilhelm III,
composed a letter and testament to his "beloved son Sasha" advising
him to guard against "the fulfillment of the evil designs" of his enemies (obviously, an attempt on his life). He warned Alexander, who
was still young, of the possibility that the sad experience of his own
accession to the throne might be repeated: "If, God forbid, unrest or
disorder should occur, mount your horse immediately and go boldly
wherever you are needed, calling on your troops if necessary, and put
it down, without shedding blood if possible. But if it should persist,
do not spare the rebels, for by sacrificing a few you will save Russia."[1]
His fears proved unfounded. Alexander II's accession to the throne
was peaceful; he had no need to walk across a square drenched in
blood to take his "ancestral" throne; he did not need to execute
anybody to announce that he had become emperor of Russia. As he
addressed the State Council for the first time on 19 February 1855,
however, the new tsar declared: "My late father told me in the final
hours of his life, 'I turn my command over to you, but unfortunately

not in the good order that I would wish. I am leaving you many worries and troubles.' "[2] The fall of Sevastopol in August 1855 put an end to the system Nicholas I had created. Russia emerged from the Crimean War exhausted by the tremendous struggle, with depleted finances and a ruined monetary structure. The war had revealed many shortcomings in both military and civil administration. It showed that the Russian colossus stood on clay feet. The country had been stripped of its "preeminent position" in Europe, held since the Napoleonic wars; the Holy Alliance had fallen apart, leaving Russia diplomatically isolated. As a result, Russia's authority abroad declined, as did its people's confidence in the government's power and ability. Alexander II confronted the task of wooing public opinion in both Russia and Europe.[3] Whereas in 1846 there had been talk in the Secret Committee (over which Alexander presided) of the undesirability of creating a "great hue and cry" or attracting "the attention of all Europe" in dealing with the peasant question,[4] such attention had become indispensable at the beginning of Alexander's reign.

"The previous system has outlived itself"—this was the general verdict pronounced by the historian M.P. Pogodin, one of the ideologists of the system, three months after Nicholas I's death. So in early 1856 Pogodin called on Alexander II to adopt a new approach to find a way out of the crisis. "Freedom! That is the word that ought to ring out from the height of the Russian autocratic throne!"[5] he proclaimed. The appeal itself was a revelation, a fundamental change in the consciousness of those who ruled Russia or stood close to "the top." Alexander II saw this more clearly than others. In 1846 the Secret Committee, which he chaired, had recoiled from the very mention of the word "freedom" in dealing with the peasant question: "The very word is more dreadful than the deed."[6] Ten years later, the word "freedom" appeared to be magical—the key to a new life.

Day-to-day political needs conflicted with the ideological foundations of Nicholas's system. "Even if the government had desired a return to recent tradition following the Crimean War, it would have encountered insuperable obstacles—if not open resistance, then at least passive resistance, which in time might even have shaken the people's loyalty, the broad foundation on which the principle of Russian monarchy is built,"[7]—this was realized "at the top."

The first-born of the princely family of Nicholas I and Alexandra Fedorovna, Alexander was born in Moscow's Kremlin on 17 April 1818. On that day, Emperor Alexander I was in Warsaw in connection with the opening of the first Sejm of the Kingdom of Poland.

Alexander Nikolaevich was declared heir to the throne on 12 December 1825, and two days later witnessed the Decembrist uprising. Nicholas I carried the boy in his arms out to the soldiers of the Life Guards sapper battalion standing in the court of the Winter Palace.

As Alexander I's birth had been saluted by G.R. Derzhavin, Alexander II's was hailed by V.A. Zhukovskii, who wished that he become a kind person: "May he live a life full of honor! May he take a splendid part in glory! And in his lofty realm may he never forget that most sacred of callings: *human being.*" This poetic reading was by no means the only or the principal act that accompanied the birth of Grand Duke Alexander Nikolaevich. Much stronger and more important to the House of Romanov were military traditions. Several days after Alexander entered this world, he was named head of a Life Guards hussar regiment; at age seven the rank of cornet was "conferred" upon him, and later during his childhood and adolescence, he was promoted to second lieutenant, lieutenant, staff major, and cavalry captain.[8]

The education of the six-year-old heir to the throne was assigned to Captain K.K. Merder. A combat officer commended for bravery at Austerlitz and repeatedly wounded, Merder had served since 1809 as a duty officer in the cadet corps. He spent the last ten years of his life as the young tsarevich's inseparable companion. Contemporaries unanimously evaluate Merder as a highly moral, kind, intelligent, even-tempered, and strong-willed man (this is also confirmed by his diary). His character combined firmness and strictness with humanity (in an 1831 diary entry commenting on his pupil's lack of compassion for the poor, Merder blamed this on himself and set himself the goal of ensuring "that he come to consider helping the unfortunate his only true pleasure").[9]

Immediately after ascending the throne, Nicholas I began to provide for his heir's general education and chose as one of his mentors Zhukovskii, a man well known for his enlightened ways and pedagogical experience and close to the royal family: from 1817 to 1820 he had taught Russian to Alexandra Fedorovna, at that time still grand duchess. He was recommended by the empress mother, Maria Fedorovna, Paul I's widow, whom he had served as reader.[10] The trust that Alexander's grandmother and mother placed in Zhukovskii influenced his appointment. During the eighteen months that followed, Zhukovskii drew up the special "Plan of Instruction" for the next twelve years, and Nicholas I approved it. The declared purpose of the upbringing and instruction was "education in virtue." Zhukovskii believed that "His Highness should be *enlightened* rather than learned."[11] The heir's religious education was assigned to religion instructor G.P. Pavskii.

As a result, Alexander received a rather well-rounded education. Special attention was paid to history. Zhukovskii believed that "history is the most important of all the sciences, more important than philosophy, for it embodies the best philosophy—that is, practical and hence useful philosophy," and that "the treasure house of royal enlightenment is *history*, which teaches using the experience of the past, explains the present, and foretells the future. History acquaints the sovereign with the needs of his country and of his age. It should be the *principal subject* of the heir to the throne."[12] Both Russian and world history were taught, and a special course was included in French, entitled "Introduction to the History of the Revolution" (the 1789 Revolution in France). Alexander himself preferred history to his other subjects. Nicholas I often gave his son history books as birthday presents or on other occasions.[13]

From the very beginning, the elaborate program for the heir's upbringing and education clashed with court tradition—which was alien to it—and with the tsar's mindset. Soon after undertaking his duties as tutor (while completing the compilation of the "Plan of Instruction" in Dresden), Zhukovskii detected a threat to both his cause and his pupil and poured out his anxiety in a letter to the empress mother dated 2 (14) October 1826:

> In the newspapers I read an account of the changing of the guard, in which our little grand duke appeared on horseback and so forth [referring to the daily changing of the guard—L.Z.]. This episode, Your Majesty, is completely superfluous to the beautiful poem on which we are working. For God's sake, let there be no such scenes in the future. Naturally, the spectators must have been delighted by the appearance of the charming child, but consider the feelings such an event must have produced in his mind. Is he not being compelled in this way to end his childhood prematurely? Is he not being subjected to the danger of considering himself a man already? ... In addition, are these warlike games not bound to spoil in him that which ought to be his primary purpose? Is he to be a military man only, and function in the narrow horizon of the general? When are we ever to have lawgivers? When are we ever to look respectfully at the people's real needs—law, enlightenment, morality?! Your Majesty, forgive me these outbursts, but a passion for the military profession will constrain his soul; he will become accustomed to seeing the people only as troops and his fatherland as a barracks. We have seen the fruits of this: armies do not make

a powerful state. If the tsar concerns himself solely with the organization
of the army, it will serve only to produce a fourteenth of December.*

In his "Plan of Instruction" Zhukovskii proclaimed: "A sovereign's
true power lies not in the number of his troops but in the well-being
of his people."[14]

"I should like to hope," Merder himself commented three years
later, "that His Highness's frequent appearance at parades, where he
sees that the affairs of state consist of parades, will not have dire
consequences for him. He could easily acquire the idea that these
really do constitute the business of the state, and he may come to
believe that." But reality proved otherwise. From childhood Alexander loved inspections, parades, military holidays, and war games, in
which Nicholas I and his brothers frequently participated, and this
fondness lasted the rest of his life. If Nicholas I sometimes showed
anxiety over his son's excessive enthusiasm for the parade side of the
military, his reasons were quite different from those of the boy's
teachers. In 1832 he reproached Merder: "I have noticed that Alexander is showing little zeal for the military sciences; I want him to know
that I will be adamant if I find that he is less than diligent in these
subjects; he must be military in spirit, otherwise in this age of ours he
will be lost."[15]

It is understandable, therefore, why Zhukovskii's attempt to limit
classes in military science to six summer weeks per year was unsuccessful from the start. The adolescent who had been so active in military
exercises became a dashing and skillful officer. He loved the Field of
Mars and took pleasure in showing off at parades, evoking delight in
his associates and unending shouts of "hurrah." The service record
carefully records each day's frequent military events, one after another, weekdays and holidays, with unfailingly regularity. Alexander
was shaped as a military man by his habits, his world view, and his
environment.

The atmosphere of Nicholas I's large family was distinguished by
good will, spontaneity, and sincerity. The young Alexander was never
threatened with the divided nature that had characterized his uncle
Alexander I. "One of the finest qualities of the grand duke is his
tender feelings for his parents," Merder concludes. Alexander was
equally affectionate toward his sisters and brothers, for whom he
organized fireworks and other amusements and to whom he wrote

---

*A reference to the start of the Decembrist uprising in 1825.—D.J.R.

letters when they were apart. He loved his home very much. In 1828, returning from his first trip abroad to see his grandfather, the king of Prussia, on sighting Tsarskoe Selo the boy "was beside himself with joy." He delighted in the beauty of nature: "on hearing the singing of larks in the field he would jump for joy." Even a composition he wrote on history (about Alexander Nevsky) began with a description of the beauty of nature.[16] The royal heir's teachers commented on his good-heartedness, sensitivity, happy disposition, sociability, natural behavior, good manners, and bravery.

His mental abilities were also evident to those around him, although they were accompanied by a lack of zeal and consistency, an absence of any profound inner interest in reading or studies; the slightest difficulty or obstacle would put him "into a kind of drowsiness and inaction." After Alexander passed his yearly examination to Nicholas I's satisfaction in the winter of 1828, Merder commented that this success was less the result of Alexander's own efforts than of his teachers', and that the grand duke was deficient in "constant endeavor, and too often he has to be 'compelled'" to pay attention to his work. This also worried Zhukovskii, who admonished his pupil: "Get control of yourself, love your work, and be diligent."

Alexander sometimes promised to straighten up; then he became more diligent—for a while. Sometimes, in despair, he even told his teachers that he wished he had not been born a grand duke, and he confessed that "quite often he gets intensely angry with those who remind him of his duties." In the end, Merder concluded that "Alexander Nikolaevich's laziness is his worst fault, from which all the others derive"; these others included arrogance, lack of persistence, and occasionally apathy.[17] Alexander spent his leisure time, holidays, and birthdays with friends, including Merder's sons, children of the nobility and of high-ranking officers among Nicholas I's immediate circle, the Adlerberg and Frederiks brothers, and students of the cadet corps. Occasionally girls were permitted to accompany the adolescents. At ten or eleven, the heir to the throne was sometimes invited to his parents' grand table; he knew how to behave, for which he was praised, and he delighted the women. Sociability and a love of high society characterized him in his mature years as well.

Day after day throughout his years of study, the formation of the heir's personality may be followed in the artless, childish diary entries.[18] The cheerful, healthy, sentimental, open, well-disposed boy studied without eagerness but of necessity, often wept, inwardly rebelling against his tutors' demands and the burden of his "obligation" to prepare himself for the role of monarch. But the pressure of his teachers, instructors, and tutors, eventually evoked a greater interest in learning and business, and his considerable innate capabilities bore fruit. Zhukovskii's goal—to raise an enlightened and humane person—was in large measure fulfilled, although Alexander also became, as his father wished, "military in spirit."

On the day he came of age (at sixteen), Alexander "took the oath of the heir to the throne" in the great church of the Winter Palace, and in St. George's Hall in solemn assembly on the occasion of entering active service. M.M. Speranskii, on orders from Nicholas I, had prepared him for the oath. In writing about the events of this "important day" to Merder, whom Alexander considered his "second father," the grand duke did not neglect to list the gifts he had received as well: "a collection of Russian historical medals and two Turkish sabers from Papa, and a big inflatable globe ... and a clock showing times around the world from Mama.... Kostia gave me various hunting things, and my dear sisters gave me portraits of themselves done by Briullov."[19]

On that very day, the Finnish mineralogist N. Nordenskjöld discovered a precious mineral in the Urals and named it alexandrite in honor of the heir's coming of age.

Alexander's "final period of instruction" commenced when high-ranking state officials began instructing the future emperor in the practical courses he would need. Over an eighteen-month period, Speranskii conducted "discussions of law" with him. Although by then the former constitutionalist had become a completely loyal advocate of "pure monarchy," he nonetheless endeavored to inculcate in his pupil a respect for the law and for the "limits of power," drawing a distinction between autocracy and despotism. Three other courses were given, one by Finance Minister E.F. Kankrin entitled "A Brief Survey of Russian Finances"; one by Ministry of Foreign Affairs Counsellor F.I. Brunov concerning the foundations of Russian foreign policy since Catherine II's reign; and one by General A. Jomini concerning Russia's military policy and strategy. The educational program ended in the spring of 1837; all that remained was the travel that would acquaint Alexander with Russia and Europe.

Alexander's travels around Russia lasted from May through December 1837, in accordance with Nicholas I's personal instructions; in the company of mentors, teachers, and an entourage. In Zhukovskii's words, and this experience amounted to "a public betrothal between the heir and Russia." The group visited twenty-nine provinces of European Russia (chiefly the central ones), the North Caucasus, the

Transcaucasus, the Crimea, and Western Siberia as far as Tobolsk. Given the lack of railroads, these travels afforded few opportunities for penetrating observations, especially considering the numerous ceremonial meetings, inspections, and festivities. Nevertheless, Alexander saw the country and accepted sixteen thousand petitions; he visited the Decembrists in Siberia and, filled with compassion, petitioned his father to alleviate their lot.

Alexander's travels to other countries lasted more than a year (from May 1838 to June 1839). First, he and Nicholas I visited Berlin and Stockholm, and then, at his father's instruction, Alexander continued on to Sweden, Denmark, a dozen German and Italian duchies and kingdoms, Austria, Holland, and England. It is noteworthy that his itinerary did not include France. During his travels, the heir to the Russian throne was awarded many orders and diplomas (honorary member of the Danish Academy of Fine Arts and the Roman Academy of Italian Literature, doctor of laws of Oxford University, and others). These joined his variegated list of Russian titles (chancellor of Alexander University in Finland from 1825, honorary member of the Imperial Academy of Sciences from 1837, honorary member of St. Petersburg University from 1841 and of Moscow University from 1851).

His travels abroad decided Alexander's personal fate. Attracted by the fifteen-year-old Princess Marie of Hesse-Darmstadt, whom he chanced to see at the theater, he wrote to his father the next day. The betrothal was announced in March 1840, and the wedding took place on 16 April 1841. The future empress (named Maria Alexandrovna in Russia) was the niece of Empress Elizaveta Alekseevna, Alexander I's wife. Dynastic ties to German ruling houses were a Romanov tradition. This marriage brought Alexander II six sons, and a daughter "whom he adored."[20]

Alexander's mood and feelings during that period are vividly revealed in his letters to his closest friend, Alexander Adlerberg. (From 1870 to 1881, Adlerberg served as minister of the Imperial court and estates; Alexander corresponded with him from age seven to the end of his life.) Soon after his marriage, the tsarevich's letters to "Dear Sasha" ("It's been so long since I've had anybody to talk to") were filled with exclamations of delight. The young husband was happy and constantly urged his friend to get married ("When, my dear Sasha, will I ever see you married too?"). The same letters also contain delighted descriptions of the beautiful women of whom they were both once fond. Another object of interest, which the author of the letters himself called "serious," was inspections, maneuvers, and visits to camps. In these letters the future monarch shows himself to be dashing and full of joie de vivre but not one to burden himself with serious state matters.[21]

Although Alexander himself showed no great interest in or zeal for politics, he gradually became involved in it. After his return from abroad in 1839, he was named an attending member of the State Council; the next year he was appointed to the Committee of Ministers; and in 1841–42 he became a full member of these ruling institutions. The heir to the throne began to be assigned increasingly important tasks, among which the peasant question was of particular importance.

Appointed chairman of the Secret Committee on Peasant Affairs in 1846, the twenty-eight-year-old heir to the throne manifested an unswerving adherence to the existing order. The committee journal states: "Until such time as Russia, due to unforeseen circumstances, shall lose her unity and power, other states cannot serve as an example to her. This colossus requires a different foundation and different concepts of freedom with regard not only to peasants but to all stations"; freedom in Russia must consist of "obedience to all the laws issuing from a single supreme source."[22] The result of another secret committee—the Secret Committee on Household Serfs (1848), which also functioned under Alexander's chairmanship—was not much different. In reaction against the revolutionary events in Europe, the tsarevich tried to strengthen censorship by instituting the secret "Buturlin" Committee (to censor the censors). Insisting that Baron M.A. Korf be part of it, Alexander said: "It is a matter of waging a fierce battle [i.e., against literature and the press—L.Z.] . . . and now you suddenly retreat from the field of battle."[23]

It may be that the heir to the throne's position reflected not so much his real convictions as his dependence on his father, his lack of independence. Before his accession to the throne he never showed any desire to emancipate the peasants nor even an inclination toward liberalism, unlike his brother, Grand Duke Constantine. Only a dramatic change in actual circumstances, one beyond the control even of an autocratic monarch, would one day compel him to forgo his traditional concepts.

Civil affairs were not of top priority in Alexander's state activities. As before, he focused most of his attention and interest on the army. He continued to rise in the military hierarchy and to accumulate titles and positions: in 1844 he became "full general"; in 1849, after his uncle Grand Duke Mikhail Pavlovich died, he took over the post of commander in chief of the military schools and assumed command of the Guard Corps, which on Nicholas I's orders was sent to suppress revolution in Hungary. In 1852 Alexander was promoted to commander in chief of the Guard and Grenadiers Corps. On more than one occasion, Nicholas I sent his son a rescript expressing his "sincere gratitude" for his "untiring efforts on behalf of the troops."[24] On 21 February 1854, when St. Petersburg Province was placed under martial law because of the "presence of the Anglo-French fleet within sight of Kronstadt," the heir to the throne was given charge of all the troops dispatched to the defense of St. Petersburg.[25]

Alexander ascended the throne at the age of thirty-six. His outward appearance at that time left an impression on A. White, a secretary in the American embassy: "He was tall, like all the Romanovs, good-looking and with a very distinguished bearing, but he had much less of his father's majesty and was completely devoid of the latter's misplaced severity."[26] Everyone who described Alexander II noted his pleasant looks. Many people, however, criticized his cold and reserved manners and his desire to emulate his father, an attempt that made him seem a "poor copy" or a "lifeless mask."

Of the numerous characterizations of Alexander II, those of lady-in-waiting A.F. Tiutcheva, the daughter of the famous poet, are most profound and perspicacious. "The emperor," she wrote in her diary in January 1856,

> is the best of men. He would be a wonderful sovereign in a well-organized country and in a time of peace, if such could ever be preserved anywhere. But he lacks the temperament of a reformer. The empress lacks initiative as well. . . . They are too kind, too pure, to understand people and to rule them. They do not have the energy or the impulse to take charge of events and direct them as they see fit; they lack passion. . . . Without realizing it himself, he has become involved in a struggle with powerful forces and dreadful elements he does not understand. . . . They [the royal couple—L.Z.] do not know where they are going.[27]

Alexander II's first steps reinforced and continued his father's policies.[28] After the fall of Sevastopol, Alexander II traveled to Nikolaev, where he personally observed the construction of fortifications, inspected the Ochakov Fortress and the reinforcements in Odessa, and visited the main quarters of the Crimean Army at Bakhchisarai. But by that time, his efforts were in vain. Russia could

Alexander II

not continue the war. In the international arena, Russia was isolated, her internal strength was undermined, and dissatisfaction had spread to all segments of society. Because he possessed a sound and sober intellect, a certain flexibility, and no inclination at all toward fanaticism, Alexander II, with the aid of competent, high-ranking officials, began empirically—without any general program whatso-ever—to make decisions out of tune with the old system, even directly opposed to it; he embarked on the path of reform.

The Treaty of Paris and the Manifesto of 19 March 1856, which ended the Crimean War, signaled an important step for Alexander II toward a new governmental policy. Russia's long-standing reliance on the Holy Alliance was over; a new deployment of forces was taking shape in Europe. The Congress System that had ended the Napoleonic wars had outlived its usefulness; France's role on the Continent had strengthened, and Russian diplomacy was forced to acknowledge this. K.V. Nesselrode, the aged chancellor who had served Nicholas I throughout his thirty-year reign and who personified the old system, was replaced by a man of a different bent—A.M. Gorchakov.

In announcing the manifesto listing the terms of the peace treaty, the tsar cautiously mentioned the necessity of improving the domestic situation and Russia's well-being, as well as drawing up laws that would provide "equal justice for all." This vague statement was enough to alarm and excite the nobility. Responding to widespread concerns that had reached his ears, Alexander II on 30 March 1856 addressed the marshals of nobility in Moscow: "Rumors are circulating that I intend to declare the emancipation of the serfs. . . . I cannot tell you that I totally oppose this; we live in an era in which this must eventually happen. I believe that you are of the same opinion as I; therefore, it will be much better if this takes place from above than from below."[29]

Gradually, the outlines of the new course of action became more distinct. First of all, the ban Nicholas I had placed on the printed word was lifted: on 3 December 1855 the Supreme Censorship Committee was dissolved. Alexander II agreed with Korf, the committee's chairman, who reported that censorship "sometimes leads to the opposite of what was intended. Literature is disseminated in manuscript form, which is much more dangerous, for it is avidly read and all police measures are powerless against it."[30] "Sevastopol struck a blow against stagnated minds," and after the "ghastly numbness in which the country had been sunk until that time" (V.O. Kliuchevskii), the printed word, as an expression of inner emancipation, became a social force that dispelled fear. Glasnost became the first manifestation of thaw.

This was followed by abolition of the restraints imposed on the universities since 1848, the authorization to issue passports for travel abroad, and the creation of joint-stock companies and firms. Russian subjects were encouraged to expand trade ties with foreign states, and at Alexander's coronation amnesty for political prisoners was declared. This affected those Decembrists who were still alive, the Petrashevtsy,* and those who had participated in the Polish uprising of 1830–31; in all, nine thousand men were released from police surveillance.[31]

Alexander II's coronation took place on 26 August 1856 at the Dormition Cathedral in the Kremlin. The French ambassador, Duc Charles de Morny, was the first of the diplomats to quit his carriage long before it approached Dormition Cathedral; he journeyed the rest of the way on foot with his head uncovered to demonstrate his government's special respect and sympathy for Alexander II. In fact, France and Russia were beginning to overcome the burden of tradition and endeavoring to strengthen their ties. In January 1857 Alexander II informed his brother Constantine in confidence: "I foresee in an alliance with France a guarantee of future peace in Europe."[32] The coronation commenced on 14 August and continued through 22 September, but it was not the only event of importance. There, in Russia's first capital city, amid a gathering of the highest-ranking noblemen and civil servants from all parts of Russia, possible solutions to the peasant question were being cautiously explored.

Not long before the coronation, with Alexander II's consent, the minister-designate of internal affairs, S.S. Lanskoi (who had been involved in the Decembrist movement in his youth), had negotiated with the marshals of the nobility about the possibility that the highest estate might initiate peasant emancipation by petitioning the tsar. Alexander II, who often acted autocratically, sought, in this "delicate" and at the same time "frightening" matter, to do everything necessary not only to gain the nobility's support but also to encourage them to take the initiative. The first noble of the empire (as Alexander II viewed himself to be) wished to use the will of the first estate to back

---

*Followers of M.V. Petrashevskii, an idealistic socialist dreamer who fell under the influence of Fourier. The police uncovered the circle in 1849, and many of its members were sentenced to death, including the young Fedor Dostoevsky, whose sentence was commuted just moments before the execution was to have taken place.—D.J.R.

up his own actions in a matter that touched upon the very foundations of society and state.

The truth of this is evident in the tsar's speech to the State Council on 28 January 1861. Urging the council to approve the reform, he drew its attention to two circumstances: that "any further delay could be fatal to the state" (i.e., carried the risk of peasant uprisings—L.Z.), and that "the undertaking of this matter was at the behest of the nobility itself."[33] In 1856, however, the nobility was in no hurry to approve the emancipation. Only one man, Vilna's governor-general, V.I. Nazimov, a personal friend of Alexander II from his military associations, promised to try to persuade the nobility in his provinces (Vilna, Kovno, and Grodno) to undertake the initiative the government needed.

Expecting the nobility's "initiatives," Alexander II failed to take decisive steps, although he knew of specific plans to abolish serfdom—for example, the proposal to emancipate the peasants on his aunt Grand Duchess Elena Pavlovna's estate in Karlovka, Poltava Province, a plan intended as a model for a future general reform. This project, developed by N.A. Miliutin, a leader of the enlightened bureaucracy and the director of the Economic Department of the Ministry of Internal Affairs, was signed not by him but by Elena Pavlovna to avoid irritating Alexander II, who considered Miliutin a "Red." The attempt to lull the tsar's suspicions failed. Alexander guessed that its author was Miliutin, and he did not want the initiative to come from the government, as the proposal recommended. Noting in his resolution that the project had obviously been developed by "one of the department directors," he rejected it. "I will wait for the right-thinking owners of large estates themselves to declare to what extent they consider it possible to improve the lot of their peasants," he said in explaining his position.[34]

The rejected project called for emancipating the peasants and granting land for which the people would pay, thus turning them into small landowners while allowing the large landowners to retain their holdings. It assigned a vital role to state authority, which was to draw up the initiatives, for which it would have to draw support from the "enlightened" nobility, creating an "initiative monarchy" that would carry out progressive reforms.[35] Two years later, in October and November 1858, under the pressure of circumstances and a new deployment of forces, the abolition of serfdom proceeded along exactly those lines, but near the end of 1856, Alexander II, indecisive and expecting petitions from the nobility, began with that which he knew from personal experience: in the Nicholaevan tradition he instituted the new Secret Committee on Peasant Affairs.

The Secret Committee, composed chiefly of advocates of serfdom, dragged its feet, but the tsar's resolve proved unshakable. This is attested by both his actions and memoir accounts. In the summer of 1857, vacationing abroad with his family, Alexander met and talked with eminent statesmen and public figures, both Russian and foreign, concerning the peasant question in Russia. He spoke with his ambassador to France, who had been a minister under Nicholas I (his "chief of staff" for peasant affairs), Count P.D. Kiselev, who insisted that the peasants should be emancipated and given land; he spoke with Grand Duchess Elena Pavlovna and with Baron A. Haxthausen, the well-known German scientist and agrarian expert who had visited Russia in the early 1840s and written a study of the Russian peasant commune and whose conservatism and monarchism were mingled with a certainty that the abolition of serfdom was inevitable; he also discussed the problem with others. He acquainted himself with the first issues of *Kolokol* (The Bell),* which had just appeared. He immediately ordered the papers of the Secret Committee dispatched from St. Petersburg, and he appointed his brother Constantine, an advocate of reform and a patron of the enlightened bureaucracy, to serve on the committee. He appointed law professor K.D. Kavelin, author of one of the first tracts advocating the emancipation of the serfs and, until recently, a liberal who had fallen from favor, as the teacher for the heir, Nikolai Alexandrovich.

Returning to St. Petersburg, he urged the Secret Committee to decide. Nazimov, with whom Alexander II had met as he was leaving for vacation, at that moment hastily delivered to the capital the long-awaited "initiative" from the nobility of his provinces—an extremely humble petition to emancipate the peasants (although, to be sure, without land). But the terms stipulated by the nobility held no interest for the tsar. More important was the mere fact that the petition had been submitted. Alexander II demanded an immediate decision from the Secret Committee. Unable to oppose the monarch, the committee approved a rescript addressed to Nazimov, although the program embodied in this vital governmental document had been drawn up outside its chambers. Moreover, in its confusion the Secret Committee authorized the minister of internal affairs to distribute the

---

*A revolutionary tocsin put out by Alexander Herzen (in exile), which openly attacked autocracy and the institution of serfdom.—D.J.R.

document to all provincial governors (predetermining the question of publishing the rescript). The openness of this first step along the path of resolving the peasant question cut off any retreat by the government. Contrary to the true will of the nobility of St. Petersburg and Moscow, similar rescripts were imposed on both capitals (formally, this was done in response to petitions from them). The business of emancipating the peasants from the yoke of serfdom was under way. In reaction, Herzen wrote of Alexander II, "Thou hast conquered, O Galilean!"

The establishment in 1858 of committees of the nobility in forty-six provinces of European Russia to discuss the reform projects revealed that most of the nobility advocated serfdom, while a liberal minority confronted Alexander II with the necessity of clarifying his own position. Meanwhile, reports poured in from all over the country concerning the peasantry's tense anticipation of emancipation. The tsar had an especially powerful reaction to the news of disturbances in Estland Province [Estonia] (adjacent to St. Petersburg) caused by rejection of the local reform, which failed to provide the peasants with land.

Alexander II's attempt to encourage the landowners to increase the pace of reform by his own example—issuing a decree emancipating crown peasants without land (on 20 June 1858)—proved unsuccessful: the peasants refused to accept that kind of emancipation. It took little foresight to predict that landowners' peasants would share their position. Alexander II's personal observations during his travels through the central provinces of Russia in August and September 1858 convinced him of this—as did the peasantry's abiding hope in their tsar. Alexander II was also strongly influenced by his closest friend, Adjutant General Ia.I. Rostovtsev, who had already approved the liberal demand that the emancipated peasants be allowed to redeem land. Under strong pressure from Alexander II—one might say, at his demand—the Main (formerly Secret) Committee specifically adopted such a program of emancipation.

The tsar even gave his consent in March 1858 (after refusing it twice) to N.A. Miliutin's appointment as assistant minister of internal affairs. Simultaneously, he approved the membership of a new, untraditional state institution to prepare proposals for peasant reform—editing commissions, chaired by Rostovtsev. Although the discussion of the proposals in the Main Committee and the State Council led to their amendment under pressure from reactionary and conservative forces, Alexander II signed the Statute of 19 February 1861 over the objections of the majority of the State Council.

This, the main accomplishment of Alexander II's reign, caused his contemporaries to hail him as Tsar–Liberator.

Alexander II's letters to his brother Constantine reveal that in his mind the concerns of state, numerous and diverse as they were, were directed at a single goal, one that dominated and absorbed everything else—restoring the prestige and greatness of "Our precious Russia" after its defeat in the Crimean War. By "greatness" he meant further expansion of the empire and strengthening of its power abroad. Alexander II expressed satisfaction with Russian diplomatic successes in the Far East and new acquisitions along the Amur; he joyfully reported to his brother the victory of Russian arms in the Caucasus and the capture of Shamil* in the summer of 1859. In 1861 he kept all the armed forces that had been under the command of the governor-general of the Caucasus, Prince A.I. Bariatinskii, in the region, despite the critical state of Russia's finances and the amount spent on Caucasian affairs, which constituted one-sixth of the national budget. Moreover, Alexander II was ready to invade Asia Minor in the event of war or the collapse of Turkish domination in the Balkans.[36]

The tone of the reports on internal affairs, finances, and the peasant question in these letters is different—restrained, pithy, and conscious of the necessity of change, but devoid of the vivid emotion characteristic of his accounts of military and foreign affairs. The priority given to imperial ambitions in the concerns and ideas of the Tsar–Liberator is obvious. His goal was not "to improve the life and lot" of his subjects, as was officially proclaimed, but to further expand and strengthen the empire. Otherwise, it is impossible to explain why the state did not invest a single ruble in peasant reform, why more than one-third of the budget was spent for military purposes, and why the redemption payments so ruinous to the peasantry were considered beneficial for the state. Apparently, Nicholas I's desire to have his son become a man who was "military in spirit" had borne fruit.

Quite characteristic was Alexander II's reaction to the peasants' unhappiness with the terms of the reform, which reduced their allotments but brought heavy obligations and redemption payments. Speaking on 15 August 1861 to peasant elders in Poltava, he declared: "I hear rumors that you are expecting another emancipation. There will be no emancipation other than the one I have given you. You are

---

*Leader of a Muslim resistance movement in Dagestan who for over two decades led his mountaineers in guerilla warfare against tsarist troops.—D.J.R.

to do what the law and the statute require. You are to work and labor. You are to obey the authorities and landowners." The Ministry of Internal Affairs, in a circular sent to the provincial governors dated 2 September 1861, stipulated that in their explanations to the peasants the local authorities were to refer to these statements by the emperor. Alexander II also failed to heed the anxieties of the minister of finance, who told him repeatedly how difficult the redemption payments were for the peasants and how burdensome the continued unproductive spending, particularly on the military, was to the budget. Thus, in a most humble report in 1866, Reutern noted: "The slowness with which the redemption payments are being collected derives, at least in some cases, from the fact that these payments exceed the peasants' means."[37]

The tsar's tough position reflected his patriarchal, sentimental attitude toward the people: "You are my children, and I am your father and pray to God for you, as I do for all those who are, like you, close to my heart," he said in 1863 to a delegation of Old Believers who had come to petition the Tsar–Liberator.[38] The grand act of abolishing serfdom had not shaken his traditional attitude toward the people, whom he saw as the principal means to strengthen the monarchy, expand the empire, and enhance its prestige. The Tsar–Liberator's spiritual kinship with his enthroned predecessors was also manifest in his notions about the inviolability and absolutism of autocratic rule in Russia, which were fully revealed during the reform years.

Alexander II's liberalism in regard to the peasant question was combined with an autocratic hatred of the mounting trend of glasnost and dissident thinking, with a willingness to interfere with "our unbridled literature, which ought to have been curbed long ago."[39] This was no momentary outburst of irritation. His hostility to liberalism surfaced often. He told his brother—the governor-general of Poland—"not to pay attention to criticism from foreign journals or from our own liberals and those who imagine themselves to be progressives."[40] In abolishing serfdom, he used his will, his autocratic word, to force the Secret and the Main Committees to make the necessary decisions, crushing the opposition of the advocates of serfdom. But in exactly the same way, as the autocrat, he closed down the liberal Editing Commissions—surprising their members, who had met for their regular sessions. Moreover, commission members from other cities were told to leave St. Petersburg.

Alexander II dismissed N.A. Miliutin, the principal figure behind the peasant reform, six weeks after the abolition of serfdom; he then turned over the Ministry of Internal Affairs (that is, the agency responsible for the implementation of peasant reform and the preparation of zemstvo [local government] reform) to Miliutin's opponent P.A. Valuev, author of a counterproposal. In 1861 he made some unexpected appointments to the Ministry of Public Education as well. During several months of reactionary and even ridiculous administration, Admiral E.F. Putianin, the new minister, and General G.I. Filippson, the head of the St. Petersburg Education District, actually fueled a student movement. The Council of Ministers, which Alexander II had created in 1857 at the same time as beginning open preparations for the abolition of serfdom, never became a government cabinet. Totally subservient to its chairman—the monarch—it convened only when he commanded. Meetings were closed, no minutes were kept, and sessions were frequently adjourned if Alexander II became tired or found the proceedings uninteresting. The idea of a unified government did not take hold: in fact, as Valuev put it, Alexander II pursued a policy of "thoughtless about-faces" in his work.

Nonetheless, in regard to the main tendencies of the early 1860s, the fact remains that the reforms did continue. In 1862 the state budget was opened to scrutiny, and D.A. Miliutin, a supporter of reforms, was placed in charge of the War Ministry to prepare military reforms. In 1863 corporal punishment was abolished (on 17 April, the emperor's birthday), and a new university charter was instituted. In 1864 the zemstvo and judicial reforms were implemented. Except for the monarch's prerogatives and the highest organs of authority, reform was under way in all areas of state and society.

While he recognized the inevitability of incorporating all social estates and strata in state affairs via an electoral system, representation, and a law-governed state, Alexander II had no doubts about the inviolability of autocratic rule. He was also forced to confront the question of a constitution, an issue raised by the nobility, which wished to recoup the losses it had sustained in the peasant reform, by individual civic and state leaders, and by the liberation movements in Poland and Finland. The tsar expressed his own attitude toward a constitution in no uncertain terms. In the autumn of 1859 he reacted with irritation to the humblest noble petition—whether liberal or reactionary—if it contained even a hint of a constitution. He ignored a project that Valuev submitted to him in 1863 calling for the implementation of limited constitutional reforms in the system of higher consultative bodies.

Especially indicative is the tsar's conversation with Otto von Bismarck, then Prussia's ambassador to Russia, on 10 November 1861. Responding to a question about the possibility of a constitution and liberal institutions in Russia, Alexander II said:

> The people see their monarch as God's envoy, as their father and all-powerful master. This idea, which has the force almost of religious feeling, is inseparable from their personal dependency on me, and I am inclined to think that I am not mistaken. The crown gives me a feeling of authority; to forgo it would be to damage the nation's prestige. The profound respect that the Russian people have accorded the throne of their tsar from time immemorial, arising from an innate feeling, cannot be dismissed. I would not hesitate to curtail the government's authoritarianism if I wanted to bring representatives of the nobility or the nation into it. God knows where we will end up regarding the question of the peasants and landowners if the tsar's authority is insufficient to exercise decisive influence.[41]

In fact, the monarch's unlimited power served to promote the implementation of reforms, but that was by no means Alexander II's only consideration as he stubbornly rejected even the possibility of a Russian constitution for twenty-five years. He had inherited the entrenched tradition of authoritarian, patriarchal rule; he had grown up and been educated in that system; his intellect and his whole psychological and spiritual makeup had been shaped under Nicholas I's watchful eye and influence at the apogee of autocracy.

While he had a sound and practical mind, Alexander II evidently lacked depth and perspicacity. In contrast to the most farsighted statesmen he failed to understand that "the tree (serfdom) had put down deep roots: it overshadowed both Church and Throne." He also failed to understand that the sudden abolition of serfdom shattered the monolith of empire: "Peter I's building is being shaken," and "portions may break away—the Baltic provinces, even Poland itself." (S.S. Uvarov wrote these words to M.P. Pogodin in 1847.)[42] When this danger actually emerged, Alexander II assessed the strength of the liberation movement and made concessions. In Finland, under pressure from a broad, well-organized, and peaceful opposition, he reinstated the Diet [Parliament], which had not convened for half a century; he opened it in person in Porvoo on 18 September 1863, giving a speech in which he twice mentioned constitutional monarchy.

In Poland and the northwest provinces, the course of events had been dramatic. Speaking in Warsaw in 1856, Alexander II had uttered the words, "*Pas de rêveries*" ["Stop dreaming"]: in a region that Nicholas I had stripped of all autonomy after the 1830–31 uprising and subjected to harsh regulation; in a year of thaw, when "Russia began to breathe free," and of political amnesty, for participants in the Polish uprising in particular. Yet five years later, when the tsar issued the decree of 14 (26) March 1861 on reforms designed to restore "autonomy" in Poland, the time was past, and the appointment of Grand Duke Constantine Nikolaevich to the governor-generalship did not help. Moreover, Alexander II ordered martial law retained in the region.

These concessions did not satisfy the Polish liberation movement. The 1863 uprising that spread throughout Poland and spilled over into the northwest provinces compelled Alexander II to take more decisive action. He remained steadfast, his own position defined in advance as the rejection of any opinion "not in accord with the general trends of monarchical government and contrary to the interests of the empire."[43] He categorically refused to restore the Sejm, and decided to end the system introduced in Alexander I's reign, with which Grand Duke Constantine Nikolaevich was in sympathy. Here, too, the tsar took the path of agrarian reforms, for which he again summoned N.A. Miliutin, who had returned from a lengthy vacation abroad; Alexander sent him to Poland along with his closest associates Iu.F. Samarin, V.A. Cherkasskii, V.A. Artsimovich, and Ia.A. Soloviev (all of whom had assisted with the 1861 reform).

In conversation with Miliutin, the emperor acknowledged that to Russia, Poland was more a source of difficulties than an element of strength, and that many Russians would willingly leave the Poles to themselves, give them broad autonomy and even complete independence, if they could only count on the Poles' being reasonable—that is, renouncing any claim to their ancestral territories. As far as Alexander II was concerned, he could no longer trust the Polish aristocracy; "the Russian government ought to rely for its principal support on the mass of the rural population."[44] The reforms of 1864, which granted Polish peasants land and property in return for a token payment, were in effect revolutionary. The peasantry abandoned the uprising.

But Alexander II did not grant Poland a constitution, following through on a warning he had given Miliutin (for all their divergent political convictions, on this matter their views coincided). In the northwest provinces, peasant reform reached its legislative culmination in the peasants' obligatory redemption of their fields as property. Once the peasant question was settled, Alexander II brutally suppressed the Polish uprising; this was in accord with those sentiments of the ruling circles and social forces that were consolidated around great-power ideas. The uprising of 1863 had a substantial impact on strengthening the reactionary tendencies in the "upper crust" and in society as a whole.

Alexander II could hardly fail to notice the worsening of the political situation in the years immediately following the abolition of serfdom. But he apparently did not understand the possible consequences, nor the risk posed to state authority by the confrontation of political forces under way in society. He failed to heed the protests and resignations of a group of liberal professors at St. Petersburg University in response to the ministry's reactionary measures in the autumn of 1861, the persecution of the liberal administration in Kaluga Province, and the oppressive treatment meted out to liberal arbitrators by the new minister of internal affairs, Valuev. He sanctioned the arrest of liberal arbitrators led by A.N. Unkovskii in Tver Province in 1862. With one stroke of the pen, the tsar removed liberal ministers and statesmen from their posts, while simultaneously employing their programs and plans. He did so because he was not acting out of conviction but responding to the force of circumstances, to the constantly changing correlation of forces in the top echelons of government and society.

The concern N.A. Miliutin and his associates felt over the weak guarantees for the liberal course of action that had been undertaken and their view that a centrist party was necessary to back up the restructuring launched in the country were foreign to Alexander II. He did not perceive that the polarization of political forces, the strengthening of reaction and activation of revolutionary extremism, the spread of nihilism, and the weakening of the liberals posed a catastrophic threat to the reforms and to him personally. Then D.V. Karakozov's gunshot rang out at the gates of the Summer Garden on 4 April 1866. This act of revolutionary terror marked the end of the first decade of the Tsar–Liberator's reign. The well-known English journalist and *Daily Telegraph* correspondent Edward Dicey, who saw Alexander II in 1866, left this sketch: "A tall, majestic, very dignified man with clearly defined facial features and dark hair; I think he could be called a King of Kings."[45] In the full bloom of his physical and intellectual powers, at the height of his glory, Alexander II had become a target. He was a brave man who had demonstrated his fearlessness more than once, but he was shaken by this first attempt on his life. This was not because he feared for his own life; the realization that the man who had fired at the Russian tsar, the Anointed of God, was a Russian and not a Pole, as he had thought at first, came as a revelation beyond his understanding. Many of his contemporaries reported—and this was later confirmed by historians—that from then on Alexander II's policies were marked by reaction.

In fact, 1866 was a watershed—not only in politics, moreover, but also in the tsar's personal life. In 1865, at age twenty-two, the tsar's eldest son and heir to the throne, Grand Duke Nikolai Alexandrovich, died of meningitis; the heir, Kavelin's pupil, had been by all accounts a mild, humane, and liberal man. Empress Maria Alexan-drovna's health was shattered. After prolonged inner struggle, Alexander II surrendered to his love for a young princess named Ekaterina Mikhailovna Dolgorukaia, and they began a romance in July 1866.[46] This was different from the emperor's previous transient infatuations and numerous liaisons, to which everyone had become accustomed, not excluding the empress. This was a love affair between a mature, forty-eight-year-old man and an enchanting young woman of eighteen. Their attempt to remain apart for half a year to avoid a scandal and cool their feelings did not help.

The shock he had experienced in connection with the attempt on his life, his marital infidelity, and the passion that absorbed all his spiritual and physical powers—all had their impact on Alexander II's emotional state, his perception of the world. His contemporaries noted that the emperor was more contemplative than he had been previously, sometimes even apathetic; in the early 1870s, physicians spoke of exhaustion and prescribed treatment. It is natural to assume that these circumstances could hardly fail to affect his handling of matters of state. His energy and interest had declined, and he had begun to doubt the correctness of his previous course of action. In an attempt to oppose these vacillations and the pressure of reaction rising in the "upper echelons," D.A. Miliutin submitted to Alexander II a memorandum, written by Kavelin, entitled "On Nihilism and Measures Necessary to Combat It." The memorandum argued that only consistent reforms could put a halt to the revolutionary movement in Russia.

Alexander II ignored the memorandum, leaning instead toward reaction and conservative forces. In a rescript dated 13 May 1866 addressed to P.P. Gagarin, the chairman of the Committee of Ministers, he stated that his task was "to protect the Russian people from the seeds of insidious, false teachings that could in time undermine the social order." The issue of further reforms was passed over in silence; purely protective goals formulated by Chief of Police P.A. Shuvalov were proclaimed. In his diary, Valuev clearly expressed his view of the rescript and the intended course of action: "The principle and the idea in our country now are identical. They consist of protecting the rulers. It is a defensive position. Power is viewed not as a means but as an end, like a right or property. . . . We demand obedience, but for what? Solely for the duty to obey and the right to command."[47]

The Tsar–Liberator's environment began to change. Despite the country's glasnost and Europeanization, the role of the Third Section [secret police], far from declining, actually increased after 1866. Chief of Police Shuvalov, who had been appointed head of the Third Section, acquired decisive influence in the upper echelons and over Alexander II himself. The lack of will that was generally characteristic of the tsar became especially noticeable during these years. Until his resignation in 1874, Shuvalov held inordinate power and authority in his hands, playing a role like that of tsar's favorite. Indeed, contemporaries dubbed that period the "Shuvalov era." A.F. Koni called Shuvalov's reign "a dominion over the fate of Russia's domestic policy and over the soul of the sovereign, who had been frightened by Karakozov's attempt on his life."[48]

Changes in personnel affected many key posts. Synod Senior Procurator of the Holy Synod, D.A. Tolstoy, an open advocate of reaction, became minister of public education; K.I. Pahlen became minister of justice; and A.E. Timashev, supported by Shuvalov, became minister of internal affairs. D.A. Miliutin lost all hope of opposing Shuvalov's omnipotence and was ready to resign on more than one occasion. The so-called "amendments" to the reforms of the 1860s introduced reactionary correctives to legislative acts passed not long before. Rule by decree intensified everywhere, control over the zemstvos and the printed word became harsher, the primary schools came under the supervision of ministerial bureaucrats, and independent judges were subjected to administrative pressure.

But even in this conservative atmosphere, Alexander II continued his reforms, albeit listlessly and sluggishly. Legislation on municipal governments was passed in 1870 (six years after the law on zemstvos). Preparations for military reform dragged on until 1874 when, at long last, decisive steps were taken to modernize the army through a law on universal military service. The impetus for this decision was the Franco–Prussian War of 1870–71, which demonstrated the advantages of modern organization and equipment for the armed forces.

Alexander II and the government were gradually losing their initiative in implementing the large-scale transformations launched by the abolition of serfdom. At the same time, moreover, repressive measures were increased to combat not only the revolutionary but also the social movement. Speaking of the period after 1866, Minister of War D.A. Miliutin said: "In the past fourteen years of stagnation and reaction, all the strict measures adopted by the police, far from putting down sedition, have actually created a mass of malcontents among whom people of ill will can select their recruits." He said this at a conference of Alexander III's ministers on 21 April 1881 that was convened to deal with the question of the government's further policy and program of action. "I argued," he continued in his diary, "that the failure to complete the reforms that were undertaken, and the absence of an overall plan, had brought about a sense of total chaos in all parts of the state organism."[49] Many public figures involved in the reforms, both advocates and opponents, shared this opinion.

During that period, Alexander II's attention was focused not so much on legislative activity as on the accomplishment of imperial tasks—the acquisition of new territories, especially in Central Asia, the settlement of border problems, and European policy, including the revision of the terms of the Treaty of Paris so burdensome to Russia.

The year 1866 marked the peak of the development of friendly relations between Russia and the United States, evident in the decision to sell Russian America. The idea that Russia's future was as a continental rather than a maritime power (the decision not to acquire distant overseas territories) appeared as early as 1818, when a proposal to impose Russian dominion on the Hawaiian Islands was rejected. Alexander II favored strengthening relations with the United States in every way. Russian squadrons were sent to America during the Civil War, visiting New York, Philadelphia, and Boston in 1863–64 and demonstrating Russia's support for the Union. Although the expedition's immediate purpose was to organize a cruiser operation in case England and France declared war against Russia in connection with the Polish uprising of 1863, it nevertheless confirmed both countries' desire for closer relations.

The United States' response to Karakozov's attempt on the tsar's life was not confined to the kind of diplomatic procedure usual in such cases. Congress unanimously passed a special resolution, and an extraordinary embassy headed by Assistant Secretary of the Navy G.V. Fox, which submitted it formally to the emperor. In N.N.

Bolkhovitinov's estimation, "Fox's mission, which marked the culmination of Russian–American rapprochement, did much to foster the widespread opinion that a natural alliance existed between Russia and the United States," which in turn influenced discussion of the sale of Russian possessions in America. This did not exclude other considerations, including financial ones (although $7.5 million could not provide significant aid for Russia's budget). The government's strategic purpose in this transaction was to eliminate a dangerous hotbed of possible future conflicts.[50] A few years later, another important question of border demarcation surfaced with Japan. After China agreed to Russia's annexation of Ussuri Territory (in the Peking Treaty of 2 November 1860), Sakhalin's importance to the empire's Far Eastern territories increased. However, the question of who owned South Sakhalin was a stumbling block in the long-drawn-out negotiations with Japan. Finally, on 25 April 1875, a convention was signed in St. Petersburg exchanging the northern part of the Kurile Islands, which belonged to Russia, for South Sakhalin.[51]

During that period of his reign, Alexander II attached great importance to the conquest of Central Asia, where Russia's interests conflicted with England's. A substantial portion of the ruling circle and of society as a whole thought that expanding into this region and developing economic relations with other Eastern countries would make it possible to restore Russia's military and political prestige while exerting pressure on her principal rival—Great Britain. Alexander II's interest in and attention to this sphere of state activity never flagged; while he shared the overall goal of advancing into Central Asia, he nevertheless restrained the hotheads from short-sighted or hasty actions and fanciful plans to march on India.

After the Caucasus War* ended favorably, a systematic push into Central Asia began in the mid-1860s. Turkestan and Chimkent were taken in 1864, and Tashkent fell in 1865 to the initiative of General M.G. Cherniaev, an event which Valuev described in his diary on 20 July 1865: "Tashkent has been taken by General Cherniaev. Nobody knows why or what for. . . . There is something erotic in everything we are doing on the far periphery of the empire."[52] And although D.A. Miliutin informed the governor-general of Orenburg on 1 November 1866 that the tsar did not want "any new conquests," soon thereafter the assignment to Central Asia of General K.P. Kaufman, a

---

*The decades-long pacification of the Caucasus, which was brought to an end with the capture of Shamil in 1859.—D.J.R.

close confidant to Alexander II and the minister of war invested with the broadest powers, portended decisive action. On 13 November 1867 Kaufman reported that he had temporarily halted his advance in order to administer the territory, but then found it necessary to advance further against the emir of Bukhara. "I totally approve," was Alexander II's response.[53]

In 1868 Kaufman took Samarkand, and the emir of Bukhara submitted to Russia. In 1869, in accordance with Alexander II's orders, Krasnovodsk fell; this clearly portended further movement into Central Asia as Russia gained a foothold on the eastern shores of the Caspian Sea. Reporting on the tsar's orders to Kaufman, P.N. Stremoukhov, the director of the Asiatic Department of the Ministry of Foreign Affairs, stated that "a new expansion of the borders would do the greatest harm to our fatherland"; General Svistunov, who had supervised the operations of the Krasnovodsk detachment, also characterized the government's policy as "a damaging infatuation with the toy rattle of cheap laurels."[54] The advance nevertheless continued; in 1873 the Khanate of Khiva became a vassal state, and in 1876 the Khanate of Kokand was liquidated and the Fergana Region incorporated into the governor-generalship of Turkestan. Further operations were temporarily halted in connection with Russia's reentry into European politics and the impending Russo-Turkish War.

In his imperial ambitions, Alexander II went beyond the intentions and admonitions of Nicholas I, who had warned his son in his testament of 1835: "Always remain on good terms with foreign powers. All of your concern from now on should be to secure Russia's regions rather than to make new conquests."[55] His father's counsel was not heeded—or, more likely, simply forgotten. In Alexander II's reign, the empire's borders expanded considerably in the Far East, Central Asia, and the Caucasus. Despite all these successes and acquisitions in Asia, however, St. Petersburg continued to accord the situation in Europe incomparably greater interest and attention than the situation on all the other continents combined. This was only natural. The vital centers of the empire lay in Europe.[56]

Alexander II's policy in Europe was not invariable; Russia's rapprochement with France in the late 1850s and early 1860s proved short-lived. The cooling of relations between the two powers and their rulers, adversely affected by the Polish question in the early 1860s, became even more strained as time went on. To a considerable extent this reflected Alexander II's growing pro-Prussian orientation. Neither Prussia's militarization and strengthening under Bismarck's leadership nor the Iron Chancellor's obvious hegemonic ambitions in Europe alarmed Alexander II. Gorchakov's attempt to improve relations with France ended unsuccessfully.

Alexander II's visit to Paris in the summer of 1867 dashed these hopes. The French capital greeted the tsar coldly on 3 June (people in the crowd shouted, "*Vive la Pologne!*" [Long Live Poland]), and on 6 June a Pole named A.I. Berezowski shot at Alexander II, who was returning from a parade in an open carriage with Napoleon III. The tsar was not wounded, but none of the tokens of pity and sympathy, none of the attempts by the French emperor and his empress, Eugénie, could dispel the tsar's bad mood. The situation deteriorated with France's obstinate resistance to Russian diplomatic attempts to repeal the restrictive articles of the Treaty of Paris. In 1870 Alexander turned a deaf ear to the appeals of the French government for aid and protection. The tsar did not conceal his Prussian sympathies, even though a substantial portion of Russian society and its ruling bureaucracy did not share them.

To some extent, Alexander's attitude toward Prussia can be explained by his hope, from the beginning of the Franco-Prussian War, that France would repeal the most burdensome articles of the Treaty of Paris, the "Black Sea articles." Counting on support from Prussia, he proposed to the Council of Ministers a plan by which Russia would unilaterally reject the articles that restricted its rights in the Black Sea. Tiutcheva commented on the tsar's initiative in this matter and, likewise, the considerable restraint of almost all the ministers.[57] Gorchakov's circular of 19 (31) October 1870 accomplished its purpose. Bismarck, although unhappy with this action, proposed to set up a London Conference of the powers concerned, and on 13 March 1871 the conference adopted a convention repealing these articles, which constituted a great diplomatic victory.

Although Alexander II calculated successfully, it would be a mistake to explain his attitude toward Prussia by that alone. His personal feelings and sympathies for his uncle, the king of Prussia, were also of great importance. D.A. Miliutin recalled that Alexander II could not conceal his delight in every telegram reporting victory by the German troops. He immediately sent Wilhelm telegrams of congratulation and, from time to time, Saint George crosses—and in such large quantities, moreover, that the action provoked complaints and ridicule in St. Petersburg society. The tsar's obvious sympathy toward Prussia also explains why, despite Russia's neutrality, Russian officers, physicians, and field hospitals served the German army. Even after the German victory at Sedan, and despite Alexander II's growing apprehensions over the possible consequences of such rapid Prussian successes, his position did not change. On 6 November 1870 he wrote to Grand Duchess Elena Pavlovna: "Like you, I mourn the latest losses by the glorious Prussian Guards."[58]

Thiers, visiting St. Petersburg in an attempt to win Russia's active support for France, left with nothing. When during the peace negotiations vanquished France tried to enlist Russia's support against Prussia's immoderate claims, Alexander II remained unapproachable. The Marquis de Gabriac, the French ambassador to St. Petersburg to whose lot fell the difficult task of combating this Prussophilia, sent the following assessment of the situation to his minister of foreign affairs, Jules Favre, in a telegram dated 19 February 1871: "You may be convinced from the exchange of telegrams between the king of Prussia and Emperor Alexander—an exchange that even here has produced a foul impression—that we have nothing to hope for from Russia. . . . Russia is neutral, but its neutrality is friendly to France; the emperor is neutral, but his neutrality favors Prussia. Emperor Alexander administers a country that is devoid of initiative and is in addition accustomed to absolutism. The country may arrange a conspiracy when it is pushed to the limit, but it is incapable of openly pressuring the authorities."[59]

Alexander II completely failed to sense the threat posed by the formation of the German Empire, the danger posed to Russia by the presence of a strong, militarized, neighboring power. He failed to understand that the Treaty of Frankfurt, which redrew the borders of Central Europe, was fraught with instability and in the long run portended a general European war—something foreseen by many politicians and diplomats. In only one instance did he abandon his position of indifferent contemplation: when he perceived the danger that the communist movement posed to all of Europe. After the fall of the Paris Commune,* Alexander II agreed with the French government's demand that commune members who had taken refuge in other countries be extradited. "I view this question as one of the utmost importance to the future of *all* governments," states his resolu-

---

*In 1871, when conservative forces crushed the forces of revolution in radical Paris. The commune later served as an inspiration to V.I. Lenin and other Russian revolutionaries in 1917.—D.J.R.

tion on a report by V.I. Vestman, the man in charge of the Ministry of Foreign Affairs. "On my orders, the minister of justice has drawn up a memorandum concerning this matter, which I myself have passed on to the king–emperor in Berlin, since I desire that the initiative should come not from me but from Prussia."[60] Even before the Paris Commune, impressed by the overthrow of the monarch in France in September 1870 and the proclamation of the Republic, the tsar, like Bismarck, acknowledged the necessity of organizing a joint international struggle against the socialist movement.[61]

A rapprochement with Austria–Hungary was also achieved. The Three Emperors' League was formed in October 1873 by Russia, Germany, and Austria–Hungary. Alexander II returned to an alliance that he had rejected early in his reign. The tsar's opposition to Germany's new claims against France in 1875 smoothed over France's previous resentments, but it did not change the overall situation. Although the alliance of the three emperors did not constitute a revival of the Holy Alliance, Alexander still, given the new international conditions, preferred an agreement with his former partners to any decisive changes in diplomacy—he preferred, as he put it, the "traditional alliance," despite Gorchakov's apprehensions and the opinions expressed in the press, which almost unanimously preferred a rapprochement with France. In addition, the alliance with Germany and Austria–Hungary would make it easier for him to carry out his imperial plans.

The magnitude of imperial ambitions required substantial military forces and financial strain. The military focus was reflected in the state budget, which, incidentally, began to be published for the first time after the abolition of serfdom. Military expenditures constituted one-third of the country's budget. From the very beginning of his administration of the Ministry of Finance, Reutern tried to convince Alexander II that the budget was weighed down with military expenses, and that it would be necessary to place the ruble on the gold standard and carry out monetary and currency reform if reforms were to be successful and Russia's renovation secured. Imperial policies and traditional thinking, however, carried the day.

A decisive event was the Russo–Turkish War of 1877–78. The tsar declared war, although not suddenly and not without reservations. Before departing for vacation in Livadia in August 1876, in a conversation with the minister of finance concerning political matters, "he [had] strongly expressed his resolve, as before, not to allow Russia to be lured into a war. He spoke with some bitterness about the

Slavophile agitation—the desire of some persons to have someone other than he represent Russia's interests." But a month later, his mood had changed. The efforts of the Pan-Slavic committees and society's consolidation around the issue of Russia's mission of liberation of Slavic coreligionists could hardly fail to exert considerable influence on Alexander II. In early October a dramatic face-to-face meeting took place between Alexander II and Reutern (who had been summoned to Livadia), during which the emperor's position was finalized.

Alexander II demanded that the finance minister provide funds for the forthcoming war. For his part, Reutern undertook a desperate attempt to oppose the influence exerted on the tsar by the military and all others who favored settling the Near Eastern crisis by military means. He submitted to Alexander II two memoranda in which he argued that a war would "call a halt to the proper development of the civil and economic initiatives that are the glory of His Majesty's reign; a war would inflict irreparable ruin on Russia and bring it into financial and economic disarray, which would provide fertile soil for revolutionary and socialist propaganda of the kind toward which our era is already too inclined." Reutern suggested that, in addition, the European powers would never permit Russia to enjoy all the fruits of victory. Alexander II returned this memorandum with irritation and hostility, without discussing it with other ministers, and, as Reutern recounts it, reproached him, maintaining "that I had said nothing about funds for waging a war and proposals to humiliate Russia. And that neither he nor his son would allow this."[62] The tsar scorned his minister's arguments (Reutern immediately decided to retire after the war ended). The monetary and currency reform he had prepared was derailed.

On 21 May 1877 Alexander II left St. Petersburg to join the army on active duty; he did not return until 3 December, after the fall of Plevna, which decided the outcome of the war. He considered it his duty to remain at the rear of the army with the wounded, and on leaving the capital he said, "I am going as a nurse." The emperor bore up patiently under the difficulties of life in the field and the bad roads, keeping a strict daily schedule and arising at seven or eight o'clock in the morning, even if he had gone to bed in the middle of the previous night. He went among the tents where the wounded were, sometimes visited the operating rooms, comforted the despairing, gave awards to those who had distinguished themselves, and cheered everyone; his eyes were frequently moist with tears. For his humanity and mercy Alexander II must be given his due. But the emperor's attempts to interfere in the direction of military operations and his impulses to "take part in combat," to the great distress of Minister of War Miliutin, led only to tension and confusion.[63]

The war played a tremendous liberating and progressive role in the fate of the South Slavic peoples. For Russia, the consequences of this war were ambiguous. Undoubtedly, the military victories and acquisitions restored Russia's imperial prestige and wiped out the painful memory of its defeat in the Crimean War. But the war had demanded a tremendous effort. It cost more than 1 billion rubles (as comparaed to an 1878 budget that totaled 600 million rubles); the ruble's rate of exchange declined from eighty-six gold kopecks to sixty-three. Reutern resigned, realizing that his policy, designed to continue the course of reforms, had been defeated completely. The war was concluded by the Treaty of San Stefano, followed by the disappointing decisions of the Congress of Berlin, which drastically reduced the fruits of the victory. Chancellor Gorchakov, who represented Russia at the congress, stated in a note to Alexander II: "The Congress of Berlin is the worst page in my service career." The emperor added: "And in mine too."[64]

Russia's obvious diplomatic defeat did nothing to resolve the domestic political situation, as the government had expected when it started the war. On the contrary, the confrontation worsened. The surge of patriotism evoked by the war to liberate the Slavs succeeded in muffling the underground's activities only for a short while, and it was reactivated with new force. Terror became the principal means of struggle, and the principal target was the emperor himself. Attempts on the tsar's life followed one after another: A.K. Soloviev's attempt on 20 April 1879; the death sentence pronounced against Alexander II by the Executive Committee of the People's Will on 26 August of that year the attempt to blow up the tsar's train that autumn and the explosion in the Winter Palace on 5 February 1880, which cost many lives.

The final and most dramatic year in Alexander II's life began. At his bodyguards' insistence, he changed itineraries, gave up pedestrian outings, and drove only in the garden of the Anichkov Palace in an open carriage surrounded by Cossacks. Increasingly he immersed himself in his private life, also filled with trauma. Living under one roof in the Winter Palace were Empress Maria Alexandrovna, racked with consumption, and the young, beautiful Dolgorukaia, without whom the emperor could not bear to spend a single day and with whom he had three children (two daughters, Olga and Ekaterina, and a son Georgii; a second son died). The empress passed away in late May 1880, and Alexander II, barely forty days later, entered a morganatic marriage with Princess Dolgorukaia on 18 July. Prince V. Bariatinskii, brother-in-law of Ekaterina Alexandrovna, the youngest daughter of Princess Iurievskaia and Alexander II, recorded the words the tsar uttered on his wedding day: "For fourteen years I have waited for this day; I am afraid of my happiness! May God not deprive me of it too soon."[65]

On the same day, he signed a decree in which he announced what he had done, ordered that Dolgorukaia be given the title of Her Highness Princess Iurievskaia (named for Iurii Dolgorukii, from whom her family descended), and decreed that his progeny by her would have the same rights as legitimate children. This decree, like the marriage itself at first, was known to only a few trusted persons who attended the betrothal ceremony. After them the first to learn of the marriage, from the lips of the emperor himself, were M.T. Loris-Melikov and Crown Prince Alexander Alexandrovich, followed by the other sons; Alexander's daughter, living in England, did not find out until November. The marriage upset many within the emperor's family and, in general, within the "upper crust."

After the 5 February 1880 attempt to assassinate the tsar, Loris-Melikov was appointed to serve first as chairman of the Supreme Administrative Commission; later, as minister of internal affairs, this former governor-general of Kharkov and hero of the Russo–Turkish War (because of his seizure of Kars) became a kind of dictator. An intelligent and energetic man who was also flexible and liberal, he believed the root of the evil lay in the dissonance between unlimited autocratic authority and the enlightened segment of society. His new, dual-purpose policy was designed to suppress the revolutionary movement definitively while simultaneously continuing reforms—expanding local self-government, mitigating censorship, completing the peasant reform with obligatory redemption, retiring the reactionary minister of public education, D.A. Tolstoy, and so on.

But the principal point of Loris-Melikov's plans was to grant representation to zemstvo and municipal governments in the spirit of the Editing Commissions of 1856–60. Loris-Melikov's plan, which can only provisionally be called a constitution, amounted to no more than instituting a "General Commission" under the State Council that would have included persons appointed by the government as well as representatives of the zemstvos and towns and would have had two subcommissions, one for finance and one for business and administration. After examination, bills were to supposed to have been submitted for final discussion by the State Council, to which Loris-Melikov also proposed to add representatives of public institutions.

Aware of Alexander II's obstinate unwillingness to give the country a constitution, Loris-Melikov cautiously sought a way to approach the monarch. Bariatinskii recounts that in Livadia Loris-Melikov had long conversations with the sovereign, in his wife's presence, concerning political affairs and the new reforms. Sometimes during their talks, just in passing, he made vague remarks about how the people would be happy to have a tsaritsa who was Russian by blood. As he made these hints, Loris-Melikov realized that he was touching upon the tsar's cherished intentions: Alexander II dreamed of crowning the princess and, once he had accomplished his planned state transformations, abdicating the throne to the tsarevich and taking his wife and children to Nice.[66] This information comes from stories passed down by Princess Iurievskaia's family, which need to be verified and confirmed.

The two "dictatorships of the heart" (beloved wife and strong ruler) became intertwined in the last year of Alexander II's life and held sway over him. Still as much in love as ever, Alexander was immersed in his private life and absorbed in the smallest details of its organization—up to and including the livery that the servants wore at the palace at Livadia, which the Princess Iurievskaia was visiting for the first time since the wedding. Yet exhausted by the burden of affairs of state and by the conflict in society, pursued by terrorists, the tsar was leaning toward a decision that categorically negated all the years of his reign. As Grand Duke Vladimir Alexandrovich told D.A. Miliutin two months after the emperor's final act of state: "On the very morning of that fateful day, 1 March, the late emperor, having signed a report submitted by the Secret Commission and having waited for Loris-Melikov to leave the office, addressed the grand dukes thus: 'I have given my consent to this representation, even though I myself realize that we are heading down the path to a constitution.'"[67]

Before making the government report public, however, Alexander II decided to have the draft examined on 4 March in the Council of Ministers.

That plan was wrecked by the terrorist act of 1 March. M. Aldanov writes that Princess Iurievskaia begged Alexander II not to drive out to the changing of the guard because of a possible attempt on his life. As he left, however, he cheerfully told her that a fortune-teller had predicted that he would die on the seventh attempt—and if there were one today it would be only the sixth. A short time later, two explosions sounded on the Catherine Canal. The organizers of the assassination on 1 March were A.I. Zheliabov, a peasant by origin, and S.L. Perovskaia—a member of an aristocratic family, the daughter of Count L.A. Perovskii, one of Nicholas I's eminent officials, and niece of Count L.N. Perovskii, a prominent official during the first years of Alexander II's reign.

The first bomb, thrown by N.I. Rysakov, exploded next to the carriage, and Alexander II remained unharmed. His personality and nature were very characteristically manifested in the final moments of his life. "Despite the driver's urging that he not get out of the carriage," P.A. Kropotkin writes, "Alexander II got out anyway. He thought that military dignity required him to look after the wounded Circassians and say a few words to them. . . . I was able to peer deep into his complicated soul . . . and understand this man, a man who possessed a soldier's bravery but lacked a statesman's courage."[68] A second bomb, thrown by I.I. Grinevitskii, hit its target.

The tsar was taken to the Winter Palace, where at 3:30 P.M. he died from loss of blood. Alexander II died on a soldier's bed, covered with the old military overcoat that had served him as a housecoat. The first of March also tragically cut short the state transformations designed to crown the "Great Reforms" as well as the monarch's romantic dreams of personal happiness. The day before Alexander II's remains were moved from the Winter Palace to the Peter and Paul Cathedral, Princess Iurievskaia cut her magnificent hair and placed it in the hands of her deceased husband.[69] At Alexander III's insistence, she and her children soon left Russia. She lived abroad in Paris and Nice, where homes had been purchased for her. Alexander II had provided for her in advance: two months before his death he had transferred to her name about 3.5 million rubles from his own capital, which amounted to 14.6 million rubles.[70] She died in Nice on 15 February 1922, in the seventy-fifth year of her life; according to memoirists, she remained faithful to her love till the end of her days.

Equally as tragic as Alexander II's personal fate was the outcome of his final endeavors on behalf of the state. Eyewitnesses testify that the mood in the Winter Palace changed with astonishing swiftness, on the very day Alexander II died: "There was a feeling that all of the late emperor's associates, if they were not already in disfavor, would not continue to be involved in affairs of state for very long."[71] Loris-Melikov was openly blamed for what had happened. The meeting that Alexander II had scheduled for 4 March was held on 8 March in Alexander III's presence. The dramatic clash between those who backed Loris-Melikov's plan (Grand Duke Constantine Nikolaevich, D.A. Miliutin, A.A. Abaza, and P.A. Valuev) and the opposition, which was most vividly reflected in the darkly accusatory speech made by K.P. Pobedonostsev, is well known. No decision was taken at the meeting, but in effect the issue was predetermined. Any peaceful path of movement toward a law-governed state and a constitution was blocked.

The tragedy of the Tsar–Liberator became the tragedy of Russia. "Russia's position is truly sad," and "it is frightening to think of what is in store for her in the future," D.A. Miliutin wrote in his diary in June 1881. He had left St. Petersburg permanently and settled in the Crimea, as had Alexander II's brother, Grand Duke Constantine Nikolaevich, who was in disfavor. What was it that so frightened one of the most brilliant statesmen of the era of the "Great Reforms?" "What kind of program will they have?" D.A. Miliutin asked himself as he assessed Pobedonostsev and his associates and the start of a new administration. And his answer, two weeks after the tragedy of 1 March, was: "Reaction under the mask of nationalism and Orthodoxy—the sure path of ruin for the state."[72]

S.S. Tatishchev, the first and most balanced biographer of Alexander II until our own days, created a highly idealized image of the monarch in his two-volume work. Having defined his task as that of "resurrecting the unforgettable, majestic, and charming image that the Tsar–Liberator held for his contemporaries," whom he had served truly and faithfully for seventeen years, Tatishchev reached this conclusion in his research: "Truly Alexander II was for Russia that 'Good Shepherd' who, in Christ's words, shall 'lay down his life for his sheep.' "[73] But Tatishchev himself realized that in the late nineteenth and early twentieth centuries, when the chronicle of Alexander II's life and reign was being compiled, the time for a historical assessment of the Tsar–Liberator and his reforms was not yet at hand. He saw his task as that of making "the first cutting in the dense forest of Russian society's lamentable ignorance regarding the actual content of the reign" of Alexander II.[74] As the twentieth century draws to a close, more than 100 years since he died and 130 years since the most important of his reforms—the abolition of serfdom— "the time for historical assessment" is at hand.

Alexander II was a tragic individual. In the act of 1 March 1881, the tragedy of a man's fate, a monarch, and a country were oddly intertwined. This act marked the beginning of the bloody trail to the tragic dénouement of Russia's history in the twentieth century. It was there that the course of reforms that had been undertaken for the peaceful construction of a state governed by law came to an abrupt end. In terms of his character, temperament, world view, and calling, Alexander II was no reformer. He became a reformer by force of circumstances; in his character and personality, his unbridled, repellant, autocratic "ego" accommodated attractive human traits, but in affairs of state it often suppressed them. He remained, in effect, a prisoner of the very system the foundations of which he began to undermine with his reforms. In his sympathies and passions, in his inclinations and orientations, the "military spirit" dominated the lawgiver.

The emperor and autocrat, genetically and historically linked to his predecessors from Peter the Great to Nicholas I, predominated over the emancipator. This was not due so much to Alexander II's personal qualities as it was to the weakness of the social forces capable of taking charge of and carrying out reform. Society's expectations, its faith in the leadership's ability to restore the country the place it deserved and in cooperation between the intelligentsia and the leadership, sentiments characteristic of the early pre-reform years of Alexander II's reign, were disappointed. In reality, the "Great Reforms" were not designed to foster economic prosperity, "improve the life" of the people, develop the principle of elective representation, or lay the foundations of a state ruled by law; they were designed to entrench the autocracy, strengthen military power, and expand the empire for the sake of Russia's greatness as Alexander II and his closest associates understood it.

Notes

1. *Krasnyi arkhiv*, 1922, bk. 3, pp. 292–93; GARF, f. 678 (Aleksandr II), op. 1, d. 818, l. 3 ob.

2. GARF, f. 678, op. 1, d. 572, l. 2 ob.

3. M.P. Pogodin, *Istoriko-politicheskie pis'ma i zapiski v prodolzhenii Krymskoi voiny* (Moscow, 1874), pp. 333–34, 336–40, 355–58.

4. RGIA, f. 1180, op. 15, d. 148, l. 29.

5. Pogodin, *Istoriko-politicheskie pis'ma*, pp. 315, 317.

6. RGIA, f. 1180, op. 15, d. 148, l. 19.

7. Ibid., f. 560, op. 14, d. 294, l. 1.

8. Ibid., f. 523, op. 1, d. 2189.

9. "Zapiski K.K. Merdera, vospitatelia tsesarevicha Aleksandra Nikolaevicha, 1826–1832," *Russkaia starina*, 1885, bk. 2, p. 343; bk. 6, p. 507.

10. V.A. Zhukovskii, *Sochineniia*, vol. 6 (St. Petersburg, 1885), p. 348.

11. *Gody ucheniia ego imperatorskogo vysochestva naslednika tsesarevicha Aleksandra Nikolaevicha nyne blagopoluchno tsarstvuiushchego gosudaria imperatora, 1826–1838* (St. Petersburg, 1880), vol. 1, p. III.

12. Zhukovskii, *Sochineniia*, p. 348.

13. *Russkaia starina*, 1883, bk. 2, p. 538; bk. 7, p. 42.

14. Zhukovskii, *Sochineniia*, pp. 261–62, 349.

15. *Russkaia starina*, 1885, bk. 3, p. 553; bk. 12, p. 514.

16. Ibid., bk. 2, pp. 256, 273, 356; bk. 4, p. 88; bk. 6, pp. 298, 496.

17. Ibid., bk. 2, p. 358; bk. 6, p. 489; bk. 3, p. 537; bk. 5, p. 504; bk. 8, p. 238.

18. GARF, f. 678, op. 1, d. 268–281.

19. Ibid., 1886, bk. 2, p. 405.

20. A.F. Tiutcheva, *Pri dvore dvukh imperatorov. Dnevnik 1855–1882* (Moscow, 1929), p. 41. Nicholas (1843–65); Alexander (1845–94)—the future Emperor Alexander III; Vladimir (1847–1909); Aleksei (1850–1908); Maria (1853–1920), who married the Prince of Edinburgh, the youngest son of the English Queen Victoria; Sergei (1856–1905), the future governor-general of Moscow, killed by SR [Socialist Revolutionary Party member] I.P. Kaliaev; and Paul (1860–1919), shot by the Bolsheviks in the Peter and Paul Fortress. The first child (a daughter, Alexandra) died in infancy.

21. RGIA, f. 523, op. 1, d. 2149, ll. 18–21.

22. Ibid., f. 1180, op. 15, d. 148, l. 39.

23. GARF, f. 728, op. 1, d. 2149, l. 32.

24. RGIA, f. 523, op. 1, d. 2149, l. 32.

25. Ibid., l. 40; d. 2222, l. 12.

26. A. White, *Autobiography* (London, 1905), vol. 1, p. 470.

27. Tiutcheva, *Pri dvore dvukh imperatorov*, pp. 105–7.

28. GARF, f. 728, op. 5, d. 2265, l. 4; RGIA, f. 1101, op. 2, d. 394, l. 1.

29. *Golos minuvshego*, 1916, no. 5–6, p. 393.

30. GARF, f. 728, op. 1, ch. 2, d. 2479, ll. 7–8.

31. RGIA, f. 1284, op. 66, 1857 g., d. 11a, ll. 3–4.

32. GARF, f. 722, d. 681, l. 62 ob. (letters from 20 January [1 February] 1857).

33. *Zhurnaly i memorii obshchego sobraniia Gosudarstvennogo soveta po krest'ianskomu delu s 28 ianvaria po 14 marta 1861 g.* (Petrograd, 1915), pp. 3–5.

34. GARF, f. 722, op. 1, d. 230, ll. 21 ob.–22.

35. See L.G. Zakharova, "Zapiska N.A. Miliutina ob osvobozhdenii krest'ian (1856 g.)," in *Voprosy istorii Rossii XIX—nachala XX veka* (Leningrad, 1983), pp. 24–33.

36. GARF, f. 722, d. 681, ll. 117–118 ob.; Manuscript Department of the Russian State Library, f. 169. 61. 25, l 32.

37. RGIA, f. 560, op. 14, d. 294, ll. 6–8, 28.

38. *Russkii arkhiv*, 1889, bk. 5, p. 159.

39. GARF, f. 722, d. 681, l. 104; *Sbornik pravitel'stvennykh rasporiazhenii po ustroistvu byta pomeshchich'ikh krest'ian, vyshedshikh iz krepostnoi zavisimosti* (Moscow, 1861), vol. 2, pt. 2, pp. 51, 59, 129.

40. *Dela i dni*, 1920, bk. 1, p. 124.

41. *Die politischen Berichte des Fürsten Bismarcks aus Peterburg und Paris (1859–1862)* (Berlin, 1920), p. 130.

42. N. Barsukov, *Zhizn' i trudy M.P. Pogodina* (St. Petersburg, 1896), bk. 9, pp. 305–8.

43. *Dela i dni*, 1920, bk. 1, p. 124.

44. P.K. Shchebal'skii, *N.A. Miliutin i reformy v Tsarstve Pol'skom* (Moscow, 1882), p. 49.

45. E. Dicey, *A Month in Russia During the Marriage of the Czarevitch* (London, 1867), p. 47.

46. See Maurice Paléologue, *Roman Imperatora* (Moscow, 1990).

47. *Dnevnik P.A. Valueva* (Moscow, 1961), vol. 2, pp. 140–41.

48. A.F. Koni, *Sobranie sochinenii* (Moscow, 1968), vol. 5, p. 287.

49. *Dnevnik D.A. Miliutina* (Moscow, 1950), vol. 4, p. 57.

50. N.N. Bolkhovitinov, *Russko-amerikanskie otnosheniia i prodazha Aliaski, (1834–1867)* (Moscow, 1990), pp. 183, 202.

51. See E.Ia. Fainberg, *Russko-iaponskie otnosheniia v 1697–1875 gg.* (Moscow, 1965). It is clear from Nicholas I's instructions to Putiatin that in 1853, at the time of the demarcation, Russia did not own the whole Kuriles chain: the islands south of Urup belonged to Japan (K. Sarkisov and K. Cherevko, "Putiatinu bylo legche provesti granitsu mezhdu Rossiei i Iaponiei. Neizvestnye ranee istoricheskie dokumenty o spornykh ostrovakh Kuril'skoi griady," *Izvestiia*, 4 October 1991).

52. *Dnevnik P.A. Valueva* (Moscow, 1961), vol. 2, pp. 60–61.

53. Quoted in A.L. Pavlov, "Iz istorii zavoevaniia Srednei Azii," *Istoricheskie zapiski*, vol. 9, pp. 213–16.

54. Ibid., pp. 225, 229.

55. *Krasny arkhiv*, 1922, bk. 3, p. 293.

56. N.A. Khalfin, *Prisoedinenie Srednei Azii k Rossii (60–90-e gody XIX v.)* (Moscow, 1965), p. 126.

57. Tiutcheva, *Pri dvore dvukh imperatorov*, p. 204.

58. GARF, f. 647, op. 19, d. 674, l. 63.

59. *Tsarskaia diplomatiia i Parizhskaia kommuna 1871 goda* (Moscow, 1933), p. 64.

60. Ibid., p. 176.

61. See S.V. Obolenskaia, *Franko-prusskaia voina i obshchestvennoe mnenie Germanii i Rossii* (Moscow, 1977), p. 34.

62. A.N. Kulomzin and V.G. Reutern—Baron Nol'ken, *M.Kh. Reutern: Biograficheskii ocherk* (St. Petersburg, 1910), pp. 158–59, 177–90.

63. M.M. Chichagov, *Dnevnik prebyvaniia Tsaria-Osvoboditelia v Dunaiskoi armii v 1877 godu* (St. Petersburg, 1887), pp. 86–89, 146, 157, 229–30.

64. See *Istoriia SSSR s drevneishikh vremen do nashikh dnei* (Moscow, 1968), vol. 5, p. 266.

65. V. Bariatinskii, "Liubov' i prestol," *Novoe russkoe slovo*, 25 December 1976.

66. *Russkaia mysl'*, 18 July 1963; 13 March 1956, etc.; *Novoe russkoe slovo*, 25 December 1976.

67. *Dnevnik D.A. Miliutina*, vol. 4, p. 62.

68. P.A. Kropotkin, *Zapiski revoliutsionera* (Moscow, 1988), pp. 417–18.

69. *Novoe russkoe slovo*, 25 December 1976.

70. RGIA, f. 1614, op. 1, d. 105, ll. 1, 12 ob.

71. *Russkaia mysl'*, 13 March 1956.

72. *Dnevnik D.A. Miliutina*, vol. 4, pp. 37–41.

73. S.S. Tatishchev, *Imperator Aleksandr II, ego zhizn' i tsarstvovanie* (St. Petersburg, 1903), vol. 1, p. 18; vol. 2, p. 662.

74. Ibid., vol. 1, pp. xvi-xvii.

Emperor Alexander III, 1881–1894

Valentina Grigorievna Chernukha's judicious portrait of Alexander III and his thirteen-year reign presents this imposing autocrat as yet another tragic figure in Russian history. In her view, Russia was already heading down the road to revolution when Alexander ascended the throne in the wake of his father's murder by the People's Will. Be that as it may, the revolution's impact, she argues, "could have been softened by a more flexible and progressive policy." But this was not to be; in this lies Alexander's personal tragedy and, by implication, Russia's collective one.

The Imperial family did not think "Little Bulldog" was cut out for statesmanship. Like Nicholas I, Alexander III had been poorly prepared to rule. A man of limited intelligence "who had to struggle to climb each rung on the ladder of knowledge," Alexander III's sympathies lay with the nationalist opposition that opposed many of his father's reforms and views. Alexander III disapproved of his father's policies not only because of his fundamental ideological disagreement with the Tsar-Liberator, but also because of the strained relations within the royal family that had come about as a result of Alexander II's romance with and subsequent marriage to E.M. Dolgorukaia. Chernukha laments Alexander's animosity toward Count Mikhail Loris-Melikov's plan to introduce a modicum of representative rule, and his lack of flexibility and unwillingness to compromise. While she suggests that not all of his policies were reactionary, the more powerful image she evokes is that of a limited, unfit ruler whose "personality dominated the statesman in him." His policies were doomed from the start, and they pushed Russia further along the path to revolution.

D.J.R.

Alexander III

Valentina Grigorievna Chernukha

We have been left many descriptions of the physical appearance of the next-to-last Russian monarch, sketched by both admirers and critics, hypocrites and sincere people. Of course, all have features in common, but they differ in their attitudes and their assessments. Let us consider the words of a man endowed with the keen eye of an artist. "It was there [in the theater] that I first saw Alexander III up close," A.N. Benois wrote as he recalled an event in 1889:

> I was astonished by his "bulk," his weight, and—despite that—his grandeur. Until that time I had greatly disliked the rather "cloddish" aspect of the sovereign's appearance, which was familiar to me from his official portraits. . . . And the sovereign's clothing (his uniform) in those portraits seemed to me downright ugly—especially in comparison with the elegant appearance of his father and grandfather. . . . But when I saw him in the flesh I forgot all about that. Moreover, the sovereign's face was remarkable for its size. I was especially struck by the gaze of his clear (gray? blue?) eyes. . . . That cold, steely gaze, in which there was something terrible and alarming, struck one like a blow. That imperial gaze! The look of a man who stands taller than everyone else, yet carries a monstrous burden and must be anxious every second for his own life and the lives of those near and dear to him! In the years that followed I had several opportunities to be near the emperor, to answer his questions, to hear his speech and jokes, and at such times I did not experience the least timidity. In more ordinary circumstances (when visiting our exhibitions), Alexander III could be gracious, and simple, and even . . . "warm." But that evening in the Mariinskii Theater, the impression he made was something else—I would even call it strange and awesome.[1]

This portrait is astonishingly reminiscent of another, the mounted statue of Alexander III sculpted by P. Trubetskoi. This is the "awe-inspiring and alarming" figure of a giant whose approach could evoke nothing but fear and the desire to move aside. That was how his subjects perceived him, that was how he appeared to foreigners, and that was what he was like to many—even the closest—members of the ruling dynasty, whom, as S.Iu. Witte put it, he knew how "to keep respectful." Nevertheless, Alexander III had many attractive features that were relegated to the background when he was "on duty." This happened because this kind and decent fellow and wonderful family man bore—literally!—someone else's burden, the burden of an autocratic ruler, yet lacked any of the qualities necessary to bear it except for his imposing appearance, which, incidentally, later contrasted so greatly with that of his son and heir.

Alexander III was sufficiently critical of himself to sense this internal discrepancy, which is why this next-to-last monarch is a tragic figure in Russian history. Equally tragic were the consequences of his thirteen-year reign. The saddest thing is that history probably could have unfolded rather differently, and the impact of the Revolution, which was apparently already inevitable, could have been softened by a more flexible and progressive policy. After all, not Alexander but his brother should have occupied the throne. But it was as if an evil fate were hovering over Russia: during the nineteenth century the country busied itself with matters that wasted the time available for reform, and that was the fault of Russia's monarchs. Alexander III made his own contribution to the tightening of these tangled knots, albeit with the best of intentions, thinking that he was guaranteeing the futures of his own family, the dynasty, Russia, and even Europe.

The future emperor of Russia grew up in a family of many children. Counting only Alexander II's sons, there were six: Nicholas, Alexander, Vladimir, and Alexei—all born between eighteen months and two years apart—and Sergei and Paul, born somewhat later. The second son, named in honor of his father and born in February 1845, was the third child in the family of the heir to the throne (the first was a daughter, Alexandra). This family had no great problem concerning the heir, as in the case of Alexander I or Nicholas II. The principle of succession according to seniority designated the eldest brother, Nicholas, born in 1843, as heir to the throne, and his parents' attention was focused primarily on him. In early childhood, all the children received a similar upbringing in the care of English nannies and military officers. Their grandfather insisted upon it, and their father agreed.

The two oldest brothers, Nicholas and Alexander, began their schooling and military training at the same time. Their governess, V.N. Skripitsyna, gave them their first lessons in reading and writing, arithmetic, and religion, while their military instructors, supervised by Major General N.V. Zinoviev and Colonel G.F. Gogol, taught them drill formation, marching, the manual of arms, and the changing of the guard. From the moment of their birth (or, more accurately, the day of their christening), all the grand dukes were assigned to the same Guards regiments and were immediately appointed as commanders over others. But that marked only the beginning of their military service. Later, numerous state and family celebrations served as occasions for the bestowing of commands and assignments to regiments, advancements in the service, and promotions through the officers' ranks. Alexander received the rank of second lieutenant at age seven, was awarded the rank of lieutenant at age ten, and was promoted to colonel at age eighteen. Nominal military service conferred the right to wear elegant regimental uniforms, and military training gave the little boys the right to stand sentry duty on solemn occasions, which was a touching sight. The two older brothers received only their primary education together; soon the difference in their ages made itself felt, and the tasks they were assigned were also different. In the nineteenth century, great importance was attached to the education of the heir to the throne.

Having had enough of the numerous instances of despotism into which absolute power all too often turned, by the eighteenth century European thinkers—and Russian thinkers too—urgently sought legal guarantees against the extremes of unlimited rule. They began to formulate theories of constitutional law. This circumstance, reinforced by arguments made during numerous European revolutions, forced the autocracy to adjust and demonstrate its sense of responsibility. This made it essential, therefore, to ensure the heirs to the throne an appropriate upbringing and education. Catherine II understood this well and made a serious effort to prepare her own grandson for affairs of state. Nicholas I turned over the supervision of the upbringing of his heir, the future Alexander II, to V.A. Zhukovskii. Nikolai Alexandrovich (Alexander's son Nicholas) also received a thorough education.

Heirs to the Russian throne attained their majority at two separate ages—legally at age sixteen and actually at age twenty-one. The coming of legal age involved the triumphant conferral of the rank of heir, and the recipient at that time took two oaths in the presence of his family and officials—the civil oath and the military oath of fealty to tsar and fatherland. Nikolai Alexandrovich took the oath and was separated from his brothers (until then they had lived together) and given separate apartments in the Winter Palace. The finale in the education of the heir to the throne was a lengthy tour of Western Europe, during which he became acquainted with various countries, public figures, and state systems, paid official visits to numerous relatives, and at the same time kept his eye out for a bride befitting his heart and rank. In 1864 the heir to the Russian throne completed his courses in the sciences "with distinction" and set off for travel abroad. His tour had a secondary purpose as well—healing baths at the seaside, for Nicholas had begun to suffer from back pains.

The countries he visited included Denmark, where he proposed to Princess Dagmar in September, and she accepted. After traveling around northern Europe the tsarevich stayed for a while in Italy and spent the winter in Nice, where Empress Maria Alexandrovna came to see him, for the heir's state of health was not improving. In early April 1865 he became so severely ill that members of his family were summoned, including Alexander II and his sons. Dagmar and her mother also came. They spent only two or three days with him, during which he alternated between regaining and losing consciousness. His mother, his brother Alexander, and his betrothed were at his bedside at all times. The doctors concurred that the heir to the throne had developed cerebrospinal meningitis. Nicholas breathed his last on 12 April 1865. On the same day, in accordance with the Law of Succession, Alexander became heir to the throne. The throne thus passed from a strong candidate to a weak one.

Within his family (where his nickname was "Little Bulldog"), Alexander was not considered cut out for statesmanship. The emperor's aunt, Grand Duchess Elena Pavlovna, "announced publicly that the state administration ought to go to his brother Vladimir,"[2] although the latter was altogether lacking in talent. Grand Duke Constantine Nikolaevich (after Alexander had already ascended the throne) noted his total lack of preparation for ruling, stating that both Alexander and Vladimir had been "left almost entirely to their own devices during their childhood and young manhood."[3] A.I. Chivilev, Alexander's teacher, was "horrified" at the prospect of his accession to the throne, and B.N. Chicherin, after several meetings with Alexander, fell into "complete despair," having heard from him "not a single bright thought nor even one sensible question."[4]

Nothing about Alexander gave anyone reason to think that he might be capable of running a country. In his official biography, assigned to S.S. Tatishchev, who was supposed to model it on his own work on Alexander II, we find this thoroughly touched-up characterization:

> In the qualities of his mind and manner, Alexander Alexandrovich was the complete opposite of his older brother. As Grot commented, he did not manifest any outward brilliance, quick understanding, or mastery; yet he was possessed of a clear and lucid common sense of the sort

that distinguishes the Russian man and a remarkable quickness of mind which he himself called "native wit." He did not learn things easily, especially at first, and it took a considerable amount of effort on his part. . . . In class, Alexander Alexandrovich distinguished himself by his attentiveness and concentration, his diligence and persistence. He loved to study and to learn from his lessons . . . , to get to the root of things and to master them, and while it was not easy he did learn thoroughly and firmly. What was hardest for him was the theory of languages; his favorite activity, on the other hand, was reading, primarily stories and travels.[5]

Even this generous and apologetic account depicts a mediocre man, one of limited intelligence who had to struggle to climb each rung on the ladder of knowledge.

Alexander was simpler and more down-to-earth than his brother; he liked military science and reading for entertainment. He was a boy who did not like school very much, preferring to play. The children of courtiers were allowed to play with the grand dukes, and they would play horses, hunting, and war, using a toy fortress that had been specially built in Tsarskoe Selo. That was how things were in his childhood, and so they remained in his final years of schooling. The aforementioned Tatishchev, contradicting himself, quotes excerpts from letters from Alexander's tutor, Count B.A. Perovskii, written between 1862 and 1863. He complained constantly to the emperor about his pupil, saying that he was utterly unable "to make him understand that studies do not consist solely of sitting still for a certain number of hours." He did everything he could to get the emperor to "understand" that "even with the use of the utmost efforts and strivings it is hardly possible, in his position, to attain the level of education that young persons of his years generally possess; to get the emperor to understand that, in every subject we are forced to focus on things that are generally taught only to children, and consequently we are wasting time." Perovskii, moreover, concluded: "unfortunately, he still looks upon this from a most childlike perspective."[6]

Until April 1865 the situation remained tolerable, because Alexander was still just one of the grand dukes, whose entire lives were spent in military service rather than in state service, and for whom knowledge of history, literature, economy, and law was of no consequence. Alexander's succession to the throne, to which he had never given a thought, came literally like a bolt out of the blue. He was greatly saddened by the death of his brother, whom he had loved very much. He was staggered by his new calling. Despite the whole family's grief and the fact that the funeral had not yet been held (the deceased's body was shipped to St. Petersburg by sea), Alexander immediately assumed the task of carrying out various kinds of ceremonies, procedures, receptions, and presentations relating to his new status as crown prince. He was obliged to take an oath in the chapel at the Winter Palace, to be presented to deputations both in St. Petersburg and in Moscow, and to take part in festivities associated with this.

By April 1865 Alexander had become a colonel and an aide-de-camp; the title of crown prince brought him the rank of major general, which also made him a member of the emperor's entourage and hetman of all the Cossack troops. By this time he had grown to manhood, but he was not prepared for his new duties and lacked the talents of a statesman. There was no way to correct the latter failing, but his training (equivalent to the education offered by a mediocre gymnasium) could be supplemented. Historians, legal experts, and economists took the tsarevich's education vigorously in hand. He was tutored by K.P. Pobedonostsev, S.M. Soloviev, F.I. Buslaev, I.K. Babst, and F.G. Terner. As an individual, the heir to the throne had many attractive traits. He was direct, honest, sincere, unpretentious, decent, and kindly disposed toward those around him, but at the same time clumsy, shy, and awkward. Moreover, he had a great sense of responsibility, of which he made use both while he was heir to the throne and during his reign.

Alexander's views were already shaped by the time his older brother died. V.P. Meshcherskii has left an interesting description of him during that period (here again, the memoirist, like others, could not refrain from making comparisons). "His older brother," Meshcherskii remarked, "was not the least bit philosophical; on the contrary, with his sensitivity to and perception of all nuances in the world around him, his subtle and penetrating mind . . . , he fully perceived life's influences on him, or he reckoned with it and realized its force. The younger brother . . . , in contrast, did not submit, so to speak, to the force of the life around him and did not mold himself to it."[7] Many called this obstinacy, but in reality it was his static way of thinking; the traits of the emperor-to-be were already apparent in the twenty-year-old Alexander.

Although Alexander's courses in the various sciences provided him with the rudiments of knowledge, they could not change significantly a character already formed. Opportunities for him to engage in studies were, in addition, severely limited. His position now demanded that he attend numerous official meetings and receptions, weddings and funerals, balls and military reviews, diplomatic parties, and meetings of all sorts. Moreover, only shortly afterward, in October 1866, he married his late brother's betrothed, who after her baptism [into Orthodoxy] took the name Maria Fedorovna. In order to marry her, Alexander had to renounce his feelings for the charming lady-in-waiting Princess M.E. Meshcherskaia, for whom his affection was so great that he was even willing to renounce the throne. Perhaps that is why his parents decided not to seek his bride from afar or to delay the wedding. The marriage was an "alliance," for each of them confessed to having feelings for someone else (Dagmar was still in love with the deceased Nicholas), but unexpectedly it turned out to be a happy one. Unanimously, people commented on the couple's cozy family life and warm relationship. Soon afterward, the heir to the throne was not only a newlywed and a family man but also a father. Alexander loved his home and his children.[8] "The birth of a child," he wrote to Pobedonostsev when his daughter was born, "is the most joyful moment in a man's life, one that is impossible to describe, because it is a totally unique feeling."[9]

Alexander's preparation to rule was practical and occurred through his participation in current affairs. In order to get the heir to the throne involved in politics, Alexander II decided to start accepting reports from ministers only when the heir was present; at first this was more the exception than the rule. By 1868, however, Alexander had become a member of the top state institutions—the Committee and Council of Ministers and the State Council. To be sure, he left very few traces of active participation in the discussions, and he did more listening than thinking. In general, heirs to the throne did not play a decisive role in nineteenth-century politics. What compelled Alexander to keep silent—his own diffidence, his incompetence, or his father's commanding position—is difficult to say. But in December 1873 at a meeting of the Council of Ministers, which discussed the question of the marshals of the nobility's control over the activities of the public schools, the emperor turned to his son and asked for an opinion, which surprised the minister of defense so much that he noted in his diary: "The sovereign has never asked him for his opinion during any previous council meeting."[10]

In casting a glance over the entire fifteen-year period during which Alexander was heir to the throne in order to understand his place in the political life of that period, a conclusion presents itself: he represented the opposition of the political right—not the opposition of the so-called aristocratic party, whose members looked admiringly at

English forms of handling both social and state issues, but rather the nationalist opposition. The heir's opposition was more ideological than real, but there is no question that he opposed his father's policies. Relations between the crown prince and his father were not such that he could argue with him in public, much less act against him openly, yet all too often they found themselves in opposite camps, and not just because their views were different (that much is indisputable!) but also because Alexander II, who possessed a statesman's qualities, often acted contrary to his own desires and views for the sake of the state.

Father and son took different positions in regard to the nationalities. Whereas Alexander II saw the extraordinary measures under way in the Kingdom of Poland and the western provinces as temporary and tried to steer a course of compromise in Finland and the Baltic region, so as not to deepen their hostility to Russia, the heir to the throne favored harsher measures. To Alexander II the "propriety" of political decisions and European public opinion had great importance; the tsarevich, in contrast, was inclined to ignore them. In the late 1860s, through the efforts of several ministers from the western provinces, P.N. Batiushkov and I.A. Shestakov were recalled in order to weaken the policies of Russification with respect to land ownership and the church (policies that were part of the extraordinary measures); in the crown prince's eyes this was a "disgraceful" decision. "At a time like this, nobody can be assured that he will not be driven from his post tomorrow," he complained.[11]

Although Alexander II made use of the services of M.N. Muraviev ("the Hangman") at difficult times, the tsar did not like him and when the country was at peace tried to keep him out of state affairs. The crown prince, however, considered Mikhail Nikolaevich an outstanding authority.[12] During preparations for the military reform, the emperor endorsed the "democratic" plan of War Minister D.A. Miliutin, a plan that had been drafted in accordance with the needs of the time; the heir to the throne, however, gathered around himself people who opposed the plan and defended feudal models of military organization. On the eve of the Russo–Turkish War of 1877–78, Alexander II, heeding his ministers, did everything he could to avoid military conflict; the tsarevich, in contrast, was in the "party of action." The tsar-reformer inwardly renounced Russia's feudal past, while the heir to the throne searched for its positive features. The father implemented judicial reforms that have been acknowledged as being among his greatest contributions; the son, while still heir to the throne, planned to revise them. The Ministry of the Navy earned Alexander II's approval, while the heir could hardly find words strong enough to condemn it.

With the passage of time, the importance of the tsarevich's reactionary stance grew, because in addition to the fact that like-thinkers were beginning to gather around him, even people of a different persuasion began to look him over in the belief that the future belonged to him. Alexander went through his "probationary period" while taking part in the discussion and implementation of domestic and foreign policies in the late 1860s and the 1870s, and at particular moments he took charge of important endeavors which left their good stamp on the history of that time.

In late 1867 and early 1868, for the first time since the emancipation, the government encountered bad harvests in a couple of dozen provinces. The abolition of serfdom absolved the landowners of the responsibility of taking care of their peasants, shifting it, consequently, onto the state. The Ministry of Internal Affairs (trying not to draw attention to itself, of course) collected information about the grain situation and simultaneously prevented reports about the harvest failures from being published. Naturally, the public began to talk about famine and to criticize the authorities. A compassionate man, the tsarevich felt sorry for the peasants whose granaries stood empty, and he yearned to help them in some way. The situation also afforded the emperor an excellent opportunity to link, for the first time, the heir to the throne to a noble endeavor, one that could hardly fail to inspire universal approval. Without any consultation whatsoever with the minister of internal affairs (itself a blatant expression of dissatisfaction with his inaction), on 23 January 1868 a rescript addressed to the tsarevich was published, directing him to create a commission to collect donations for the purchase and distribution of grain. The rescript spoke of the heir's role as initiator of the undertaking: "In appointing Your Imperial Highness to the honorary chairmanship of this undertaking it is gratifying to Us to see the sincerity and warmth of your heartfelt participation as a guarantee of the successful accomplishment of the proposed charitable goal."

The rescript was published in the newspapers, a donation box was hung on the Anichkov Palace, and a commission was formed, consisting of what we today would call businessmen. The first meeting of the commission was devoted to strategy, and the idea of distributing the grain free of charge was rejected as demoralizing; the commission decided to purchase the grain in large quantities in order to ensure stable grain prices in the provinces afflicted by crop failures. This would require money right away (even though volunteer donations were coming in), and the tsarevich "wheedled" a million rubles from his father. The appropriation of funds and the purchase of a large amount of grain were successfully kept secret, and the grain was shipped to where it was needed. The actions of the commission, the emerging zemstvo system, and the local authorities successfully relieved the urgent grain shortage and forestalled the peasant resettlement movement that had begun because of the crop failures. Considering the events surrounding the food aid vastly overblown, an offended Minister of Internal Affairs P.A. Valuev resigned.

The biggest event in the heir to the throne's life was the Russo–Turkish War. During the initial stages when the liberation movement of the Slavs against the Ottoman Empire flared up in the Balkans, both military men and Russian society as a whole responded quickly to it. The movement in support of the Slavs was not universal. There were many who, although they did not contest the idea of helping their coreligionists, nonetheless opposed Russia's military intervention in the struggle, as they believed that war would impose a heavy burden on the country's economy and finances, not to mention human losses. The minister of internal affairs, the war minister, and the minister of finance opposed the war. The last, in fact, asked to resign because he was personally unwilling to do anything that would destroy the delicate budget balance that he had tried to achieve for more than ten years.

At first, Alexander II also proved unwilling to plunge Russia into a serious war. Yet the heir to the throne and the empress argued that Russia ought not to leave her poorly armed coreligionists to the tender mercies of the Turkish army. For quite a while, both the emperor and his minister of internal affairs, A.E. Timashev, tried to force the Russian press not to discuss Russia's Balkan policies and not to push the country toward entering the war. One of the troubadours of Pan-Slavism and Russia's mission of liberation was a man very close to the tsarevich—V.P. Meshcherskii. The position of his paper, The Citizen, with which the emperor was not in sympathy and which was subject to administrative penalties several times during that period, was close to that of the heir to the throne.

In the autumn of 1876, Alexander II held continuous conferences in Livadia with the ministers involved in foreign policy. One of the regular participants was the tsarevich. At one such meeting, the tsar complained about the difficulty of the situation and, defying the rules of propriety, directly reproached the heir to the throne, who was present, because he and Maria Alexandrovna were going against his will. At the time, the tsarevich himself wrote to Pobedonostsev from Livadia:

> Yes, there were a few difficult moments of indecisiveness and uncertainty, and outright despair set in. The situation could not be more abnormal than it is now: none of the ministers in St. Petersburg knows anything, while here everything hinges on two ministers, Gorchakov and Miliutin. The chancellor has grown too old and does not know how to act decisively, while Miliutin, of course, would like to avoid war, because he feels that it could break too much out into the open. Fortunately, when I arrived here I found Ignatiev, who opened everybody's eyes so wide that finally they came up with a plan of action.[13]

As a result, arguments in favor of military intervention carried the day, and Russia went to war. Many members of the Imperial family headed for the war zone, with the tsar and the tsarevich in the forefront. During the entire campaign on the front, which lasted almost a year, the tsarevich commanded the Rushchuk detachment (one of three that made up the Danubian Army). He had two corps under his command (around seventy-five thousand men). His chief of staff was P.S. Vannovskii (whom Alexander later made war minister). The cavalry was commanded by I.I. Vorontsov-Dashkov (who served as minister of the Imperial court under Alexander III). The detachment commanded by the heir to the throne fought along a relatively quiet sector of the front (compared with Shipka and Plevna, where the outcome of the war was decided), but there, too, there were combat operations—attacks and withdrawals, reconnaissance and the repelling of Turkish sorties.

The Rushchuk detachment carried out its combat mission successfully without allowing the Turkish forces to break through the front and reach the crossings. The forces commanded by Alexander repelled the Turkish detachments and forced them onto the defensive. "We never thought the war would drag on for so long; we were so successful at the start, and everything was going so well and promised a swift and brilliant outcome, and then suddenly that wretched Plevna! That nightmare of the war!"—wrote the heir to the throne on 8 September 1877,[14] a cry of frustration that perfectly conveys his comprehension of the military experience. The mood of joyful expectation was replaced by sober consideration, because he was seeing not a mere exercise but real war; he came to recognize its confusion and to witness the shortsightedness of the military command (his uncle, Nikolai Nikolaevich, was the commander in chief) and the corruption of the quartermasters; he saw his friends and those close to him die. During a reconnaissance that he led on 12 October 1877 his cousin Sergei Leikhtenbergskii died right before his eyes.

The tsarevich conducted himself well in the war and did not interfere in the affairs of the high command. He became attached to "his" detachment and hated to part with it when the Guards, to which he belonged, arrived at the front. He was open and democratic within the circle of his entourage and staff officers. According to those who participated in the events, Alexander's tent was a center where as many as forty men would gather for breakfast and dinner and pass the time in relaxed conversation. It was a real comradeship born of combat. Alexander devoted his free time—and in fact there was some free time at the front—to amateur archeological digs. His participation in the war was rewarded with medals: in September 1877 he received the Order of Saint Vladimir with swords; in late November he was awarded the Order of Saint George, Second Degree; and in February 1878 (this time in St. Petersburg, to which he had by then returned) he was given a golden saber decorated with diamonds and inscribed "For Distinguished Command."

After returning from the war, the tsarevich embarked on a major undertaking—the Volunteer Navy. His closest associate in this undertaking was Pobedonostsev. The reason for the creation of the Volunteer Navy, which survived until 1917, was that the heir to the throne was highly dissatisfied with the performance of the Ministry of the Navy in the field of shipbuilding. "The Ministry of the Navy refuses to focus on good ships; it has concerned itself exclusively with those rotten round-hulled coastal-defense gunships, squandering tens of millions on them," he said in one of his letters.[15] Meanwhile, Fleet Admiral Grand Duke Constantine Nikolaevich enjoyed the tsar's complete confidence. This meant that the only possible solution was to create a private merchant marine based on voluntary contributions. The society could travel abroad to purchase ships that had already been built or order them from abroad and use them as transport vessels during peacetime, converting them to warships in wartime. It was decided to purchase high-speed, ocean-going vessels of the cruiser type.

The tsarevich became the patron of the Volunteer Navy, and matters proceeded successfully. By 1878, three million rubles had been collected and the first three steamships had been purchased. But that was just the beginning. The earnings from shipping were spent on enlarging the fleet, and naval personnel were recruited to make up the crews. The heir to the throne devoted considerable attention and energy to this undertaking, kept track of the press and the movements of vessels, and met with the men who sailed on these steamships. After he became emperor, Alexander transferred the administration of the Volunteer Navy to the Ministry of the Navy and subsidized it, but during the initial period of the fleet's existence it was maintained by the donors' enthusiasm and the tsarevich's efforts.

Alexander also deserves credit from historians, because to a considerable extent they have him to thank for the creation of the Russian Historical Society, which, during its half-century of activity, published some hundred and fifty volumes of documents and an encyclopedic reference work, *The Russian Biographical Dictionary*. The creation of scholarly societies was no easy matter, because like any other institution they required at least a modest staff and funds to cover their expenses. Often there were not enough funds from private contributions. Whenever the state refused to finance the activities of such a society and private contributors had trouble securing the necessary funds, the latter resorted to an old, tried-and-true technique of solving the problem: they would induct a highly placed patron whose name would both inspire new members to join and encourage voluntary donations.

Having an honorary chairman did not, by any means, automatically guarantee prosperity for such an organization, but it did allow it to survive. This device was used in the mid-1860s, when certain people close to the heir to the throne had the idea of establishing a professional–amateur historical society, especially since the Economic Society, the Geographical Society, and several juridical societies already existed. The Historical Society was intended to foster interest in Russia's history and to promote the study of it.

In March 1866, twelve founding members (including K.N. Bestuzhev-Riumin, Prince P.A. Viazemskii, A.F. Bychkov, M.I. Bogdanovich, M.A. Korf, D.A. Tolstoy, and E.M. Feoktistov) convened to agree on the principles of the organization and activity of the society. Initially, stewardship of the society came from the Ministry of Foreign Affairs (in any event, the ministry submitted the proposal to establish the society to the Committee of Ministers); the ministry was also willing to provide aid to the society. But the Committee of Ministers argued in favor of placing the Historical Society under the jurisdiction of the Ministry of Public Education, at that time headed by A.V. Golovnin (he was replaced by D.A. Tolstoy soon afterward). The Historical Society's charter states: "As well as an actual chairman, the society may have an honorary chairman if one of the members of the Imperial family is willing to favor the society by accepting that title."[16] The society was supposed to maintain itself by means of one-time and annual dues and contributions. The tsarevich assumed the honorary chairmanship.

From the very beginning, the Historical Society decided to specialize in study of the post-Petrine period, in particular the eighteenth century. The society described itself as "general educational" and "scholarly"—that is, broad in scope. Members of the society, the number of whom was unlimited, were to convene for meetings "on a regular, an extraordinary, and an annual basis." Alexander III loved history, and both during his tenure as heir to the throne and after he ascended the throne he read historical works with pleasure, took part in the meetings of the Historical Society, and gave aid to it; he invited members of the Historical Society to his home in the Anichkov Palace, his official residence; hence, his chairmanship and membership were not by any means nominal, as so often happened in situations of that sort. In all this, Alexander III was courteous and cordial; we may presume that he enjoyed the respite from duties that were mandatory and unpleasant. As Grand Duke Nikolai Alexandrovich grew older, he was invited to meetings of the society and took pleasure in listening to discussions of Russia's history.

In his youth, Alexander had another enthusiasm that likewise produced tangible results. He proved to be one of the organizers of a type of instrumental ensemble that had never before been heard within the palace walls—a brass band. His parents had conscientiously tried to ensure that their children loved music, and musical training was included among the mandatory subjects of their education. Nicholas, Alexander, and Vladimir all began to learn to play the piano, but the latter two did not find it to their liking. They came to hate their music lessons, which were discontinued. Alexander, however, had a strong military streak and liked military music, and it was not long before his interest in music performed by others turned into an attempt to play instruments himself. First he gathered around him a brass septet, in which he played the cornet. Later, the septet grew to nine players, and finally into a full brass band.[17]

In the late 1870s, the heir's responsibilities increased. When the emperor had to leave St. Petersburg, Alexander took over the duties of receiving reports and overseeing current policies. All this took place during the onset of a deep domestic crisis, as the economic, social, and political situation deteriorated. "A grievous and frightfully difficult situation," was how he assessed it in December 1879.[18] During that period, in fact, all Russia was in a state of dissatisfaction and expectation. Expenditures on the war led to a budget deficit, which deprived the government of freedom in financial maneuvering. The war, plus agrarian reform, which had stalled, worsened the situation in the countryside. The peasantry, most of whom saw no possibility of alleviating their shortage of land through their own efforts, began to nurture illusions of enlarging their allotments from manorial lands. This gave rise to rumors of a "black repartition"—that is, land free of charge—which posed a risk of mass upheaval.

The Populists,* in despair and lacking normal political means of struggle, began to resort to terrorist activities. Added to this was opposition from the elite, some of whom demanded measures to solidify the nobility's land ownership and confer political rights, while others demanded more rapid progress toward middle-class democratic reforms. Chief among these was the reform of the state system, the creation of a form of statewide representation. A series of attempts to assassinate the emperor began in 1879, and these made the ruling circles nervous and compelled them constantly to discuss measures to stabilize the situation, including proposals ranging from extensive repression to substantial concessions to the social movement for the sake of "tranquillity."

The troubled situation within the tsar's family, and indeed in all court and governmental circles, was further complicated by the emperor's lengthy romance with E.M. Dolgorukaia and the fact that he had a second family which, with the passage of time, began to affect governmental policy. The aging monarch became increasingly attached to this woman who was thirty years younger than he and to the children he had by her. The private desires and passions of this aged and ailing man increasingly crowded out the statesman. In order to simplify interaction with his second family, he moved it into the Winter Palace. Maria Alexandrovna, who had known about her husband's liaison for a long time, was so deeply hurt that she became reclusive. In addition, she was in an advanced stage of consumption. In May 1880 she died in the Winter Palace, all alone, for Alexander II was not even in the city; he had gone to Tsarskoe Selo, where Dolgorukaia was.

---

*Or *Narodniki*, members of the revolutionary intelligentsia who combined an idealistic faith in the Russian peasantry with a determination to overthrow the autocratic social and political order.—D.J.R.

People at the court gossiped about the emperor's affair, which was widely known. Many denounced him as "senile," some highly placed persons had to adapt to the circumstances, and some even tried to take advantage of the situation by going through Dolgorukaia, who had enormous influence on the tsar. The tsarevich, both because he loved his mother and because he held very strict views on family ties, was indignant. He became still more indignant when Alexander II secretly married Dolgorukaia immediately after the traditional forty-day mourning period, thus officially recognizing his children by her and conferring on her entire family the title "Royal Princes of Iuriev." Despite the secrecy of the marriage and the monarch's repeated insistence that it represented the marriage of a private person, it became well known in society, especially after Alexander II appeared with Dolgorukaia in public and introduced her to the people closest to him. There was a real danger that she would be crowned and that her children would be completely legitimized.

Relations within the royal family became extremely strained. The emperor took his new family to the Crimea, to Livadia, leaving the heir to the throne in St. Petersburg to take his place. But the tsar continued to deal regularly with the most important business even while in the Crimea; papers were sent to him, and ministers came to see him. The tsarevich's relations with his stepmother were poor, and in hopes of reconciling them the father summoned his eldest son to Livadia. When he arrived, however, the heir to the throne was hit by another blow: his stepmother was occupying his late mother's chambers in the palace. No reconciliation took place, and the tsarevich avoided meetings with his stepmother. A.N. Kulomzin, who at the time served as deputy minister of state domains and represented the tsar in Livadia in that capacity, recalls:

At the time I found the following circumstances. Emperor Alexander II had installed Princess Iurievskaia, who had formerly been living in a separate dacha near Yalta, in his own palace—that is, in the chambers that had been previously occupied by the Empress Maria Alexandrovna, because there were no other rooms. The heir to the throne, whom the sovereign had summoned to Livadia, did not want to go, and Count Loris-Melikov, in order to carry out the sovereign's wishes for a reconciliation, lured Alexander Alexandrovich by falsely assuring His Highness that the princess was not living in the palace. Once he got there, however, it was impossible to turn back. The following procedure was established. Every Sunday, the sovereign invited to his table various ministers and other high-ranking officials who had come to Yalta. On one Sunday the seat to the sovereign's right was occupied by Tsarevna Maria Fedorovna and the seat to his left by the heir to the throne; on the following Sunday the tsarevich and his wife went hunting or for a ride in the mountains, and Princess Iurievskaia sat at the table and guests were presented to her.[19]

All this took place after the explosion in the Winter Palace,* that is, under the extraordinary legal circumstances that began to develop in February 1880 with the creation of the Supreme Administrative Commission headed by M.T. Loris-Melikov. Characteristically, the tsar had not wanted to resort to extraordinary measures, but he did so at the insistence of the heir to the throne, who was inclined to employ strong-arm methods. He placed great hopes in Loris-Melikov, a field general, believing that the man would know how to establish order with a firm hand. At first, Loris-Melikov seemed to justify those hopes, as attested by the hasty execution of I. Mlodetskii, who had tried to assassinate him. Repressive measures, however, were not the only tactics of this virtual Russian dictator. Very soon he accepted the idea, shared by the liberal bureaucracy and the liberal public, that the most important thing under such circumstances was to grant certain political rights to the public, which had already been living under the emancipation settlement for twenty years, and to give them the right to participate in central governmental organs.

Once he reached this understanding, Loris-Melikov gradually began to promote the idea of getting the zemstvo and city representatives involved in the process of drafting laws. This was not a new idea, for it had been discussed in governmental circles on at least four occasions—in 1863, 1866, 1874, and 1879–80—but it was rejected: Alexander II found the situation ambiguous and postponed any decision on the matter. But in early 1881 the situation changed; the constitutional idea had by then acquired many advocates, and under pressure from them the emperor decided to use this means to establish civil peace.

A special commission, which included the heir to the throne (who until recently had believed that "nothing" needed to be done along those lines), formulated a general proposal on creating deputy commissions and a Drafting Commission to take part in the initial discussion of bills, the essence of which was to be suggested by senatorial audits organized by Loris-Melikov. By that time he had already taken charge of the Ministry of Internal Affairs. The more he revealed his constitutional intentions (the word "constitution" itself, naturally, was never uttered), the more his relations with the tsarevich, which had been quite warm at first, deteriorated, although the heir to the

---

*That is, after an attempt to assassinate the tsar.—D.J.R.

throne, now isolated, did withdraw his objections to Loris-Melikov's draft. Meanwhile, the atmosphere in ruling circles reached a peak of tension. On the one hand, Alexander II's marriage was increasingly splitting both the Imperial family and the dignitaries, and, on the other hand, the draft project of representative institutions had been in preparation for a long time but was not yet approved. Its passage signaled a turning point in domestic politics. The country faced an opportunity to take a more civilized, constitutional path, without confrontation between society and its rulers.

On 1 March 1881 Alexander II approved the plan of Loris-Melikov's commission, and scheduled a meeting of the Council of Ministers to be held on 4 March under his chairmanship to reach final agreement on the draft of an announcement concerning the convening of the deputy commissions. Afterward, the tsar left for the Riding School. He was carried into the palace, mortally wounded by a bomb thrown by the People's Will, and one hour later he died in the arms of his wife and son from loss of blood. The people in Alexander II's entourage perceived his death in various ways. Many assessed the assassination as Minister of the Imperial Court A.V. Adlerberg did: "It may be that the sovereign's martyrdom ... saved his brilliant reign from an inglorious and humiliating finale."[20]

The fate of Loris-Melikov's plan, and with it the prospects for Russia's constitutional development, was now in jeopardy. The hastily published manifesto announcing Alexander III's ascension to the throne mentioned the government's course of action in vague terms. The new emperor gave no pledge that he would continue his father's cause. All he did was proclaim his intention to take care of Russia "according to the covenant of our forefathers." Yet Russia—and all the world—was trying to guess what the new tsar would be like and what to expect from him. All kinds of assumptions were expressed, including that he favored a constitution. There was a grain of truth in all this gossip, but there were obvious absurdities as well.

Yet one man during those days did discern Alexander III's character and prophetically foretold the tsar's policy direction. This was the writer I.S. Turgenev. Turgenev had spent much time abroad and was European in his political sympathies, but he had not lost any of his Russian nature, and he dreamed of a Europeanized Russia, of a constitutional monarchy conferred from above, of genuine liberty, and of the country's appropriate development. He also had a very keen sense of nationalism. In the summer of 1879, Turgenev had met the tsarevich in Paris, and he understood Alexander with

Alexander III

the perception of a trained psychologist. To be sure, the writer also made use of stories such as those told by N.A. Orlov, Russia's ambassador to Paris.

Under a pseudonym, Turgenev wrote an article titled "Alexander III," which appeared in the French press on 26 March—that is, it was written during the first weeks of the new reign. The article was intended for the French people, and its purpose was to create the most favorable image possible of Russia's new emperor.

Turgenev focused his readers' attention on Alexander III's unquestionably positive qualities—his health, his sincerity, his honesty, and so forth; however, he never stretched the truth or resorted to extolling traits that the tsar did not possess. He said—very delicately!—that the tsar was inadequately educated, and that he had received a primarily military training. "This sovereign appears to have been born with definite abilities to rule," Turgenev wrote, but he also cautioned that Russia could not, nevertheless, count on a "great sovereign." The author carefully but unambiguously wrote about the tsar's nationalism, his "sympathy" for certain nations and his antipathy toward others: "All that can be said about him is that he is a Russian and nothing but a Russian." Turgenev also wrote that the emperor would play the role of a people's tsar. Even though he had not yet heard about the fate of the Loris-Melikov plan, Turgenev dispelled liberals' hopes. "Anyone who expects a parliamentary constitution from the new tsar is bound to lose these illusions quickly," Turgenev warned. "His extremely close relations with the ultranationalist party point to a definite distrust of the constitutionalists. Ideas about limiting the authority granted to the monarchy, which are generally accepted in Europe, have always been foreign to Russia and will continue to be so for a long time. Imperial rule prefers to carry out important reforms by granting them from above, via edicts." Turgenev added, quite reasonably: "These reforms, incidentally, are essential; they have been in the works for a long time and are completely ready."[21]

For Alexander III, the first few months of his reign were a time when he was obliged to concern himself with an incredible amount of current business, and this relegated major concerns to the background. He had to endure the ritual of his father's funeral and the procedures of his coronation and undertake an intensive search for revolutionaries and swift retribution against the participants in the assassination. Toward the latter he was merciless. In the best traditions of the Russian intelligentsia, V.S. Soloviev tried a Christian appeal to Alexander's Russian heart and soul, declaring in a public lecture that Christian morality required the rejection of the death penalty and mercy toward the conspirators. But an autocrat's cruelty stirred in the new monarch. "You may rest assured," he said, "that nobody had better dare to approach me with proposals of this sort, and that all six are going to be hanged, I guarantee you that."[22] And in fact, in 1881 and afterward, drastic measures were taken against radical elements in society.

The new tsar also busied himself with arranging the Iurievskii family's fate. Hoping to evict them as soon as possible from St. Petersburg, he instructed Loris-Melikov to undertake negotiations with his stepmother. Alexander III was forced to offer her yearly support and place her in an appropriate situation, not only because of her official status as his father's wife but also because of his father's touching letter to him, written in late 1880, in which he instructed his son to take care of the family after his death. Not long afterward, Iurievskaia and her children went abroad to live; from time to time she attracted attention from the tsar's family and the Ministry of Foreign Affairs.

Although busy with everyday affairs, Alexander III made it clear from the very start of his reign, at first to his closest associates and then to all his subjects, just what course of political action he intended to follow. At that time, Russia had only two choices, and both were obvious to politicians. Germany's ambassador to Russia, General Hans von Schweinitz, outlined them as follows:

> In actuality, the choice that can be made today is only between two paths—either reforms in the European sense, from St. Petersburg, or autocratic rule in Moscow. With few exceptions the newspapers in the northern capital are calling for liberal reforms and are angrily dismissing Katkov's and Aksakov's resounding calls to transfer the government to the Kremlin. I agree that the latter proposal has a grain of soundness in it, but I do not believe that it will be accepted; it would be too inconvenient.[23]

As Alexander's policies showed, he chose the second path, though without, in a certain sense, rejecting the first: he tried to be the tsar of Moscow in St. Petersburg, under conditions of empire and developing capitalism.

By that time, the fundamental question for Alexander III had been decided—namely, the well-worn European road or the old Russian road with its ruts and potholes but also with Russia's autocratic Father-Tsar and its poor peasantry, guarded against shortages of land by its inalienable allotment of communal land. This is confirmed by his actions at the 8 March meeting of the Council of Ministers. He did not long postpone the meeting that had been scheduled by his father; in fact, he convened it in the Winter Palace after a three-day delay. The fact that Pobedonostsev and S.G. Stroganov were unexpectedly invited to the meeting, although they had not previously taken part in discussions of the matter, indicated that the emperor was strengthening the opposition to the Loris-Melikov plan. It seems that Alexander III's sense of filial duty and the fact that the matter was predetermined obliged him to treat the discussion of the proposal as a simple formality, one that by his signature automatically clinched his father's political legacy.

Alexander III warned the members of the council, however, that they must proceed on the basis that the plan's fate had not been decided, and, consequently, that it was a matter not of editing the document but rather determining what to do with it. Stroganov and Pobedonostsev took upon themselves the role of "principal opponents." The arguments they advanced were traditional ones: Loris-Melikov's proposals were foreign to Russian customs, they were untimely, they would weaken the autocracy. The last argument—the usurpation of the monarch's absolute rights—was always lethal. It amounted to an accusation of political unreliability, a fatal blow to any statesman's career. It was no accident that the authors of any project for governmental constitutionalism always began with a declaration of loyalty and concern for the consolidation of the autocratic principle. Alexander III conducted the meeting like a skilled chairman of a ministerial college who knew exactly what he wanted. Taking advantage of the categorical opposition of some people and the caution of others, he proposed, despite the majority's support for the project, that discussion of it be postponed indefinitely.

The supporters of the project who took part in the discussion, despite the tsar's hostility to constitutional measures (of which they were aware), openly risked their careers as they argued in favor of both the timeliness and the necessity of changing the existing procedures for drafting laws. Their conviction that the moment to implement political reforms had come compelled them to struggle and, without immediately tendering their resignations, to entertain mild hopes for the success of a renewed discussion. This is also linked to the final attempts by Loris-Melikov and his supporters A.A. Abaza and D.A. Miliutin to get the emperor to agree to set up at least an ersatz cabinet of ministers that would hold sessions without the emperor present, make decisions on a majority basis, and submit them to him for examination. In this way they were trying to weaken the influence of Pobedonostsev, who at that time was still isolated in government circles. At a conference on 21 April 1881 at Gatchina (where Alexander III had moved in late March), they received such permission.

While the advocates of reform were hoping for civilized activity by an informal cabinet, the autocracy showed the liberal ministers that it did not intend to cultivate a state based on the rule of law, and was perfectly capable of operating by the old methods. Finally, the emperor decided to announce publicly to the country and to the world (and he was forced to do this by both the declarations of the liberal press and the ultimatums of the People's Will) that he would not back down. In a note to his brother Vladimir he explained with utmost clarity the content of the future Manifesto of 29 April: it must proclaim that he would "never permit limitations on autocratic rule."[24] He said the same thing in his note to Pobedonostsev on 21 April. "Our meeting today made a sad impression on me," Alexander III wrote, showing that he was not deceived about the tasks of the "cabinet." "Loris, Miliutin, and Abaza are actively promoting the same policy and would somehow like to lead us to a representative government, but until I am convinced that such a thing is necessary for Russia's happiness, of course, it will not happen. I will not allow it."[25]

When Bismarck, in consideration of German interests, spoke out in favor of retaining the autocracy, in favor of the "Russian path" for Russia's development, Alexander III noted the following on the Russian ambassador's report concerning it: "I hope to God every Russian, and in particular our ministers, understands our position as Prince von Bismarck understands it and does not indulge in vain fantasy and rotten liberalism."[26] After that, of course, the liberals among the ministers became irrelevant. A decisive blow to Alexander II's entire corps of ministers was the almost simultaneous resignation of the minister of internal affairs, the war minister, and the minister of finance immediately after the 29 April manifesto that proclaimed Alexander III's intention to do without society's cooperation and preserve autocratic rule.

Each of these had been a major figure among the liberals. Only Loris-Melikov had become a reformer by accident, but he managed to demonstrate his ability to respond to the dictates of the times and his ability to gather active statesmen close around him, something extremely important for a statesman. Miliutin had stayed with Alexander II almost throughout his entire reign. For twenty years, he had spent every day transforming the Russian army. But not every minis-ter was up to the task of engaging in this kind of everyday, routine activity devoted to a unified, formulated plan. The resignation of such a man, who was replaced by P.S. Vannovskii (a much less edu-cated and rather mediocre entity), was a serious loss to Russia, as was the departure of A.A. Abaza from the Ministry of Finance (to which he had been appointed only in 1880) and the transfer of N.Kh. Bunge to that post. Bunge had been one of Alexander's teachers. He was a learned man who had a sound understanding of the tasks of financial policy; a "man of the 1860s," yet an outsider in the ministe-rial community in general and in the new company of ministers in particular. He and Abaza could have made an excellent pair, with the minister's comrade drawing up programs and projects, and the minister himself, with his characteristic intelligence and energy, im-plementing them and skillfully defending them in the State Council and the Committee of Ministers. The intellectual Bunge, who lacked a fighter's qualities, had a very hard time as minister of finance, especially since he soon became the object of attacks by the press, or, more accurately, by M.N. Katkov, who rightly saw him as something alien to the new course of action, a remnant of the liberalism of the previous period.

The process of replacing the statesmen of the previous administra-tion proved to be rapid, and was accompanied by the advancement of "real Russians," in Alexander III's terminology—for he included him-self in that category. His touching statement concerning this subject has come down to us: "There are some gentlemen who think that they alone, and no one else, are Russians. Surely they don't imagine that I am a German or a Finn? It's easy for them to indulge in farcical patriotism when they do not have to answer for anything."[27]

That was when Grand Duke Constantine Nikolaevich, Fleet Admi-ral and chairman of the State Council and the Main Committee for Rural Affairs, should have been removed from his numerous posts. In fact, he was advised in no uncertain terms to resign—through intermediaries, to be sure (Alexander III refused to see him). Con-stantine Nikolaevich was one of the few eminent members of the Imperial family whose statesmanship was marked by broad experi-ence, intelligence, and consistency. Since 1865 he had been in charge of the country's top lawmaking institution—the State Coun-cil—through which all the most important laws passed, and, partly thanks to his position as Alexander II's brother, he knew how to maintain the worthy status and prestige of that form of authority. As a presiding officer he did have his shortcomings, to a large extent the result of his being a grand duke—abruptness, lack of restraint, and arrogance. Nevertheless, having him replaced as chairman of the State Council by Grand Duke Mikhail Nikolaevich (another of Alexander III's uncles) signaled the ascent to leadership of a man who was ignorant, unprepared, and disinterested in legislation, a man who preferred military affairs and court life.

The role of head of the Russian fleet was transferred to Grand Duke Alexei Alexandrovich. The Imperial family member closest to Alexander III was his brother, Grand Duke Vladimir Alexandrovich. Alexander's uncles, except for Mikhail Nikolaevich (with whom his nephew also had very little to do), were kept out of government and even out of St. Petersburg. Like many other things, this signaled that Alexander rejected the policies to which they had been privy and that he intended to transform. The older generation of Romanovs noticed and assessed this rather early. Once in the autumn of 1882, Grand Dukes Constantine and Mikhail Nikolaevich got together in the Crimea and began talking about the "truly abnormal state of affairs," about the "breakdown" of everything that Alexander II had done, and in casting about for the causes of this phenomenon, which seemed so strange to them, they reached the conclusion that the causes were purely emotional and rooted in childhood: Alexander III's hurt feelings because his parents did not give him enough attention. "Hence, he has an unconscious desire to modify everything that exists, if only to return to something that existed once upon a time and is now forgotten."[28]

The natural first steps along those lines consisted of a shake-up in the ranks of the higher bureaucracy. The next man who did not fit the designation of "real Russian" after Constantine Nikolaevich was P.A. Valuev, the chairman of the Committee of Ministers, a man who came from a venerable Russian family but was a Westernizer in terms of his convictions and program. Count A.V. Adlerberg, the minister of the Imperial court, was dismissed in an insulting way and replaced by I.I. Vorontsov-Dashkov, with whom the tsar was on intimate terms. The post of chief of the monarch's bodyguard went to General P.A. Cherevin, who was a great lover of the bottle, which from Alexander III's point of view was a definite virtue, for he saw his chief bodyguard additionally as a resourceful drinking buddy who could bring his sovereign a pair of boots in which a flask of cognac was hidden.

The process of changing ministers and officials of ministerial rank was difficult and rocky, and it demonstrated that the opposition and the administration demanded different qualities in people. One of the first to be appointed after Alexander III assumed the throne was N.M. Baranov, who became governor of St. Petersburg. Much liked by the emperor because of his previous battles with the Ministry of the Navy and Grand Duke Constantine Nikolaevich, Baranov turned out to be a totally inept administrator; he was soon posted farther away from the capital city. Another of the "real Russians," N.P. Ignatiev, who had found his way into Alexander's affections in 1876 because of his Pan-Slavism, was removed from the post of minister of internal affairs as soon as he revealed his intention to convene—in full accordance with Slavophile doctrines—an Assembly of the Land.

Finally, from 1881 through 1882, Alexander III formed the nucleus of his closest associates. They were Pobedonostsev, the procurator-general of the Holy Synod who served as prime minister (an event unimaginable in the eighteenth and nineteenth centuries); D.A. Tolstoy, who was ostentatiously reinstated to government activity by Alexander III; and M.N. Ostrovskii and I.D. Delianov, who did not enjoy the respect of their colleagues outside that nucleus. The circumstances that took shape at that time were aptly described by an employee in Volf's bookshop, where the upper crust of St. Petersburg placed subscriptions and, at about the time of Loris-Melikov, had started to order books on constitutional law from abroad:

> The events that followed the assassination of the tsar on 1 March 1881, and the reactionary direction which had the upper hand in Russian statesmanship during Alexander III's reign, had a noticeable impact on the conversations of highly placed functionaries who visited Volf's store. Most of the functionaries who were Volf's clients found themselves out of a job; some of them went away, a few went abroad and some retreated to the countryside. Others who remained in St. Petersburg in honorary posts ceased to play a role in the machinery of state, and those who did manage to hold on to their positions under the new policies became more restrained in what they said. In general, after the animated discussions on political themes during the first months after Alexander III ascended the throne came a time of despondency, silence, and dread. Even highly placed officials were afraid to say too much.[29]

Thus society's despondency, fear, and hopelessness marked the beginning of the reign of Alexander III, who had ascended the throne in his maturity. What can we say about this man who began single-handedly to command the destiny of this vast country standing at the crossroads? Certainly both the nature of the country and the characteristics of the times demanded that the new tsar not only have the qualities of a statesman but also those of an outstanding figure who knew how to balance the desirable with the possible and the essential with the attainable, who knew how to view goals from a short- and a long-term perspective, and to select the people who would accomplish them according to the tasks rather than his personal sympathies. There was very little of this in Alexander III. As a human being, however, he had a striking and a solid personality; he was a person of firm principles and convictions.

In private, the tsar had many sincere friends, because almost all his human qualities evoked sympathy. The external appearance of this huge, clear-eyed man with his direct, firm gaze was in perfect harmony with his direct and open character, which was therefore easy to guess. The tsar's personality clearly dominated the statesman in him, and it was therefore clearly reflected in his policies, through which, in turn, his character could be discerned. When the tsar's human qualities and convictions coincided with the goals of governmental policy and were sufficient for them, his policies were successful. But where far-sightedness, flexibility, and compromise were needed, his policies were doomed, and that applies to the historical perspective as well.

As a man, Alexander III was simple, sincere, and true to his word. He felt most at ease in the company of military men and in his family circle, among his own and other people's children, but he had to spend much time reading tedious and barely comprehensible official papers—reports, journals, memorials, proposals, and notices. He found it difficult to compare and to contrast different points of view and discern any grain of reason in them; he had neither the requisite knowledge nor the necessary abilities, and was unwilling to trust specially selected professionals. This explains his search for people whom he could trust and whose proposals he could accept, as well as his unwillingness to convene the Council of Ministers in which opinions would clash in his presence.

This also explains why the State Council declined in importance during his reign. His view regarding that legislative college was very simple: the State Council was to help him carry out his intentions by endorsing projects that he and his ministers had already developed in private. Alexander III became angry when the council subjected one project or another to criticism—sometimes very severe criticism—or even to a serious and prolonged discussion that meant the passage of a law would have to be deferred. That happened with the bills on the land captains* and the judicial counterreforms, which Alexander pushed in every possible way. Loyal, gray-haired dignitaries were simply indignant when the emperor, without batting an eyelash, signed into law something that was merely a minority opinion, ignoring the viewpoint of the majority on the State Council. For this reason, during his reign the Committee of Ministers became the major legislative body (or, more accurately, legislative–advisory body), because its simpler procedures of discussion and narrower circle of participants made it easier to pass a bill there.

A similar pattern was visible during the reign of Nicholas I, whom Alexander III much resembled despite their outward differences. They had the same kind of mentality—that of the master of a large estate who was single-handedly responsible for everything on it. This "master" mentality, of course, had its positive aspects. In the first place, Alexander III was a workaholic; he personally pulled the cart of state, and he became involved in all domestic and foreign matters. He was always loaded down with urgent, major business, and for this reason he was not very fond of social entertainments such as the balls and receptions that he had to attend; even after he made an appearance he would try to slip away unobserved. Second, the emperor was as frugal as a housewife. The story of his patched and repatched trousers, which a servant made for him, is well known. N.K. Giers, the minister of foreign affairs, was shocked to see the tsar stooping over and revealing a "great big patch" on his riding breeches.[30]

This took place while all kinds of people hoped to share in available state funds. Once in late 1885, Bunge complained to Pobedonostsev: "Everybody wants money . . . from the state treasury . . . both for state needs and for industrial enterprises, as well as for their own well-being. . . . If we take . . . more from the population than the people can give, naturally we are going to increase the number of people begging for alms. . . . There are also people grabbing for money who only want to have fun at the treasury's expense."[31] Like any thrifty manager, Alexander III tried to economize for everyone—the bureaucracy and the landowners, the grand dukes and the entrepreneurs. He felt burdened by his inflated retinue, the spendthrift habits of the court, and the established everyday routine of handing out medals to people for time in service and in connection with anniversaries. He did everything he could to combat this,

---

*Introduced in 1889, the office of land captain (*zemskii nachal'nik*) furthered bureaucratic supervision over the peasants.—D.J.R.

mercilessly striking from the lists names of persons whom ministers had nominated for awards.

He also tried to fight the spendthrift habits of the Imperial family, which was not in the least inclined to operate according to the laws, and continued to consider itself the elite of high society. A.A. Polovtsov, a man close to Mikhail Nikolaevich by virtue of his position as state secretary, related that Grand Duke Mikhail Mikhailovich, once he came of age, decided to set up his own house, for which he intended to build a new palace, and he cited his own father as the example for this. Polovtsov, having had his fill of observing idle and pretentious society at the mansions of the grand dukes and understanding the whole monstrous discrepancy between the upper crust's way of life and the life of everyone else, tried to instill some reason in the young grand duke. He told him: "Your father's position belongs to the sixteenth century, but you belong to the twentieth, if any, because it is impossible to foretell what the future has in store for you and what the grand dukes' position will be before long."[32]

Disturbed by the Imperial family's rapid expansion, Alexander III decided to change the law [on the Imperial family] instituted during Paul I's reign and to reduce the number of potential "highnesses." What impelled him to make this decision was the increased expenses charged against the Imperial estates to maintain the royal family; after all, the emperor saw both the treasury and the revenues of the estates as his own purse. He was motivated not by abstract considerations of state but rather by the fear that his own family might wind up in the poorhouse. This fear was compounded by his unwillingness to be officially related to certain members of the Imperial family. In short, the dynastic character of the policy here was especially apparent. Alexander III prepared the draft of the new law in great secrecy, in the company of persons who were especially trustworthy—his brother Vladimir, Polovtsov, Vorontsov-Dashkov, and Adlerberg; they discussed it repeatedly. Almost three years were spent drafting and passing the law, in accordance with which the title of grand duke was reserved solely for the emperor's children and grandchildren, while his great-grandchildren would become mere "princes of the Imperial blood," with reduced stipends and privileges.

The law's passage was preceded by an edict announcing that a law was in preparation, in which everything had already been worked out in detail. The edict (like the law itself) provoked suppressed dissatisfaction among the grand dukes and their circles, yet it provoked no open clashes with the emperor. Among the titled nobility of St. Petersburg, however, Alexander III's measure met with approval: the result of an outbreak of the three-hundred-year-old enmity of the old Riurikovich dynasty toward the upstart Romanovs. Mikhail Nikolaevich complained: "Only the old St. Petersburg upper crust rejoices in this measure. They say they are Riurikoviches and we are just Holstein Germans with not a drop of Romanov blood left in us. But what would the Dolgorukiis or the Obolenskiis say if their own progeny were deprived of their rightful titles, with no recourse to the courts, with no crime having been committed?"[33] Incidentally, this law of Alexander III's demonstrated that the policies of his reign need not be assessed exclusively as a series of reactionary measures.

The reduction in redemption payments and the conversion to mandatory redemption, the laws on peasant migration, the establishment of state mortgage banks, and the gradual abolition of the poll tax—all these measures constituted not only an elaboration of the reforms of the 1860s but also an implementation of various projects that had, to one degree or another, been examined during those years. But for that very reason, the contrast with the laws that preserved the peasant commune and introduced the land captain's stewardship over the peasantry in a way that virtually resurrected the pre-reform system of relations, only slightly modified, seemed even greater. There were also several reforms and counterreforms that Alexander III simply failed to implement: his attempt to transform the system of promotion in the ranks ended in failure; members of General P.E. Kotsebu's commission, which the tsar had established in 1881, could not bring themselves to break up the military organization formed over such a long period and obviously efficient. In short, it was a rather eclectic policy, a mixture of what Alexander III wanted to do and what could actually be done.[34]

If one asks which personal convictions exerted the greatest influence on Alexander III's policies, first place goes to his blind faith in the need to preserve the autocracy. He perceived power as his own property, and he viewed those who talked about popular rule as thieves who would try to steal the shirt off his back. A democratic nature and the monstrous arrogance of a supreme ruler were blended in him, and sometimes manifested themselves in astonishing forms. Consider this statement, made in 1881: "Constitution? Is the tsar of Russia supposed to take an oath to a bunch of cattle?"[35]

He blocked any possibility of constitutional development in Russia and assessed the reforms that his father had implemented from the standpoint of their compatibility with absolute power. He insisted on judicial counterreform precisely because, in his eyes, the 1864 reform had been the brainchild of the constitutionalists who had started by limiting the tsar's judicial powers. Another of Alexander III's striking ideas concerned nationality; it influenced both his foreign policy and his policies with respect to the country's border districts, from which he began to remove any remnants of autonomy. It even influenced the way he selected his closest associates. The estate principle, which he professed, also strongly affected his policies. That principle came to replace the caste-free approach of the preceding reign and had an especially strong impact on Alexander III's policies with regard to the nobility, which were designed to support and revive the landed nobility even though it obviously lacked potential.

Despite Alexander III's firmness and persistence, and his deep resolve to provide his family and his country with peace and prosperity, his policies took shape slowly and with difficulty. He was constantly disappointed both in how matters were progressing and in his sluggish and incompetent ministers. He found inspiration in his family, which generally resided either at Gatchina or in the Anichkov Palace. He was not fond of the officialdom and court life of St. Petersburg, and every summer he would escape it by taking his family on a yacht trip among the coastal islands of Finland. He spent his whole life heavily guarded, with bodyguards stationed in the palaces and the suburban parks, although, unlike his father, he did not feel fear because of a series of attempts on his life. Only once, on 1 March 1887, might such an attempt have been successful.

The famine of 1891 proved to be a hard lesson for him. After all, he had started his reign with the intention of improving the position of the peasantry—yet in ten years he was confronted with a nationwide famine. Another disaster, but one of which he was not aware, was the conflict between the system he had established and the intelligentsia. The reforms of the 1860s turned out so well because, as soon as Alexander II and his government manifested their intention of carrying out progressive transformations, all Russia's intellectuals considered it their duty to take part in them. Alexander III's policies, on the other hand, drove all the country's intelligentsia into the opposition. University students joined the opposition not because they demanded that a parliament be convened but rather because they were refused the right to dining facilities, libraries, and scholarly societies. The loyal professorial community, which did not accept revolutionary methods, were persecuted and humiliated by their lack of rights. The intelligentsia began to wonder whether the autocracy possessed any common sense. The consequences of all this made themselves fully felt during Nicholas II's reign.

Many Russian monarchs have gone down in history with sobriquets firmly stuck to them. Alexander III has become known as the "peace-making tsar." This perception by his contemporaries reflected one of the most outstanding features of his reign—the absence of wars, a life under peaceful conditions. Yet his reign was far from cloudless and serene. During the 1880s, the tsar was greatly tempted to meddle in Balkan affairs. After all, he had personally served at the front and defended the freedom and statehood of Bulgaria, and so he had to take offense when Alexander Battenberg and his successors decided to worsen relations with Russia in order to draw closer to Austria–Hungary. In 1885 Russia was literally teetering on the brink of an Afghan war, which was fraught with the danger of conflict with England. And although there were always people among his military men who would prefer to speak in the language of warfare, the emperor heeded the arguments of reason and decided on the language of diplomacy.

Alexander III's foreign policy bore the stamp of his personality as clearly as did his domestic policy. He busied himself every day with intergovernmental relations, which were affected by his frankness, verging on rudeness; his straightforwardness; his extravagance; and his dislike of maneuvering and diplomatic protocol. Not for nothing did the high-level officials of the Ministry of Foreign Affairs constantly feel awkward because of the tsar's directness or try to conceal documents containing his resolutions, which threatened to provoke international scandals. But those of Alexander III's qualities that were dangerous in terms of policy were balanced by his common sense and his loathing for war, because he had personal knowledge of the true, horrific cost of war.

His foreign policy was also strongly affected by his well-known Germanophobia. It was related—but only in part!—to Russia's sharp about-face in relations with its allies. Russia's departure from its traditional alliance with Germany and Austria was a lengthy and painful process. Objectively, it was based on Germany's growing might and aggressiveness, its increasing use of strong-arm methods in its foreign policy with respect to Russia, its hostile tariff policy, and its attempts to link the issuance of credits to political conditions. Under these circumstances, Russia was increasingly obliged to view France as a possible ally, an idea that M.N. Katkov, the ideologist whom the tsar most respected, had long promoted. But the continuous maneuverings of the German chancellor blocked any swift reorientation. Two kinds of diplomacy confronted one another: the straightforward, curiously honest diplomacy of Alexander III and the sly, subtle diplomacy of his opponent, Bismarck. All the open-hearted monarch could do was exclaim, "Archbeast!" For that reason, the Franco–Russian alliance was not drawn up until 1891–93, after Bismarck had left the political arena. Alexander III signed the Franco–Russian military convention in December 1893, on the eve of his fatal illness, as if closing the books on the most important endeavor of his life. He made Russia safe from Germany's growing aggressiveness, while simultaneously taking a step toward a future world war.

S.Iu. Witte, Alexander III's fervent admirer, who saw in him the firm hand that would make it possible for Witte to mobilize the country's economic potential in order to transform it, assumed that the emperor would at long last see the necessity of liberal reforms. But that was unlikely. In any case, there was not enough time left in his life for that. Fate was merciless to Alexander III. In early 1894 his illness (nephritis, which is thought to have developed owing to injuries that he received during a wreck of the Imperial train at Borki Station) began progressively to worsen. This huge, powerful man, who once inspired fear, grew emaciated and gaunt; his temples were sunken and his ears stuck out. Owing to his ailment he became forgetful even while talking, and he lived between despair and hope; periodically he would begin to believe in some kind of simple treatment. He was not yet fifty years old when he died in the Crimea in October 1894, leaving his vast country to his eldest son, whom he himself considered just a boy clearly unready for affairs of state.

Notes

1. A. Benua [Alexandre Benois], *Moi vospominaniia*, bks. 1–3 (Moscow, 1990), p. 591.

2. Quoted in A.A. Polovtsov, *Dnevnik gosudarstvennogo sekretaria*, vol. 2 (Moscow, 1966), p. 426.

3. E.A. Peretts, *Dnevnik (1880–1883)* (Moscow–Leningrad, 1927), p. 46.

4. B.N. Chicherin, *Vospominaniia: Zemstvo i Moskovskaia duma* (Moscow, 1934), p. 109.

5. S.S. Tatishchev, "Imperator Aleksandr III. Ego zhizn' i tsarstvovanie," RGIA, f. 878, op. 1, d. 4, l. 55.

6. Ibid., l. 327.

7. V.P. Meshcherskii, *Moi vospominaniia* (n.p., 1898), pt. 2 (1865–1881 gg.), p. 4.

8. Alexander III and Maria Fedorovna had three sons and two daughters: Nicholas (1868–1918), emperor from 1894 until his abdication in 1917, who was shot in 1918 in Ekaterinburg; George (1871–1899), who died of tuberculosis; Xenia (1875–1933), who married Grand Duke Alexander Mikhailovich and emigrated; Michael (1878–1918), in whose favor Nicholas II abdicated, but who never ascended the throne and who was executed in Perm in 1918; and Olga (1882–1960), who first married Duke P.A. Oldenburgskii, then an officer named N.A. Kulikovskii, and who emigrated.

9. *K.P. Pobedonostsev i ego korrespondenty* (Moscow–Petrograd, 1923), vol. 1, pt. 2, p. 1008.

10. D.A. Miliutin, *Dnevnik*, vol. 1 (Moscow, 1947), p. 116.

11. *K.P. Pobedonostsev i ego korrespondenty*, vol. 1, pt. 2, p. 1009.

12. *Starina i novizna*, bk. 2 (St. Petersburg, 1898), pp. 256–66.

13. Miliutin, *Dnevnik*, vol. 2 (Moscow, 1949), p. 102; *K.P. Pobedonostsev i ego korrespondenty*, vol. 1, pt. 2, p. 1016.

14. *K.P. Pobedonostsev i ego korrespondenty*, vol. 1, pt. 2, p. 1019.

15. Ibid., p. 1041.

16. *Imperatorskoe Russkoe istoricheskoe obshchestvo, 1866–1916* (Petrograd, 1916), p. 7.

17. *Starina i novizna*, bk. 3 (St. Petersburg, 1900), pp. 314–38.

18. *K.P. Pobedonostsev i ego korrespondenty*, vol. 1, pt. 2, p. 1035.

19. A.N. Kulomzin, "Perezhitoe," RGIA, f. 1642, op. 1, d. 189, ll. 32 ob.–33.

20. Miliutin, *Dnevnik*, vol. 4 (Moscow, 1950), p. 79.

21. I.S. Turgenev, *Polnoe sobranie sochinenii i pisem* (Moscow, 1982), vol. 10, pp. 288–89.

22. *K.P. Pobedonostsev i ego korrespondenty*, vol. 1, pt. 2, pp. 46–47.

23. H.-L. von Schweinitz, *Denkwürdigkeiten des Botschafters* (Berlin, [1927]), vol. 2, p. 157.

24. *Konstitutsiia grafa Loris-Melikova i ego chastnye pis'ma* (Berlin, 1904), p. 75.

25. *K.P. Pobedonostsev i ego korrespondenty*, vol. 1, no. 2, p. 49.

26. *Krasnyi arkhiv*, 1927, no. 3, p. 250.

27. *Russkii arkhiv*, 1906, no. 4, p. 624.

28. Miliutin, *Dnevnik*, vol. 4, p. 155.

29. S.F. Librovich, *Na knizhnom postu. Vospominaniia. Zapiski. Dokumenty* (Petrograd, 1916), pp. 298–99.

30. V.N. Lamsdorf, *Dnevnik, 1891–1892* (Moscow–Leningrad, 1934), p. 274.

31. *K.P. Pobedonostsev i ego korrespondenty*, vol. 1, pt. 2, p. 542.

32. A.A. Polovtsov, *Dnevnik gosudarstvennogo sekretaria*, vol. 1 (Moscow, 1966), p. 243.

33. Ibid., pp. 287–88.

34. Portrayals of this policy are reproduced in S.N. Valk's generalized study and in P.A. Zaionchkovskii's monographic study. See S.N. Valk, "Vnutrenniaia politika tsarizma v 80-kh–nachale 90-kh godov," in *Istoriia SSSR: Rossiia v period pobedy i utverzhdeniia kapitalizma (1856–1894)* (Moscow, 1951), pt. 1; P.A. Zaionchkovskii, *Rossiiskoe samoderzhavie v kontse XIX stoletiia* (Moscow, 1970).

35. A.S. Suvorin, *Dnevnik* (Moscow–Petrograd, 1923), p. 166.

Emperor Nicholas II, 1894–1917

Russian readers waited long for a historical portrait of Nicholas II written by serious historians. B.V. Ananich and R.Sh. Ganelin, both corresponding members of the Russian Academy of Sciences, have devoted their careers to illuminating the reign of Nicholas II and in this regard are well qualified to author this essay. Their dispassionate approach to Nicholas results in a succinct account of his reign that will be familiar to readers who know the Western literature. Avoiding broad generalizations and even a unifying argument, the authors draw heavily on firsthand accounts and on Nicholas's own correspondence. Weak-willed and distrustful, Nicholas shared many of the views of his father and of his tutors, especially K. P. Pobedonostsev. More comfortable in his private life than in his role as emperor, Nicholas fell under the influence of the empress. Be that as it may, the authors deemphasize Alexandra's role and the health of the tsarevich in bringing down the monarchy. They also relegate Rasputin's indiscretions to a footnote. Like French historian Marc Ferro,[1] the authors underscore the influence (often pernicious) of the grand dukes and the royal family, observing that conflict characterized it on the eve of the February Revolution. Although there has long been speculation over the private papers of Nicholas and Alexandra held in Soviet archives, Ananich and Ganelin do not discuss these materials and it is unclear to what extent they might have used them.

The authors seem to suggest that no matter how sympathetic one might be to Nicholas and his plight (they are not), it is difficult to present him in anything other than a negative light. Ananich and Ganelin back the long-held view that Nicholas granted concessions only when confronted with revolution but later renounced them when the revolutionary wave had subsided and he once again had gained the upper hand. Ascending the throne without a program or policy other than the firm conviction that he must defend the autocratic order, Nicho-

las and his empress shared a "psychological reliance on Divine Providence." Convinced of their divine right to rule, Nicholas and Alexandra are depicted not as tragic figures or as pawns in the historical drama, but as victims of circumstance. But to a large extent, the circumstances were of their own making.

D.J.R.

Note

1. Marc Ferro, *Nicholas II: The Last of the Tsars* (New York, 1993).

Nicholas II

Boris Vasilievich Ananich and Rafail Sholomovich Ganelin

Works on Russia at the beginning of the twentieth century present Nicholas II not as a politician and thinker but rather as the last representative of a dynasty that has since left the stage of history, a man with a tragic fate, imbued with a mystic sense of doom.[1]

The eldest son of Crown Prince Alexander Alexandrovich, who became Emperor Alexander III in 1881, and his wife Maria Fedorovna, the daughter of Danish King Christian IX (Princess Maria Sophia Frederika Dagmar prior to her marriage), Nicholas was born on 6 May 1868 at Tsarskoe Selo. On that day, a ceremonial salute was arranged in St. Petersburg and Tsarskoe Selo. By established tradition, the birth of a grand duke was celebrated by 301 shots (201 for a grand duchess). On this occasion, forty guns were fired in salute from the fortress at St. Petersburg. The grand duke was baptized on 30 May in the court chapel of the Grand Palace in Tsarskoe Selo. On that day he was awarded the Order of Andrew the First-Called (with chain), the Order of Alexander Nevsky, the Order of the White Eagle, the Order of Anna, first degree, and the Order of Stanislav, first degree. Thus, the future emperor's military service began from the day of his birth. By Alexander II's order he was registered in all regiments and units of the Life Guards in which his father was registered, and he was also appointed chief of the Sixty-fifth Moscow Infantry Regiment. At age seven he was promoted to second lieutenant in the Life Guards of the Preobrazhenskii Regiment. One year later, on the occasion of the 150th anniversary of the Academy of Sciences, he was elected an honorary member.

The heir to the throne started his schooling in 1877 under the supervision of Adjutant General G.G. Danilovich, who had previously served as inspector of instruction for the cadet corps and director of a military gymnasium. He drew up a primary-education curriculum consisting of twenty-four lessons per week: four classes each in Russian, arithmetic, and penmanship; three classes each in English and French; and two classes each in religion, history, and drawing. For six days a week, between nine o'clock in the morning and five o'clock in the afternoon, the heir to the throne had to spend four full hours at his studies, with breaks for lunch, for a walk outside, and for gymnastic exercises. This schedule also seems to have later governed Emperor Nicholas II's daily business routine.

The overall educational plan spanned twelve years. The first eight years were devoted to a gymnasium course of study, with ancient languages replaced by mineralogy, botany, zoology, anatomy, and physiology, and expanded studies in political history, Russian literature, French, and German. The last four years, to which one more had to be added, were devoted to a "course in the higher sciences"— military, juridical, and economic. The tsarevich received religious instruction from Archpriest I.L. Ianyshev, the royal family's confessor. The economic sciences were taught by Professor N.Kh. Bunge, the minister of finance and a thinker of liberal-reformist orientation, while the juridical sciences were taught by K.P. Pobedonostsev, a leading ideologist of conservatism who taught law to several of the grand dukes, including the future Alexander III. M.N. Kapustin taught international law. Political history was taught by E.E. Zamyslovskii, who lectured in Russian history at St. Petersburg University and the St. Petersburg Historical and Philological Institute. He was the author of several studies of foreigners' accounts of Muscovite Russia as well as a major authority on sources. N.N. Beketov taught chemistry.

The military cycle of studies was especially full, and the various subjects in it were presented by the most outstanding representatives of the various branches of military science—N.N. Obruchev (military statistics or military geography, providing a comprehensive geographical, ethnographical, military–economic, and political knowledge of possible theaters of operation), M.I. Dragomirov (troops' combat training), G.A. Leer (strategy and military history), N.A. Demianenko (artillery), P.L. Lobko (military administration), O.E. Shtubendorf (geodesy and topography), P.M. Gudim-Levkovich (tactics), Ts.A. Kiui (fortifications), and A.K. Puzyrevskii (history of military science).

In 1884, when Nicholas turned sixteen, he was promoted to the rank of lieutenant and made an honorary member of the Russian Archeological Society and St. Petersburg and Moscow universities. In order to gain experience in front-line service and become acquainted with military life, he attended two camps with the Preobrazhenskii Regiment, serving first as a subaltern ("half-company officer"—that is, junior officer in the company) and then as company commander. He spent two summer seasons in the cavalry as a platoon officer and squadron commander in a hussars regiment, spent one camp serving in the artillery and, prior to ascending the throne, commanded the First Battalion of the Preobrazhenskii Regiment in the rank of colonel. Nicholas II considered himself of this rank when he was on the throne as well. He had been promoted to colonel in 1892.

To become acquainted with the state administration, starting in 1889 the tsarevich began to participate in the work of the State Council and the Committee of Ministers. With the same purpose in mind, he also accompanied his father on travels around the country, and from October 1890 to August 1891 he traveled to the Far East, going there by sea[2] and coming home overland, across Siberia; in Vladivostok he took part in launching the construction of the Trans-Siberian Railroad. In connection with this journey by the heir to the throne, a royal edict declared a partial amnesty for persons serving time in Siberia. In late 1891 Nicholas was appointed chairman of the Special Committee to Aid the Needy in famine areas, and in 1892 he was made head of the Siberian Railroad Committee.

When Alexander III fell gravely ill in April 1894, Nicholas became betrothed to twenty-two-year-old Princess Alix, the daughter of the grand duke of Hesse-Darmstadt, the granddaughter of England's Queen Victoria and the sister of Ernst Ludwig, also grand duke of Hesse-Darmstadt. The bride arrived in Russia one and a half weeks before Alexander III's death, which came on 20 October. On the next day, 21 October, she converted to Orthodoxy, taking the name Alexandra Fedorovna; the wedding took place on 14 November.

A change of rulers in Russia was almost always accompanied by the public's hopes for changes of a liberal character, hopes that liberties would be granted. The press and the public looked for the slightest grounds for such hopes, and were ready to perceive them even in so insignificant an episode as Nicholas's buying gloves for his bride in a

Nicholas II

shop on Nevskii Prospekt. Both the Russian and the European press used this episode as evidence that the young emperor had democratic leanings.[3]

Nicholas II, however, ascended the throne with the firm intention of strictly following his father's political course. On 17 January 1895, at a triumphant reception of zemstvo deputies who had come to offer congratulations on his wedding, Nicholas II cautioned against "senseless dreams about the participation of zemstvo representatives in matters of domestic administration." "Let everyone be aware that as I devote all my efforts to the people's well-being, I will defend the principle of autocracy just as firmly and unswervingly as my unforgettable late father did," he stated. This was the new tsar's response to the Tver zemstvo, which had hinted at the possibility of a constitutional future. This meeting with the tsar distressed most of those who had taken part in the ceremony. One of them said, "This little officer came out; he had a piece of paper in his cap. He began to mutter something, glancing at the piece of paper from time to time, and suddenly he yelled, 'senseless dreams'—and we realized that we were being scolded for something, but why did he have to snarl?"[4]

The tsar's speech not only caused disappointment and unhappiness among society's liberal circles, but nurtured the process of consolidation. Nicholas II's statement received full approval only from Pobedonostsev in Russia and Wilhelm II in Germany. On the eve of the coronation, Pobedonostsev published a treatise defending the national character of the autocracy. He devoted many pages in this work to exposing bourgeois democracy as a mechanism of "parliamentary hypocrisy," and to arguing that any constitution is "the biggest lie of our time."[5]

Preserving the inviolability of the autocratic principle of government was an article of faith for the royal couple, who were sincerely convinced of their divine right to rule. Affirming the widespread belief that Pobedonostsev was a major influence on the tsar, Grand Duke Alexander Mikhailovich wrote: "His cynical mind influenced the young emperor in ways designed to teach him to fear any innovation."[6] In this regard, moreover, Alexandra Fedorovna played a considerable role, because of her character (A.A. Vyrubova, who was close to the royal family for many years, believed that the empress understood people better than her husband did and could not help noticing flattery and perfidy in members of the tsar's entourage),[7] because she was a neophyte to Orthodoxy, and because of the particular position she held within the royal family. In general, both Nicholas and Alexandra felt an inherent suspicion toward the various manifestations, even trivial ones, encroaching on tsarist absolutism. This was true concerning the actions not only of democrats or liberals but even of relatives. Later, people began to call them the "Grand-Ducal Party," by sarcastic analogy with the various political parties that opposed the monarchy. On the day Alexander III died, his heir said to Grand Duke Alexander Mikhailovich, "What will happen to Russia now? I am not yet ready to be tsar. I do not know how to run the empire. I don't even know how to talk to the ministers."[8]

The emperor was the head of the royal family, which included more than forty of his relatives, uncles among them. According to Alexander Mikhailovich, during the first ten years Nicholas II listened to their advice and instructions "with a feeling that bordered on horror." "He was afraid to be left alone with them," Alexander Mikhailovich wrote. "They were always demanding something. Nikolai Nikolaevich fancied himself a great military commander. Alexei Alexandrovich was ruler of the seas. Sergei Alexandrovich wanted to convert the governor-generalship of Moscow into his own patrimony. Vladimir Alexandrovich was a patron of the arts. Each of them had his own favorites among the generals and admirals, who had to be promoted and elevated in rank out of turn; each had his own ballerinas who would have liked to arrange a Russian season in Paris; each had his own remarkable missionaries thirsting to save the emperor's soul; each had his own miracle-working doctors requesting an audience; each had his own clairvoyant sages sent from above . . . , and so forth."[9]

Among the grand dukes, of course, some were held in high public regard—for example, the poet Constantine Constantinovich and the well-known historian Nikolai Mikhailovich, a Francophile and advocate of parliamentarianism who, nevertheless, feared that introducing it into Russia would prove unsuccessful. Alexander Mikhailovich considered his own father, Mikhail Nikolaevich, highly experienced in matters of state administration: he was chairman of the State Council and an inspector general of artillery who served for more than twenty years as the head of the administration in the Caucasus, although he had acquired the habit of blind obedience to anything the tsar said or did.[10]

One of the most bitter conflicts within the royal family erupted in 1896, over the catastrophe at Khodynka Field in Moscow during the coronation ceremonies that resulted in more than 2,600 casualties, including 1,389 deaths. The younger grand dukes, the four sons of

Mikhail Nikolaevich, demanded the cessation of ceremonies and the immediate resignation of Sergei Alexandrovich, who was supported by the older members of the Imperial family. Nikolai Mikhailovich warned the tsar not to go to the French ambassador's ball, but Nicholas II attended it. "The radiant smile on Grand Duke Sergei's face prompted foreigners to remark that the Romanovs lacked judgment," Alexander Mikhailovich wrote later.[11]

When Nicholas II ascended the throne he had no particular domestic policy program. This created disorganization in the functioning of the state apparatus. Because Russia did not have a united government, the political course of action developed out of rivalry among the ministers and was defined by the policies of the ministries, in particular the Ministry of Finance and the Ministry of Internal Affairs, which were in charge of the empire's economic might and domestic security, respectively. During the early part of Nicholas II's reign, he was influenced by Procurator-General of the Holy Synod K.P. Pobedonostsev, Chairman of the Committee of Ministers I.N. Durnovo, Minister of Finance S.Iu. Witte, and also I.L. Goremykin, who was appointed minister of internal affairs in 1895.

Although not a stupid man, Goremykin was "extremely lazy . . . , shallow, and conceited." He would "undertake any job without a definite plan," guided only by the general rule of "accommodating commands from above, no matter how often they change[d]."[12] He combined a desire to please and "to hold onto his job" with a rather cynical attitude not only toward the other representatives of the higher bureaucracy but even toward Nicholas II himself. When A.N. Kulomzin, the business manager of the Committee of Ministers, reprimanded Goremykin for not submitting timely explanations in response to "the sovereign's notes on the reports" of the Ministry of Internal Affairs, Goremykin said, "Why should we have to answer every one of his scribbles?"[13] In the late 1890s, Goremykin openly complained to War Minister A.N. Kuropatkin about the "domestic squabbling," for which he mostly blamed the tsar. Witte described the tsar as a man "without a strong will," a man who was ill-prepared and who dealt with everything "on the spur of the moment" without giving the least thought to the "importance of preparatory work for any particular decision."

In December 1897 Grand Duke Mikhail Nikolaevich explained to Kuropatkin, who had taken over the War Ministry from P.S. Vannovskii, that "everything needs to be settled without getting the sovereign involved in the decision." "You'll have a lot of worries," he said to Kuropatkin; "the ministers foul things up. Each one tries to circumvent the law."[14] The royal family was kindly disposed toward Kuropatkin; he was often invited to lunch.

Alexandra Fedorovna hardly ever spoke Russian during the first years of her reign, although she understood spoken Russian very well. The tsar himself took part in her instruction in the language. In the evenings he would read to her Leo Tolstoy's *War and Peace*, Gogol's *Taras Bulba*, or N.K. Shilder's works about Alexander I's reign. As a joke, Nicholas II ordered Kuropatkin to converse with Alexandra Fedorovna only in Russian. But when Kuropatkin tried to address the tsaritsa in Russian in December 1898 she answered him in French "that her progress in the Russian language had been minor and she found it hard to learn."[15] To be sure, after a few years she spoke Russian fluently.

Descriptions of meetings with the royal family occupy much space in Kuropatkin's diary; he also reproduced the reports he sent to Nicholas II while in charge of the Transcaspian region, and later while war minister—not only in substantial detail but even with conversations as he remembered them. In these entries, the tsar seems more like a well-informed and lively conversationalist than a major state figure with a well-thought-out military and foreign policy program. Nicholas, incidentally, definitely adhered to at least two principles: Russia must expand its influence in the Near, Middle, and Far East; and "Nicholas I was right when he said that 'where the Russian foot has trod, it shall not be moved.'" Nonetheless, the tsar listened attentively to Kuropatkin when the latter warned against military adventurism, and often agreed with his arguments.

When Nicholas II asked, "What should we do in Afghanistan?" Kuropatkin said decisively, "There is no reason to take a single inch of Afghan soil," and the tsar not only agreed with him but added, "It's easy to advance, but it's hard to stop." Kuropatkin told him about the "physical and ethnographic" characteristics of war conditions in Afghanistan: the "inevitability of having to fight the mountain population . . . , the fact that topographic borders do not match ethnographic borders," the lack of roads, and the inevitability of enormous losses in the event of a war. Nicholas II accepted these explanations with full comprehension, and responded, "So again it would be the Russian peasant who would have to pay for all this."[16]

Kuropatkin and the tsar, however, disagreed on the problem of the Straits. The tsar allowed himself to be pulled into the dubious project of seizing the Bosporus in the autumn of 1896. The project was canceled only thanks to active opposition from Witte, backed up by Pobedonostsev. Nicholas II, however, could not give up the seductive idea of taking possession of "the Bosporus and the Dardanelles at the same time." Kuropatkin was among those who advocated the seizure of the Bosporus, but he tried to convince the tsar that it would be dangerous to seize the Dardanelles and might lead to a European war. Nicholas II thought that the seizure of the Straits was "a matter of a few hours." "You have half convinced me that we do not yet need the Dardanelles," he responded to Kuropatkin's arguments.[17]

By the end of the 1890s, Witte's influence came to dominate governmental policy. He produced a program for the accelerated modernization of Russia's economy. The minister of finance promised that if the reforms he mapped out were implemented, Russia would overtake the industrially developed countries of Europe in ten years. He introduced the gold standard into the country, opened the economy to foreign capital, effected the mobilization of domestic resources by increasing indirect taxation and exploiting the government monopoly on alcohol, and instituted protective tariffs for Russia's industry. Drawing on the Franco–Russian alliance in Europe for support, the tsarist government embarked on active economic expansion in the Far and Middle East with the aim of capturing markets for Russia's developing industry.

In implementing his political course of action, Witte enjoyed Nicholas II's support. The tsar accepted his economic program because it was supposed to strengthen Russia's economic might without encroaching on the foundations of the autocratic system of state administration. Witte's attempts in 1898 to accomplish a revision of the government's agrarian policy, however, met with significant resistance from opponents in the Ministry of Internal Affairs and did not receive Nicholas II's approval. By 1902, when V.K. von Plehve was appointed to the post of minister of internal affairs, Witte's influence had begun to decline. In August 1903 he was removed as minister of finance and appointed to the unimportant post of chairman of the Committee of Ministers. The initiative in defining the country's political course moved to the Ministry of Internal Affairs. Witte's influence and that of Minister of Foreign Affairs V.N. Lamsdorf also began to decline as Russia advanced in the Far East, Manchuria, and Korea. The levers of policy wound up in the hands of the "Bezobrazov gang," as Witte called the group of persons headed by State Secretary A.M. Bezobrazov, people who did not hold official posts but exerted influence on the tsar. This kind of "unofficial influence," which grew inordinately during Nicholas II's reign, was one manifestation of an obvious crisis of authority.

At the very beginning of his reign when the tsar deferred to his mother, the dowager empress Maria Fedorovna, thereby making Empress Alexandra Fedorovna unhappy, hostile relations developed between her and Maria Fedorovna's numerous supporters. These relationships became even further strained because Alexandra Fedorovna was unable to achieve the kind of popularity that her mother-in-law continued to enjoy. The young tsaritsa said, "Empress Maria Fedorovna is beloved because the empress knows how to elicit that love and feels relaxed in the context of court etiquette. But I do not know how to do so, and it is difficult for me to be among people when I am distressed."[18] For all that, Alexandra Fedorovna was convinced of the omnipotence of imperial authority. On one occasion she demanded that the well-known international reference work published in Germany, the *Almanach de Gotha*, refrain from printing under the rubric "Russia" the words "the dynasty of the Holstein-Gottorp–Romanovs." A letter was sent to the editors, but they answered that Paul I had been the son of Duke Peter of Holstein-Gottorp. Then Alexandra Fedorovna demanded that the *Almanach* be banned from Russia, despite its quite legitimate character, but doing this would have provoked a scandal of European scope.[19]

As with all relations within the royal family, Alexandra Fedorovna's position in it could not help but affect the tsar's behavior. This alone, however, did not account for his secretiveness, his evasiveness in dealing with business, his effort to avoid open polemics or political struggle, and his tendency instead to announce his decision to the person or persons whom it concerned at the last possible moment—all traits that caused his contemporaries to speak of his devious character. "I always consult with everybody about everything, and then I do things my way," he acknowledged once.

"Nicholas II," wrote General A.A. Mosolov, the head of a chancellery of the Ministry of the Imperial Court in 1900–1917,

> did not like to argue, partly owing to his painfully developed pride and partly owing to his fear that someone might show his views to be wrong or convince others that they were, and he, being aware of his inability to stand up for his views, considered that offensive. This defect of Nicholas II's character caused him to act in ways that many considered dishonest; in reality, however, these were nothing more than manifestations of a lack of civic courage. . . . He dismissed persons, even those who had served him a long time, with remarkable ease. All it took was for people

... to start slandering someone, without even producing factual information, and the tsar would consent to dismiss the person. The tsar never tried to determine for himself who was right and who was wrong, what was truth and what was slander.... Least of all was the tsar inclined to defend any of his close associates or to try to determine what motivated slander that was brought to his, the tsar's, attention. Like all weak individuals, he was mistrustful.[20]

Directly manifesting strength of character was not easy for Nicholas II. Describing how he put down the ministers' "mutiny" against the removal of Grand Duke Nikolai Nikolaevich from the post of supreme commander in chief and his own assumption of these duties, A. Vyrubova wrote:

I dined with Their Majesties prior to the meeting, which was scheduled for that evening. At dinner the sovereign was agitated, and he said that no matter what arguments were presented to him he would remain adamant. When he left, he said to us: "Well, pray for me!" I remember taking off my icon and placing it in his hand. Time passed; the empress was becoming nervous.... The clock struck eleven, but the tsar still had not returned.... They were serving tea when the sovereign came in, very happy, threw himself into his armchair, and extending his arms to us said, "I was adamant. Look how much I've sweated!" He gave my icon back to me, laughed, and continued, "I kept squeezing it in my left hand all the time. After listening to all the ministers' long, boring speeches, I expressed myself approximately as follows: 'Gentlemen! My will is firm, I am leaving for Headquarters in two days!' Some of the ministers really looked crestfallen!"[21]

Pobedonostsev considered the tsar impatient with "general problems" and capable of evaluating "the importance of a fact only in isolation, without relation to the rest, without any link to the aggregate of other facts, events, tendencies, and phenomena." Nicholas II himself once acknowledged to Kuropatkin that he made "hard work of trying to choose what he needed from what he had heard," that he found "it difficult to focus his mind," and that he thought that "this effort of the mind, if it were to pass to a horse (when he was mounted on it) would alarm it greatly."[22] Statements of this sort, exaggerated and generalized in the tradition of public affairs writings, earned Nicholas II a reputation as a man who was not very intelligent.

According to many contemporaries, however, the tsar had an excellent memory and a fairly good education in the humanities; he was interested in archeology and literature, he knew the history of the Church and was well versed in matters of theology. "My personal conversations with the tsar," wrote the well-known Russian scientist and legal expert A.F. Koni,

> have convinced me that this is a man who is undoubtedly intelligent, unless we consider the highest development of the mind to be the faculty of reason, the ability to encompass an entire aggregate of phenomena and conditions, rather than just to develop one's thinking exclusively in one direction. We might say that of the five stages of a person's thinking ability—instinct, judgment, wit, intelligence, and genius—he possessed only the middle one and, perhaps unconsciously, the first. . . . Meetings with him in ordinary life, if he were Colonel Romanov, might arouse some lively interest.[23]

Many of those around him thought Nicholas II's characteristic behavior and way of doing things were to a considerable extent caused by doubts about his level of state experience and his lack of a royal demeanor. He had inherited his small stature from his mother. When exchanging Easter kisses with his soldiers, Nicholas II "was obliged to stand on tiptoe in order to kiss a tall guardsman, while the soldier would have to bend politely toward the emperor."[24] This is probably why Minister of the Imperial Court V.B. Fredericks, according to Mosolov, always insisted that Nicholas II be on horseback when he showed himself to the crowd. "Despite his small stature," Mosolov wrote, "Nikolai Alexandrovich was an excellent horseman, and he really did make a more magnificent impression on horseback than on foot."[25] Meanwhile, the other Romanovs were distinguished by their height; Alexander III possessed an especially regal appearance, one in harmony with the reputation of an omnipotent sovereign. According to Alexander Mikhailovich, Nicholas II "gazed longingly at the portrait of his father and lamented that he could not speak the language of that awesome first lord of Russia."[26]

The tsar felt most comfortable in his private life. Daughters were born into the royal family one after another: Olga in 1895, Tatiana in 1897, Maria in 1899, and Anastasia in 1901. They were waiting for a male heir. A son, Alexei, was born in 1904, but it turned out that he suffered from incurable hemophilia. This inherited disease, which afflicts males but is transmitted through the female line, was widespread in the English royal house and was called the "Victorian disease." The family tragedy was compounded by certain of Alexandra Fedorovna's character traits, such as a tendency toward hysteria and fanatic religiousness along with a proclivity for superstition and strict puritanism.[27]

It was Kuropatkin's impression that Alexandra Fedorovna took an active part in dealing with important state matters from the very beginning of her reign, and that she acted as an adviser even with respect to issues that one would think were far outside her interests. She exerted influence on her husband's decisions and actions in various spheres of state administration. This is attested both by their correspondence and by the reminiscences of contemporaries. Even more important was that they both had the same cast of mind, with a psychological reliance on Divine Providence, as well as—and this cannot be ignored—a faith in "holy fools"* and charlatans who appeared at court, from the French quack "Doctor" Philippe to Grigorii Rasputin.[28]

In 1907, Nicholas II, clarifying his reliance on his own intuition in matters of state, wrote the following to P.A. Stolypin:

> I hereby return to you, unapproved, the journal of the Council of Ministers that relates to the Jewish question. . . . [The Council of Ministers had proposed the abolition of certain restrictions on the rights of Jews.—B.A., R.G.] Despite very convincing arguments in favor of approving this matter, my inner voice ever more insistently tells me that I must not take this decision upon myself. Until now my conscience has never deceived me, and I therefore intend to follow its dictates in this case. I know that you also believe that "the tsar's heart is in God's hands." . . . So be it. For all the rules I have laid down I shall answer in full before God on Judgment Day, and I am ready at any time to answer Him.

V.N. Kokovtsov, who served for many years as minister of finance and succeeded Stolypin as chairman of the Council of Ministers, wrote: "In not one of the documents in my hands have I seen such a clear manifestation of the mystical cast of mind in assessing the nature of his royal authority as is expressed in this letter from the sovereign to his chairman of the Council of Ministers."[29]

Nicholas II's reliance on God was combined with his naive belief that the ordinary people were inalterably devoted to their tsar. Even the events of 1905–7 failed to shake this belief in any substantial way. During discussion of the Statute on Elections to the State Duma in the summer of 1905, one of the conservative officials proposed that literacy be eliminated as a condition for election to the Duma. "Illiterate peasants," he said, "whether old men or young persons, have a more solid perception of the world than literate persons do."

---

*People who sought spiritual purification by committing foolish acts that would earn them public condemnation. In Russia, "holy fools" were highly revered, and even people who were merely simple-minded were often venerated.—D.J.R.

Despite Kokovtsov's remark that illiteracy does not guard peasant deputies against revolutionary influences ("they will only repeat in epic style what others tell them or suggest to them"), the tsar decided in favor of illiterate peasants having a "solid perception of the world."[30]

After the Manifesto of 17 October 1905, which proclaimed the creation of legislative representation and conferred political liberties, Nicholas II issued the Manifesto of 3 November, which halved the redemption payments stipulated in the 1861 reforms for 1906 and abolished them altogether as of 1907. It was his opinion that the latter was "incomparably more important than the civil liberties granted to Russia the other day."[31] There was a grain of truth in this, to be sure. However, his faith in the peasants' loyalty, like his belief in the common people's wholehearted love for the royal family, was nourished by a flood of loyal messages mostly inspired by the authorities or by monarchist civic organizations, as well as by impressions gained by Alexandra Fedorovna and Nicholas II during ceremonial occasions as they traveled around the country and especially when they visited holy places.

For the tsar the press did not play a big role as a reflection of public opinion. But he was interested in using the press as a means of shaping public opinion. In 1905–6, according to A.A. Spasskii-Odynets, the secretary of the Council of Ministers chairman, Witte, Nicholas II used to read the conservative *New Times* and *Society* and also, "however surprising it may seem," the liberal *Stock-Market Gazette.* The rest he called "rubbish," "trash," and even worse. Someone read them for His Majesty—most likely, General Trepov. This can be judged on the basis of remarks noted on pages sent to the chairman of the Council of Ministers, for example: "Sergei Iulievich! Can my government really be so helpless that it does not have the legal means to prosecute this revolutionary sh— in court?" (The word sh— was written with special clarity.) All these things served as a reason to publish a newspaper called *The Russian State* as an evening supplement to *The Government Herald.* This was the fourth newspaper which the sovereign read carefully.[32]

The way of life in the palace and the presence of guards made it hard for the royal family to have much contact with reality. The governmental apparatus, as personified by the ministers and governors, as well as several other persons who enjoyed the tsar's particular trust, for example, Prince V.P. Meshcherskii and agronomist A.A. Klopov, were those to whom the tsar turned in order to find out about various aspects of Russian life. Neither the tsar nor the members of his family had the slightest idea of the value of money. Only when they went abroad did they themselves make purchases; in Russia all their bills were paid by the treasury. The royal children were astonished once when they were given change in a store, wanting to know why the storekeeper did not take all the money for himself.

Nicholas II could draw about twenty million rubles a year. This amount came from appropriations to maintain the Imperial family from treasury funds (eleven million rubles), revenues from estate lands, and interest earned on capital invested abroad. However, the maintenance of the royal family, its numerous palaces and residences, Gatchina and the Grand Kremlin Palace in Moscow, along with their numerous staff, support of the Imperial theaters, receptions, and balls cost so much money that only about 200,000 rubles per year remained to meet the tsar's personal needs. Nicholas II never touched the 200 million rubles that had been invested in England since Alexander II's time. He did not spend any of that money until World War I, and then to provide for the needs of suffering families and the wounded. But shortly before the war, Minister of the Imperial Court Fredericks transferred to Berlin seven million rubles from the royal children's pensions which had also been left untouched.[33]

A total of twenty thousand rubles per year constituted the tsar's "own funds for domestic expenditures." This money was spent on his wardrobe, gifts, awards, and various kinds of grants and contributions. In addition, the tsar had at his personal disposal what was known as "economic capital." As of 1 January 1896 that sum amounted to more than two million rubles or 355,000 francs.[34] Nicholas II held a considerable quantity of internal and railroad bonds, four percent annuities, and other securities. The tsar also had a current account in the Volga–Kama Bank.[35]

To a considerable extent, the life of the royal family was spoiled by the *Okhrana* [secret police]—in particular because the family itself was the principal object of its surveillance. "Her Majesty found this 'protection' especially oppressive, and she protested. She said that she and the sovereign were worse off than prisoners," wrote A. Vyrubova. "Every step Their Majesties took was recorded, and even their telephone conversations were monitored. Nothing afforded Their Majesties more pleasure than to give the police the slip and successfully evade the surveillance."[36] The Okhrana, under the supervision of a palace commandant, included the palace police, an escort, and a combined regiment. Everyone who entered the palace was registered, then the visit was reported by telephone to the chief's office. Anybody whom the tsar or tsaritsa met and with whom they exchanged even a few words while taking a walk was later subjected to interrogation by Okhrana agents.

It was argued that these agents protected the tsar from terrorists; however, there was sometimes a close link between terrorists and the police department. After the Revolution of 1905–7,* A.V. Gerasimov, head of the St. Petersburg branch of the Okhrana, would not give the tsar permission to ride from his suburban residence to the capital city until he received assurance from E. Azef, who was simultaneously the leader of the militant organization of SRs [Socialist Revolutionaries] and a police informant, that his guerrillas were not in St. Petersburg that day. Hence, the tsar's security was largely in the hands of a provocateur. Moreover, danger could also come from the leadership of security.

A.A. Lopukhin, director of the police department, recalled a conversation he had had with Witte in 1903. Witte, just removed from his post as minister of finance, told him, tongue in cheek, of course: "The director of the police department, you know, essentially holds everyone's life and death in his hands, including the tsar's. So why not give some terrorist organization or other the chance to do away with him? The throne would go to his brother. [At that time Nicholas II still had no son.—B.A., R.G.] I, S.Iu. Witte, enjoy favor with him, and I could provide protection for you as well."[37]

The very fact that Lopukhin allowed himself to hold such a conversation and was willing to listen to Witte's hints testifies to the kind of mood that prevailed in the police department. B.V. Nikolskii, one of the leaders of the Black Hundreds who enjoyed Nicholas II's trust but was dissatisfied with his policies, contemplated the possibility of not only overthrowing the tsar but also of "something Serbian"—referring to the assassination of the Serbian king Alexander Obrenovich and his wife Draga on 29 May 1903 as a result of an officers' conspiracy.[38]

The royal couple lived in an atmosphere of suspicion and mistrust. Not without reason, Nicholas II doubted his ministers' sincerity, and generally he was not above butting heads with them; he kept track of what they were saying and writing. The ministers' diaries and other papers were generally confiscated after they died. Some of the journals of Minister of Internal Affairs D.S. Sipiagin were destroyed by the tsar, who blamed it on his adjutant general. When he served as minister of internal affairs, D.P. Sviatopolk-Mirskii prudently kept his own

---

*A revolutionary explosion breaking out as Russia suffered defeat in the Russo–Japanese War, the Revolution of 1905–7 forced Nicholas to introduce a limited parliamentary system, which he soon tried to subvert.—D.J.R.

diary in the form of his wife's; essentially he dictated what she wrote in it almost every day.[39] After Witte died in February 1915, his office in St. Petersburg was sealed immediately, and while its caretakers were away his vacation home in Biarritz in the south of France was searched by agents of Russia's secret service abroad. The agents hunted for the manuscript of Witte's memoirs, but they were unaware that he had prudently hidden it in a safe in a French bank.[40] Although the tsar was a cultivated man who knew how not to let his feelings show, he was nevertheless unable to conceal his happiness at Witte's death. After Witte insisted on publishing the Manifesto of 17 October 1905 and became the first to occupy the post of prime minister, the tsar saw him as an enemy of the autocracy.

Nicholas II considered it his duty to pass on to his own son the authority he had inherited from his father, in all its inviolability. This adherence to the idea of autocracy drew upon a tradition of many years, both secular and ecclesiastical, on a conservative historiography and social thought, and, finally, on the sincere conviction that the existing system was essential to the general welfare. Not only the principles of popular representation but even the idea of a united government were profoundly alien to the tsar.

Before the Revolution of 1905, nothing in the country resembled either a representative institution or a united government. Although he enjoyed the exclusive right to convene the legally constituted Council of Ministers and determine the representation therein, Nicholas II—just like Alexander III, incidentally—never did convene it. Instead, he preferred to receive his ministers' most loyal reports face to face, in private, lest they unite even under his own chairmanship. The threat of revolution forced the tsar to opt for reform; when the revolutionary movement declined, he renounced the concessions he had made earlier. Evidently failing to recognize the seriousness of the warning from Minister of Internal Affairs D.P. Sviatopolk-Mirskii concerning the dimensions of the revolutionary threat, the tsar gutted the Edict of 12 December 1904 and with his own hand rescinded the paragraph convening representation.

After "Bloody Sunday,"* people on all sides persistently warned Nicholas II about the need for reforms. On two occasions during the second half of January, A.S. Ermolov, the minister of agriculture and state domains, talked with him in no uncertain terms regarding this

---

*The government's brutal suppression of a peaceful workers' demonstration in January 1905, usually considered the opening salvo of the Revolution of 1905–7.—D.J.R.

issue—and Ermolov was a man who, because of his character and lack of political ambitions, could never be suspected of wishing to encroach on the tsar's prerogatives, as Witte generally was. Finally, on 3 February the tsar convened the Council of Ministers. In opening the meeting, he said that he was torn ("I'm tossing and turning") between the desire not to deviate in any way from the autocratic method of government ("to postpone it to a calmer time," which actually meant refraining as much as possible from making concessions) and the fear of "losing everything." Referring to the fact that he had removed the paragraph on representation from the Edict of 12 December 1904, Nicholas II explained this as due to "weighty considerations" that continued to guide his actions, which he summarized in the elaborate formula "a parliamentariland of attorneys." Each element in the formula—parliament, Finland with its special status and rights, and attorneys—represented a concept that irritated him.

The tsar's understanding of history was also pressed into service as he argued against the necessity of changes ("we did not have feudalism, we always had unity and trust"), a conception that corresponded to the idea almost universally accepted in prerevolutionary historiography of the traditional absence of conflict among political interests in Russian society. From the very beginning, Nicholas II did not conceal his attitude toward representation ("I do not understand representation. Nobody understands the Assembly of the Land").[41]

The tsar always explained the appearance of the Manifesto of 17 October by reference to the hopelessness of his position. On 16 October he had written to one of his personal representatives, General D.F. Trepov, "Yes, Russia is being granted a constitution. Too few of us fought against it. We received no support in our struggle from anywhere; each day, a larger number of people turned away from us, and eventually the inevitable happened. Nevertheless, in conscience I prefer to give away everything at once instead of being forced in the near future to give way on petty things yet end up in the same place."[42]

Nicholas II hated the State Duma from the moment of its creation. This is attested by recollections about the opening of the Duma on 26 April 1906. According to A.F. Koni, the representatives of the ruling house viewed the opening ceremony itself as the funeral of the autocracy.[43] Even then, Nicholas II expressed his attitude toward the newly formed "parliament." On the day the First Duma was dissolved, the tsar wrote in his diary: "It's done! Today the Duma is closed down."[44]

Nicholas II took an active part in preparations for the coup on 3 June 1907. In a letter delivered at two o'clock in the morning on 2

June 1907, sent from Peterhof to St. Petersburg, where the ministers were waiting in Stolypin's summer residence for a courier bringing the manifesto that dissolved the Duma, the tsar demonstrated the qualities, seemingly uncharacteristic, of a firm and resolute politician. "I waited impatiently all day for your report that the dissolution of the damned Duma was accomplished," he wrote. "But at the same time, my heart told me that it could not be done cleanly and that there would be delays. That is unacceptable. The Duma must be dissolved tomorrow, Sunday morning. Firmness and resolve—that's what Russia needs to see. The dissolution of the Duma right now is correct and urgently necessary. Not a single delay, not a moment's wavering!"[45]

Any cooperation between the autocracy and the First and Second State Dumas proved impossible. Relations also remained strained between Nicholas II and the first Council of Ministers, formed in October 1905, and its chairman, Witte. The only thing that united them was the need to oppose the revolution. The Council of Ministers simulated the activity of bourgeois government, while Nicholas II received loyal reports from his ministers in strict accordance with the established ritual.

Cooperation—or, more accurately, coexistence—between the united government and the representative institution, on the one hand, and the autocracy, on the other, became more or less stable only after the coup of 3 June 1907. Stolypin, a master politician, wanted to reconcile the irreconcilable: the legislature and the autocracy. Many of his governmental reform projects relating to the completion of the reforms of the 1860s—for example, the introduction of zemstvos into the western district—were unsuccessful. Stolypin's policy annoyed Nicholas II, who did not want to have to cope with the recently emerged political parties of the Russian bourgeoisie. The people around the tsar turned him against Stolypin, just as they had earlier turned him against Witte, by encouraging the royal couple's suspicion of the head of the united government which, with the Duma in place, was becoming an influential repository of power. And although the tsar and tsaritsa were enthusiastic in their reception of Stolypin's words—"You need major upheavals; we need a great Russia"—and although Nicholas II liked the prime minister, he once remarked over tea, "Stolypin would be happy to take my place."[46]

Witte and Stolypin were masters at adapting the feudal form of government to the developing bourgeois attitudes, and they were political pragmatists. Their successors did not even try to emulate them. By the eve of World War I, the government no longer had a specific political program, either bourgeois liberal or conservative.

The people who led the government were not statesmen of sufficiently broad views. The political course of action was dictated by the interests of the moment and by principles founded on the desire at least to preserve the supremacy of tsarist authority if not actually to restore the autocratic order that had existed before 1905. In 1915 this became the subject of bitter conflict between the tsar and his ministers, when Nicholas II dismissed Grand Duke Nikolai Nikolaevich (who had been favored by the Duma members) from his post as supreme commander in chief and took over the post himself. He refused to satisfy public demands for the creation of not only a government responsible to the Duma but also a ministry of trust comprising ministers who enjoyed the Duma's support.

Nicholas II's assumption of the post of supreme commander in chief was explained officially as necessary to "raise the army's morale." According to the testimony of Georgii Shavelskii, the archpriest of the army and navy stationed at the Supreme Command Headquarters in Mogilev, this event caused rejoicing only in the Rasputin camp. "In military affairs," the tsar "represented, to say the least, an unknown quantity; his military talents and knowledge have never been in evidence anywhere," and "his overall spiritual makeup was least suited for that of supreme military commander."[47]

At Headquarters, Nicholas II spent a considerable part of the day surrounded by his retinue. He rose at nine o'clock, dressed and groomed himself, and after morning prayers went to the mess hall for tea, where members of his retinue were already waiting for him. At eleven o'clock the tsar went to receive reports and familiarize himself with the operational situation, and conferred with the chief of staff General M.V. Alekseev to discuss and to decide matters concerning the army. After twelve o'clock, Nicholas II returned to the palace. "Strictly speaking," Shavelskii wrote,

> that hour-long report session constituted all of the sovereign's work as supreme commander in chief. His participation in ordinary work was, of course, out of the question. That work was done by the chief of staff, with or without the participation of his aides, and the finished reports and decisions were brought to the sovereign, who was free to accept or reject them. The chief of staff hardly ever had emergency reports. In all the time the sovereign spent at Headquarters, General Alekseev went to the palace with an emergency report only once or twice. Generally he issued urgent orders and commands on his own, without the sovereign's prior approval, and did not report on them until afterward.[48]

Lunch began at 12:30. His Majesty's lunches and dinners were attended by more than twenty people—grand dukes who happened to be at Headquarters, his retinue, foreign military agents, and the governor of Mogilev. Although it was wartime, the lunch and dinner ceremonies were quite lengthy. Because of this, General Alekseev requested that he be excused from mandatory attendance at them. After lunch the tsar received reports from the minister of the Imperial court or other ministers if they had come to Headquarters, and later, around three o'clock, he went out for a drive accompanied by the palace commandant and several members of his retinue. Usually they drove out of town in cars and then walked about ten kilometers; sometimes they took boat rides on the Dnieper.

Tea was served between five and six o'clock in the afternoon. Then Nicholas II received his ministers' reports and wrote letters. Dinner began at 7:30. Both at lunch and at dinner the tsar usually drank one or two glasses of vodka and one or two glasses of wine. After dinner, conversations with dinner guests continued, frequently until nine o'clock in the evening. Tea was served at ten o'clock in the evening, after which, unless there were urgent matters, they played dice.

The press began to report that Goremykin, the chairman of the Council of Ministers (he had not taken part in the "ministers' mutiny"), had started to travel regularly to Tsarskoe Selo, reporting on affairs of state to Alexandra Fedorovna, who then wrote letters of advice to the tsar at Headquarters, and that in them she also made reference to Rasputin. In September 1915, when his ministers expressed their opposition at a meeting in Mogilev, Nicholas II muttered: "What is this, a strike against me?"[49] He started to replace his ministers and prime ministers at an ever-increasing rate. A game of "ministerial leapfrog" was under way, and people began to call the Council of Ministers "the somersault college."

Meanwhile, a rumor began to circulate widely—and spread rapidly—both at the front and at the rear that Alexandra Fedorovna, despite the war, maintained ties with her highly placed German relatives. She considered it essential to refute these rumors.[50] The tsar ordered a secret investigation of matters abroad. "Through a network of Russian agents in Switzerland and Germany," it was learned—though the explanation was rather unreliable—that the rumors had been fomented specifically by the German General Staff.[51]

After Nicholas II assumed the post of supreme commander in chief, "it was no longer the grand dukes' Headquarters but the tsar's." Besides Nikolai Nikolaevich, Sergei Mikhailovich, and Georgii Mikhailovich, the appointed hetman of the Cossack troops, Boris

Vladimirovich, and his brother Kirill Vladimirovich were generally to be found there. Alexander Mikhailovich, who was in charge of aviation, Prince A.P. Oldenburgskii, the supreme chief of the medical unit, and other members of the Imperial family also showed up at Headquarters. The tsar's brother, Michael, was away at the front. In the summer of 1916, General Alekseev complained to Shavelskii that the grand dukes interfered in the work at Headquarters. Boris Vladimirovich demanded a special train for himself, traveled around sectors of the front, and did nothing but "bother the troops." Grand Duchess Maria Pavlovna persuaded the tsar to provide the same kind of train for Kirill Vladimirovich, and only a vigorous protest from Alekseev, who explained to Nicholas II that "all the rail lines are overloaded" and "every car has to count," quashed this notion.[52]

The resignation of Nikolai Nikolaevich strengthened the influence of the empress, the retinue, and the "Rasputin party." Both verbally and in written form, the grand dukes warned Nicholas II and Alexandra Fedorovna against continuing the old policies. It was more than just a matter of ridding themselves of Rasputin. On 1 November 1916 Nikolai Mikhailovich demanded in the most decisive manner that the tsar not give in to the influence of "dark forces," including the empress. On 26 November an attempt was made to influence Alexandra Fedorovna as well. Kirill Vladimirovich's wife, Viktoria Fedorovna, tried to convince her of the necessity of getting G.E. Lvov, N.N. Pokrovskii, A.D. Samarin, and A.V. Krivoshein to serve as members of a government responsible to the Duma. But the tsaritsa stated that they were all enemies of the dynasty. "Who is against us? Petrograd and a gang of aristocrats who play bridge and understand nothing. I have been sitting on the throne for twenty-two years. I know Russia. I have traveled all over the country, and I know that the people love our family," she responded indignantly.[53]

Conflict was brewing in the royal family. It could hardly keep from being exacerbated by the long-standing problems in the relationships between Nicholas II and the grand dukes, caused by his obligation to keep track of the matrimonial aspects of their lives and not to allow them to contract morganatic marriages—that is, to marry persons who did not belong to the ruling houses of Europe.[54] Later, however, Nicholas II was obliged to recognize these marriages. Mikhail Alexandrovich's wife became Countess Brasova (named for an estate that belonged to him). And Grand Duke Pavel Alexandrovich wrote a letter to the tsar requesting that his wife, O.V. Pistolkors, be elevated to the rank of princess and attached a note from Rasputin supporting his petition.

It was Rasputin's influence on the tsar and tsaritsa that brought the conflict in the Romanov family to a critical point on 17 December 1916. Rasputin was murdered in the palace of Felix Iusupov, who had married the tsar's niece, the daughter of Alexander Mikhailovich and the tsar's sister Xenia. Grand Duke Dmitrii Pavlovich participated in planning the murder. Iusupov and Dmitrii Pavlovich were expelled from the capital city without trial or investigation, and the latter was assigned to General Baratov's detachment in Iran. Rasputin's murder proved to be a kind of harbinger of the approaching revolution. A split occurred among the Romanovs. Most of the grand dukes came to Dmitrii Pavlovich's defense. Just before the new year, 1917, Grand Duke Nikolai Mikhailovich was also exiled to the estate of Grushevka in Kherson Province.

On 1 March 1917 Nikolai Mikhailovich returned to Petrograd and announced his support for the Provisional Government. Kirill Vladimirovich, Nicholas II's cousin, who had been best man at his wedding and who was a close friend of Mikhail Alexandrovich, became the first of the grand dukes to recognize the Provisional Government in the Tauride Palace during the February Revolution. Several days later he gave an interview to the correspondent of *The Russian Will.* Kirill Vladimirovich was happy, the correspondent reported. "At last I'm free," Kirill Vladimirovich told him, "and I can speak freely on the telephone. Before, they interrupted me every minute. We were living almost publicly under police surveillance."[55]

The conflict in the Romanov family on the eve of the February events reflected the overall crisis of authority as well as its paradoxical character. The feudal system of family governance not only failed to bring prosperity and well-being to the country, but even weighed heavily on the members of the Imperial family themselves.

It may be that Nicholas II's main character traits and his demeanor as a statesman were most fully manifest in his behavior during February and March 1917, first at Headquarters in Mogilev and later at the headquarters of the Northern Front in Pskov. The tsar was usually slow in evaluating the reports on the events taking place at that time in Petrograd. Even though he sent a telegram on 25 February to General S.S. Khabalov, commander of the Petrograd Military District, with instructions to "put a stop to the disorders in the capital city, as they are unacceptable in this difficult time of war with Germany and Austria" (which Khabalov interpreted as an order to fire upon the people), his anxious remark about the events in Petrograd and his decision to go back to Tsarskoe Selo did not appear in

Nicholas II's diary until 27 February, along with some comments about a ride along the highway to Orsha on a sunny day.[56]

On the same evening, the tsar moved as if to satisfy the opposition's demand, repeated by Duma Chairman M.V. Rodzianko, that a government responsible to the Duma be created.[57] Nicholas II talked with General N.I. Ivanov from midnight to two o'clock in the morning (that is, on 28 February), then dispatched him to Petrograd with a detachment to restore order there. Concerning their conversation, the court historian, General D.N. Dubenskii, wrote,

> "I was not concerned about autocratic rule, but about Russia. I am not convinced that changing the form of government will bring tranquillity and happiness to the people," the sovereign said, concerning his innermost thoughts as to why he persisted in refusing to authorize a parliamentary system. Then the sovereign noted that now he considered it essential to consent to the Duma's demand, because the disorders had reached the point of rebellion, which it was beyond his power to oppose.[58]

The members of the court expressed the "hope that the forthcoming parliamentary system will bring tranquillity to society."[59] It became clear the next morning, however, that Nicholas II had in mind a government responsible not to the Duma but to the tsar. In addition, the appointments of the minister of the court, the war minister, the minister of the navy, and the minister of foreign affairs were to remain the tsar's prerogative.[60] In essence, Nicholas was again rejecting any changes in the state structure. It was not until late in the evening of 1 March that the commander in chief of the Northern Front, General N.V. Ruzskii (denied entry to Petrograd, the tsar's train arrived at Ruzskii's headquarters in Pskov) managed to persuade Nicholas II to consent to the creation of a government that would be responsible to the legislative chambers.

For one and a half hours, Ruzskii tried to convince the tsar that he "had to compromise with his conscience for the sake of Russia and of his own heir." "The sovereign's basic argument," Ruzskii said of the tsar's objections,

> was that he desired nothing for himself or for his own interests, nor was he trying to hold on to anything, but believed that he did not have the right to turn the whole business of governing Russia over to persons who might do the greatest harm to the Motherland today while they were in power and then wash their hands tomorrow and "resign along

with the cabinet." "I am responsible to God and to Russia for everything that has happened and will happen," the sovereign said; "whether the ministers are responsible to the Duma and the State Council is inconsequential. Seeing that what the ministers are doing is not for the good of Russia, I will never be in a position to agree with them or to console myself with the thought that it is not something that I have done, not my responsibility."

Ruzskii [in his memoirs, dictated to General S.N. Vilchevskii, references to Ruzskii are in the third person—B.A., R.G.] tried to persuade the sovereign that his thinking was erroneous and that he should accept the formula, "The sovereign reigns and the government governs." The sovereign said that he could not understand that formula, that he would have had to have been brought up differently, to have been reborn, and again he emphasized that he personally was not hanging onto power, but he could not make a decision that went against his own conscience, and, if he did slough off his responsibility to the people, he would be unable to believe that he himself was not responsible before God. With unusual clarity, the sovereign reviewed the positions of all individuals who might be able to govern Russia in the near future as ministers responsible to the chambers, and he expressed his own conviction that the public figures who would undoubtedly constitute the first cabinet were persons totally inexperienced in the matter of government, who if they did assume the burden of rule would not know how to cope with their task.[61]

Meanwhile, the revolutionary wave in Petrograd had reached the point where a "responsible ministry" no longer served to satisfy public demands as it had with the Manifesto of 17 October 1905 on which Ruzskii had counted. It became necessary for Nicholas II to abdicate the throne, and around ten o'clock on the morning of 2 March the general informed the tsar of that fact. The decision to abdicate, which Nicholas II then made, apparently came more easily to him than authorizing a "responsible ministry." During the 1920s, one author explained that for the tsar, the sort of authority that would be limited by his ministers' parliamentary responsibility had no value; Nicholas II simply could not "turn himself into a constitutional monarch on the West European model" (which is how Ruzskii characterized Russia's future state system).[62]

On the afternoon of 2 March, the tsar reconsidered his original decision to abdicate in favor of his son with Grand Duke Mikhail Alexandrovich acting as regent, and decided to abdicate in favor of his brother. "I cannot part with my son," he said to A.I. Guchkov and V.V. Shulgin, delegates to the Provisional Committee of the State Duma. "I hope you will understand."[63] Four years after triumphantly celebrating the three-hundredth anniversary of the Romanov dynasty in 1913, Nicholas II signed the Abdication Manifesto without fanfare, thereby closing the final page in the dynasty's history.

According to the succession laws, the tsar could abdicate only on his own account and did not have the right to abdicate on behalf of his son. The grand dukes recognized the illegality of his decision. P.N. Miliukov noted that it was then that he concluded that this was a deliberate move on the tsar's part.[64] But in Pskov, Guchkov and Shulgin, after conferring with one another, and without giving any thought to the tsar's innermost thoughts, decided to agree with him. "Let it be wrong! Maybe it will serve to gain time. . . . Michael will rule for a while, and then, after everything settles down, it will become clear that he is incapable of ruling, and the throne will go to Alexei Nikolaevich," Shulgin reasoned.[65]

Guchkov and Shulgin also discerned other advantages to the tsar's abdication in favor of Mikhail Alexandrovich. The situation in Petrograd was becoming more heated with each passing hour, and it was no longer enough to think just about saving the monarchy; they must think about saving the lives of the members of the dynasty as well. This might require that the new monarch swear allegiance to the constitution or even that he abdicate. The only one who could do either of these was Mikhail Alexandrovich; the underage Alexei could not. In addition, if Alexei were to ascend the throne it would be necessary to decide whether his parents would remain with him or be separated from him. In the former case, the abdication might seem fictitious; in the latter, the new tsar would assume that his father and mother had been taken away from him.

On the morning of 3 March Nicholas II's Abdication Manifesto, which with difficulty had been concealed from the enraged workers who had arrested Guchkov at the railroad station, was delivered to the home of Princess O.B. Putiatina on Millionnaia Street, where Mikhail Alexandrovich was in hiding after arriving there on 27 February dressed as a commoner. It was there that negotiations concerning the autocracy's future took place.

Miliukov desperately attempted to preserve the monarchy, with Guchkov providing his only support; meanwhile, it was clear to all those attending that the monarchy was irretrievably lost. Miliukov, according to Shulgin, was "pale as a ghost," and he "cawed like a raven." "The monarch is the axis. . . . The country's only axis!" he insisted, prophesying that Russia would perish without the monarchy.[66] "It was like a filibuster!" another eyewitness recorded.

"Miliukov simply would not end it. He could not, he was afraid. . . . He wouldn't let anybody speak, he interrupted anyone who objected to him; he interrupted Rodzianko, Kerensky, everybody."[67] Later, Miliukov essentially confirmed these details, though he did say that Shulgin had "exaggerated a little." "Anyway, there was some method in my cawing," Miliukov insisted.

Although Miliukov had not the slightest chance of success, in his memoirs he explained his hopes at that moment. His plan consisted of departing immediately for Moscow, whence he would wage a battle to preserve the monarchy. "Perhaps even Ruzskii's attitude toward the defense of the new emperor who has been thrust upon him will be different from his defense of the old one," he wrote.[68] However, Michael declared that he was refusing the throne. Around four o'clock in the afternoon, he signed his abdication. The act did, to be sure, provide for the possibility of his assuming the throne if the Constituent Assembly so decided. For Miliukov this served as a kind of consolation ("in this way, the form of government remained an open question").[69]

Nicholas II reacted to his brother's abdication in a manner that made it obvious that what most horrified him at the time was not the fate of the throne but rather the irreversible change in the state system. "So Misha has abdicated. His manifesto ends with a call for the election of a Constituent Assembly in six months. God knows what possessed him to sign such a vile thing!" the former tsar wrote in his diary on 3 March.[70]

On 9 March he and his family began living under guard at Tsarskoe Selo in an atmosphere of steadily mounting antimonarchical sentiments. Their stay at Tsarskoe Selo proved to be a prelude to lengthy wanderings to Tobolsk, then to Ekaterinburg. The danger threatening him because of the rapid leftward movement of the masses was something that Nicholas II had realized even before going to Tsarskoe Selo. He asked the Provisional Government for permission to remain there until his children recovered (they had come down with the measles), then to proceed onward to the port of Romanov from which he would take his family to England.

Miliukov, serving as minister of foreign affairs in the Provisional Government, reported this to the English ambassador Sir George Buchanan on 6 (19) March. Miliukov said that the former tsar's requests would be satisfied and asked whether preparations were being made for the tsar's journey to England. The next day, Buchanan informed London that Miliukov was insisting that the former tsar sail to England, and that he was certain that Britain would send a vessel for him. On 9 (22) March the English government decided to invite Nicholas II and his family to England, emphasizing that the initiative must lie with the Russian government; it also inquired as to the former tsar's property and means. ("It is most desirable that His Majesty and his family have sufficient means to live according to their status as members of an Imperial family.")[71]

Meanwhile, the protests of the revolutionary organizations against the former tsar's departure grew stronger and reached England. King George V, a cousin both to Nicholas II (their mothers, who had been princesses of Denmark, were sisters) and to Alexandra Fedorovna (her mother and the king's father were children of Queen Victoria), was frightened by the revolutionary turn events in Russia had taken and the English public's negative attitude toward inviting the tsar's family. He categorically demanded that the government rescind the invitation. On 6 April (New Style) his secretary wrote to Foreign Minister Lord A.J. Balfour: "Buchanan must be instructed to tell Miliukov that objections against allowing the emperor and the empress to come here are so strong that we will have to take the liberty of withdrawing the consent that was earlier given to the Russian government's proposal."[72]

The permanent undersecretary for foreign affairs Lord Ch[arles] Hardinge addressed a private inquiry to England's ambassador to Paris, Lord Bertie, as to whether the former tsar would be allowed into France, and he emphasized the difficult position of the English government. The king's secretary wrote to Bertie that George V opposed the tsar's coming, but that the government had accepted Miliukov's proposal, and now the public believed that it had been the king's idea from the very beginning. Bertie, however, answered that in his opinion, the arrival of the tsar's family in France would not meet with approval there in view of Alexandra Fedorovna's Germanophile reputation.

England's refusal to receive the former tsar and his family was actually advantageous to the Provisional Government in April and May, inasmuch as it was apprehensive about public indignation over their departure from Russia—just as George V was afraid of protests against their arrival in England. But in the summer, the Provisional Government repeated its request, and in June or July, A.F. Kerensky recalled, Buchanan came with tears in his eyes to inform the minister of foreign affairs that England had definitely refused to receive the former emperor.[73] "King George Slams the Door" was the title of one chapter in a book by two English authors, who state that this "sealed the fate of Nicholas II and all his family."[74]

The tragic fate of the last emperor of Russia gave rise to a vast literature, primarily of émigré origin. In the last few years this has been supplemented by numerous articles by Russian and Soviet authors, mainly journalists and writers who have beaten the professional historians to it. One achievement of glasnost has been the uncovering of a number of facts and documents about the brutal murder of the tsar, the tsaritsa, their children, Doctor E.S. Botkin, and their servants. The generally accepted version of their deaths is that they were all shot on the night of 16 and 17 July 1918 in the Ipatiev house in Ekaterinburg.

The investigative material confirming this story was used by the one investigator of the White government who had the opportunity to complete his task.[75] (Others were forced to stop their endeavors at the insistence of the White command.) Testimony obtained during the course of the investigation relating that the female members of the tsar's family were in Perm after 17 July and that one of the grand duchesses had tried to make an escape, however, was not taken into account by N.A. Sokolov. Meanwhile, the English authors who researched the material that wound up in Western archives believe that the women were not murdered until the beginning of September[76]; before then, their fate was the subject of negotiations between the Soviet government and Germany, conducted by K.B. Radek on the Soviet side. No documentary data concerning this matter have as yet come to light.

Summers and Mangold also analyzed the arguments of Anna Anderson, who for many years lodged claims in Western courts demanding that she be recognized as Grand Duchess Anastasia, and who was even recognized as such by several members of the royal family. Of particular interest among these arguments is the pretender's claim that she had seen her uncle, her mother's brother Ernst-Ludwig, grand duke of Hesse-Darmstadt, who had come to Petrograd during the war. In the opinion of Summers and Mangold, it was this report of a delicate secret mission that forced the duke not to identify Anderson as Anastasia.

The English authors have brought together several reliable sources confirming that such a journey did take place. On the road to Russia and Tsarskoe Selo, Ernst Ludwig was seen by a number of witnesses whose trustworthiness is not subject to doubt. It also turned out that Wilhelm II, who sent the duke to Russia, told his relatives about this visit, which took place in 1916. The kaiser was trying to get Russia out of the war by means of a separate peace while preserving the inviolability of the tsarist regime, rather than by fomenting revolution, as the German government was doing and on which it was relying. The tsar, however, refused to entertain any proposals for a separate peace.[77]

The book by Summers and Mangold is also interesting because the authors have researched the reaction of the Entente and Germany to the murder of the tsar's family. But the authors' main idea is probably incorrect. In any case, the recently published memoirs by Ia. Iurovskii, who supervised the shooting in the Ipatiev home, confirm that the whole family and others were killed there on the night of 16 and 17 July 1918. This is also backed by the account of two brothers, Cheka members A.G. and M.G. Kabanov, who took part in the execution, which confirms the testimony published previously. The report that the tsar alone was shot in Ekaterinburg, which appeared in several documents of Soviet organs, in public statements, and even in a private letter by Ia.M. Sverdlov,[78] can be explained only by the bloody nature of the event and the desire to conceal the actual circumstances.

Notes

1. See L.G. Zakharova's description of him in "Krizis samoderzhaviia nakanune revoliutsii 1905 g.," *Voprosy istorii*, 1972, no. 8, pp. 119–40; R. Wortman, "Nikolai II i obraz samoderzhaviia," *Istoriia SSSR*, 1991, no. 2.

2. When he met Grand Duke Alexander Mikhailovich hunting elephants in the jungle near Colombo, the tsarevich envied him, and said bitterly that his trip had been stupid. "Palaces and generals are the same all over the world," he explained, "and those are the only things they show me. I might just as well have stayed home" (Grand Duke Aleksandr Mikhailovich, *Kniga vospominanii* [Paris, 1933], vol. 2, p. 169).

3. V.V. Vedernikov, *Problema predstavitel'stva v russkoi publitsistike rubezha XX stoletiia* (Ph.D. dissertation, London, 1983), p. 62.

4. V.N. Lamsdorf, *Dnevnik, 1894–1896* (Moscow, 1991), p. 126.

5. *Moskovskii sbornik* (Moscow, 1896), pp. 34–35, 41–42.

6. Aleksandr Mikhailovich, *Kniga vospominanii*, p. 178.

7. A.A. Vyrubova, "Neopublikovannye vospominaniia," in *Novyi zhurnal* (New York, 1978), vol. 131, p. 178.

8. Aleksandr Mikhailovich, *Kniga vospominanii*, p. 171.

9. Ibid., pp. 174–75.

10. Ibid., p. 136.

11. Ibid., p. 174.

12. A.N. Kulomzin, "Perezhitoe," RGIA, f. 1642, op. 1, d. 195, l. 108.

13. Ibid., l. 111.

14. *Krizis samoderzhaviia v Rossii, 1895–1917* (Leningrad, 1984), pp. 28–29.

15. "Dnevnik A.N. Kuropatkina. Kopii. 1897–1902 gg.," RGVIA, f. 165, op. 1, d. 1871, ll. 20, 25, 40.

16. Ibid., d. 1769, ll. 170–72.

17. Ibid., d. 1871, l. 31.

18. N.L. Zhevakhov, *Vospominaniia* (Munich, 1923), vol. 1, p. 305 (erroneously given as 350 in the book).

19. A. Mosolov, *Pri dvore poslednego imperatora* (St. Petersburg, 1992), pp. 98–99.

20. Ibid., p. 72.

21. *Freilina ee velichestva. "Dnevnik" i vospominaniia Anny Vyrubovoi* (Moscow, 1990), pp. 156–59.

22. Quoted in B.A. Romanov, *Ocherki diplomaticheskoi istorii russko-iaponskoi voiny* (Moscow–Leningrad, 1955), pp. 163–64.

23. A.F. Koni, *Sobranie sochinenii* (Moscow, 1966), vol. 2, p. 377.

24. Vyrubova, "Neopublikovannye vospominaniia," *Novyi zhurnal,* vol. 130, p. 136.

25. Mosolov, *Pri dvore,* p. 70.

26. Aleksandr Mikhailovich, *Kniga vospominanii,* pp. 175–76.

27. Alexandra Fedorovna did not even allow her daughters to engage in light flirtation (Vyrubova, "Neopublikovannye vospominaniia," *Novyi zhurnal,* vol. 130, p. 141).

28. G.E. Rasputin (Novykh) arrived at court not long after the explosion caused by the SRs at Stolypin's dacha on 16 October 1906 as a result of which Stolypin's daughter was injured. On the same day, Nicholas II wrote to him: "Petr Arkadievich! The other day I received Grigorii Rasputin, a peasant from Tobolsk Province; he brought me the icon of St. Samson of Verkhoture. He made a remarkably strong impression on both me and on Her Majesty, and so instead of five minutes I spent more than an hour talking with him. He will be departing soon to return home. He has a strong desire to visit you and to bless your injured daughter with the icon. I do hope that you can find a moment to receive him this week. His address is: St. Petersburg, 2-ia Rozhdestvenskaia 4. He is staying with Father Iaroslav Medved" (*Vozrozhdenie,* 1957, no. 63, p. 137).

29. V.N. Kokovtsov, *Iz moego proshlogo* (Paris, 1933), vol. 1, pp. 238–39. Nicholas II's patronage of the Black Hundreds organizations, which contributed significantly to his political disorientation, gained him a reputation as an anti-Semite. V.L. Burtsev attributes part of the tsar's anti-Semitism to Alexander III's influence. Nicholas II was strongly influenced by the forged document "The Protocols of the Elders of Zion." But after an appraisal carried out at Stolypin's instructions by the police department revealed that the "Protocols" were fake, and the leaders of the Black Hundreds nonetheless still tried to get permission to use them in their propaganda, the tsar wrote: "The 'Protocols' are to be withdrawn. A clean cause cannot be defended by dirty methods" (V.L. Burtsev, *"Protokoly sionskikh mudretsov." Dokazannyi podlog* [Paris, 1938], p. 106).

30. *Petergofskie soveshchaniia o proekte gosudarstvennoi dumy* (Petrograd, 1917), pp. 156–58.

31. *Krizis samoderzhaviia v Rossii,* p. 249.

32. The memoirs of A.A. Spasskii-Odynets are kept in the Bakhmetev Archive at Columbia University in New York.

33. Evidently, General V.V. Biskupskii, the head of the Russian "government" under Grand Duke Kirill Vladimirovich who later became the director of Hitler's Department for Russian Émigré Affairs, tried to get these funds from Hitler's authorities out of the Mendelssohn Bank. In this attempt he referred to an agreement on the Russian–German partition of Europe signed by him and General Ludendorf in the early 1920s, and preceded by Ludendorf's receipt of money from Russian émigré sources. Even though Biskupskii emphasized that the Molotov–Ribbentrop Pact was not in conflict with that agreement, his petitions were refused (W. Laqueur, *Russia and Germany* [London, 1965], pp. 109, 340; R.C. Williams, *Culture in Exile: Russian Émigrés in Germany, 1881–1914* [Ithaca and London, 1972], pp. 349–50).

34. GARF, f. 601, op. 1, d. 1707, ll. 3–5; d. 1718, l. 3.

35. As of 1 January 1903 this "economic capital" exceeded 1,484,000 rubles, and the Volga–Kama Bank account held about 85,000 rubles (GARF, f. 601, op. 1, d. 1732, l. 1–6, 9).

36. *Freilina ee velichestva*, p. 162.

37. A.A. Lopukhin, *Otryvki iz vospominanii* (Moscow–Petrograd, 1923), p. 73.

38. B.V. Nikol'skii, "Iz dnevnika 1905 g.," *Krasnyi arkhiv*, 1934, no. 2 (63), pp. 71–83.

39. Between October 1905 and April 1906 Witte, who held the post of chairman of the Council of Ministers, gathered together a collection of orders that the tsar had addressed to him regarding the suppression of the revolution. Nicholas II demanded ("would you be so kind") that Witte, who was resigning, return his notes to him. "Later," Witte "very much regretted" that he had done so, because in those documents "posterity would read a number of thoughts and ideas that reveal the character of the sovereign" (S.Iu. Witte, *Vospominaniia* [Moscow, 1960], vol. 3, pp. 349–50).

40. See B.M. Vittenberg, "K istorii lichnogo arkhiva S.Iu. Vitte," in *Vspomogatel'nye istoricheskie distsipliny* (Leningrad, 1985), vol. 17.

41. *Arkheograficheskii ezhegodnik. 1989* (Moscow, 1990), pp. 296–99.

42. Quoted in E.D. Chermenskii, *Burzhuaziia i tsarizm v pervoi russkoi revoliutsii* (Moscow, 1970), p. 144.

43. Koni, *Sobranie sochinenii*, vol. 2, pp. 355–59.

44. *Dnevniki imperatora Nikolaia II* (Moscow, 1991), p. 323.

45. Chermenskii, *Burzhuaziia i tsarizm*, p. 408.

46. Vyrubova, "Neopublikovannye vospominaniia," *Novyi zhurnal*, vol. 130, p. 148.

47. Father Georgii Shavel'skii, *Vospominaniia poslednego protopresvitera russkoi armii i flota*, vol. 1 (New York, 1954), p. 324.

48. Ibid., pp. 343–44.

49. A.I. Spiridovich, *Velikaia voina i Fevral'skaia revoliutsiia*, vol. 1 (New York, 1960), pp. 208–9.

50. F. Vinberg, *Krestnyi put'* (Munich, 1922), pt. 1: *Korni zla*, p. 181.

51. S. Andolenko, "Kleveta na imperatritsu," *Vozrozhdenie*, 1968, no. 204, p. 111.

52. Shavel'skii, *Vospominaniia*, pp. 328–30.

53. "Lichnost' Nikolaia II i Aleksandry Fedorovny po svidetel'stvam ikh rodnykh i blizkikh," *Istoricheskii vestnik*, vol. 148 (April 1917), pp. 170–75.

54. Probably the most tragicomic marriage was that between the tsar's brother Michael and N.S. Vulfert, the daughter of a Moscow attorney; her first married name had been Mamontova. Nicholas II forbade the marriage, and the authorities were instructed to prevent it from taking place. Early in 1909 it became known to the palace commandant's office that the grand duke had found a priest who would agree to perform his wedding. Gerasimov, head of the Petrograd Department of the Okhrana, summoned the priest to him and threatened to let him rot in the Peter and Paul Fortress. But when the grand duke and Vulfert went abroad, Minister of the Imperial Court Fredericks sent Gerasimov after them. He was told that in the event that the wedding actually occurred, he was to walk up to Michael in church, tell him that he was under arrest, and demand that he return immediately to Russia. Gerasimov took the same train as the grand duke to Paris, where he had at his disposal some detectives in the Paris department of Russia's security service abroad. But their efforts proved to be in vain. When he learned that Michael had left for Nice, where he intended to marry, Gerasimov went there also, but once there he received a telegram informing him that the grand duke had gone in another direction. A few days later it was learned that the wedding had taken place in Vienna (A.V. Gerasimov, *Na lezvii s terroristami* [Paris, 1985], pp. 179–80; "Brak v[elikogo] k[niazia] Mikhaila Aleksandrovicha. Sysknoi nadzor za bratom tsaria. Dok[lad]," in *Nikolai II i velikie kniaz'ia* [Leningrad–Moscow, 1925], pp. 127–30).

55. "Lichnost' Nikolaia II," p. 177.

56. *Otrechenie Nikolaia II. Vospominaniia ochevidtsev. Dok[lad]*, 2d enl. ed. (Leningrad, 1927; repr. Moscow, 1990), p. 33.

57. Ibid., pp. 49–52.

58. Ibid., p. 53.

59. Ibid., p. 52.

60. Ibid., p. 98.

61. Ibid., p. 153.

62. Ibid., pp. 17–18.

63. Ibid., p. 170.

64. P.N. Miliukov, *Vospominaniia* (Moscow, 1990), vol. 2, p. 270.

65. *Otrechenie Nikolaia II*, p. 183.

66. *Fevral'skaia revoliutsiia*, 2d ed. (Moscow–Leningrad, 1926), pp. 44, 146–59.

67. M. Aldanov, "Tret'e marta," in P.N. Miliukov, *Sbornik materialov po chestvovaniiu ego semidesiatiletiia, 1859–1929* (Paris, n.d.), p. 31.

68. Miliukov, *Vospominaniia*, pp. 317–18.

69. Ibid., p. 319.

70. *Dnevniki imperatora Nikolaia II*, p. 625.

71. A. Summers and T. Mangold, *The File on the Tsar* (New York–London, 1976), p. 247.

72. Ibid., p. 250.

73. Ibid., p. 252. When Kerensky's memoirs were published, they provoked a storm of indignation. Both D. Lloyd George, the former prime minister of England, and Buchanan contradicted Kerensky, saying that the agreement to offer asylum to the tsar had never been rescinded. In 1927, in response to a parliamentary request, the Foreign Office accused Kerensky of lying and submitted as "irrefutable evidence" the early telegrams offering asylum to the tsar, while omitting the later telegrams that refused it. When the former secretary of the British Embassy in Petrograd stated that he remembered receiving a telegram of refusal from London, the Foreign Office responded that his memory had failed him. In 1932, however, Buchanan's daughter related that her father had been threatened with the loss of his pension if he did not falsify the account in his memoirs so as to conceal the true facts of the matter.

74. Ibid., p. 245.

75. N.A. Sokolov, *Ubiistvo tsarskoi sem'i* (Berlin, 1925).

76. Summers and Mangold, *File on the Tsar*, p. 300.

77. Ibid., pp. 218–89.

78. Ia.M. Sverdlov told someone close to him in the party that only the tsar had been killed, while his family had been removed to Alapaevsk ("Pis'ma iz 1918 g.," *Oktiabr'*, 1982, no. 11, p. 175).

Suggestions for Further Reading

Alexander, John T. *Catherine the Great: Life and Legend* (New York, 1989).

Anderson, M. S. *Peter the Great* (London, 1978).

Anisimov, Evgenii V. *The Reforms of Peter the Great; Progress through Coercion in Russia*, trans. and ed. John T. Alexander (Armonk, 1993).

Catherine II. *The Memoirs of Catherine the Great* (New York, 1955).

Charques, Richard. *The Twilight of Imperial Russia* (London, 1958, 1974).

Cherniavsky, Michael. *Tsar and People: Studies in Russian Myths* (New Haven, 1961).

Cracraft, James, ed., *Peter the Great Transforms Russia*, 3d ed. (Lexington and Toronto, 1991).

de Custine, A. *Journey for Our Time: Russia—1839*, ed. and trans. P.P. Kohler (London, 1980). Reprint.

De Madariaga, Isabel. *Catherine the Great: A Short History* (New Haven, 1990).

———. *Russia in the Age of Catherine the Great* (New Haven, 1981).

Dziewanowski, M.K. *Alexander I: Russia's Mysterious Tsar* (New York, 1990).

Egan, David R., and Melinda A. Egan, *Russian Autocrats from Ivan the Great to the Fall of the Romanov Dynasty: An Annotated Bibliography of English Language Sources to 1985* (Metuchen, NJ, and London, 1987).

Ferro, Marc. *Nicholas II: The Last of the Tsars*, trans. Brian Pearce (New York, 1993).

Gasiorowska, Xenia. *The Image of Peter the Great in Russian Fiction* (Madison, 1979).

Grey, Ian. *The Romanovs: The Rise and Fall of a Dynasty* (Garden City, NY, 1970).

Griffiths, David M. "Catherine II: The Republican Empress," *Jahrbücher für Geschichte Osteuropas*, vol. 21 (1973), pp. 323–44.

Harcave, Sidney. *Years of the Golden Cockerel: The Last Romanov Tsars, 1814–1917* (New York, 1968).

Hartley, Janet M. *Alexander I* (London, 1994).

Hughes, Lindsey. *Sophia: Regent of Russia, 1657–1704* (New Haven, 1990).

Klyuchevsky, V. O. *Peter the Great* (New York, 1964).

Leonard, Carol S. *Reform and Regicide: The Reign of Peter III of Russia* (Bloomington, 1993).

Lieven, Dominic C. *Nicholas II: Emperor of All the Russias* (London, 1993).

———. *Nicholas II: Twilight of the Empire* (New York, 1994).

Lincoln, W. B. *In War's Dark Shadow: The Russians before the Great War* (New York, 1983, 1994).

———. *Nicholas I* (Bloomington, 1978).

———. *The Romanovs: Autocrats of All the Russias* (New York, 1981).

Lipskii, Alexander. "A Re-examination of the 'Dark Era' of Anna Ivanovna," *American Slavic and East European Review*, vol. 25, no. 3 (1965), pp. 477–88.

————. "Some Aspects of Russia's Westernization during the Reign of Anna Ioannovna," *American Slavic and East European Review*, vol. 18, no. 1 (1959), pp. 1–11.

Massie, Robert K. *Nicholas and Alexandra* (New York, 1967).

————. *Peter the Great: His Life and World* (New York, 1980).

————. *The Romanovs: The Final Chapter* (New York, 1995).

McConnell, A. *Tsar Alexander I: Paternalistic Reformer* (New York, 1970).

McGrew, Roderick E. *Paul I of Russia, 1754–1801* (New York, 1992).

Meehan-Waters, Brenda. *Autocracy and Aristocracy and the Russian Service Elite of 1730* (New Brunswick, 1982).

Mosse, W.E. *Alexander II and the Modernization of Russia* (New York, 1958).

O'Brien, C. Bickford. *Russia under Two Tsars, 1682–1689* (Berkeley, 1952).

Obolensky, Chloe. *The Russian Empire: A Portrait in Photographs* (New York, 1979).

Palmer, Alan W. *Tsar Alexander I: Tsar of War and Peace* (London, 1974).

Pares, Bernard, ed. *The Letters of the Tsar to the Tsaritsa, 1914–1917* (London, 1929).

————. *The Letters of the Tsaritsa to the Tsar, 1914–1916.* (London, 1923).

Presniakov, A. E. *Emperor Nicholas I of Russia: The Apogee of Autocracy, 1825–1855*, ed. and trans. Judith C. Zacek (Gulf Breeze, FL, 1974).

Radzinsky, Edvard. *The Last Tsar: The Life and Death of Nicholas II*, trans. Marian Schwartz (New York, 1992).

Raeff, Marc. *Imperial Russia 1682–1825: The Coming of Age of Modern Russia* (New York, 1971).

Ragsdale, Hugh, ed. *Paul I: A Reassessment of His Life and Reign* (Pittsburgh, 1979).

————. *Tsar Paul and the Question of His Madness: An Essay in History and Psychology* (New York, 1988).

Rasmussen, K. "Catherine II and the Image of Peter I," *Slavic Review*, vol. 37 (1978), pp. 51–69.

Riasanovsky, Nicholas V. *The Image of Peter the Great in Russian History and Thought* (New York, 1985).

————. *Nicholas I and Official Nationality in Russia, 1825–1855* (Berkeley, 1959).

Rieber, Alfred J. "Alexander II: A Revisionist View," *Journal of Modern History*, vol. 43, no. 1 (1971), pp. 42–58.

Rogger, Hans. *Russia in the Age of Modernization and Revolution, 1881–1917* (New York, 1983).

Soloviev, S.M. *History of Russia*, vol. 29: *Peter the Great: The Great Reforms Begin*, ed. and trans. by K. A. Papmehl (Gulf Breeze, FL, 1981).

Stavrou, Theofanis G., ed. *Russia under the Last Tsar* (Minneapolis, 1969).

Steinberg, Mark D., and Vladimir M. Khrustalev, *The Fall of the Romanovs* (New Haven, 1995).

Sumner, B.H. *Peter the Great and the Emergence of Russia* (London, 1951).

Tolstoi, A. *Peter the First* (New York, 1959). (Historical novel written by Soviet author.)

Verner, Andrew M. *The Crisis of Russian Autocracy: Nicholas II and the 1905 Revolution* (Princeton, 1990).

Wortman, Richard. *Scenarios of Power: Myth and Ceremony in Russian Monarchy* (Princeton, 1995).

Zaionchkovskii, Petr A. *The Russian Autocracy under Alexander III*, trans. D.D. Jones (Gulf Breeze, FL, 1976).

Index